GHANA

GHANA

A Political and Social History

Jeffrey S. Ahlman

ZED

LONDON • NEW YORK • OXFORD • NEW DELHI • SYDNEY

ZED BOOKS
Bloomsbury Publishing Plc
50 Bedford Square, London, WC1B 3DP, UK
1385 Broadway, New York, NY 10018, USA
29 Earlsfort Terrace, Dublin 2, Ireland

BLOOMSBURY and Zed Books are trademarks
of Bloomsbury Publishing Plc

First published in Great Britain 2024

Portions of Chapter 5 have previously appeared in a different form in Ahlman,
Jeffrey S. "'The Strange Case of Major Awhaitey': Conspiracy, Testimonial Evidence,
and Narratives of Nation in Ghana's Postcolonial Democracy." *International
Journal of African Historical Studies* 50, no. 2 (2017): 225–49.

Cover design by Adriana Brioso
Cover image © Sakchai/Adobe Stock

A catalogue record for this book is available from the British Library.

A catalog record for this book is available from the Library of Congress.

ISBN: HB: 978-1-7883-1422-0
         PB: 978-0-7556-0156-1
       ePDF: 978-0-7556-0158-5
      eBook: 978-0-7556-0157-8

Typeset by Integra Software Services Pvt. Ltd.

To find out more about our authors and books visit www.bloomsbury.com
and sign up for our newsletters.

To those who introduced me to the study of History

CONTENTS

Part I

Part II

ILLUSTRATIONS

PREFACE

Ghana: A Political and Social History emerged on a bit of a lark in early 2017. At this time, I had recently submitted my first book, *Living with Nkrumahism: Nation, State, and Pan-Africanism in Ghana*, to Ohio University Press. As I awaited the copy-edits, I was exploring what to do next. I had recently returned from Ghana, where I spent nearly a month mostly in the Western Region towns of Essiama, Nkroful, and Sekondi investigating a potential project on public memories of Ghana's first president Kwame Nkrumah. Circuitously and indirectly, portions of that research made their way into my 2021 biography of Nkrumah, *Kwame Nkrumah: Visions of Liberation*, also published by Ohio University Press.

While reflecting on paths forward, Jo Godfrey, then at I.B. Tauris, approached me about writing a history of Ghana for a series I.B. Tauris ran on modern national histories. Skeptical about the genre of national histories, I remained intrigued about what it would mean to write a history of Ghana spanning a so-called modern era largely defined by the nineteenth and twentieth centuries. Over the past five years, this question has proven one of the most challenging of my academic career, as it has forced me to reflect much more broadly on foundational questions within the historical discipline, namely what histories and whose stories get privileged, how do we tell these stories and with what sources, and at what scale (temporal and geographic), and in the case of so-called national histories specifically, what are the confines of the "nation" itself. As I approached these questions, the central theme that emerged, at least for me, became that of what does it mean to be a "Ghanaian" or earlier a "Gold Coaster." As I aim to show in this book, the idea of the "Gold Coaster" or "Ghanaian" is fundamentally a moving target, and one deployed strategically for some and, at times, just as strategically against others, as those living in what became Ghana sought to make their way through the changing realities of the nineteenth and twentieth centuries. *Ghana: A Political and Social History* is simply one way to tell this history.

I should also note that, as originally envisioned, the book aimed to speak to more than an audience of academic historians. Rather, as per the original vision of I.B. Tauris's Modern Histories series, it sought to be accessible to both undergraduate students and the general public. Despite the book's move to Zed Books, the book still has this ambition. Not a synthetic work by any means, *Ghana: A Political and Social History* is, however, still a distillation of decades of work by scholars—Ghanaian and non-Ghanaian alike—put in conversation with a wide array of archival, oral, governmental (colonial and postcolonial), and journalistic sources, among others. In keeping with the aim of this to be a teachable book, many of the sources highlighted were selected because they are relatively accessible to students and others alike. They include the featuring of such sources as published oral traditions collected during the 1960s and 1970s; published memoirs, autobiographies, and personal accounts; archival databases like those of the Endangered Archives Programme of the British Library; and the bevy of newspapers digitized in Gale's *Nineteenth Century Online* and *Nineteenth Century British Newspapers* collections as well as those by the Center for Research Libraries. Unfortunately, paywalls still do limit some of this access.

Finally, a quick note on terminology. Throughout the text, I refer to locations and groups by the names used at the time period under discussion (e.g. Gold Coast pre-March 1957; Ghana post-March 1957). If a name has changed since, the contemporary version is included in parentheses after the initial reference in each chapter. In addition, the use of the term "modern" should not be read as a reference to a moment when or path by which "Ghana" or "Ghanaians" became modern, as some may be inclined to do. There was no specific moment when Ghanaians became modern; by the historical times under discussion, they were by definition modern, as they were part of and active agents in a world constructed via the processes of modernity: most notably, the *longue durée* of capitalist expansion and all its political, economic, social, cultural, and intellectual reverberations. Finally, since the 1960s, scholarly convention has recognized two spellings of "Nkrumahism": "Nkrumahism" and "Nkrumaism." This book will use the spelling "Nkrumahism," except when quoting directly.

ACKNOWLEDGMENTS

There are many challenges in writing a book and, as the cliché goes, one accumulates many debts along the way. Most directly, this book would not exist without the urging of Jo Godfrey, now of Yale University Press. Jo encouraged me to reflect on how one might tell Ghana's history in a way that would be accessible to a wide-ranging audience. Jo's guidance during the project's conception helped me envision how I might do so. At Bloomsbury/Zed, I have also benefited from the patience, advice, and encouragement of Nick Wolterman, who took on this project in 2022. Olivia Dellow expertly guided the book through the production process.

More broadly, this work would have been impossible to complete without the community of scholars that make up the Ghana Studies community—past and present. Nana Osei-Opare, Alice Wiemers, Nana Osei Quarshie, Jennifer Hart, Gerardo Serra, and Bianca Murillo all shared sources and advice that enriched the text. As part of a long-standing writing group, Lacy Ferrell, Julia Cummiskey, and Alice Wiemers read several of the book's chapters. Abdulai Iddrisu and Kwame Essien generously answered questions when I had them as well as hosted me during previous trips to Ghana. Numerous scholars including Jean Allman, Kofi Baku, Owusu Brempong, Sara Berry, Tshepo Masango Chéry, Frank Gerits, Trevor Getz, Matteo Grilli, Bright Gyamfi, Leslie James, Tanvi Kapoor, Keri Lambert, Chris Lee, Dan Magaziner, Liz McMahon, Stephan Miescher, Adwoa Opong, Nate Plageman, Elisa Prosperetti, Richard Rathbone, Paul Schauert, Elizabeth Schmidt, Ben Talton, Lessie Tate, Habtamu Tegegne, and Brian Yates have assisted in ways they may and may not know of. Furthermore, from 2020–2, I benefited from the knowledge and wisdom of Abdul-Garafu Abdulai as, together, we co-edited *Ghana Studies*, the journal of the Ghana Studies Association (GSA). Carina Ray, who preceded us, helped guide us through the editing process. Additionally, Nana Akua Anyidoho and Kwasi Ampene proved supportive colleagues and partners during their GSA presidencies.

My debts in Ghana are equally as numerous. In addition to Abdulai's and Kwame's generosity while hosting me, Emily Asiedu opened her home to me on several occasions. Soale Iddrisu introduced me to Tamale in 2006. At the George Padmore Research Library on African Affairs, Edward Addo-Yobo and James Naabah introduced me to the library and its collections, also in 2006. James has welcomed me back to the library during every trip I have made to Ghana since. At the Public Records and Archives Administration Department (PRAAD) branch in Accra, I benefited from the assistance of Judith Botchway and Bright Botwe during their tenures in the archive's reading room. Numerous additional archivists have helped me in PRAAD's regional branches in Sekondi, Kumasi, Cape Coast, and Sunyani. In 2007–9, Kwesi Asiedu and Ben Cudjoe each helped with interviews and transcriptions. Meanwhile, early in my graduate student career, Nana Arhin Brempong invited me into his home, sharing his perspectives on the Ghanaian past. Among those who have kindly allowed me to interview them about their experiences, S. Kofi Asiedu, Lawrence Bessah, Kofi Duku, Thomas Daniel Laryea, Victoria Laryea, E. B. Mensah, Ben Nikoi-Oltai, M. N. Tetteh, N. Sifah, and Jacob Sesu Yeboah also welcomed me on multiple occasions into their homes and shops.

At Smith College, where I have made my academic home since 2012, I have been lucky enough to be part of an intellectual community that not only challenged me to think more deeply, but has also been a model of support. In the History Department, my colleagues Marnie Anderson, Ernest Benz, Josh Birk, Darcy Buerkle, Sergey Glebov, Jennifer Guglielmo, Richard Lim, and Liz Pryor have been there every step of the way as I have sought to complete this project. Darcy Buerkle deserves particular note, for, following the College's Covid shutdowns, she worked to ensure I had access to a microfilm reader during her tenure as department chair. Without her efforts, much of the book would have been impossible to complete. Likewise, Liz Pryor regularly served as a sounding board for ideas. In the African Studies Program, I have benefited from the guidance and wisdom of Kuukuwa Andam, Colin Hoag, Aaron Kamugisha, Caroline Melly, Albert Mosley, Katwiwa Mule, Anna Mwaba, Camille Washington-Ottombre, Greg White, and the late Louis Wilson. Similarly, Pinky Hota has been a pillar of my time at Smith, providing advice, friendship, and wisdom from the time we arrived on campus together. The book also benefited from participation in a Louise W. and Edmund J. Kahn Liberal Arts Institute seminar on democracies in 2021–2. Anjali Biswas, Kendra Bonde, Priya Dalal-Whelan, Jona Elwell, Liz Haas, Liz Hoffmeyer, Emma Jewel, Rehana Nazerali-Ruddy, Freda Raitelu, and Sowon Yoon each provided research support for parts of this book via Smith's generous undergraduate research assistantship program.

At home, Katie and Emmanuelle have endured the mess created as I sprawled across the floor encircled with books, a spiral notebook, and a mechanical pencil writing.

Finally, this book is dedicated to those who introduced me to the study of history. It was Walter Rucker who first displayed for me what it meant to be a historian early in my undergraduate career at the University of Nebraska-Lincoln. James Le Sueur took me under his wing shortly thereafter by providing me a research assistantship and showing me what it meant to do serious research. Jean Allman introduced me to Ghana during the mid-2000s. Likewise, the late Joe Miller encouraged me to think deeper and more broadly about the African past, while Elizabeth Schmidt modeled how to write political histories from below.

ABBREVIATIONS

ADM	Administrative Files
AFRC	Armed Forces Revolutionary Council
AME	African Methodist Episcopal
ARPS	Aborigines' Rights Protection Society (Gold Coast)
BAA	Bureau of African Affairs
CPP	Convention People's Party
EAP	Endangered Archives Programme
ECOWAS	Economic Community of West African States
ERP	Economic Recovery Programme
GCP	Ghana Congress Party
GCR	Gold Coast Regiment
HIPC	Heavily Indebted Poor Countries
IMF	International Monetary Fund
INEC	Interim National Electoral Commission
JFM	June Fourth Movement
KAR	King's African Rifles
MAP	Muslim Association Party
MP	Member of Parliament
MSRC	Moorland-Spingarn Research Center
NAL	National Alliance of Liberals
NCP	National Convention Party
NDC	National Democratic Congress
NLC	National Liberation Council
NLM	National Liberation Movement
NPP	New Patriotic Party
NRC	National Redemption Council
NUL	Northwestern University Libraries
OFY	Operation Feed Yourself
PDA	Preventative Detention Act
PDC	People's Defence Committees
PFP	Popular Front Party
PNDC	Provisional National Defence Council
PNP	People's National Party
PP	Progress Party
PRAAD	Public Records and Archives Administration Department
PUA	Princeton University Archives
RG	Record Group
RWAFF	Royal West African Frontier Force
SC	Special Collections

SCUA	Special Collections and University Archives
SMC	Supreme Military Council
TNAUK	The National Archives—United Kingdom
TUC	Trades Union Congress
UAC	United Africa Company
UGCC	United Gold Coast Convention
UMASS	University of Massachusetts-Amherst
UP	United Party
VRP	Volta River Project
WANS	West African National Secretariat
WDC	Workers' Defence Committees
YUL	Yale University Library

Part I

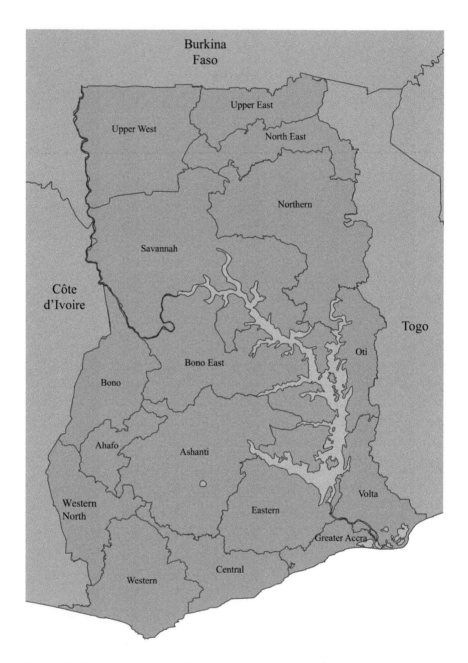

Figure 0.1 Map of contemporary Ghana.

INTRODUCTION:
BELONGING AND NATION IN MODERN GHANA

On March 6, 2007, Ghana celebrated the fiftieth anniversary of its independence from British colonial rule. The series of events leading up to the festivities were years in the making and ultimately cost the government more than $60 million.[1] In the capital of Accra, the epicenter of the Golden Jubilee celebrations, the city was readied for the event with the hurried completion of a range of beautification and infrastructure projects in preparation for what was to be a yearlong celebration of the nation. Similarly, outside the capital, more modest projects accompanied those pursued in Accra, including the construction of Jubilee Parks in each of the country's regional capitals. Meanwhile, in public forums, on the country's university campuses, in newspapers, on television, and, most importantly, on the radio, debates over the progress of the Ghana@50 celebrations, as they came to be popularly known, dominated the country's political discourse in the months leading up to the festivities and for several years afterwards. At the same time, in bars, homes, workplaces, and schools, Ghanaians used the occasion to comment on the progress—or lack thereof—of the country's present and past governments in living up to the promises of independence.[2]

For those planning the country's anniversary festivities, the nature of Ghana's postcolonial independence posed many challenges as they struggled to create a coherent narrative for the maturing country. For, in the 1950s and 1960s, few places in Africa had garnered the international attention and notoriety that Ghana—the colonial Gold Coast—had in its transformation from what, in the mid-1940s, colonial officials had marketed as a "model colony" to that of a colony of supposed rebellious nationalists during the final years of the decade. As such, in 1949, Gold Coasters would come to form one of Africa's first mass political parties, the Convention People's Party (CPP), which, in 1951, would win the colony's first popularly contested elections. The election results would catapult the party's then-imprisoned leader, Kwame Nkrumah, into the newly created position of "leader of government business." A year later, Nkrumah would accept the new title of prime minister, while, over the next five years, he and the CPP would spend much of their time and energy agitating for the future Ghana's full independence. At the same time, however, through two additional general election victories (1954 and 1956), they worked to run a government of their own under a constitutionally constructed Anglo–African dyarchy that gave the CPP government control over most of the colony's domestic affairs. Even more importantly, with independence in March 1957, Ghana became the first sub-Saharan state to emerge from European colonial rule, setting, in the eyes of many, a path for the rest of the continent.

The reaction to Ghana's independence both inside and outside of Africa was dramatic. Invitations to the country's independence were heavily vetted, resulting in intense negotiations between the CPP government, the British, and other interested parties in order to ensure all local and international contingencies were accounted for.[3] Meanwhile, in both academic and popular publications, journalists and activists alike heralded the newly independent country. Writing in a 1957 issue of the *Phylon Quarterly*, for instance, the British journalist Russell Warren Howe openly celebrated the monumental nature of the country's independence, noting somewhat opaquely and perhaps even with a bit of hyperbole how "other things … of perhaps greater world and human significance than even the Emancipation of Africa" emerged from Ghana's independence.[4] Likewise, in the USA, the editors of the National Association for the Advancement of Colored People's *Crisis* magazine similarly commemorated Ghana's independence. In doing so, the magazine offered a short history of its path to independence, highlighting both the CPP's rise in the then colony and the centrality of women to the party's success. As a result, the magazine's editors not only aspired for "Ghana's success [to] foreshadow the independence of the rest of Africa," but also suggested that Ghana had the potential to serve as a model for the rest of the continent.[5]

In the years following Ghana's independence, Nkrumah and the CPP sought to capitalize on the country's growing international notoriety. In doing so, they aimed to transform the West African state into a continental and global epicenter for mid-century anti-imperial politics by welcoming expatriates and freedom fighters from throughout Africa and beyond to the young country. In the newly christened state, they thus sought to commit themselves and Ghana as a whole to the broader struggle for African self-government. Among those making their way to Ghana at the time were figures including George Padmore, T. Ras Makonnen, Frantz Fanon, Malcolm X, Maya Angelou, Pauli Murray, Robert Mugabe, Félix Moumié, Shirley Graham Du Bois, and Che Guevara, among many others. Similarly, in 1961, with the Nkrumah government's offer to support his long-anticipated *Encyclopedia Africana*, the doyen of twentieth-century pan-Africanism, W. E. B. Du Bois, also made his way to Ghana. Du Bois would ultimately spend the final years of his life in Accra, where he remains buried.

Half-a-century later, the legacies of Ghana's decolonization and first decade of self-rule continued to echo throughout Ghana and Africa as a whole. For those planning the country's Ghana@50 celebrations, the question of how to address the legacies of the 1950s and 1960s haunted their proceedings. For them, the jubilee was a balancing act as they sought to weigh the interests and ambitions of the then-governing New Patriotic Party (NPP) with the expectations and policies of a public at home and abroad reading the Ghana@50 festivities through the lens of the Ghanaian past. In Africa, for instance, independence-era Ghana, particularly through the imagery and legacy of Kwame Nkrumah, continues to resonate throughout the continent as an icon for both the hope and dashed dreams of independence. Nkrumah's unabashed and perceived unrelenting support for African liberation and unity—buttressed by his independence-day proclamation that Ghana's "independence is meaningless unless it is linked up with the total liberation of the African continent"—anchors this belief.[6] The Nkrumah government's willingness to materially support, fund, and coordinate with anticolonial movements in numerous locales throughout the continent only reinforced Ghana's singular status in the African political imagination. As former Tanzanian President Julius Nyerere insisted in a 1997 speech commemorating the fortieth anniversary of Ghana's independence, the importance of Ghana's independence to the continent had not waned during the preceding decades, for he recounted, "Ghana was more than just the beginning [of African liberation]. Ghana," he recalled, "inspired and deliberately spearheaded the independence struggle for the rest of Africa."[7]

Further complicating the Ghana@50 planners' deliberations was the internal history of the CPP and many of the NPP's elders' historical relationships to the CPP and Nkrumah. Evolving out of what is colloquially known as the "Danquah–Busia tradition" of Ghanaian politics, the NPP in part has its roots in a series of parties and political organizations that, during the 1950s and 1960s, were bitterly opposed to the CPP, Nkrumah, and vast portions of the Nkrumah-era domestic and international agenda, including key aspects of its pan-Africanism. To many within the NPP, some of whom and their families had suffered greatly under Nkrumah, the legacy of independence-era Ghana did not ring of hope or inspiration. Rather, it was one of emerging despotism, and Nkrumah, for them, was the face of that tyranny. In reflecting on the era, then, many regularly recounted tales of the closing prospects of postcolonial democracy under Nkrumah and the rise of a government embodied in not only the one-party state that emerged during the 1960s, but, perhaps more importantly, also in the personal and familial tragedies resulting from the government's policies of preventative detention. Others, likewise, complained of the Nkrumah period as an era of widespread corruption, false promises, and even godlessness.[8] The result during the Golden Jubilee's planning was the attempted and at times awkward construction of a delicate balance during the fiftieth anniversary celebrations as the official program at once sought to celebrate the achievements of the first decade of Ghanaian self-rule, while, at the same time, it also sought to elide the towering figures of the independence era into a broader national narrative culminating in NPP governance during the first decade of the new millennium.[9]

The challenges before the Golden Jubilee planners in their attempts to construct a coherent national narrative—even for just the five decades since independence—in many ways, added up to an impossible task. At its foundation, it required a dissection of what was meant by "Ghana" and what it meant to be "Ghanaian."[10]

However, these were questions that those living in the area that came to be known as Ghana had been debating even before the contemporary idea of "Ghana" came into political focus during the late 1940s and 1950s. In previous decades, the question was one about what constituted a "Gold Coaster" and what his or her relationship was to Africans elsewhere on the continent, especially in West Africa. Tied to these debates was also the more politically nettlesome question of what was the Gold Coaster's place within the British Empire itself and his or her position within the colonial project more broadly.

At the heart of these colonial-era debates were attempts by those living in the Gold Coast to push back against a colonial regime that sought to categorize them as mere colonial subjects. In doing so, Gold Coasters sought to claim and engage with a range of political, social, and cultural identities that aimed to add new dimensions to their relationships with one another, the British Empire, West Africa, and the international community writ large. As such, they regularly tapped into even longer-standing notions of belonging and self-identification—ones constructed out of a constantly evolving set of negotiations over what it meant to be part of a community or precolonial state in the region. By the twentieth century, many of these debates over belonging and self-identification would in turn inform colonial-era reflections on what it meant to be a "Gold Coaster" and, by mid-century, what it meant to be a "Ghanaian."

Ghana: A Political and Social History argues that much of Ghana's nineteenth- and twentieth-century history is a history of these debates. At its most basic level, the idea of Ghana itself—as understood at its most literal in the contemporary imagination—was formed in the aftermath of World War II. As historians Jane Burbank and Frederick Cooper have illustrated, it was during this period that a world marked by global empires began its long, uneven transformation into one of nation-states.[11] Internationally, no institution better embodied this metamorphosis than that of the newly created United Nations, representing on its most idealistic level a community of nation-states. As a result, with its independence in 1957, Ghana formally entered the emergent world of nation-states. Moreover, within Ghana, the first months following independence read as an archetypal recitation of what it meant to be a nation-state in the mid-twentieth century as the Ghanaian National Assembly debated everything from the country's citizenship and nationality laws to the continued presence of colonial holdovers in many of the new state's government institutions. Even before independence, debates over such symbols of the modern nation-state as the flag, the national anthem, and even what the new "Ghanaians" should call themselves—"Ghanatian," "Ghanese," "Ghanian," and "Ghanatta," among others bandied about by some at the time—presaged the legal debates that marked the post-1957 period.[12] Meanwhile, highlife bands, state dance ensembles, and concert parties performed for the Ghanaian public the hopes and anxieties (official and unofficial) of the nation-state's construction.[13] It was thus in these debates that the then colony sought to intellectually, culturally, and politically come to grips with the meaning of independence and the complexities of nationhood.

However, the formal establishment of the nation-state and the symbolic measures taken to accompany it disguise the deeper debates over the meaning of "Ghana" or of being "Ghanaian" in the historical imagination. Furthermore, these are debates fundamentally and simultaneously shaped by the interactions forged out of an intersecting array of local and transnational networks connecting Ghanaians to West Africa, precolonial Atlantic and Saharan trade networks, the former British Empire, and the international community over the last several centuries. Key to these debates, then, are the histories and legacies of the international gold trade in the region, slavery and the slave trade, and the subsequent development of the "legitimate trade" in such commercial goods as palm oil, rubber, kola, and timber during the nineteenth century and eventually cocoa. For the Gold Coasters/Ghanaians engaged in the commodity trade, these trading networks helped integrate them into the broader world of the Atlantic, the West African Sudan, and beyond, in turn reshaping how they related to one another and the many groups of strangers arriving in and along the Gold Coast over the last four- to five-hundred years. Moreover, as the colonial state gradually began to come into being over the second half of the nineteenth century, the Gold Coast did not cede its place as a site of international importance in colonial West Africa and within the British Empire. By the early to mid-twentieth century, the colony possessed one of Africa's most educated populations and, for some, resulted in a standard of living with few African equivalents.[14] At the same time, the cocoa revolution of the early twentieth century not only helped quench a growing global hunger for chocolate, but, at home, also allowed for the growth of an independent and influential class of farmers, who, for much of the next century, would serve as the economic engine for the colony and later country.[15]

The pan-African and socialist agenda of the Nkrumah government only accentuated the centrality of and tensions within the national and transnational conceptions of "Ghana" articulated during the twentieth century. However, even after Nkrumah's 1966 overthrow, subsequent governments did not fully shy away from such conceptions of Ghana, with some, at various points, even seeking to resurrect the legacies of Nkrumah's pan-African vision in their own attempts to consolidate their base of influence. Likewise, during the 1980s, Flight Lieutenant Jerry John Rawlings, who came to power in coups in 1979 and 1981, aimed to cultivate his own vision of a radical Ghana that would be able to exert political, economic, and cultural influence in the region and Africa more broadly. Rawlings's tone and political repertoire may have changed with Ghana's democratization during the early 1990s, but his ambitions for presenting Ghana as a regional and continental power rarely wavered. Rawlings's successor, John Agyekum Kufuor, who presided over a period of genuine, if yet uneven economic growth, doubled down on this vision of an internationally influential Ghana during his eight years in office. Even more importantly, though, over the course of the Rawlings and Kufuor administrations, many Ghanaians adopted such beliefs. However, in doing so, they often integrated them into powerful critiques of the priorities of the country's post-democratization governments.

History, Ghana, and the Problem of Periodization

There are many challenges in writing Ghana's modern history. The question of periodization is just one. As numerous scholars have shown, it is often difficult to establish clear demarcations between the "precolonial," "colonial," and, in some cases, even "postcolonial" periods in Africa as the definitional boundaries between these eras are often fuzzy and, in many cases, are difficult to transplant on to the African historical scene. Likewise, scholars often disagree quite vociferously about whether such distinctions are even appropriate in the African context, with some, such as the prominent Nigerian historian Jacob Ade Ajayi, openly questioning what he viewed as a scholarly overemphasis on colonial rule in Africa. To this end, he called for a better contextualization of European colonialism within the *longue durée* of African history.[16] Others, in contrast, have emphasized what, from their perspectives, were the rapid, if not dramatic changes to African life brought forth by colonial rule.[17] Additional questions surround the postcolonial era. Writing on Africa more broadly, political scientist Mahmood Mamdani—not entirely dissimilar, at least in principle, from Ajayi, who focused on the distinction between the precolonial and the colonial—suggested in 1996 that the formal granting of independence represented little more than a superficial dividing line in scholarly reflections on the recent African past. Much more important to him in terms of understanding the twentieth-century African experience were the real and perceived continuities of exploitation, violence, and inequality embedded in European colonial rule and African postcolonial governance.[18] Still others, meanwhile, question historians' seeming lack of interest in Africa's most recent past, abiding instead by a process of historical periodization that rarely looks beyond the height of African decolonization during the 1950s and 1960s.[19]

For Ghana specifically, questions of periodization are of particular importance, for reflected in them are even more fundamental issues of intersecting forms of local, national, regional, and even continental self-identification. Coming into the international imagination as a coherent geographic entity during what scholars have defined as the early modern period, the "Gold Coast" conceptually was a creation of the Atlantic trade with both cultural and geographic implications. At its most literal, the Gold Coast referred to a region of the Gulf of Guinea coast that, over the course of the late fifteenth and sixteenth centuries, became known in Europe as a site rich in gold. Over the next several centuries, explorers, traders, and cartographers would reify this rendering of the region in the early modern Atlantic imagination. As a result, the Gold Coast (literally in name) and, by extension, the people who lived there largely became defined by the region's gold supply for outsiders looking in until, during the eighteenth century, slaves overtook gold in importance in the region's trade. To this end, in the mid-eighteenth century, one Danish merchant even went so far as to lament what he viewed as the region's loss of identity with the rise of the slave trade, or, more specifically, the political and economic instability that drove it. According to him,

> fifty to sixty years ago [circa 1700], the whole Gold Coast, from Cape Three
> Points [in far western Ghana] to River Volta [in the east], could have been called

a gold mine. The reason that not a thousandth part of the gold formerly brought from there is not brought today is not that the land is no longer as rich in gold as it was in former times, but that millions of people have been beaten to death, that entire nations have been destroyed, and that the Akim people, who had actual expertise in digging gold, have, in fact, since 1747, all fled from their country.[20]

On the ground, those living in the newly demarcated Gold Coast did not necessarily dissuade such mineralogically oriented definitions of the region. Throughout the coast, trading communities popped up, many of which established elaborate and often highly profitable relationships with the handful of European powers that arrived on the coast. In these coastal communities, forts were built, intermarriages took place, and, ultimately, multigenerational trading relationships emerged—all of which reinforced externally derived notions of the area as one largely defined by the gold trade. Meanwhile, inland, an intricate social and economic system emerged for the extraction and transportation of the region's gold to the coast for export, while, at the same time, merchants from elsewhere in West Africa also distributed Gold Coast gold, along with other goods, to markets within the West African Sudan to the north. Moreover, at its most intimate, this extractive economy worked its way down to the familial level as families supplemented their much more foundational agricultural labor with the mining of gold. Furthermore, the economic system that emerged in the early modern Gold Coast was one that regularly relied upon local slaves and their labor, for, as historian Ivor Wilks noted during the early 1960s, internally, the relationships between the gold and slave trades were reciprocal. Gold production and the gold trade, he argued, bought slaves, and the unfree—through their labor (agricultural, mining, and reproductive)—reproduced wealth.[21] To this degree, the early modern gold trade became a defining feature in how those living in the region related to one another well into the seventeenth century.

However, at the same time, those living in the region also carried with them more personal and fundamental forms of self-identification that developed and operated on different scales—time and otherwise—than those forged through the Atlantic trade. In most cases, it would not be until as late as the late nineteenth and early twentieth centuries that even a fraction of those living in the region would begin to think of themselves as "Gold Coasters." Instead, at the individual level, they understood themselves to be parts of a cascading array of networks of belonging that, according to some, dated to the beginning of time and, for others, to a deep past characterized by migrations from lands as far afield as the Nile.[22] Individuals were also part of families that had their own genealogies and entanglements. Additionally, they were also part of specific communities and groups of communities with their own histories and interests. Some had political and military ties. Some shared languages. Others, meanwhile, were part of distinct religious communities: indigenous, Islamic, syncretic, and Christian. Moreover, by the middle of the second millennium, an increasing number of these communities came together to comprise the many different linguistically, ethnically, and religiously defined states that would characterize the region's political and cultural landscape through much of the nineteenth century.

The intersecting ways in which these various networks of belonging interact with one another—both historically and in the present—are key to understanding Ghana's and the Gold Coast's modern history. Even more importantly, they are central to understanding how Ghanaians themselves reflect upon their own past individually and collectively, for Ghanaians almost definitionally view their pasts as operating on multiple timescales. Such temporal eclecticism, however, challenges historians as they aim not only to explain the past, but also to order that past in ways that reflect the truly layered nature of the Ghanaian historical imagination.[23] Indirectly, philosopher Kwame Anthony Appiah highlights this challenge in his 1992 *In My Father's House*. As Appiah argues throughout his text, too often African peoples are constrained to a particular set of idioms of identity in academic studies. These can take the form of race (Appiah's foremost focus), ethnicity, nationality, or religion, among others. Moreover, as Appiah notes, in many of these cases, such a process is often externally derived and reflected in the stereotypes and politics that even certain well-meaning groups have of Africa and Africans. The result, for Appiah, is a paradigm in which individuals and communities tend to become boxed into necessarily incomplete and often ahistorical definitional categories that may—even if only temporarily—force them to deny or overshadow a part of themselves.[24]

With the arrival of Europeans along the Gulf of Guinea coast, the process of constructing the intellectual framework by which the identities and histories of those living in the region became homogenized in the international imagination began to take shape, at least in the form that features so prominently in the world today. Key to this process was the flourishing number of reports, travel logs, correspondence, and other forms of communication sent to and from the Gulf of Guinea coast by European explorers, traders, administrators, and others from the fifteenth through nineteenth centuries. Meanwhile, as the Atlantic trade gradually began to overtake that of the West African Sudan in influence for many in the region, a slowly growing trickle of would-be Gold Coasters began to turn their attention to the ideas, politics, and, in certain cases, even cultural models articulated by European arrivals. However, in only the most exceptional cases did these ideas or political models—and the forms of belonging and self-identification built into them—gain dominance on the community or even individual levels. Instead, in the vast majority of cases, those who encountered them viewed them as one would an *à la carte* menu, picking and choosing what fit their interests and ambitions at a particular moment. As a result, at most, these ideas and beliefs were additive, built into individuals' and their communities' own, already existing political, social, and cultural models. They were also, then, strategically deployed.

At various times, the emerging colonial state of the late nineteenth and early twentieth centuries aimed to both promote and dissuade this political and cultural *bricolage* among its African subject population. On its most literal level, colonialism gave demonymic power to the idea of the "Gold Coaster," as, for the first time, the Gold Coaster came into view as a clearly defined political being—a legally defined subject of the British Empire. In the late nineteenth and early twentieth centuries, as subsequent chapters will show, prominent groups of newly anointed Gold Coasters actively adopted the moniker as they sought to make political and social claims against the developing colonial state. However, the colonial state, for its part, often sought to weaken these claims by de-emphasizing the "Gold Coaster" as a political identity with the promotion and even, to borrow Terence Ranger's and Eric Hobsbawm's famed term, "invention" of so-called traditions.[25] In doing so, new ethnic groups, while not necessarily created out of thin air, were newly delineated, gained internally and externally sanctioned political and social structures and rights, and/or, in certain cases, even new forms of political and social authority over others.[26] In other cases, such as in Accra, which, in 1877, would become the capital of the colonial Gold Coast, political figures, whose traditional powers may have previously been more circumscribed, gained new authority over land and people. They acquired this power as colonial authorities sought to force Gold Coasters' traditional institutions into the colonial government's often quite narrow definitions for what African political, social, and cultural life should look like.

Independence and the promotion of such a thing as the Ghanaian "nation" further complicated the Gold Coast/Ghanaian political and historical picture during the mid- and late-twentieth century. From the perspective of not only the Nkrumah government, but also most of its successors, a particular, often narrowly defined Ghanaian national identity was required should the country wish to thrive in the international community of the twentieth and early twenty-first centuries. The nature and shape of this national identity may have shifted as new governments came into power and outlined new sets of priorities for the country and its peoples. However, in nearly every instance, these state-sanctioned visions of the Ghanaian national identity were contested as Ghanaians again viewed them as additive and in turn sought to integrate them—often in different and/or unintended forms— into the many different networks of belonging already embedded within their own contemporary and historical imaginations. Ultimately, what this book argues is that these twentieth-century debates over what it meant to be "Ghanaian" are historical debates as Ghanaians themselves played with—and still do—various methods of periodization as well as time and geographical scale in their attempts to define for themselves the meaning of "Ghana."

Ghana, Nation, and National Histories

Among the other challenges for historians writing Ghana's history is the broader question of writing national histories themselves. Like many formerly colonized territories, Ghana's history does not easily fit within the intellectual and structural confines of a genre largely defined in terms of the territorial nation-state. Over the last two-plus decades, the historical profession as a whole has increasingly become more skeptical of the utility of the nation-state as a unit of historical analysis. However, this skepticism has a much deeper history in the study of Africa as scholars have long openly decried what they presented as the historical, cultural, and political artificiality of the nation-state on the continent.[27] Even more importantly, key continental political and intellectual figures maligned this artificiality as they used the opportunities of decolonization to explore a range of postcolonial potentialities. Nkrumah himself would take up this question throughout the 1950s and 1960s. In doing so, he regularly insisted that the nation-state, as transplanted onto Africa, only served to weaken the continent and its peoples by dividing them into "small, uneconomic and non-viable States [*sic*]."[28] Nkrumah's pan-Africanism was thus an attempt to address this balkanization as he and others—inside and outside of Ghana—experimented with an array of political configurations that sought to simultaneously operate within and beyond the confines of the territorial nation-state.

Key to much of the skepticism surrounding the territorial nation-state was the nation-state's real and perceived colonial genealogy. For Nkrumah specifically, the influx of balkanized states that emerged from decolonization was indicative of colonialism's attempts to modernize itself during the post-World War II era. Moreover, according to him, it did so under the guise of a political process that commonly became known as "neocolonialism." Taking on the issue of neocolonialism directly in his 1963 *Africa Must Unite*, Nkrumah described it as a fundamentally deceptive process aimed at subverting Africa's political and economic independence. "It acts covertly," he argued in the book, "manœuvring men and governments, free of the stigma attached to political rule." The result, he firmly asserted, was the establishment of "client states, independent in name but in point of fact pawns of the very colonial power which is supposed to have given them independence."[29] As such, Nkrumah viewed the African nation-state, including the Ghanaian nation-state, as a colonial creation. As a result, he was among many who argued that not only were most of the boundaries for the new states established by the then largely retreating imperial powers, but, in most cases, the states were also direct reflections of the lack of imagination implicit in the borders themselves—borders that, from Nkrumah's perspective, promised little more than the continued redirection of the continent's wealth to the former colonial powers.[30]

Thus, at the heart of both the scholarly and continental frustrations with the nation-state structure was (and still is) the continuing legacy of the continent's late nineteenth-century partition in the twentieth- and even twenty-first centuries. Foremost for Nkrumah, the tensions within the nation-state system were both political and economic as Ghana and Africa more broadly sought to negotiate a world constructed out of what he understood as a global political economy of capitalist and imperial exploitation. Basil Davidson, the prominent British historian of Africa, picked up on Nkrumah's argument several decades later, arguing that, in the mid-twentieth century, "nation-statism looked like a liberation, and really began as one. But it did not continue as a liberation. In practice," he lamented, "it was not a restoration of Africa to Africa's own history, but the onset of a new period of indirect subjection to the history of Europe." For Davidson, the key question surrounding the rise of the African nation-state was that of what was lost. Through its policies, boundaries, and administration, Davidson argued, colonialism had thwarted Africa's postcolonial development, disrupting what he suggested to be the organic evolution of Africa's precolonial states.[31] Others, meanwhile, have examined how colonial boundaries bisected major cultural and linguistic groups, thus dividing peoples and communities with shared histories between two or more colonial powers.[32] In some cases, these borders grouped peoples with little or no shared past together in newly created colonial states.[33] The result, if one follows political scientist Crawford Young, was a process of reconfiguring Africa's diversity—political, cultural, and social—for European gain. Moreover, Young, much like Mamdani, insists that African decolonization did not liberate the continent from this process, but instead reinvented it.[34]

In many ways, the genre of national histories, with its focus on the territorial nation-state, has the potential to reinscribe the colonial legacy of partition upon the personal and cultural histories of formerly colonized peoples. In doing so, the genre has often constrained how historians have sought to tell and even conceptualize the histories of places like Ghana. As discussed in the previous section, Ghanaians held and deployed a variety of intersecting visions of and for themselves, all of which were in constant negotiation. At various times, it may be relatively easy to interlay these visions on top of or within the political and cultural apparatus of the Ghanaian nation-state. Even Nkrumah and his government, despite their skepticism of the nation-state, ultimately accepted nation-statism as, at least for that moment, an unavoidable political reality. They in turn went to great lengths not only to cultivate a particular image of what it meant to be Ghanaian at the time, but also to establish the bureaucratic and administrative machinery necessary for the new government to explore and eventually utilize well-worn mechanisms of state power—including deportations, arrests, and detentions—to ensure state security. To varying degrees, all of Ghana's subsequent governments followed in Nkrumah's and the CPP's path as they sought to define "Ghana" on both the domestic and international stage.[35] Moreover, the Ghana@50 celebrations of the early twenty-first century, which were to mark the country's reemergence on the international and continental stage, were foremost celebrations of the Ghanaian nation-state as the NPP government sought to manufacture a clear, official narrative for the jubilee that sought to coalesce Ghana's political, social, cultural, and historical diversity into the modularity of the nation-state.

However, at other times, the nation-state dissipates as a meaningful category of analysis altogether in understanding the Ghanaian recent past. As a result, this book seeks to expand the genre of national histories in its telling of Ghana's nineteenth- and twentieth-century history. As concepts, nation and the nation-state each become important analytical categories for the book, albeit they do not operate synonymously. In Ghana, there is only one nation-state—the one created with the country's independence. Foremost, the nation-state is a political entity that carries with it important political, bureaucratic, and legislative functions in the name of Ghana's approximately thirty-one million people.[36] Moreover, the Ghanaian nation-state operates in an international system largely built around the nation-state as an entity. As such, the Ghanaian nation-state has clear international functions, with Ghana maintaining a place within such international institutions as the United Nations, the African Union, and the Economic Community of

West African States to name a few. Likewise, the country's president is recognized throughout the world as the country's official and sole head of state. Furthermore, the cultural and symbolic significance of the nation-state cannot be ignored, for the vast majority of Ghanaians happily tout their connection to the country, proudly fly the Ghanaian flag, joyfully sing the national anthem, root for the country's football team, as well as take part in other exhibitions of national pride—all of which represent clear embodiments of the abstract concept of the nation-state in Ghanaian daily and public life.

The nation, by contrast, is a much more nebulous historical, cultural, and sociological concept. This is not only the case in Ghana, but in world history more broadly. Scholarly definitions of the term have varied widely, with many of the most prominent scholars of the nation focusing on the process by which certain forms of collective identities are constructed and politicized in the modern era, often under the guise of nationalism. For instance, writing in the early 1990s on the concepts of national identity and nation, sociologist Anthony Smith notes that the concepts foremost "signify bonds of solidarity among members of communities united by shared memories, myths and traditions that may or may not find expression in states of their own but are entirely different from the purely legal and bureaucratic ties of the state." For Smith, a fundamental "multidimensionality" underpins the real-life expressions of nation and national identity, which in turn provides the phenomena with the malleability to become "such a flexible and persistent force in modern life and politics."[37] Benedict Anderson, with his famed theorization of nations as "imagined communities," adds even more flexibility in how one defines the nation through his interrogation of how, through the power of print culture, previously disparate groups of communities came together through processes of imagination to claim shared, albeit contested heritages.[38] Others, most famously including Partha Chatterjee and, more recently, Elleni Centime Zeleke, question the applicability of the political and scholarly quest for defining the nation at all outside of the West.[39]

It is precisely the ambiguity in the structure and confines of the nation that make it such a useful concept in thinking through the multiplicity of forms of African political identities that marked the nineteenth and twentieth centuries. In different ways, Smith, Anderson, Zeleke, and Chatterjee, among others, have provided scholars with the analytical space with which to think both inside and beyond the nation-state in their reflections on the many different forms of belonging and self-identification that make up modern Africa. Citing Smith and Anderson specifically in her study of decolonization-era Asante nationalism, historian Jean Allman credits each with constructing historical and sociological frameworks for the nation that break from the rigidity of what she views as the Eurocentric statist definitions coming out of decolonization. For her, it was this Eurocentrism that had plagued many of Anderson's and Smith's equally prominent contemporaries and only by eschewing it could scholars begin to "leave the dead some room to dance."[40] In Ghana, more broadly, such formulations of the nation ultimately allow scholars to both think bigger and smaller than the conventional narrative structures offered by most national histories. They also open the possibility to question whether the concept of the "nation" is even the most appropriate when discussing differing features of the Ghanaian experience. As such, they provide a space for an equally important and worthwhile interrogation of the many different forms of identities—religious, imperial, familial, ethnic, migrant, and linguistic, among others—that do not fit neatly within the traditional analytical confines of the nation-state, but, in nearly every situation, interact with varying conceptions of the nation articulated by Gold Coasters and Ghanaians over the past 150 to 200 years.

Structure of the Book

Ghana: A Political and Social History is divided into eight chapters. In a broad sense, the chapters are chronologically arranged, tracing Ghana's history from the mid-nineteenth century to the country's 1990's transition to the Fourth Republic. More importantly, each chapter also focuses on the changing meanings of the "Gold Coaster" and "Ghanaian" during the period as Gold Coasters/Ghanaians developed and negotiated these emergent political identities in the context of the region's own political, social, and cultural eclecticism. Chapter 1 provides the historical background to the Gold Coast's and Ghana's nineteenth- and twentieth-century history by tracing the region's history from the fifteenth-century European arrival along the Gulf of Guinea coast to approximately 1900. By no means was the European arrival the beginning of the region's history. However, it was the European arrival that eventually helped transform the region into a coherent geographical space in the international imagination through their trade, cartographic commitments, and travel logs. Broadly, it is the legacy of this geographical image of the Gold Coast/Ghana, expanding in concert with the interests of expansionist states such as Asante during the eighteenth and nineteenth centuries and later the British colonial state, that persists with us today. At the same time, the chapter also shows that, slowly over the course of the early modern period, the Atlantic trade— replete with all its political, cultural, and social implications—gradually drew ever-more attention from those living in the region, eventually overshadowing the previously dominant inland trade.

Chapter 2 traces the development of the Gold Coast colonial state from the mid-nineteenth century to approximately 1920. Even more importantly, the chapter also details the emergence of the "Gold Coast" and "Gold Coaster" as distinct political geographies and identities in the late nineteenth- and early twentieth-century political imagination. As the chapter illustrates, politically and intellectually, the period was strongly influenced by a prominent group of intellectuals who sought to interpret and reframe aspects of the burgeoning colonial project in ways that met their own needs, interests, and expectations. In doing so, they not only challenged the young colonial state on such things as land, taxes, and political representation, but they also experimented with multi-layered conceptions of belonging and civic representation that were at once connected to the Gold Coast as a territorial unit and to the Gold Coast as part of a larger civic network embodied in British-controlled West Africa and the British Empire writ large. Chapter 3, meanwhile, traces the cultural politics of early- to mid-twentieth century commodity production in the Gold Coast. No commodity has been more important to the Gold Coast/Ghana over the last hundred-plus years than cocoa. Using cocoa as its framing device, the chapter explores the political, social, and cultural networks created through the production process. More than a mere economic endeavor, the chapter details how cocoa production emerged as a site where key networks of familial relations, labor, migration, colonial and national interest, and generation intersected in Gold Coasters' and Ghanaians' understandings of their presents and visions of their futures.

Chapters 4 and 5 interrogate the politics of decolonization and state-building in an emergent Ghana, focusing on the period between the end of World War II and the 1966 overthrow of the Nkrumah government. Specifically, Chapter 4 focuses on the many conceptions of the nation articulated and mobilized during World War II and its immediate aftermath. Key to the emergence of these varied mid-century conceptions of the nation was the sense of possibility unleashed by the war's end as a variety of new and old institutions—colonial, continental, and international—came together to create new opportunities for political, social, and cultural mobilization. Politically, this was a period of widespread political eclecticism as Gold Coasters toyed with and tested a wide variety of ways through which to reconceive their relationship to the Gold Coast and British Empire, with the United Gold Coast Convention ostensibly headed by J. B. Danquah and Kwame Nkrumah's CPP representing just two political models in an era of innovation. Chapter 5, meanwhile, details the construction of the postcolonial Ghanaian state under Nkrumah. Driving this chapter is the process by which the Nkrumah government at once used the mechanisms of state power, which for all intents and purposes, were sanctioned by the nation-state system, in order to shore up its authority inside Ghana and the international community, while, at the same time, promoting and materially supporting a pan-African agenda aimed at the continent's postcolonial unification.

The book's final three chapters shift the focus to the interconnected politics of debt, dependence, and development from independence to the birth of the Fourth Republic. At the political level, the 1960s and 1970s increasingly represented a period where Ghanaians endured widespread political and economic instability marked by an escalating debt burden and a rotating array of military and civilian governments. For most Ghanaians, the instability of the period led to extensive economic insecurity as both local and international pressures forced Ghanaians to look for and establish new networks of political, social, and economic exchange in order to survive. For its part, Chapter 6 explores the development ambitions that drove Ghana's eventual debt burden, while themes of precarity guide Chapter 7's examination of Kofi Busia's and I. K. Acheampong's governments' attempts to escape it. Under Busia, this process included a continuation of Ghana's post-Nkrumah economic liberalization and a nativist expulsion of upwards of 200,000 West African immigrants from the country. Acheampong, meanwhile, sought to eradicate Ghana's presumed dependence by both repudiating much of Ghana's pre-1966 debt and embarking upon an ambitious program of national self-reliance.

The politics and experiences of the December 31st Revolution in 1981 guide the book's eighth chapter and set the stage for its conclusion. Orchestrated by Flight-Lieutenant Jerry John Rawlings—who had overthrown Acheampong's successor, Fred Akuffo, in 1979 before handing over power to a short-lived civilian government—the coup that led to the December 31st Revolution promised not only to tackle the country's longstanding economic troubles. It also vowed to bring Ghanaians closer to their government via the construction of a so-called people's democracy. However, as the chapter shows, an array of political, economic, and environmental crises during the early 1980s complicated the construction of this envisioned people's democracy. During this time, drought and bush fires exacerbated the already existing shortages of food, goods, and other supplies in Ghana's markets. By the end of 1983, nearly all of Ghana would experience devastating food shortages and threats of famine. Moreover, the 1983 expulsion of "illegal aliens" from Nigeria, which returned upwards of a million refugees to Ghana, further destabilized the lives of Ghanaians expelled from a country many considered home as well as those who never left. In response, Rawlings and the government he oversaw responded to the crises with an economic stabilization program that aimed to promote macroeconomic growth alongside the withdrawal of the state from much of Ghanaian economic life. The result was the emergence of Ghana's neoliberal age. By the early 1990s, political neoliberalization in the form of the birth of Ghana's Fourth Republic accompanied its economic neoliberalization, culminating in the hopes, contradictions, and contingencies of Ghana's return to multi-party democracy.

Chapter 1

MAKING THE GOLD COAST: THE GOLD COAST TO THE TWENTIETH CENTURY

In his 1954 account of his travels through the then decolonizing Gold Coast, the African-American novelist and journalist Richard Wright provides a short history of the Gold Coast's emergence in early modern West Africa. In doing so, Wright connects the Gold Coast's rise to that of an African population manipulated into participation in a growing Atlantic trade. In Wright's history, the Europeans who arrived along the Gulf of Guinea coast during the fifteenth century did so not out of any particular interest in Africa, but out of a desire to find a more efficient trade route to India. However, according to Wright, while in West Africa, the Europeans "had become distracted by the incredibly rich gold dust to be found on the Guinea coast."[1] The result, Wright related, was the development of a long-standing trade between the Europeans and the communities and states they encountered, yet one rooted in "a kind of coy and furtive bargaining between the predatory Europeans and the frightened but gullible natives." In this so-called silent trade, Wright continued, "Europeans would leave heaps of cheap trinkets upon the ground and then retire a half day's march away; the Africans would steal out, examine the shoddy merchandise, and place tiny piles of gold dust upon each heap." This ritual—the historicity of which is in doubt—would supposedly continue until a satisfactory price could be determined.[2]

A few pages later, Wright shifted his focus specifically to the Gold Coast in a reflection on the establishment of the Portuguese settlement in the coastal town of Elmina. As Wright related in his history, the Elminans—despite what he portrayed as an African naivety—knew enough to distrust the Portuguese, even to the extent of protesting the Europeans' presence in the town. However, Wright asserted, "the Portuguese had long before made up their minds that it was well worth their while to risk the terrible climate, and, pretending to be spokesmen of the Gentle Jesus, they hankered not for peace, but for victory."[3] As other European powers arrived along the Gold Coast over the sixteenth and seventeenth centuries, Wright further suggested, similar processes played out as Gold Coast Africans protested various European settlements, only to be hoodwinked, overpowered, or further victimized by the introduction of new European powers into their respective communities. As such, Wright declared:

> The European campaign against the mainland of Africa, buttressed by a mixture of religious ideology and a lust for gold, had begun in earnest; there had been no declaration of war; there had been no publicly declared aims save those of soul-saving, which even the Portuguese didn't believe, and, as time passed, European governments *per se* were not even involved in these calculated assaults, for it was the right endorsed by no less than the Pope, of any individual merchant, criminal, or adventurer to buy a ship, rig it out, muster a crew, and set sail for Africa and try his luck.[4]

For Wright, the history he recounted served to orient him to West Africa and specifically the Gold Coast during his decolonization-era travels, in part helping to explain for him what he perceived to be the cultural oddities and, in his eyes, even seeming backwardness of the Gold Coasters he encountered. The narrative constructed in Wright's history was thus one defined not only by European interactions with the coast's African communities, but, more importantly, by a process of European duplicity, exploitation, and oppression that would characterize what he viewed as the fundamental nature of the capitalist modern world.

Wright's narration of his voyage to the late-colonial Gold Coast only serves to further reinforce such an image of West Africa and the early modern Gold Coast by proffering it as an allegory for Africa's ultimate subjugation to capitalism, exploitation, and violence. Beginning his expedition on a train from London to Liverpool, the money and power of the Atlantic slave trade continuously haunt Wright as he journeys to and eventually embarks upon his West African voyage from a port city defined by its role in the slave trade. "Once slavery had become a vested interest in Liverpool," Wright reminded his audience, "its importance stretched far beyond the mere buying and selling of slaves. Britain's merchant navy was nursed and reared in the slave trade; her seamen were trained in it; shipbuilding in England was stimulated by this trade in flesh. ... And Liverpool itself flourished."[5] For Wright, his trip to West Africa was not a return "home"—a quest the prominent African-American writer Saidiya Hartman, half-a-century later, would also find elusive—but a reliving of the history of global capitalism and the political and economic processes by which Africans simultaneously built the foundation of the modern world and were excised from the riches of that world.[6] Decolonization, for him, was therefore an African attempt to reinsert the continent and its people back into this modern world.

After more than half-a-century of fruitful and rich scholarship on Africa's early modern and modern history, it is largely cliché to pick apart the fallacies, weaknesses, and half-truths in histories of early modern West Africa like Wright's. Included here is the superficiality of Wright's narrative, its removal of or at least minimization of African agency, and its presentation of the European powers on the coast as overpowering actors with a clear agenda for how to extract the most out of their relationships with the Africans they encountered. In very few places in West Africa did any European power ever play such a hegemonic role. Not even in the communities hosting the numerous massive forts and castles that continue to dot the Ghanaian Atlantic coast today did any European power ever maintain such authority.[7] Instead, in nearly every instance, the European powers operated at the discretion of their African hosts. In doing so, they were forced to pay tributes and rents to the communities and states they interacted with, relied on the labor and tolerance of the communities' peoples in order to maintain even the forts' most basic functions, and subjected themselves to the rituals and legal structures of the kingdoms and states with which they engaged. For instance, in one 1681 dispute with the King of Fetu over the behavior of a Danish bookkeeper, the Danes had little choice but to pay the king a fine of say (a type of woolen fabric), a cow, brandy, gold, and gunpowder so as to avoid being cut off from wood and water.[8] A little more than a century later, the Dutch similarly complained about conflicts with Fetu, among others, and a "stifled" trade in the region.[9]

The value in Wright's analysis, however, rests in its efforts to reflect upon the historical moment in which the territory that came to be known as the Gold Coast first entered the international imagination. Even more important is the journalist's emphasis on the long-term political, social, and economic reverberations of this burgeoning international interest in West Africa for not only those living in the region, but also, more broadly, the emerging global political economy of the early modern period. As Wright makes abundantly clear, he views the Gold Coast, as an idea, as a European creation, one manufactured out of the extraction of African wealth—gold and slaves—for European benefit. For him, the history that led to the formation of the Gold Coast was ultimately a history of global capitalism's rise. Over the years, many scholars—none more important in the study of Africa than Walter Rodney—have echoed Wright, offering similar and often much more sophisticated iterations of the journalist's general argument. In doing so, they too have sought to highlight for audiences that generally underestimate the importance of Africa in world affairs the centrality of Africa in the making of the modern world.[10]

This chapter traces the Gold Coast's history from approximately the fifteenth century through the nineteenth. In doing so, it argues that the making of the modern world and the development of the Gold Coast as a defined place in both the international and West African imagination were reciprocal, building off of each other. At least as popularly conceived in the twentieth and twenty-first centuries, no concept of the Gold Coast as a singular, coherently defined political, cultural, or geographic space existed within the West African imagination prior to the European arrival. Europeans named it and, while doing so, established a set of trading relationships that, over time, would come to reap the most out of the region's wealth as they could—first in gold and, later, in slaves.

However, it would be facile and even wrongheaded to argue that the early modern history of the region was dominated or even defined by Europeans and that European ideas regarding the Gold Coast were of foremost importance to those living in the region. Rather, it would be centuries before those living in the area would begin to identify themselves as Gold Coasters in even the most

Figure 1.1 Map of Upper Guinea or Proper Guinea in Africa, 1734.

perfunctory terms. Instead, most viewed themselves as part of a complicated web of political, social, cultural, and economic networks from which they derived their sense of self. With that said, recognition of the Gold Coast's rise as a quasi-defined place in the West African imagination can be seen in the shifting geographical orientation of those living in the region as, over the course of several centuries, they increasingly—albeit unevenly and never fully—turned their attention away from the historic wealth of the African interior toward the seeming promise of the emergent Atlantic trade. In doing so, they in turn sought to ensure themselves ever greater participation in a developing global political economy that would ultimately outrival anything that had preceded it.

The Gold Coast in the Early Modern World

The world of the late medieval and early modern periods was one of rapid integration, exchange, and change. For those living in what came to be known as the Gold Coast in the fifteenth century, the European arrival on the Atlantic coast was but one feature of an era of widescale transformation. On the global scale, the first centuries of the second millennium witnessed an influx of new trading and political networks, with major trading routes connecting world regions as far afield as the West African Sudan and Mediterranean to the Red and Black Seas and, at their furthest reaches, to China and Southeast Asia. Similarly vibrant networks also flourished in the Indian Ocean, linking Southeast Asia to the Indian subcontinent, the Persian Gulf, and East Africa's Swahili coast.[11] Moreover, it is also during this period that scholars can find the origins of the Ottoman Empire, which, over the course of the next six centuries, would thrive as the preeminent political and economic power in the so-called Muslim World. As such, the Ottomans positioned themselves as a global power connecting the western Mediterranean and North Africa to the Indian Ocean and Iran and as far north as the Caspian Sea.[12]

Throughout the medieval and early modern periods, West Africa was central to this process of global integration, as its ability to supply gold to markets in the Mediterranean, Red Sea, and beyond catapulted it to the forefront of the Mediterranean and Islamic worlds' political and economic imaginations. As early as the late eighth century, for instance, Arab travelers and scholars had already begun to refer to the region's foremost power, ancient Ghana (the medieval empire from which the modern state takes its name), as the "land of gold."[13] Others, meanwhile, wrote of court cultures awash in gold-adorned extravagance. "The king [of Ghana] adorns himself like a woman," the eleventh-century Iberian scholar al-Bakri reported at the time, "[wearing necklaces] round his neck and [bracelets] on his forearms, and he puts on a high cap (*tarṭūr*) decorated with gold and wrapped in a turban of fine cotton." Al-Bakri similarly described a reality in which gold existed in such magnificent abundance that the people had the ability to "accumulate gold until it lost its value."[14] Likewise, as Ghana declined and the empire of Mali overtook its northern neighbor, tales of West African gold were no less dramatic. Accounts of the wealth distributed during the Malian king Mansa Musa's fourteenth-century *hajj* still boggle the mind. En route, "This man flooded Cairo with his benefactions," the Damascus-born scholar al-'Umarī wrote. "He left no court emir ... nor holder of a royal office without the gift of a load of gold. ... They exchanged gold until they depressed its value in Egypt and caused its price to fall."[15]

In the first centuries of the second millennium, the region that came to be known as the Gold Coast largely remained on the periphery of the late medieval system. However, as archaeologist Merrick Posnansky has argued, the archaeological record suggests that the region was not fully disconnected from its Sudanic neighbors. Instead, Posnansky cites the discovery of pottery originating from the middle Niger River in dig sites as far south as the area that now comprises the southernmost reaches of the West African savanna in present-day Ghana. For Posnansky, the pottery, which dates back to at least the eleventh century, suggests a Sudanic trade presence in the region much earlier than the fifteenth-century timelines proposed by many scholars. By the late thirteenth or early fourteenth centuries, Posnansky argues, contact between the two regions intensified as a commercial gold industry began to develop on the borderlands of the forest and savanna in what is now Ghana's Bono and Bono East Regions.[16] Over the ensuing centuries, Sudanic traders in turn established long-standing and often quite intimate relationships with their local hosts, including the forming of communities of their own alongside those of their autochthonous counterparts. In doing so, as historian Ivor Wilks has shown, the traders often took local wives, learned local languages, and "tended to develop secondary identities" connected to their host communities.[17]

In contrast to what had likely been a set of relatively localized trading relationships, integration into the Sudanic trade provided those living in the region with linkages to the broader sets of relationships that, for centuries, had connected the West African Sudan to the Mediterranean and broader early modern world. For those living in these earliest Gold Coast gold-producing regions, the trade primarily took place through northern caravans operated by Mande traders originating from the Malian city of Djenné, who exchanged items including beads, cloth, and brassware for the region's gold and other forest products.[18] By the sixteenth century, the Mande further entrenched their position in the region as Mande warriors challenged existing political powers in what is now northern Ghana in order to found the state of Gonja. Over the course of the next century, Gonja would rise as a major player in the region's trade and politics, dismissing its major rival (Dagbon) west of the White Volta.[19] As Wilks and others have detailed, in Gonja's founding and expansion was not only an attempted centralization of the Sudanic trade in the region, but also the first major expansion of Islam into the area.[20] While the wider-scale Islamization of parts of modern-day northern Ghana would likely not occur until later, the Islamization that accompanied Gonja's founding signaled, at least in part, the region's increasing cultural and social integration into the broader early modern world of the West African Sudan and beyond.[21] Moreover, by at least the late fifteenth and early sixteenth centuries, Mande traders would make their way as far south as the Atlantic coast.[22]

By the time the Portuguese arrived along the Gulf of Guinea coast during the mid-fifteenth century, much of the area comprising the contemporary Ghanaian state had become integrated—if not directly, indirectly—into the Sudanic trade. For the Portuguese, who, like most Europeans, had heard tales of riches to be found in West Africa, the portion of the Gulf of Guinea that they named the "Gold Coast" offered a land of opportunity. In his early sixteenth-century *Esmeraldo de Situ Orbis*, for instance, the Portuguese explorer Duarte Pacheco Pereira chronicled a region flush in the trade of gold, cloth, metal works, and other items. Writing on the now Western Region town of Axim, Pacheco Pereira painted a picture of a trading relationship that annually supplied upwards of "thirty to forty thousand doubloons of good gold" to the Portuguese. In exchange for the gold, Pacheco Pereira further noted, those trading in Axim received "brass bracelets, basins of the same metal, red and blue cloth, linen neither very coarse nor very fine, and 'lanbens,' that is, a kind of mantle made like the shawls of Alentejo [a region of southern Portugal], with stripes of red, green, blue and white, the stripes being two or three inches wide." Nearly all of these goods, he added, had North African and southern Mediterranean origins.[23] However, more than the "cheap trinkets" Wright dismissed them as,[24] for those purchasing the items, these goods carried significant political, cultural, and social meaning and became thoroughly integrated into the region's political, social, economic, and cultural history.[25]

The 1482 construction of what is now known as Elmina Castle only foretold of even greater future wealth for the Portuguese according to Pacheco Pereira.[26] The construction of the fort was a long and frustrating process, the Portuguese explorer wrote, one apparently stalled by what he presented as "trouble with the negroes [*sic*], who wished to prevent the work." However, he proudly asserted, "it was finally finished, despite them, with all diligence and zeal." As a result, Pacheco Pereira boasted, since the fort's completion, "170,000 doubloons of good fine gold, and sometimes much more, are yearly brought thence to these realms of Portugal."[27] By the early sixteenth century, the Portuguese Gold Coast would ultimately emerge as one of the world's leading exporters of gold. In Elmina alone, the trade had transformed the once sleepy coastal town into a major trading center shipping out nearly half a ton of gold per year.[28]

Over the next century, several new European actors would arrive on the Gold Coast's shores, with each seeking to partake in the region's lucrative trade. By as early as the 1590s, the Dutch would challenge the Portuguese dominance of the region's European trade. In 1637, they would capture Elmina Castle and, not long after, push the Portuguese out of the region almost completely.[29] Likewise, the English, who had begun to make expeditions into the area as early as the 1550s, would begin construction on a fort of their own in the town of Kormantse by the early seventeenth century.[30] By the mid-seventeenth century, the Danish, Swedish, and Brandenburgers would all come to also have a presence in the region. Moreover, as with the Portuguese, nearly all of these European powers sought to establish their own trading centers, with each erecting their own forts and castles along the Atlantic coast.

Gold Coast Histories in the Era of the Atlantic Trade

With their arrival on the Gulf of Guinea coast, the Europeans opened new avenues for trade in the region, which gradually came to compete with those of the West African Sudan. For those living in the Gold Coast, though, the trade coincided with broader shifts in the region's political, cultural, and social landscape, particularly in the region's forest belt. By the late medieval period, for instance, what some scholars have posited as a forest region marked by relatively densely populated settlements dating back to at least the ninth century had given way to communities of much smaller social groupings possibly engaged in hunting and gathering.[31] However, by as early as the fifteenth century—if one follows Ivor Wilks's influential, but contested "big bang theory"—an agricultural revolution had begun to take hold in the Gold Coast's forests, with settled communities cultivating a range of food crops.[32] In the cultural realm, again following Wilks, the forest's agricultural revolution gave rise to the Akan culture, which, up to the present, has played a central role in the region's political, social, cultural, and economic history.[33] Meanwhile, along the central coast and Accra Plains, the sixteenth century marked the likely arrival of the original Ga settlers (*Ga mashi*).[34] Further east, Ewe-speaking peoples in Ghana's Volta Region also trace their roots to the period, which they mark with oral traditions highlighting a late fifteenth-century exodus from the Togolese town of Notsie.[35]

For those living in the regions comprising the emerging Gold Coast, the Atlantic trade was but one feature of the political and economic transformation that characterized the era. More broadly, local oral traditions almost invariably recount an era of widespread uncertainty, warfare, and migration. Moreover, many both directly and indirectly connect this instability to their unique founding stories. In Simbew of the Edina (Elmina) state, for instance, a 1970's informant of historian John Kofi Fynn constructed a historical narrative for the town centered on the possibilities created by an escape from instability. "What I heard from my ancestors," he explained,

> was that the founder of this town was called Nana Ngwando. And he was accompanied by his sister Adjoa Ngwando. ... When we were coming from Takyiman, there was a war which scattered most of our people but our founder always went with his sister. When we arrived on the coast they [Nana Ngwando and Adjoa Ngwando] left Elmina behind us and went into the interior; when they reached the river Surowi he told his sister that they should settle here and hence Simbew.[36]

Another of Fynn's respondents offered a similar account, insisting, "All settlers around these areas arrived from Takyiman; we left Takyiman area because of wars. When each group arrived they did not know some other groups had arrived; so it was only when [they] came in contact that it was recognised that some of their brothers had already preceded them."[37]

Other groups, meanwhile, have narrated histories connected to migrations far from West Africa. In the 1970s, for instance, then-Denkyirahene Odefo Boa Amponsem III reflected on what he presented as a past of transcontinental migration—a trek that helped shape who the Denkyira were. "We migrated from the source of [the] River Nile," the Denkyira king explained, "passed through the lands of the Moslems, and came to settle at Brong-Ahafo Nkyiraa for about two centuries. ... And because we settled at Nkyiraa for such a long time that people said we have become like the Nkyiraas. Hence 'Denkyira.'" As articulated by the Denkyirahene, the long migration westward proved necessary given the Denkyira's supposed dislike of the "Islamic religion."[38] Meanwhile, in Asante, Asantehene Osei Agyeman Prempeh II made similar claims during the mid-twentieth century. To this end, he insisted that "I know it truly to be the fact that in the ancient past Ashanti people lived by Jerusalem and removed little by little to live again in Egypt then to here."[39] However, as historian T. C. McCaskie has explained, the Asantehene did not intend to connect all Asante to this history of migration. Instead, the history the Asantehene put forward had clear class implications as he presented it as a history primarily of the Asante elite.[40]

There is a dearth of historical evidence supporting many of the claims articulated in many of the narratives of transcontinental migration. However, key to the local histories articulated by Ghana's various peoples and states is the simultaneous sense of connection and competition embodied within them, for embedded within many of Ghana's oral traditions are intersecting and, at times, conflicting themes of autochthony and relocation. In the Bono East town of Takyiman, for instance, Bono claims to be the "first-born people"[41] not only represent an attempt to emphasize the Bono's direct connection to the land, but also their independence from the subsequent powers—most notably the Asante—that encroached upon and would eventually usurp Bono sovereignty. As former Takyimanhene Nana Akumfi Ameyaw asserted during a 1970 interview with Dennis M. Warren and K. O. Brempong, "It is not true when people say that Techiman [Takyiman] had no culture or tradition of its own. Techiman taught the Asante how to wear cloth. Techiman people used to wear ornaments made of gold. The Asante used pieces of iron from the blacksmith's shop and they called it gold." As a result, he firmly asserted, "The culture of Asante came from Techiman."[42] At the heart of such portrayals of Bono history is thus a representation of a Bono collective sense of self bound to a past rooted in power and wealth that predates what would become Bono's eventual fall to its southern rival. For those holding Bono's historical knowledge and traditions, the task therefore became that of constructing a past that positioned the Bono as the genealogical forebearers to the Asante and Akan more broadly. In doing so, the Bono not only claimed ancestral status, but also asserted themselves as the cultural progenitors of that which made the Akan unique, most visibly via Nana Akumfi Ameyaw's examples of its goldworks and dress.

A similar narrative process played out in Denkyira. By the end of the seventeenth century, several major Akan states had emerged in the Gold Coast, with some like Akwamu rising in strength to overpower coastal non-Akan peoples and in turn coming to direct major portions of the Atlantic trade along the central coast.[43] Also arriving on the Gold Coast political scene during the mid-seventeenth century, Denkyira distinguished itself from its southeastern counterpart by focusing not on controlling the Atlantic trade directly, but on supplying gold and slaves for the coastal trade.[44] As such, European commentators reflected on the precipitous rise of Denkyira as a regional power. According to the Dutch merchant William Bosman, "This Country, formerly restrained to a small compass of Land, and containing but an inconsiderable number of Inhabitants, is, by their Valour, so improved in Power, that they are respected and honoured by all their Neighbouring Nations; all of which they have taught to fear them, except *Afiante* [Asante] and *Akim* [Akyem], who are yet stronger than they."[45] Similarly, a late seventeenth-century Danish daybook recounted reports, whereby, out of fear of the Denkyira, potential adversaries absconded to areas of European influence for protection.[46]

By 1701, however, Denkyira would fall to a rapidly expanding Asante. Bosman, for his part, described the Denkyira defeat as "a fatal and sudden Destruction ... [on] so potent of a Land." From his perspective, though, writing four years after Denkyira's defeat, the state's collapse appeared almost inevitable, for he explained that, in the years following its rise, "*Dinkira*, elevated by its great Riches and Power, became so arrogant, that it looked on all other *Negroes* with a contemptible Eye, esteeming them no more than its Slaves." The result was purportedly a feeling of "common Hatred" among its neighbors toward the once powerful state.[47] Moreover, so dramatic was Denkyira's downfall from the European perspective that, approximately sixty years later, one Danish merchant barely deigned to mention it in his list of influential Gold Coast "nations." Instead, he cast the defeated state off as one of among several other kingdoms that, by the mid-eighteenth century, were little more than has-beens "of no more importance than our Mountain Negroes at Accra, who also often wage war against each other."[48] A Danish official, meanwhile, offered a similar appraisal of Denkyira in 1749 as he labeled the Denkyira as simply a people "who do nothing but steal small quantities [of gold?] from the *Assiantes* [Asante]."[49]

Like with Bono, Denkyira's defeat to the Asante continues to haunt the once powerful state's oral traditions. As Odefo Boa Amponsem III recounted in his interview with historian K. Y. Daaku, military defeat exiled the Denkyira from their capital of Abankeseeso near the Ofin River.[50] At its peak, Abankeseeso was a major cosmopolitan center with significant political and spiritual importance.[51] However, as Odefo Boa Amponsem III related, few things marked Denkyira history more so than conflict, warfare, and instability. In its rise, the then-Denkyirahene argued, Denkyira arose during a period in which differing groups were constantly seeking "to swallow" one another. At this time, though, the Denkyira thrived, for, he contended, "through constant fighting we managed to increase our numbers, and our fighting force. So by the time we reached Abankeseeso, or rather by the time we fought and defeated Awurade Basa [the king of Adanse], we had quite a substantial force. And our empire too was expanding."[52] However, Denkyira's 1701 defeat to the Asante not only forced them to succumb to Asante authority, but it also represented an existential threat to the Denkyira's collective sense of themselves as a people as Asante threatened to destroy or usurp key features of what it meant to be Denkyira, including the Denkyira stool. Exile thus served as a means by which to protect the ritual symbols of the state from the Asante. The ramifications of this dispersal, however, are still felt by the Denkyira as they remain alienated from their now lost historical capital.[53]

States and Slaves in the Atlantic Trade

As the region succumbed to a period of widespread warfare and uncertainty during the mid-centuries of the second millennium, those living in the recently christened Gold Coast sought to adapt to their new political and economic realities. Through at least the mid-seventeenth century, gold continued to dominate the region's trade. In the Edina (Elmina) state town of Brenu-Akyinmu, where salt production had been key to the region's pre-Atlantic economy, one woman explained that, in order to partake in the region's emerging Atlantic trade, "We sold our salt for gold dust and used it in buying cloths, guns, gun powder and other European goods."[54] Access to these goods was not just about economic power. Rather, access carried with it key forms of political, social, and cultural power connected through the social relations and networks bound to the goods' distribution. To this end, historian Ray Kea has shown that, by the early seventeenth century, elaborate systems of local governance had emerged throughout the southern Gold Coast aimed at regulating not only the Atlantic trade, but also the distribution of its wares. This included the introduction of an array of mechanisms of revenue generation (tolls, custom duties, and taxes) in the Gold Coast's coastal communities.[55]

The introduction of the Atlantic slave trade into the Gold Coast further intensified the social and cultural uncertainties generated by the European arrival. In relative terms, the Atlantic's export trade in people was a late arrival to the region as more slaves disembarked in the Gold Coast than left it through the mid-seventeenth century.[56] However, this would change dramatically. Externally, the ever-increasing demand for slaves in the Americas drove the trade internationally as enslaved Gold Coasters, among others, toiled in New World plantation societies. For those enslaved, the journey to the Americas was a tortuous experience. Shuttling the enslaved, often hundreds of miles, from the sites of their capture, slavers forced the enslaved from market to market, where, for some, local slaveholders purchased them as part of the domestic trade. For others, they would often find themselves bought by a new set of traders who would continue to shepherd them even further south until their arrival at the coast. The horrors of enslavement persisted once aboard a slave ship. As historian Sowande' Mustakeem has argued, the slave ship was foremost a site of death, terror, and sickness. It was through such horrors, she further insists, that the slave ship served its purpose, as it sought to break down the captive's sense of self and, in doing so, "any sense of control over one's personal life in the near and far future."[57] Despite a slow start up to the mid-seventeenth century, by Britain's 1807 abolition of the slave trade, European slavers would forcibly export more than a million individuals from the Gold Coast to the Americas.[58]

For those living in the Gold Coast, the rise of the international slave trade was at once indicative of the shifting political landscape of the region and a catalyst for even further change and uncertainty. Moreover, key to Gold Coast participation in the Atlantic slave trade was the state-building initiatives of the region's early modern centralized states. As the states expanded, often via warfare, many found themselves with a surplus of captives-turned-slaves of whom they felt compelled to dispose. As Asantehene Osei Bonsu argued after his 1818–19 conquest of neighboring Gyaman, the problems associated with maintaining a population of war captives were unambiguous, for, he asserted, "Unless I kill or sell them, they will grow strong and kill my people."[59]

Meanwhile, on the coast, the trade in people offered a new source of revenue, supplementing the region's gold trade with an enslaved labor pool in increasing demand by their European counterparts. Along the Fante coast, for instance, many of the towns that had previously risen to prominence as cosmopolitan centers of the transnational gold trade, including Elmina, refashioned themselves into key sites for the international trade in people. "My own uncle who was a slave dealer bought textiles from the whites at the coast and sent them to the North and brought slaves back to the south," Adwoa Mansa of Brenu-Akyinmu recalled to John Kofi Fynn in the early 1970s.[60] Other towns, meanwhile, further to the periphery of the pre-eighteenth-century Atlantic economy—the most notable being Anomabo—utilized the slave trade's rise in order to assert themselves as new economic players on the Gold Coast political and economic stage.[61]

By the turn of the eighteenth century, accounts by European merchants and travelers—many of whom were involved in the slave trade—emphasized the destabilizing effects of the trade on Gold Coast social life. Even the "most Potent *Negroe* [*sic*]," William Bosman explained in 1705, "can't pretend to be insured from Slavery; for if he ever ventures himself in the Wars it may easily become his Lot." Following enslavement, Bosman further relayed, an individual could only hope that someone would pay the ransom required to ensure his or her freedom. If not, he could be "forced to a perpetual Slavery."[62] Others, meanwhile, seemingly turned a blind eye to the social disruption caused by the trade by insisting with little qualification that slavery was a natural part of African life. In doing so, they often suggested that the external trade in slaves had little effect on those caught up in it. Arguing in 1764, for instance, governor of Cape Coast Castle and slave trade apologist John Hippisley proposed that, "in a civilized part of the world, where liberty is considered in so rapturous a light," the slave trade and slavery may have resulted in a set of more devastating consequences for a given society by stunting its population growth and even potentially altering the "sensibility" of its men and women. "But," Hippisley insisted, "the idea of slavery is different in Africa; for independent of the almost total absence of keen sensation, the slaves of a family are considered as no unrespectable part of it." As a result, in this not uncommon rendering, only those who actively disrupted society were ever sold, thus making slavery, to his mind, a potentially stabilizing force in African society.[63]

Not dissimilar portrayals of slavery and the slave trade also made their way into local accounts, particularly among those states that were deeply involved in the trade's various facets. Along the Fante coast, for instance, accounts of the trade at times deemphasize the personal devastation and social disruptions it caused, focusing their attention instead on the supposed social qualities of those sold into slavery. In the oral traditions collected by John Kofi Fynn in the towns of the Edina state, Fynn's informants stressed that it was the region's social deviants—namely "disobedient children" and "notorious criminals"—who were sold into the trade.[64] Meanwhile, in accounts from other regions of the Gold Coast, the focus of many oral traditions often turned to how key groups of the enslaved were spared export and incorporated into the communities and families of those who captured them, particularly in the case of women. As one man in the Central Region Denkyira town of Kyekyewere-Nyameso noted in 1969, marriage—albeit without "marriage rites ... beside a bottle of gin"—served as the primary mechanism for integrating enslaved women into one's family.[65] In another Denkyira town, it was also argued that it was even possible for slaves to become local chiefs should "no royals [be] available."[66] Similar claims were made in Adanse. However, at least in the Adanse town of Dompoase, it was claimed that marriage rites of a "'small drink'" were to be performed before a slave was to be married so as to ensure that "a fine could be collected from any one [*sic*] who seduced her."[67]

For those enslaved, though, enslavement was almost invariably a deeply alienating and traumatic experience, even for those kept for domestic purposes. The historical record, however, offers few contemporaneous first-hand accounts from those enslaved of the social disruption and fear elicited by the growing slave trade of the eighteenth-century Gold Coast.[68] However, among the accounts produced a century later by former slaves, themes of danger, dislocation, and fear abound.[69] Recalling his enslavement during the 1869–71 Asante invasion of the Ewe-dominated lands east of the Volta River, former slave Aaron Kuku – whose narrative historian Sandra Greene published in 2011 – recounted in 1929 to a Gold Coast-born amanuensis a pre-enslavement life characterized by a close-knit family shattered by the Asante attack and the family's subsequent enslavement. As the Asante attacked, Kuku, who was approximately nine or ten years old at the time, recalled the chaos of the scene as his father and other men, "wielding machetes," ran to meet the Asante forces, while the "whole village gathered and started running away from the war—mostly women and children." Overwhelmed on the battlefield, Kuku continued, "My father and his colleagues who could not continue fighting retreated and joined us in the night. We had left our own village and become [*sic*] war refugees." Eventually captured, Kuku and his father were separated from his mother, who he would not see again for more than two decades, and escorted to Asante. In Asante, Kuku and his father eventually escaped and returned home only to be re-enslaved, this time in Eweland.[70]

For Kuku, enslavement carried with it an extremely high price. Throughout his life history, he spoke openly about the depression, desires for death, and suicide attempts manifested by his enslavement. Kuku's first suicide attempt came after hearing that his younger sister had died in Kumasi and after being told that all older people enslaved by the Asante were eventually killed. Assuming this would be the fate of his father, Kuku attempted to hang himself while his master was away. Later, while watching his father suffer while "fastened to a heavy piece of wood," Kuku confessed to his father his renewed intentions to kill himself, for, he lamented, "it would be better for me to die than to see him suffering all the time."[71] Even after his second escape, while living free in his hometown, Kuku could not shake his suicidal thoughts as loneliness and depression overtook him while he cared for his family members and others during a smallpox outbreak. "In the night," he explained, "I took my gun, made it ready for firing, and laid it down. I took my accordion, played it, and sang sorrowful songs, with the intention of committing suicide after the singing."[72] As with many narratives attached to those who eventually joined the church, Kuku asserted that it was ultimately God who saved him from his suicidal intentions and the church from his sorrow.[73]

The situation for enslaved women was often even more harrowing and laden with uncertainty. On the coast, not only did female captives face increased likelihood of export to the Americas, but, in major trading centers, they also faced threats of sexual exploitation, violence, and marriage to the Europeans.[74] Those enslaved domestically faced similar threats to their well-being and body. Even more fundamentally to their lives was the deep-seated personal insecurity that characterized female enslavement in the Gold Coast. As historian Sandra Greene, among others, has emphasized, arguments touting the marriage of female slaves to their masters or other members of their masters' families should not blunt the vulnerability, isolation, and even danger women faced in their enslavement. Rather, for many enslaved women, marriage was a double-edged sword. At one level, it served as a strategy for self-preservation at a moment in their lives necessarily defined by uncertainty and insecurity, while, on another level, it was a demand to which they often had little power to contest. In many enslaved women's day-to-day life, the result was a reality for these women and their children in which they were uniquely reliant on the whims of their masters/husbands to protect their interests, thus fundamentally circumscribing the options available to them even in cases of potential emancipation.[75]

As elsewhere in Africa, the Atlantic and domestic slave trades operated in tandem in the Gold Coast through Britain's 1807 abolition of the international trade. For those caught up in the trade, there was little to distinguish between the two trades at the point of capture. Chance and most notably gender often determined the likelihood of whether one would be integrated into the local trade or be exported abroad. For most male captives, of which there was comparably only a negligible internal market, the Middle Passage awaited them. A range of other options, however, existed for female slaves, including sale further north as part of the trans-Saharan slave trade. Others, as noted, were integrated into their capturers' families or those of other slave owners. As a result, by the end of the eighteenth century, less than a third of slaves shipped from the Gold Coast across the Atlantic were women and, among both the men and women incorporated into the Atlantic trade, most were between the ages of fourteen and thirty.[76] Furthermore, as historian Patrick Manning has argued, throughout much of West Africa, the gender disparities of the slave trade had broader social repercussions, particularly in the areas of labor and marriage as women now increasingly involved themselves in work previously conceived of as men's work. Moreover, in terms of marriage, the gender imbalance also shifted local and regional marriage patterns, leading to an increasing reliance on polygyny. In doing so, Manning notes, marriage ages shifted for both men and women, resulting in men marrying later in life and women earlier.[77]

The 1807 abolition of the Atlantic slave trade did little to slow the Gold Coast's domestic slave trade. Rather, through continued warfare and the shifting of the trans-Atlantic trade in people to that of so-called legitimate goods (cash crops and other commodities), the practice of slavery continued unabated through the last decades of the nineteenth century. In contrast to other African settings, however, where large plantations run on slave labor characterized much of nineteenth-century domestic slavery, the shift to the legitimate trade in the Gold Coast was buttressed through the productive capabilities of relatively small-scale producers and landholders who, with the labor of slaves and kin, cultivated and processed a rotating array of goods for international markets.[78] Economic historian A. G. Hopkins has thus described this shift in West African production as an economic revolution, as production was oriented away from groups Hopkins portrayed as "large entrepreneurs" toward a much wider array of small-scale farmers and traders involved in everything from rubber to timber to palm oil production.[79] In terms of palm oil specifically, which over the course of the nineteenth century would come to literally lubricate much of the European Industrial Revolution, slave and free labor in the Gold Coast and nearby Nigeria would result in a forty-fold increase in palm oil exports over the first half of the century.[80] Moreover, the second half of the century witnessed a renewed influx of interest in the Gold Coast and West African oil palm industry as European manufacturers sought uses for the tree's kernels, which produced an oil of their own consisting of a different chemical makeup.[81]

Meanwhile, in Asante, which, by the early nineteenth century, had secured its position as the region's unrivalled superpower, the abolition of the Atlantic slave trade initiated a reorganization of the state's economic orientation. For a state built upon military expansion, abolition left it with a surplus of slaves, which had both political and economic implications as prices for slaves dropped precipitously and, as Osei Bonsu complained of earlier, left the state with an abundance of captives. Moreover, as historian Ivor Wilks has argued, the Asante also faced a coastal trade in which European traders now insisted on trading in either gold or ivory, which for both practical (in the case of ivory) and cultural (for gold) purposes proved difficult for the Asante to collect.[82]

The Asante state responded to the situation by attempting to reorient major portions of its trade away from the Atlantic and back to the north, trading in kola to states as far afield as the Sokoto Caliphate in present-day Northern Nigeria.[83] As with the oil palm trade in the southern Gold Coast, the Asante kola trade rested on the labor of relatively small-scale producers who worked family plots cultivating and harvesting the nut for sale to local traders. As harvests took place, traders—operating under the protection of the Asante state would transport the commodity to northern Gold Coast market towns before the goods would continue even further north into the West African Sudan. Throughout its production and eventual arrival in the Sudan, the Asante kola became embedded with a range of cultural meanings as communities integrated what historian Edmund Abaka calls the "food-drug" into everything from marriage rites to healthcare and the rituals of royal gift giving.[84] For many living in the Gold Coast during the early nineteenth century, the Asante turn to the north ultimately offered an economic alternative to the regional commerce that, for the previous several centuries, had been increasingly dominated by the Atlantic trade. Moreover, it did so much to the frustration of the European merchants along the coast.[85]

Commodities and Colonization

As the economics of the Gold Coast and West Africa shifted during the nineteenth century, so too did the international politics encompassing the region. For much of the more than three-century-long European presence in the Gold Coast, European political power in the region had at best been marginal. In most cases, Europeans operated at the pleasure of their African hosts, making them subject to the whims and desires of not only the region's numerous coastal communities, but also the Gold Coast's shifting political and cultural realities.

However, the nineteenth century saw the intensity of European interest in the region—and Africa more broadly—escalate as European powers, vying for their own political and economic superiority in the burgeoning world of industrial capitalism, sought to cordon off control over a cascading array of regional import and export markets in the Global South. In the Gold Coast, particularly, competition for access to the region's commodity markets swelled during the early nineteenth century, with the British consistently seeking to stave off challenges from a variety of competing powers. Writing in 1843, for instance, one Danish official eyed the Scandinavian power's potential entrance into the oil palm trade as a mechanism for securing Denmark's position in the emerging industrial trade of the era. Not only would a Danish focus on palm oil aim to challenge Britain's oversized role in both the West African and European trade of the commodity, but it also promised to position Denmark at the center of an envisioned Baltic trading network feeding Central Europe's manufacturing sector.[86] In the Gold Coast and Nigeria, the French and Germans also sought to make inroads in the region's palm oil trade, as did other African traders. British firms, in turn, responded to these challenges by attempting to push the interlopers to the periphery of the trade.[87]

Meanwhile, politically, a gradual shift began to occur during the nineteenth century as European authorities increasingly sought to extend their reach beyond their coastal bases. The British proved the most aggressive. By the early 1820s, the first of a series of wars would break out between the Asante and the British. Lasting nearly a decade, the first of these wars culminated in a peace that drastically limited the Asante presence in what now comprises approximately the southern quarter of the contemporary Ghanaian state.[88] Moreover, in the southern Gold Coast, the British came out of the war aiming to strengthen their relationships with allied chiefs and kings in the region. In perhaps the most famous and debated instance, nine southern chiefs and kings signed an agreement with the British whereby they extended British legal and criminal jurisdiction to their territories. Known as the Bond of 1844, the agreement often unofficially marks the onset of the Gold Coast's colonial history in the Ghanaian and imperial popular imaginations, with even the date of the country's 1957 independence (March 6) chosen to coincide with the 113th anniversary of the Bond's signing. In practical terms, though, the Bond alone had only a limited impact on the Gold Coast–British relationship, with even some nineteenth-century apologists for British colonial rule hinting that its influence was often overstated.[89] Rather, the Bond should be seen as part of a broader, incremental process that gradually extended British authority in the region.[90] It was also a process that, over the course of the century, eventually drove the region's competing European powers out of the Gold Coast. As a result, by mid-century, the Danes would sell their remaining Gold Coast possessions to the British, with the Dutch following suit approximately two decades later.

The Dutch withdrawal from the Gold Coast left Great Britain as the only remaining European power in the region. Following the Dutch exodus, the British began an even more aggressive push into the region. In Elmina, the most famous and influential Dutch-allied town in the region, residents quickly protested British claims to the town.[91] In response, in June 1873, British forces—largely comprised of West Indian and Hausa soldiers—attacked the town. It would fall to the British approximately two weeks later. Elsewhere, other previously Dutch-allied towns, including Shama, Sekondi, and Axim, also rebelled against the British before they too succumbed to British authority.[92] In other parts of the southern Gold Coast, such as the Kingdom of Apollonia (Nzema) in contemporary Ghana's far southwest, long-standing local tensions coincided with this period of British consolidation. For the Nzema, these tensions culminated in the kingdom's 1873 schism.[93] Meanwhile, in Asante, another war between the British and the Asante ensued, contributing to a political crisis in the forest state.[94] Simultaneously, British authorities would continue with legal and administrative discussions on the extension of Britain's political, juridical, and even territorial rights in the region. In doing so, the British had carved out the artifice for the nascent Gold Coast colonial state. The 1901 defeat of the Asante during the final Anglo–Asante War only further solidified British colonial supremacy in the Gold Coast at the turn of the century.

Conclusion

It is tempting to draw a clear line connecting the Gold Coast Africans' precolonial relationships to the emergent Atlantic trade to the late nineteenth-century establishment of the Gold Coast colonial state. Part of the reason for which such a narrative proves so enticing is how colonialism appears from the perspectives of modern African history as simultaneously new and old. As a product of global capitalism with antecedents dating back to the early modern gold and slave trades, the extractive forces that embodied the nineteenth- and twentieth-century Gold Coast colonial state appear as logical extensions of this early modern past into the modern era. Moreover, from the viewpoint of the continental and global scale, such a model does in fact reflect a history that, over the past 500-plus years, has cultivated a fundamental inequality in relations between the Global North and Global South. For, as Walter Rodney argued in a 1969 essay on the Gold Coast gold and slave trades, regardless of the commodity (minerals or people), on the macro-scale, the result was a further impoverishing of the Gold Coast people at the expense of their trade relative to their counterparts in the Global North. More importantly, Rodney further contends, "The comparison attempted here between gold and slave exports from the Gold Coast can be repeated in other areas of West Africa by examining local products which were valuable exports, such as gum in Senegal and camwood in Sierra Leone. In every instance," he continues, "the comparison reveals those debilitating effects upon African society which were peculiar to the Atlantic slave trade, because they flowed from the unique way in which the trade was conducted."[95]

However, such a framework only tells part of the story. Most importantly, it leaves out the interests, ambitions, and desires of the Gold Coast—and, more broadly, African—communities that engaged in the Atlantic trade. For these communities, the Atlantic trade did not only provide new sources of social and economic wealth, they also created new alternatives and pathways for experimentation as they often integrated the relationships forged through the Atlantic into a broader repertoire of political, social, economic, and cultural decision-making and activities that, in their broadest formulations, linked the Atlantic, the West African forest belt, the West African Sudan, and, in some cases, even the Mediterranean. Even up to the nineteenth century, many in the Gold Coast were balancing the multiple relationships forged through these linkages, moving in and out of them as their interests, self-conceptions, or political and economic realities shifted.

In their relationships with Europeans, the result was a set of political and economic realities whereby, up until the nineteenth century, no European power could dominate the region's political and economic relations. In many cases, most could not even feel secure in the stability of their positions in the region as, in the vast majority of instances, they relied on the communities hosting them. It was only in the nineteenth century, when Great Britain, following the abolition of the slave trade and the eventual exodus of all other European powers from the region, gained the political and military power to begin what even then was the gradual and uneven process of establishing the Gold Coast colonial state. As a result, what the introduction of Europeans into the Gulf of Guinea ultimately did, from the perspective of the Gold Coast, was incrementally shift the region's focus away from the African interior toward the coast. In doing so, it began the process of integrating the region into an emerging global political economy—with its resultant political, economic, social, and cultural ramifications—formed out of the growing Atlantic trade.

Chapter 2

COLONIAL NETWORKS:
MAKING NATION AND STATE IN THE GOLD COAST

By the early twentieth century, as the colonial state increasingly became a political and administrative reality, Gold Coasters began to adapt to their new political and social circumstances. As numerous scholars have underscored, at the macro-level, colonialism was simultaneously a political and economic phenomenon designed to secure, if not control, key features of the world's import and export markets.[1] As the subsequent chapter will show regarding cocoa specifically, the situation in the Gold Coast did not differ substantially from that of the rest of the continent as the colonial and imperial governments' continuous search for new commodities and products for extraction fundamentally shaped how Gold Coasters related to the emergent colonial state. More broadly, in the new capital of Accra, colonial administrators in turn concerned themselves with everything from the stability of and productive capabilities of the colony's mining industry to the value of a rotating array of export commodities (palm oil, cocoa, timber, coffee, and rubber, among others) to the quest for ever newer sources of colonial wealth generation during the first decades of colonial rule. The administrative and political apparatus of the colonial state not only sought to serve these economic interests, but, perhaps even more importantly, also aimed to construct what from its viewpoint was the social and cultural milieu necessary for the colony's economic success.

However, for many Gold Coasters, the colonial state had a variety of other meanings as well, for it also connected them to a range of new local, regional, and even global networks. In many ways rooted in the colonial system, these networks offered key groups of Gold Coasters new avenues for political, social, cultural, and economic exploration. Missions, the extension of Western education, the advent of African-run newspapers, and the rise of African political and social clubs, among other phenomena, all helped create an environment in which Gold Coast men and women found it possible to experiment with new political and social relationships, religions, modes of self-expression, economic advancement, and mediums of self-identification. As a result, this chapter argues that it was foremost during the decades straddling the nineteenth and twentieth centuries that Gold Coasters first began to theorize the ideas of the "Gold Coast" and "Gold Coasters" themselves, transforming their meanings from mere geographic and demonymic references to ones that have specific, yet evolving political and social meanings.

The result then was a political, social, and cultural environment during the late nineteenth and early twentieth centuries whereby Gold Coasters increasingly began to reflect on their own and others' relationships to the region's complex precolonial identities and histories, those manifested by empire, and, in some cases, even the supranational possibilities promised by late nineteenth- and early twentieth-century pan-Africanism.

This chapter thus explores the interactions between the emergent colonial political economy of the late nineteenth and early twentieth centuries and the changing ways in which key groups of Gold Coasters related to one another and identified themselves during the period. Among the most important issues addressed are questions surrounding the colonial project's role in advancing ideas about what the Gold Coaster should be and how Gold Coast intellectuals, merchants, farmers, clerks, and others embraced and pushed back on these ideas. Most importantly, the chapter foreshadows that it was through the vibrancy and fluidity of this *fin-de-siècle* discourse that subsequent debates and contestations over what it meant to be "Ghanaian" in Ghana's postcolonial history would in part have their genealogical roots.

Background to Colonization

In 1911, a Cape Coast Methodist minister named Samuel Richard Brew (S. R. B.) Attoh Ahuma published a book titled *The Gold Coast Nation and National Consciousness*. Largely comprised of articles previously published in the Cape Coast-based newspaper, the *Gold Coast Leader*, Attoh Ahuma lamented the rise of a Gold Coast populace that he felt had become consumed by the shiny things offered by the European presence in the region. In doing so, he complained of African clerks obsessed with European fashion—young people whose shortsightedness had blinded them from the accomplishments of those who had come before them and engendered a society overly dependent on singular leaders.[2] For Attoh Ahuma, these social and cultural scourges had distanced many Gold Coasters from what had connected them to the land and their past. Just as importantly, it had also inadvertently helped cultivate the perception that an organic and coherent Gold Coast nation did not exist. Instead, he contended, the focus in discussions around a possible Gold Coast identity had become the presumed disunities that, some claimed, divided the populace, as commentators reflected on what they presented as the Gold Coast's "multiform composition of congeries of States and Provinces" that were artificially brought together under the single umbrella of colonial rule. For these commentators, Attoh Ahuma relayed, the Gold Coast could not be a nation, for it was simply too politically, constitutionally, and linguistically fragmented to embody the requisite sense of coherence demanded of a nation.[3]

In *The Gold Coast Nation and National Consciousness*, Attoh Ahuma fundamentally disputed such characterizations of the Gold Coast on both cultural and historical grounds. In doing so, he conceded that certain Gold Coast social and cultural realities may, on their face, stretch conventional definitions of a nation, with their focus on political, cultural, and linguistic homogeneity. Regardless, the Cape Coast minister defiantly declared: "WE [Gold Coasters] ARE A NATION." Foremost, in his critique of such reflections on Gold Coaster self-identification, Attoh Ahuma rejected the idea of a lack of political and cultural cohesion among those in the region as he trumpeted the cultural and linguistic similarities created by the centrality of the Akan language—as a possible *lingua franca*—in bringing many of the region's people together. Similarly, he celebrated the role of the empire, which he referred to as "the highest organized form of government in creation," in uniting the colony's peoples under a single flag and sovereign and in turn further solidifying the idea of a Gold Coast nation.[4] The real question for the Gold Coast, Attoh Ahuma asserted, was that of whether Gold Coasters themselves had developed a national consciousness, a recognition of themselves as a nation with their own shared pasts and futures. For him, the actions of those he deemed to be overly Anglicized was uninspiring. Instead, he called on Gold Coasters to reconnect themselves with the Gold Coast by looking back to the land, culture, and ultimately, the past. Framing this program as a politics of "Intelligent Retrogression," the Cape Coast minister ultimately asserted that this "Backward Movement" was "the only Progression that will save our beloved country."[5]

Attoh Ahuma's vision of the Gold Coast nation emerged out of the political and social malleability that marked the first decades of colonial rule in West Africa. As Charles Francis Hutchinson's famed *Pen-Pictures of Modern Africans and African Celebrities* detailed, Attoh Ahuma came of age in "one of the first families of Cape Coast." Moreover, on his father's side, Hutchinson continues, the Cape Coast minister was also "closely related to the Chief of James Town Accra"—the historical center of British activity in Accra.[6] Born to a prominent Methodist minister, Attoh Ahuma attended the Wesley High School in Cape Coast before continuing his education in Sierra Leone and London, where he preached until his return to the Gold Coast. Back home, Attoh Ahuma, along with fellow Methodist minister Kobina Asaam, established the short-lived Accra Grammar School and served as principal for the similarly short-lived African Methodist Episcopal (AME) Zion Church College in Cape Coast.[7] In the 1890s, Attoh Ahuma emerged as a prominent public figure, serving as editor of the Cape Coast-based *Gold Coast Methodist Times*. As editor of the newspaper, he not only used the newspaper as a vehicle through which to address issues related to the Methodist church, but, more importantly, he also used it as a means by which to reflect on the rapidly changing political and social context brought forth by colonial rule. Two decades later, Attoh Ahuma would become the editor of the Gold Coast Aborigines' Rights Protection Society's (ARPS) *Gold Coast Nation*.[8]

In the context of the late nineteenth and early twentieth century, Attoh Ahuma's personal history and politics were at once unique and part of a broader political and intellectual trend within the early colonial Gold Coast. Socially, Attoh Ahuma was one of a relatively few Western-educated Gold Coasters. As with elsewhere in West Africa, formal Western education during the nineteenth century had largely emerged as the purview of the mission societies operating in the region. By the mid-nineteenth century, for instance, the British operated only one government school. Based in Cape Coast Castle, the school claimed an enrollment of 194 students in 1850, all of whom were male. By contrast, the Gold Coast's missions, within whose schools Attoh Ahuma studied, operated four schools in Cape Coast alone during the same year and sixteen others in six other major coastal towns. The missions in turn claimed a total enrollment of more than 900 students—239 of them girls—during the year.[9] As for Attoh Ahuma, his mission education was almost certainly shepherded by his father who, in his 1937 biographical dictionary, Magnus Sampson describes as "the saintly minister of the Wesleyan Mission."[10] Even among those educated, Attoh Ahuma—again likely due to his family background—would have been among an even more select class of Gold Coasters who continued their education abroad, giving him access not only to the imperial metropole of London, but also the West African intellectual hub of nineteenth-century Sierra Leone.[11]

Through such experiences, Attoh Ahuma embodied a political and intellectual class of Gold Coasters who, during the late nineteenth and early twentieth centuries, would commit themselves to dissecting and reflecting upon the nature and state of the evolving British colonial project. Even as late as Attoh Ahuma's 1911 writings, formal colonial rule in the Gold Coast, like that of much of the rest of Africa, was still a relatively new phenomenon on the international stage. On the ground, it was even more so. For, throughout the second half of the nineteenth century, competing parties throughout the Gold Coast—the emergent colonial government, chiefs, merchants, farmers, and a growing class of political and intellectual leaders like Attoh Ahuma—varyingly sought to protect their interests and define new ones as they attempted to adapt to the changing political realities around them. The period, the prominent Sierra Leonean surgeon and intellectual J. Africanus Horton described in 1870, was foremost one of "feverish excitement," for it was a time in which "every month seems to bring fresh matters ... to agitate the public mind." For Horton, who spent much of his career as an army doctor stationed in the Gold Coast, the principal impetus for this excitement rested in the unintended consequences of Britain's 1868 transfer of Gold Coast properties with the Dutch, which tested the political loyalties of all involved—African, British, and Dutch.[12]

As Horton highlights in his brief book of letters, the Gold Coast's transition into an official British colony developed in fits and starts. As late as the mid-nineteenth century, for instance, the continued presence of the Dutch and the Danish in the region's major coastal centers slowed many of Britain's ambitions. The 1850 Danish sale of the kingdom's Gold Coast properties to the British, however, provided the British with the opportunity to further expand their influence, most notably by solidifying Britain's position in what would later become the colonial capital of Accra. The 1872 Dutch withdrawal furthered Britain's political entrenchment in the region, providing the British another opportunity to redefine their position in the Gold Coast. As a result, almost immediately after the Dutch exit, the British advanced a new set of diplomatic and ethnographic expeditions aimed at justifying Britain's presence and actions in the region, including its mounting colonial wars. At the same time, the British also sought to extend their juridical reach outside of what had traditionally been the European powers' historical centers of influence along the coast as it began to claim territorial sovereignty over areas of the region extending from the Volta River in the east to the Tano in the southwest and the Pra bordering Asante. As such, by 1874, Great Britain and the Gold Coast had become legally linked to each other, theoretically bestowing upon both Britain and its new subjects new obligations toward each other. The Asante defeat in 1901 provided the impetus for another extension of British influence, paving the way for the formal annexation of Asante and the transformation of what is now contemporary Ghana's northernmost regions into a protectorate of its own under British authority. The result was that, by the time of Attoh Ahuma's writings, Britain's claim in the region now reached from the Atlantic to eventually what is approximately Ghana's current border with Burkina Faso.[13]

What the first decades of colonial rule meant for individuals like Attoh Ahuma was the rise of a political and social environment rife for redefinition. In newspapers and public forums, key groups of Gold Coasters came together to debate among themselves and, in many instances, also with certain colonial figures the nature and state of their relationship with the colony and empire. Moreover, in doing so, many looked to the colonial powers' own discourse in their efforts to define their relationship. In Great Britain specifically, colonial rule was promoted as a philanthropic, if not humanitarian mission aimed at civilizing and, for many, Christianizing peoples that not only the British, but Europeans and white Americans more generally, increasingly viewed as outside the modern world. As the former Lord Provost of Glasgow, Sir James Watson, explained in an 1876 public meeting, European exploration of the continent—undertaken by individuals including Henry Morton Stanley, David Livingstone, John Hanning Speke, and others—earlier in the nineteenth century had paved the way for the continent's revitalization. "All of these gentlemen," the meeting's minutes recorded Watson asserting, "had opened up a path which he [Watson] hoped might afterwards lead to the civilisation of Africa." To this end, Watson claimed that "[b]y their explorations these gentlemen had shown that there were rich and fertile districts in Africa, which, if civilised, would not only be a blessing to the natives, but be the means of opening up new markets for their commodities, and be of incalculable advantage to this country in a commercial point of view."[14]

Throughout Africa, however, the realities on the ground were far from as straightforward as Watson and his colleagues paternalistically suggested. This was the case for both Great Britain's new African subjects and those commissioned to administer the empire's new African colonies. In the Gold Coast specifically, indecision and conflict characterized much of Britain's colony-making process as the British sought to balance the empire's lofty and often ambiguously defined ambitions with the political, social, and economic realities of the territory and Britain's own domestic interests. In 1880, for instance, in response to the colonial governor's proposal for establishing an elaborate network of regional commissioners designed "to bring the European into immediate contact with the natives of the interior," an official in the Colonial Office rejected the idea. In doing so, the official explained that "[s]uch a scheme reads well on paper and in theory is excellent," while insisting that, in practice, "it seems to me most uneconomical and impracticable." Instead, he proposed a network of traveling commissioners who would visit Britain's subject communities seasonally.[15] Similarly, conflict and indecision also followed Britain's annexation of the Dutch Gold Coast possessions as one British newspaper lambasted another for describing Britain's claim to Elmina and other previously Dutch-aligned towns as "Our New Colony."[16] Meanwhile, in Elmina, many in the town defiantly asked how they could be forced to "turn English."[17] Four years later, in 1876, the situation still appeared unsettled as the Earl of Kimberly noted quizzically the local political and cultural difficulties that arose following the annexation. As a result, he advised his colleagues in the House of Lords to be more attuned to African opinions. However, while doing so, he also seemingly minimized the particular interests undergirding these opinions by arguing that, in Elmina specifically, "[t]he Natives clung to old habits and traditions, and there was no doubt they were attached to the flag they had been accustomed to seeing."[18]

As had been the case for much of the previous four centuries, major coastal centers like Accra, Cape Coast, and Elmina, among others, endured the most intimate colonial contact during the transition to formal colonial rule. In Cape Coast in particular, which, for more than two hundred years, had served as the political and administrative center of the British presence in the region, the result of this past engagement was the emergence of an elaborately cosmopolitan city featuring an eclectic array of courts, trading firms, jurists, diplomats, missionaries, and civil servants. As described by a Freetown newspaper in 1821, Cape Coast was a town in transformation, for the newspaper described its streets as a "scene of constant bustle," particularly around the castle. The newspaper further recounted how the construction of new housing (both African and European), along with new roads, had given the town "a very different appearance to what it did two years ago."[19] Over the next half-century, Cape Coast would witness significant growth, further drawing ever more diverse groups of people into it and leading some Europeans to complain about what they saw as the town's declining order and sanitation.[20] As would be the case for African cities throughout the continent over the next century, such complaints (warranted or not) marked the culmination of a community's transformation into a modern urban center in the European mind, particularly as European officials sought to balance the changing social realities of African colonial life with their own ideas of where and how Africans should live. As such, by the late nineteenth and early twentieth century, a prominent class of African intellectuals—including Attoh Ahuma and J. E. Casely Hayford, among others—would emerge out of Cape Coast's bustling cosmopolitan environment.

For others in Cape Coast, the onset of colonial rule marked the rise of new challenges to their current and historical social positions. For the community's chiefs in particular, Britain's gradual efforts to extend its reach into the town's administration during the nineteenth century proved a clear threat. For instance, a mid-century attempt to impose a new poll tax on the Gold Coast population was met with fierce resistance, particularly among chiefs who felt that the British actions—absent input from the chiefs—had weakened the chiefs "in the eyes of the people." For the British, attempts to rectify the situation proved difficult as they sought to balance their emerging colonial ideology and desire for colonial self-financing with the interests of the chiefs on the ground. As a result, an 1856 report on the tax described the levy as key to funding the "gradual civilization" of the Gold Coast, while also highlighting Britain's own fears about what it would mean to bring the chiefs into the policy-making process. To this end, the report argued that, by incorporating the chiefs into the decision-making process, there would be a danger of "exalt[ing] the power of the chiefs" when it was "our policy to endeavour to lower" their influence.[21] By 1861, the British would ultimately deem the tax a failure and abandon it.[22] Just under three decades later, however, in an 1887 petition, another group of Cape Coast chiefs, in conjunction with representatives from the town's *asafo* companies, similarly complained about the effects of the chiefs' weakened positions in the town's affairs. For them, the dislocation of the chiefs' traditional authority, which the petition implicitly connected to British colonial rule, had cultivated an increasing sense of disarray, particularly in relations between the town's *asafo* companies.[23]

A similar situation developed in Accra. As with Cape Coast and Elmina, among other coastal communities, Accra's deep history of European interaction continued into the nineteenth century, with the British, Dutch, and Danish all maintaining a presence in the communities that comprise contemporary Accra as late as 1850. In the early nineteenth century, the English merchant G. A. Robertson in turn painted a picture of Accra as a politically, culturally, and economically vibrant town centered upon its local Ga population. Composed of three separate "districts" with approximately 12,000 residents, Robertson emphasized what he viewed as Accra's and its surrounding area's rich agricultural, fishing, and hunting grounds. As with elsewhere, the Europeans present in the town paid what the merchant described as "ground rent" to their hosts for access to their forts and the town, while he also noted how the Danish had even sought to establish their own agricultural enterprises—namely coffee—in the lands surrounding the town.[24] Meanwhile, politically, Accra's Ga community—which had previously fallen under the suzerainty of Akwamu followed by alliance with Akyem before Akyem's fall to Asante—maintained a complicated political organization of its own that comprised the town's chiefs, *asafo* companies, and priests. The result in Accra politics was an eclectic mix of Ga, Akan, and European influences in the town's precolonial administration.[25]

By the mid-nineteenth century, Accra, too, faced tensions as the political and social realities of Britain's expanding influence began to take shape. Like with the Dutch exit from the Gold Coast two decades later, the Danish decision to cede its interests in Accra (namely present-day Osu) elicited significant frustration among certain politically and socially influential groups. Writing in his 1895 history of the Gold Coast and Asante, for instance, the Basel Mission-educated Gold Coast historian Carl Christian Reindorf described both the gender and class anxieties surrounding Britain's intrusion into the Osu Ga's affairs. In particular, Reindorf emphasized local frustrations with British attempts to limit what he portrayed as men's "cruel treatment of wives." Previously, under the Danish, Reindorf argued, preference had been given to "native laws and customs" in dealing with such situations, whereas, under the British, "wives had now the option of leaving their husbands." Reindorf similarly noted anger in Accra with British "ill-treatment" of pawns and slaves, namely British attempts to emancipate some of these dependent peoples without granting "stipends."[26] Again, not dissimilar to Cape Coast, the mid-century experiment with the poll tax also piqued the ire of Accra's population, with protests—particularly in Osu—breaking out in 1854. As Reindorf described the protests, men were armed and mobilized, while, in front of Christiansborg Castle, groups congregated, singing of how "Whitemen [*sic*] dishonestly imposed [the] poll-tax on the blacks" and demanded the "white man ... come out!" Eventually, the British responded to the protests by shelling Osu during the town's Homowo celebrations—the most important festival on the Ga calendar—eventually forcing Osu's residents out of the town. Following the exodus, Reindorf reported, "The soldiers now freely entered every house, plundered everything, and pulled down several stone buildings which stood close to the castle" as well as, to the Basel-educated Reindorf's horror, looted the already damaged Basel Mission.[27]

The tensions that led to the mid-century conflicts did not resolve themselves with the British takeover of Osu. Rather, they underpinned Accra's six-decade-long transition from what historian John Parker describes as a "precolonial city-state" to that of a "colonial city."[28] By the early 1870s, Accra would overtake Cape Coast in political and economic importance as officials in both London and the Gold Coast complained about the limitations Cape Coast posed in meeting Britain's administrative needs during the region's colonial transformation. In the House of Lords, for instance, one member in 1874 argued that everything from the congestion of Cape Coast Castle to the makeup of the surrounding terrain and its climate made Cape Coast untenable as a capital for the new colony when compared to alternatives in Elmina and Accra.[29] Three years later, the British would heed such arguments and move their administration to Accra. Meanwhile, economically, Accra emerged over the second half of the century as the primary port of call for the Gold Coast, for, by 1901, the bulk of the region's rapidly growing cocoa exports flowed into the city for shipment abroad.[30] Developing alongside this export trade was also an expatriate-driven economic model that decentered Accra's historically influential indigenous mercantile class from the town's and the burgeoning colony's economic system. As Parker explains, new cultures of credit, the abolition of slavery, and growing uncertainty in global commodity markets had all weakened and, in some cases, impoverished the town's merchant class.[31]

Outside the region's major coastal towns, direct contact between the burgeoning colonial administration and the Gold Coast's African population tended to be much more sporadic and often fraught with unfulfilled expectations. In one 1900 example, the King of Adukrum in the Gold Coast's Western Frontier complained of the seeming empty promises that marked the new colonial government. As he articulated to a visiting traveling commissioner at the time, a previous official had promised to send him a flag and message stick. However, he had yet to receive the items. Moreover, he had also been promised a set of cutlasses and axes in order to replace a different set lost when an earlier shipment capsized in transit. These items, too, had not arrived in Adukrum. On top of that, he noted that he had not been paid for roof work that he—or more likely the community—had completed for the third-class officers stationed in the town. In an attempt to rectify the situation, the traveling commissioner promised to bring the issue of the missing items to his superiors before giving the king "leave to clear away clump [*sic*] of bamboo in front of [the] wharf."[32] In a similar situation in 1915, market women in Winneba seemingly attempted to go around the town's chief to a visiting assistant district commissioner to protest what they viewed as the chief's overreach in proposing a new tax on their stalls. The assistant district commissioner, however, ultimately sided with the chief who had convinced the official that, since "most of the sellers were strangers," they "ought to contribute to the town."[33]

In other instances, the new colonial system emerged as a vehicle for certain Gold Coasters to set forth an array of new political, social, and economic expectations for the evolving colonial administration to live up to. These included not only investment in such things as infrastructure, education, and other social services, but also a presumed neutrality in adjudicating certain local and regional disputes. As would be the case well into the twentieth century, chieftaincy and land disputes would dominate much of this process of adjudication. In Nzemaland in the far western Gold Coast, for instance, where turn-of-the-century colonial administrators found themselves trying to navigate a set of disputes evolving out of the 1873 schism of the Kingdom of Appolonia, officials in 1902 sanctioned the creation of "independent" eastern and western Nzema stools in Atuabo and Beyin. In the eyes of the British, the decision aimed to finally settle the three-decade-long Nzema question.[34] However, as historian Pierluigi Valsecchi notes, attempts to adjudicate the Nzema case did not resolve the matter. Instead, it resulted in the creation of a detailed popular and official archive offering competing visions of Nzema history characterized by vociferous arguments over the contesting parties' claims to land, resources, stools, and people.[35] Similar situations played out in communities throughout the regions that comprise the contemporary Ghanaian state as the colonial administration and Gold Coast populace sought to make sense of the political, social, cultural, economic, and administrative realities of the burgeoning colonial system.

Gold Coast Intellectuals and the Colonial World

For the colonial government, cases such as those in Nzemaland exemplified the challenges embedded in colonial governance. For many in the Colonial Office and beyond, at the heart of the colonial project was a delicate balancing act in which the colonial regime aimed to at once assert its authority over the diverse populace it viewed as its subjects, while, at least in theory, also respecting the rights and autonomy of a rotating class of communities over which it claimed jurisdiction. Further challenging this colonial balancing act was the colonial government's need to protect Britain's own political and economic interests. As a result, as conflicts arose between Gold Coasters and the colonial government, among Gold Coasters themselves, and across colonial borders, the relationships embedded within the colonial project had to be continuously renegotiated, often frustrating officials in London and Accra. Expressing this exasperation in 1880, Governor H. T. Ussher complained to the Secretary of State for the Colonies about what he saw as the half-hearted nature of the colonial government in its efforts to exact change in the Gold Coast. The result, he insisted, was an outsourcing of the colonial project to chiefs who had their own agendas, which often did not align with those of the colonial government.[36]

Meanwhile, on the ground, the changes brought on by colonial rule ushered in a vibrant period of debate in the new colony about not only the meaning and purpose of colonialism, but, more importantly, what it meant to be both a Gold Coaster and a subject of the British Empire. At the center of much of the Gold Coast debate was thus an attempt to make sense of the changing nature of the Gold Coast's relationship with Great Britain. Writing, for instance, in a 1906 edition of the *Gold Coast Leader*, one author emphasized what many viewed as the shared and reciprocal aspects of this relationship by highlighting what he presented as the mutual nature of the Gold Coast peoples ceding their sovereignty to the British. "When we voluntarily united ourselves with the Great Empire upon whose parts the sun never sets," he argued, "we did so upon the clear understanding that our customs and institutions would not be interfered with." For him, however, the presumed partnership connecting Britain with the Gold Coast had soured as, in his view, the British continuously sought new ways to infringe upon Gold Coasters' autonomy. As a result, he outlined a political process in the young colony that simultaneously hailed what he presented as "[o]ne of the essential principles of the aboriginal constitution"—local political representation—and actively sought to silence Gold Coasters' attempts to have their voices heard in the political process. This silencing, the author insisted, foremost occurred through the attempted burying of Gold Coasters under the weight of colonial bureaucracy.[37] Another author, this time writing in a November 1888 edition of the *Gold Coast Echo*, similarly sought to highlight the contradictions implicit in a governmental system that, at home in Great Britain, was founded upon the power of popular opinion, but, in colonies like that of the Gold Coast, provided few colonial subjects official venues through which to express their political voice. The British did this at the same time as they were promising Gold Coasters that they were "being trained … to [the] habits of self-government."[38]

In another instance, a separate commentator in the *Gold Coast Echo*, writing in October 1888 under the pseudonym "An Old Man," spoke of the many ways in which the colonial administration actively sought to subvert the contemporary and historical autonomy of those it claimed to represent. Focusing on the history of Cape Coast specifically, the author relayed a town history that dated back to the eighteenth-century reign of Bronpon Cudjoe (also known as Cudjoe Caboceer). In doing so, he established for his readers a lineage of legitimate leadership in the town that was intimately connected to a perceived cooperative Afro-European partnership that, according to him, had resulted in "so much wealth [for the king] that his riches were spoken of by all the peoples of this and adjacent countries."

As the Old Man continued, he proceeded to outline for Cape Coast a continued lineage of legitimate leadership that culminated in the 1865 accession of King John Aggery—a Christian supported by Cape Coast's educated elite—to the town's paramount office. Aggery's story, however, was one of tragedy according to the Old Man. Not only did the town's non-Christian faction challenge Aggery's legitimacy and ultimately elect its own challenger to the office, but Aggery's independence also raised the ire of the British. In the Old Man's rendition of Aggery's history, the British used the king's decision to arrest an accused adulterer with British connections to detain and deport the king to Sierra Leone. For the Old Man, Aggery's case foremost represented a break from a past Afro-European relationship exemplified, at least in his mind, by the African political and economic autonomy that had made Bronpon Cudjoe and his community so wealthy a century earlier.[39]

The Old Man's contribution to the *Gold Coast Echo* in particular was published during a period of growing Gold Coast frustrations with the widespread changes brought forth by colonial rule. Beyond the broader questions of political autonomy, attempted legislative changes in everything from marriage law to land policy outraged many within the new colony as the colonial government reached into aspects of Gold Coast life often seen as outside colonial jurisdiction. In the case of marriage specifically, the colonial government garnered a vehement response from the Gold Coast's male intellectual class as the government sought to rectify what it viewed as a growing hole in colonial marriage law, particularly as it pertained to certain Christian marriages. As historian Roger Gocking has described, prior to the 1880s, Christian marriages had almost invariably been administered by the colony's various mission societies, with the government recognizing these marriages. Yet, a reinterpretation of English law began in the late 1870s following questions arising from the Basel Mission's attempts to have the government recognize the marriages of German nationals wedded in its churches. After substantial debate, the government insisted that, under existing English law, it only had the authority to recognize marriages of British subjects conducted by Roman Catholic and Anglican clergy. In the Gold Coast, the result of this decision was the creation of a legal void for those married in nonconformist churches.[40]

As Stephanie Newell adds, the situation for nonconformist Christians proved particularly tricky in cases of divorce and adultery, for the government claimed that it did not have jurisdiction over such disputes regardless of the quality of the aggrieved party's claims. To this end, the newly created hole in Gold Coast marriage law inordinately affected the colony's Christian women by leaving them without a clear avenue through which to have their complaints addressed in court. The proposed 1884 Marriage Ordinance was to promise to bring these nonconformist Christians' marriages back within the government's purview. However, in doing so and much to the displeasure of many of the colony's elite men, the ordinance also served to sanction a broadly defined monogamist Christian ideal as the only legitimate form of government-recognized marital union. As such, in the context of the late nineteenth century, the proposed ordinance was emblematic of Victorian gender and sexual ideals and of the process by which colonial rule aimed to introduce these ideals—both intentionally and unintentionally—to its subject populations. Yet, as Newell also notes, by not incorporating customary marriages—including polygamous marriages—in the proposed ordinance, the government inadvertently sanctioned a "parallel legal system" outside official governmental channels and Victorian convention for addressing complaints arising from such marriages.[41]

The response among the colony's male educated elite to the proposed ordinance was swift. Many decried the ordinance as a mechanism for dissuading Christian marriages altogether due to its insistence upon monogamous unions. Others, meanwhile, maintained that the ordinance promised nothing more than the de-masculinization of Gold Coast men, for, in Newell's words, many men predicted that women would use the new law to attempt to "ensnare innocent men into monogamous unions and then terrorise them within the home till death do them part."[42] Even in portions of the Gold Coast press run by Europeans, the law received a lukewarm response, with the *Gold Coast News* accusing the government of seeking "to make people moral by legislation."[43] Furthermore, the questions surrounding the 1884 ordinance did not subside quickly, for, even as late as the first decade of the twentieth century, debates surrounding the ordinance would return as the government sought to amend the 1884 law. In response to the renewed intrusion into Gold Coast marriage practices, the *Gold Coast Leader* proceeded with a scathing attack on both the original law and amendment process. The newspaper therefore wondered in 1905 "whether it would not be advisable to recommend the repealing of the Marriage Ordinance altogether, seeing nine-tenths of all the trouble over the Marriage question in the country are brought about by the Ordinance, a state of things practically unknown before its advent."[44] A month later, a writer using the name of "Dick Carnis" added to the newspaper's attack by describing the ordinance as a "clumsy manufacture" and "made up law." The *Leader* in turn positioned the original law as the direct "outcome of ecclesiastical bungling aided and abetted by an administration eager to please the clergy without attemption to realise any necessity for the enunciation of proofs therefore, and without duly apprehending its own position as the Conserver of the integrity of the Native Customary Law."[45]

Even more importantly, the *Gold Coast Leader* positioned its early twentieth-century critiques of the ordinance at the center of broader questions about what it meant to be a Gold Coaster under colonial rule. In opening his 1905 challenge to the law, Carnis contextualized his arguments through references to the prominent Gold Coast nationalist J. E. Casely Hayford and his recently published book, *Gold Coast Institutions* (1903). In its intention, *Gold Coast Institutions* aimed to describe what Casely Hayford presented as the "true nature of the problem which Great Britain has to face in her administration of the Gold Coast and her hinterland," namely the challenge of how to govern another. For Casely Hayford, the only ethical path forward for the British was that of a clear respect for Gold Coast institutions and its peoples' political, social, and cultural practices.[46] As a result, in turning to Casely Hayford in framing his critique of the Marriage Ordinance, Carnis shifted the debate's stakes away from questions of marriage law alone to concerns over the preservation of the uniqueness of Gold Coast culture and life more broadly.

"Every patriotic native," Carnis declared in the *Leader*, "should therefore leave no stone unturned in assisting ... the amendment or repeal of this anomalous law," for at the heart of the law, he suggested, was a legislative quashing of an organic and deeper reflection on Gold Coast life, belief, and custom under British rule.[47]

The questions raised in the *Gold Coast Leader* and, more systematically, by Casely Hayford and others were fundamentally questions over identity, belonging, and history within the colonial sphere. Very few Gold Coast intellectuals in the period failed to recognize the systemic changes to Gold Coast life brought on by colonial rule. For Casely Hayford and John Mensah Sarbah, who, like his younger colleague Casely Hayford, published multiple treatises on the nature of Gold Coast customary law, the attempted legislative changes brought forth by colonial rule threatened a set of social and cultural patterns in ways that, for many, felt alien and arbitrary. More importantly, they also promised a potential erasure of a Gold Coast past and way of life that ultimately defined what, for them, it meant to be a Gold Coaster. As suggested earlier, Casely Hayford's 1903 text does not offer a direct rejection of colonial rule. Rather, Casely Hayford ostensibly presented it as a guide to Akan law and society with the goal of colonial reform. Mensah Sarbah, for his part, embarked upon a similar mission, focusing on Fante law and custom in first his 1897 *Fanti Customary Law* and, almost a decade later, the *Fanti National Constitution* (1906). Similar to Casely Hayford's work, which blended ethnographic analysis with policy reflections, Mensah Sarbah's 1897 text in particular offered a foundation upon which to build and formalize customary law within the burgeoning imperial system as it—through a focus on everything from land tenure to marriage and inheritance—provided an ostensible guide to a customary case law. Meanwhile, his *Fanti National Constitution* combined a historical analysis of the Gold Coast and its governmental systems with profiles of British naivety in its governance and of pathways toward greater Gold Coast African representation.[48]

For both Mensah Sarbah and Casely Hayford, colonial rule ushered in a range of legislative and policy decisions that thrust new fissures into the institutions of Gold Coast life. More fundamentally, they argued that the rapid changes brought on by the colonial administrative process manifested themselves in clear threats to the Gold Coast way of life. These threats, they suggested, were fundamentally cultural and political. Moreover, for their fellow early Gold Coast nationalist, S. R. B. Attoh Ahuma, the stakes of these threats to Gold Coast life were clear, particularly as to how they related to the way Gold Coasters connected to their culture. To this end, the Cape Coast minister offered warnings of what he perceived as a growing educated population willing to abandon all that made them uniquely Gold Coasters for the false promises of British society. As noted earlier, this included everything from their career aspirations to their dress. Kobina Sekyi, another Gold Coast polymath and later president of the ARPS, added to the nationalists' critiques of the cultural effects of colonial rule with his own scathing 1915 rebuke of the colony's purported Anglophiles in his play *The Blinkards*. Casting the colony's Anglophiles as both ignorant and obnoxious, Sekyi's play paints a picture of a society in conflict with itself. However, this conflict was only in part caused by Britain's direct policy interventions in the colony. Instead, much more deeply, Sekyi suggested that the British had introduced a value system that, as the play's closing lines proclaimed, was incompatible with the Gold Coast's needs, interests, and traditions.[49]

Colonialism, the Gold Coast, and Early Pan-Africanism

As Gold Coast intellectuals sought to make sense of the changes to life under colonial rule, many also sought to look beyond the colony as they reflected upon the new political and cultural networks forged by colonial rule. As has been noted, at its heart, the British Empire served as a vehicle for the political and economic transfer of wealth from Britain's colonies to the metropole. However, the empire was also a conduit for network building for those within both the colony and the metropole, as Gold Coasters, like others in Africa and beyond, used their status as imperial subjects not only to critique British imperial policy, but also to make connections among themselves around shared issues of colonial land and labor extraction, political representation, property, race, and, more fundamentally, personal and collective dignity. Further buttressing the colonial subjects' claims on their particular colonial governments and the imperial government as a whole was the civilizing and humanitarian discourse of the colonial mission, for, as supporters of the imperial project touted the assumed unqualified benefits of colonization to subject peoples, intellectuals and others within the empire took to the press, petitions, and conferences to chide the government for its inability and unwillingness to live up to its proclaimed ideals.

By the early twentieth century, London had thus emerged as a prominent political and cultural center for the exploration of both pan-African and pan-imperial bonds within the British Empire. As historian Jonathan Schneer has outlined, London at the turn of the century had transformed itself from a prominent industrial city into a cosmopolitan center that drew people, goods, and ideas from throughout the empire into its political and cultural sphere. As a result, Schneer notes, its streets were marked by a cacophony of accents, languages, and methods of political, social, and cultural organization that brought together groups and agendas as diverse as those of Irish and Scottish nationalists, Eastern European Jewish refugees, Malay and other South and Southeast Asian dockworkers and sailors, and many others.[50] Furthermore, by 1900, an increasing number of West African and West Indian students and workers had begun to establish themselves within the city. In doing so, they initiated a critique of the imperial government that blended the pan-African language of nineteenth-century Ethiopianism with a politics of transnational connection.[51]

This project gained its greatest visibility with the 1900 London Pan-African Conference. Initially organized by the Trinidadian H. Sylvester Williams and the newly formed African Association, the London Pan-African Conference, while not explicitly anti-imperial, sought to pressure the world's major European powers for reforms in their colonial administrations.[52] In total, thirty-two individuals attended the London conference, with one representative from the Gold Coast—A. F. Ribeiro, a lawyer and member of a prominent family of Brazilians who had repatriated to Accra.[53] Moreover, within West Africa itself, both the conference and its organizing group, the African Association, garnered significant attention during the final years of the nineteenth century. In 1898, for instance, the *Gold Coast Chronicle* celebrated the African Association's first anniversary by asking whether this "new Society … augurs well for us in common with other branches of our race." The *Chronicle*, for its part, culled much of its commentary on the Association from the *Lagos Standard*. Both the *Chronicle* and the *Standard* emphasized the Association's organization as "encourag[ing] a feeling of unity … [among] all subjects claiming African descent." Furthermore, the *Standard* also celebrated the Association's efforts to challenge, if not upend, "a political creed [advanced] by unscrupulous West African Governors" that "laid open" West African lands to "so-called empire building speculators."[54] As the conference came about in 1900, other West African publications further memorialized the meeting as an event "of great importance, one of racial signification, one that will be far-reaching in its effects, and comprehensive in its sweep." So important would the conference be, an author writing in Liberia's *New Africa* predicted, that it was sure to be one of "the new subjects to engage the pen of the 20th Century [*sic*] historian."[55] The *Gold Coast Aborigines*, meanwhile, discussed the conference in terms not dissimilar to the self-determination discourse that would envelop the continent's anticolonial nationalism several decades later, for the newspaper asserted that "we predict Africa will always remain what it has always been—the black man's continent."[56]

By the end of the first decade of the twentieth century, many of the political features, impulses, and networks that had driven the organization of the 1900 Pan-African Conference had begun to integrate themselves into the Gold Coast political scene. In the case of the Aborigines' Rights Protection Society, as early as 1905, the society expressed its own ambitions for an ultimately unrealized pan-African conference to be held in the Gold Coast.[57] In his 1911 novel *Ethiopia Unbound*, J. E. Casely Hayford reflected upon what such a conference could have looked like. For him, the imagined conference would have represented a celebration of a vision of Africa and the African intimately connected to the ideas of Edward Blyden.[58] For Casely Hayford, Blyden—born on the Caribbean island of St. Thomas in 1832 before immigrating to Liberia—offered a vision of pan-Africanism that was focused on the uniqueness of what it meant to be African. As the Gold Coast intellectual would explain at a 1903 conference honoring Blyden, Blyden's thought superseded that of his most eminent contemporaries like W. E. B. Du Bois and Booker T. Washington, both of whom Casely Hayford argued had made important contributions to the Black race globally. However, the Gold Coaster insisted, with Du Bois's and Washington's overriding focus on the American racial scene, both also tended to be "exclusive and provincial in a sense." Blyden, in contrast, the Cape Coast barrister remarked admiringly, had developed a view of the Black experience that was "universal, covering the entire race and the entire race problem."[59]

Pan-African interest in the colony intensified during the second decade of the twentieth century. As historian David Kimble details, new discussions for a pan-British West African conference began as early as 1914 with Casely Hayford leading the way, albeit now largely operating independently of the ARPS. Casely Hayford's move away from the ARPS ultimately resulted in a rift between the Gold Coast intellectual and the society over which he once presided as the two parties debated the balance between Gold Coast national particularities and the promises brought forth by pan-West African cooperation and, for some, even unity. After failing to receive cooperation from the ARPS, Casely Hayford, among others from the Gold Coast, Nigeria, and Sierra Leone, ultimately proceeded with their own plans, holding the conference in March 1920.[60] Meanwhile, as preparations for the conference were underway, Casely Hayford sought to connect what he viewed as the burgeoning West African pan-Africanism to the broader pan-African movement that Du Bois had advanced in the aftermath of World War I. Writing to Du Bois in March 1919, Casely Hayford not only advised the African-American intellectual of the plans for the West African conference and expressed his interest in the Du Bois-led movement, but also sought to entice Du Bois into reading the *Gold Coast Leader* and presumably, by extension, take a greater interest in the events occurring in West Africa.[61] Approximately a year-and-a-half later, Casely Hayford wrote to Du Bois again. This time Casely Hayford sought to persuade his counterpart of the West African's commitment to the global pan-African cause by assuring Du Bois that "We in West Africa are studying with careful attention the great strides that our brethren in America are making towards liberty and," he added, "we cannot but hope that it will be possible in the future for mutual co-operation."[62]

Meanwhile, as Gold Coast intellectuals and others planned, celebrated, and debated the political organization of West Africa's burgeoning pan-African activities during the first decades of the twentieth century, related forms of pan-Africanism had also begun to emerge within the Gold Coast. In 1910, for instance, Reverend Alexander Walters of the AME Zion Church travelled throughout much of the West African coast, stopping in Freetown, Monrovia, Cape Coast, and ultimately in the eastern Volta town of Keta. Founded in the USA during the early nineteenth century, the AME Zion Church grew rapidly among enslaved and free African Americans before eventually making inroads across the Atlantic. As he stopped in Keta, Walters, an African American who a decade earlier had also chaired the London Pan-African Conference, presided over a conference of the church that resulted in the baptism of forty new members—with another forty joining the congregation—in a church that Walters described as one fundamentally built upon "race pride and patriotism."[63]

In the Gold Coast, though, the church's message may have had different meanings from those intended by diasporic visitors like Walters. As Sandra Greene has outlined, the church had its Gold Coast origins in Cape Coast during the late nineteenth century, influencing prominent nationalist intellectuals like S. R. B. Attoh Ahuma who, as already referenced, had earlier founded a school associated with the church. Shortly after establishing itself in Cape Coast, the church made its way to Keta. However, different groups of Gold Coasters injected into the church's message a variety of distinct meanings. Among the educated elite, the church's race-conscious discourse offered a language to reflect on the broader sense of social immobility manifested by the colonial context of the nineteenth and early twentieth centuries. In doing so, the church—unlike more established Christian denominations—gave voice to the limitations created by the colonial glass ceiling. Outside of the educated elite, however, church leaders shifted their focus away from race toward a history of trans-Atlantic kinship that resurrected and re-authored oral traditions of kidnapping and enslavement still told decades later.[64]

Conclusion

Throughout the Gold Coast, the transition to colonial rule elicited feelings of alienation, social dislocation, and concern for many and, for others, opportunity as it both shut down certain political and social possibilities and opened new ones. As Gold Coasters coped with and interpreted these changes, colonial officials often found themselves—not entirely willingly—engrained in the day-to-day affairs of the communities they sought to govern as they adjudicated chieftaincy disputes, land and marriage questions, and sought to eradicate political and cultural practices that they deemed unfit for so-called civilized society. What this intrusion into Gold Coast life ultimately meant for many of those living under formal colonial rule was the rise of a desire to publicly define what was unique about being a Gold Coaster. For some, like Attoh Ahuma, Casely Hayford, Mensah Sarbah, and many of the Gold Coast's numerous and vocal African-run newspapers, the result was a turn to key political and cultural changes brought on by colonial rule—debates over political representation and autonomy, marriage, religion, and past Afro-European relationships—in the construction and promotion of a broadly defined Gold Coast national identity in the emergent colonial public sphere. Moreover, the new social and political networks of pan-African activism, in part also inadvertently created by colonial rule, offered Gold Coasters creative outlets through which to explore the possibilities of this burgeoning Gold Coast national identity in relation to those also emerging among other recently colonized peoples. Even more importantly, much of this debate actively blended clear echoes of a precolonial Gold Coast past—both culturally and politically—in often deep and highly nuanced reflections on what it meant to be a Gold Coaster during this unique moment of historical uncertainty.

Chapter 3

COCOA FUTURES:
STATE, SOCIETY, AND COMMODITY
PRODUCTION IN THE GOLD COAST

As Gold Coast intellectuals sought to make sense of the changes brought forth by colonial rule, Gold Coasters writ large also sought to adapt to the new economic environment manifested by colonial rule. As detailed in Chapter 1, since at least the advent of the early modern Gold Coast gold trade, key segments of the region's economy had centered upon the export of a rotating array of goods and commodities, including, most tragically, the trade in people during the era of the slave trade. As also outlined in the first chapter, the nineteenth century witnessed a shift in the types of goods exported abroad as Europeans—beginning with the British in 1807—moved away from the slave trade and increasingly turned to cash crops and similar commodities in their economic interactions with Gold Coasters and Africans more broadly. The advantages of the so-called legitimate trade were envisioned to be both economic and moral. As Reverend Samuel Crowther—a freed Yoruba slave educated in Sierra Leone and who eventually became the first African Anglican bishop—insisted in 1857, all individuals felt the benefits of the shift from the slave trade to the legitimate trade. Illustrating his point, Crowther reported on a recent conversation he had with an unidentified chief, who maintained "that their aged persons never remembered any time of the slave-trade [*sic*], when so much wealth was brought to their country, as has been since the commencement of the palm-oil trade during the last four years." Moreover, the Anglican clergyman asserted, the result was an increasing interest among the population to learn about "the English, their trade, their work, and the motive of their benevolent proceedings towards Africa."[1]

As with elsewhere in West Africa, including Nigeria about whose oil palm industry Crowther was likely discussing, the palm oil and palm kernel trade in the Gold Coast rapidly emerged as a cornerstone of the Gold Coast's export economy during the mid- and late nineteenth century. In 1895, for instance, the Gold Coast was exporting more than 4.3 million gallons of palm oil. Likewise, in 1894, it also exported more than 17,000 tons of palm kernels.[2] As the Methodist missionary Dennis Kemp recounted in 1898, Gold Coast palm oil was used for everything from the production of tinplate to the manufacturing of soap, candles, and margarine. Similarly, he also noted, the colony's palm kernels gained usage in the production of oils.[3] Meanwhile, as the government invested in the oil palm industry, it also looked to an array of additional agriculturally based export industries to introduce to or expand in the Gold Coast, including cotton, copra, coffee, rubber, kola, and others. However, by the first years of the twentieth century, one crop—a crop, unlike the colony's indigenous oil palm and kola trees, that was not native to the region—came to supplant all other Gold Coast agricultural products in terms of wealth and ultimately political, social, and cultural importance. That crop was cocoa.

This chapter traces the social and cultural politics of early twentieth-century commodity production in the Gold Coast, focusing foremost on cocoa. No commodity has been more important to the Gold Coast over the past hundred-plus years than cocoa as the Gold Coast quickly rose to become the world's leading producer of this essential ingredient in chocolate during the decades following its late-nineteenth-century introduction into the nascent colony. Even today, Ghana, along with neighboring Côte d'Ivoire, produce more cocoa than anywhere in the world. Together, in 2016, for instance, the two countries produced more than half of the world's supply. Furthermore, in 1961, Ghana alone controlled more than a third of the global cocoa market.[4] As a result, by using cocoa as its framing device, this chapter explores the political, social, and cultural networks created by the Gold Coast cocoa revolution. More than a mere economic endeavor, cocoa

Figure 3.1 Cocoa beans at the Bunso Plantation, Ghana, 1957.

production emerged as a site where key networks of familial relations, labor, migration, colonial and later national interests, and community intersected in Gold Coasters' and Ghanaians' understandings of their present and their visions for their futures.

Cocoa and the Cash Crop Revolution

In the late 1870s, as the popular narrative of cocoa's introduction to the Gold Coast recounts, a blacksmith by the name of Tetteh Quarshie returned to the Gold Coast from Fernando Po (Bioko, Equatorial Guinea) with a number of cocoa plants and pods. As detailed in a 1951 issue of the *West African Review*, Quarshie had made his way to Fernando Po sometime between 1873 and 1875.[5] Introduced to Fernando Po approximately a decade earlier, cocoa had rapidly transformed the island's economy as the wealth potential of the crop encouraged a general shift in the island's economic activity away from trade and toward agriculture. As a result, over the course of the 1860s and 1870s, many of Fernando Po's planters quickly abandoned experimentation with competing cash crops.[6] Quarshie, purportedly employed as a laborer for a Spanish settler on the island, would have arrived in Fernando Po at the height of the excitement surrounding the crop's potential. As narrated by the *West African Review*, Quarshie— "evidently observant, thrifty, and foresighted"—thus eluded the watchful eye of his employer and "smuggled" the plants off the island during his return to the Gold Coast. Following his arrival home, Quarshie established the colony's first cocoa farm in the small town of Mampong, approximately 40 kilometers north of Accra.[7]

Key aspects of the legend surrounding Tetteh Quarshie's role in introducing cocoa to the Gold Coast have long been contested, with some emphasizing previous attempts at Gold Coast cocoa cultivation earlier in the nineteenth century.[8] Others, including several elderly farmers in Mampong interviewed in 1960 by Polly Hill, even suggested that Quarshie himself may not have gone to Fernando Po. Instead, they argued that it was a relative or apprentice of Quarshie who made the trip. Regardless, Hill asserts, Quarshie should at a minimum receive credit for establishing the colony's first cocoa farm, which, within four years of his return, had begun to bear fruit and led the newly minted farmer to sell the resultant pods to others in nearby communities.[9] Just over a decade later, in 1885, the colony would export its first shipment of cocoa, a mere 121 lbs. that fetched £6 1s. The next shipment would not occur until 1901.[10] However, over the ensuing decade, the quantity and value of the Gold Coast's cocoa production would increase dramatically. By 1914, Gold Coast farmers would come to produce approximately 50,000 tons of cocoa for export, accounting for just under a fifth of the international crop. Gold Coast production would continue to increase in subsequent years, reaching 175,000 tons by 1919 out of 450,000 tons globally.[11] As the Liverpool-based *African Mail* would insist in 1909, with the recent takeoff of the Gold Coast cocoa industry, "The agricultural position on the Gold Coast seems full of promise if the Government will only continue their efforts to instruct the people as to the best methods of production and preparation of produce, and help them in every way to procure the best economic results."[12]

The speed by which cocoa distinguished itself during the late nineteenth and early twentieth centuries from other emerging industries surprised many early colonial officials. Like elsewhere on the continent during the last decades of the nineteenth century, colonial officials devoted much of their energy to experimenting with a range of new cash crops and industries. From the perspective of the colonial government, the development of a strong economic base for the colony largely centered around agricultural and specifically cash-crop production. Moreover, the benefits of such an economic model were viewed as at least twofold. Foremost, the growth of such an export-driven agricultural economy promised to stabilize the colony's finances, ideally paving the way for more investment—infrastructural and monetary—in the colony and thus setting the stage for what many hoped would be the colony's eventual profitability. Furthermore, many in the colonial government also viewed the rise of well-defined cash-crop industries as another avenue for the creation of the type of individual they saw as necessary for the modern world. As one 1890 report on Gold Coast agriculture suggested, there were times when claims that Gold Coasters were "too lazy to work" had "a specious air of truth" about them. However, instead of being lazy, the report claimed that Gold Coasters—due to poor infrastructure and communication—did not have the "inducement to continuous labor." Cash-crop production—via the wealth it heralded—promised to create the labor incentives necessary for instilling in the population the colonial-defined modern work ethic officials desired.[13]

However, as late as 1902, colonial reports continued to lament what their authors felt was a lack of a clear agricultural industry in the Gold Coast.[14] As noted in Chapter 1, for the previous half-century, the products of oil palm trees had dominated the region's export trade. By the early 1880s, rubber also increasingly began to draw interest from the colonial administration. However, production of each of these commodities tended not to be organized, nor systematized in ways that appeared entirely legible to many colonial officials, with both the late nineteenth-century oil palm and rubber industries largely operating via the tapping, collection, and processing of wild and semi-wild trees as opposed to production on established plantations or farms. In the case of rubber specifically, producers would climb or fell wild trees and then tap them to drain the latex.[15] In other instances, rubber collectors cut the latex-producing vines, leading to governmental concerns over the sustainability of the colony's rubber supply.[16] An intricate network of middlemen and porters then transported their hauls to the coast for export. As one group of elders in Sefwi Wiawso explained to historian K. Y. Daaku in 1974, rubber during the period would come to replace gold as the primary economic activity of their communities, with, after collection, individuals making the two-week trek south to sell their yields.[17]

A similar production structure marked the older and much larger oil palm industry at the turn of the century, with producers—often with the help of an array of dependent peoples—maintaining a role in the collection and processing of the fruits of the oil palm trees. For colonial officials, the challenge of both industries was the seemingly variable structure of a production process that in each case was largely marked by the social and economic independence of the producers. Writing, for instance, in 1910, one official complained that this independence, buoyed by many Gold Coasters supposedly being "indifferent to the value of the [oil palm] tree," resulted in individuals in some areas of the central and western forests wastefully, in his mind, tapping trees for locally produced palm wine rather than for the export trade.[18] Likewise, in the case of rubber, the same official advocated shifting the region's rubber production away from wild collection. In its place, he proposed that "[e]fforts should ... be made to induce the native communities to take up the planting of the indigenous rubber trees, *Funtumia elastica*, on a large scale." Modeled on those already operating in parts of Nigeria, these envisioned plantations would still be owned and operated by local producers, but it was presumed that they would also operate with an improved level of efficiency.[19]

At the turn of the century, cocoa promised to reinvigorate Gold Coast agriculture in the eyes of many inside and outside of the colonial government. Singing the praises of the new crop's potential in 1890, a government report insisted that it was "another project worthy of every attention." Cocoa cultivation, the report advanced, was "cheap and the preparation simple." As a result, it predicted that the crop would soon draw "the attention of small cultivators." Accordingly, "[i]ts only disadvantage" the report asserted, "is the length of time (five years) before a crop is obtainable."[20] In 1897, the African-run *Gold Coast Express* was even more blunt in its praise for cocoa's potential as it matter-of-factly declared: "There appears to be a good demand for West African Cocoa [*sic*] at present in Europe. Its cultivation in these days," the newspaper announced, "would pay very well."[21] Thus, to get the crop off the ground, the government established several experimental farms, which in turn sold pods to local farmers who were then to take over commercial production. Furthermore, government and commercial experts, including representatives from the Cadbury chocolate company, toured localities in the Gold Coast's nascent cocoa-growing regions with the aim of training farmers in key production and processing techniques in order to ensure an export-quality crop. To this end, in 1908, a representative from Cadbury proposed the development of a "cocoa house" to teach prospective farmers about market expectations and "an agricultural bank where farmers might deposit money or obtain loans."[22] A year later, the Agriculture Department, likewise, issued a set of instructions designed to train farmers in everything from proper tree-spacing practices to the benefits of regular weeding and the treatment of diseased pods, among other cocoa-care techniques.[23]

Quality issues, however, would remain a key area of concern throughout the early twentieth century. In 1908, for instance, the *African Mail* reported on complaints from the Botanical and Agriculture Department that much of the West African cocoa that reached the European market arrived "without any attempt at proper fermentation," thus affecting the prices paid when compared to the cocoa produced in more established cocoa-producing localities like São Tomé and Grenada.[24] Likewise, in 1906, another report noted that, in the Gold Coast, "trees are allowed to almost run wild, and the selection of seed for planting is done anyhow." Furthermore, like in the 1908 report, the 1906 report emphasized the purported lack of attention given to the processing of the harvested cocoa, emphasizing that farmers seemingly viewed it as being "of secondary importance to the growth of healthy pods and large beans. In short, the native is sinning through ignorance."[25] However, as originally highlighted in the German newspaper, the *Gordian*, farmers had little incentive to increase the quality of the cocoa they produced, for companies such as Cadbury argued that they could not pay more for higher quality cocoa than they did for the broader crop given the "small quantities of better cocoa ... produced at present" since "when re-selling on the European market they [merchants] cannot reckon on correspondingly higher prices." To this end, the *Gordian* asked: "How, then, is he [the farmer] to make his work pay?"[26]

Despite these concerns, cocoa took off in the Gold Coast. Within two decades of the first Gold Coast cocoa trees producing, it had become apparent that, for much of the Gold Coast, the future lay with cocoa, often at the expense of the colony's other industries. As early as 1904, observers had already begun to complain that "cocoa ... [had become] the all-absorbing cultivation," pushing to the wayside more established commodities such as the various products of the oil palm tree.[27] A little more than a decade later, a 1915 report—portions of which the *African Mail* reproduced—similarly cast cocoa as the death knell to the colony's oil palm industry. "As the cocoa industry develops," the report's author asserted, "it becomes every year more apparent that except to supply local demands as an article of food the native palm industry is being neglected and must sooner or later die a natural death." As the report's author continued, he explained that there were logical reasons for Gold Coast producers to switch to cocoa, for, in terms of both labor and monetary returns, cocoa far outperformed oil palm production when examined from the farmers' perspectives. As such, the report's author suggested, major interventions would be needed to save the oil palm industry.[28]

The Making of the Gold Coast Cocoa Farmer

For Gold Coasters, the effects of the colony's transition to the cocoa economy were wide-ranging. The earliest farms tended to have their beginnings in the areas surrounding Aburi and Mampong north of Accra. Through the early twentieth century, cocoa would spread throughout the Gold Coast's forest region, eventually taking hold as far north as the contemporary Bono and Bono East Regions. However, as it made its way throughout the forests, cocoa came not only to provide diverse groups of Gold Coasters access to new forms of economic mobility, but also simultaneously operated within and transformed existing social and cultural institutions as farmers and non-farmers alike adapted to the new economic, political, and social power created by the crop.

In cocoa's earliest years, many farmers tended to combine cocoa production with the cultivation of a range of other crops, commodities, professions, or engagement in other commercial activities. Among the early farmers interviewed by anthropologist Polly Hill during the late 1950s and early 1960s, entrance into the cocoa industry tended to be a roundabout process for most. As one man, Ofori Jyawu, described to Hill, prior to turning to cocoa, he had entered the government's Agriculture Department in 1903 and, in 1906, the government sent him to Aflao on the Togoland border to study cotton cultivation. A year later, he was commissioned to the Northern Territories "to collect rubber specimens." His first formal entry into cocoa came as an overseer for Cadbury in 1910 before returning to work in the colony's rubber industry for a company in Assin Manso until his retirement in 1925 when he established his own cocoa farm in Obodang. However, as he pursued his career, Jyawu also invested in lands previously acquired by his father in Obodang and Bepoase that produced everything from plantains and palm oil to coconuts and cocoa.[29]

Others had equally varied paths to cocoa cultivation. James Dei, for instance, began his career in the Akyem town of Bunso, where he worked for the African Products Development Company. Initially focused on kola production, the company later turned to cocoa and rubber, hiring Hausa, Ewe, Kroo, and Liberian day laborers. Dei himself acquired his first cocoa farm circa 1895 in Nsuasi, which he bought with his older brother. He subsequently acquired additional farms in Asuboi, Apirade, and Bunso. As Dei pursued his career in Bunso, the daily operation of his various farms largely rested with his elder brother and hired laborers.[30] Likewise, another farmer, Moses Addo, came to own two cocoa farms by the end of the 1930s. However, his family's entrance into cocoa production began as early as 1894 with his older brother establishing a nursery. In 1908, Addo reportedly entered a Kumasi exhibition, where he claimed his cocoa won "a prize medal." As described by Hill, Addo continued his conversations by listing a "whole lot more of exhibitions and prizes" that his cocoa won over the years. Moreover, Addo emphasized to Hill, the farm from which this prize-winning cocoa originated was still in existence at the time of his interview and was still producing about forty to fifty loads (2,400–3,000 lbs.) a season.[31]

The acquisition of farm lands for cocoa production was not a singular, nor often straightforward process. Rather, it was part of an intersecting set of processes with both contemporary and historical implications that included questions of land rights, ownership, and family and community relations, among others. In the case of an individual named Kwame Appiah, for instance, he inherited his first farm from his mother when he was about twelve years old circa 1896. According to Appiah, his mother, who "cracked [palm] kernels," had initially bought the land following the death of Appiah's father. Around 1914, she bought another, larger farm in Surum that Appiah would also inherit. In addition to these inherited lands, Appiah maintained another farm with his older brother. Appiah would later use the profits from his cocoa investments to build a prominent house in Surum "'in memory of' his mother and her enterprise." However, in his discussions with Hill, he also noted that he was not alone in such an endeavor, for he emphasized that "all the big houses [in Surum] 'came from the uneducated farmers.'"[32] Similarly, another individual by the name of E. E. Tham also stressed the role of his familial connections in introducing him to the cocoa industry. For Tham, both his paternal and maternal grandfathers had engaged in cocoa farming from as early as about

1897, and his father had established his own cocoa farms on family lands in Ahamahama and Wiamoase. Tham himself would establish his first farm in the contemporary Bono Region near Sunyani, hiring laborers to work the land. He would subsequently go on to acquire lands in travels throughout Asante, among other locales, while also maintaining inherited properties near Aburi.[33]

Many Gold Coasters similarly turned to friends, neighbors, acquaintances, family members, and others to buy land together, forming "companies" that purchased the land semi-collectively. As Hill has outlined, members of a company would buy the land together, yet would then maintain individual rights to a portion equivalent to their investment. Highlighting the loose collective framework of the company structure, companies tended to operate with a chosen leader who guided the company through the purchase process. For prospective farmers and land owners, the company structure was foremost the result of the rapidly commercializing nature of agriculture that accompanied cocoa's rise during the late nineteenth and early twentieth centuries, for it allowed prospective farmers to establish corporate arrangements that strengthened their negotiating positions.[34] For instance, in the case of Akropong farmer Okyeame Kofi Darko, the company structure helped him purchase at least five of the thirty parcels of land he would accumulate during his lifetime. Likewise, he bought a number of his other plots secondhand from land that had previously been purchased by companies. As outlined by Darko in his interview with Hill, his initial introduction to cocoa had come as a servant to the Akyem Abuakwa king, Nana Kwame Fori, during the 1880s when cocoa first arrived in Akropong. According to Darko, at the time, it was the king's servants who planted and maintained the area's first cocoa trees. However, as he "became a grown up man," Darko explained that he would come to invest in his own cocoa farms, buying land and using the proceeds to build a house, sending two of his children to the UK, and establishing a money-lending business.[35]

As with Darko, many farmers looked to cocoa as a means to enter into other industries and money-making ventures. In the case of another Akropong farmer, Opanyin (Kwaku) Ntow, his cocoa investments provided the income necessary to build "a big house" in which he once lived before eventually renting it out. Old enough to remember then Gold Coast Governor Bradford Griffith's 1892 visit to Akropong to distribute "a box of 24 pods," Ntow would attain seven farms—buying alone and, at least in one instance, as part of a company. In addition to the initial house he built with his cocoa money, Ntow also purchased a lorry and, at the time of his interview with Hill, was currently building another house in Senchi, "because," he emphasized, "his ancestors 'came from Akwamu.'" Accenting the entrepreneurial ethos of the Gold Coast's cocoa farmers, Ntow thus asserted to Hill that, in all his ventures, "Money is the main object for me." Like many others, key to Ntow's personal history was a narrative of professional ascent that, in his case, took him from a palm tapper and laborer on the Sekondi railway line to a farmer of food products like maize and fowl to a livestock farmer raising sheep and pigs to ultimately cocoa cultivation. His transition to cocoa had thus transformed his economic and social prospects as he went from what he presented as a common laborer and small-scale farmer to an individual that controlled the labor of others.[36]

As increasing numbers of Gold Coasters sought to make inroads in the cocoa industry during the early twentieth century, prospective farmers scoured the greater Gold Coast in search of new lands upon which to establish their farms. In doing so, an elaborate system of migration developed, where individuals and groups would seek land far from their natal or established homes. For Hill, these migrant farmers represented the hallmark of the Gold Coast cocoa industry. Not only did they exemplify the "rural capitalist" spirit she would come to celebrate, but, through their migration, they would construct a range of often competing, complicated networks of community building in which they simultaneously tended to view themselves as—and were regarded as—strangers and as new members of the communities where they have established farms.[37] For the widow of Kwabena Kumi, for instance, the migration to establish her husband's first cocoa farm in Dedewa remained fresh in her memory as she recalled the physical complications Kumi and his family encountered trying to get to their new lands and the leisure activities—music and "native plays"—they engaged in upon arrival. Moreover, in a symbol of the permanence of his intentions in Adeiso, where Kumi established his second farm, Kumi built a "Big [*sic*] house."[38]

Likewise, in the case of Obeng Kwadjo, cocoa cultivation served as a process of network building as he maintained lands in at least five separate communities in which he rotated living. Like many of the farmers Hill interviewed, Kwadjo built houses on a number of the lands he owned as well as made several other forms of infrastructural investments, including the construction of pump-operated wells, as signs of his long-term commitment to the lands. More broadly, the social and economic processes underpinning cocoa's rise in the Gold Coast offered him new avenues for income diversification and generational mobility. As such, Kwadjo would use portions of his cocoa profits to educate his children, opening up previously remote career possibilities for his children and grandchildren. For his son, this social mobility meant the opportunity to pursue a career as a teacher, while Kwadjo's grandson gained the ability to graduate in 1959 with a bachelor's degree from the University College of Ghana. Kwadjo himself, not dissimilar to Darko, would also use part of his cocoa profits to turn his attention to money-lending, granting loans to other farmers in Mamfe.[39]

Similar forms of investment and professional diversification also emerged further north in Asante and in what, in 1958, became the now defunct Brong Ahafo Region.[40] Arriving in Greater Asante only shortly after its spread in the southern Gold Coast, cocoa rapidly supplanted many of the central forests' other industries. By the 1910s, it had become firmly established in the region.[41] Writing in his 2001 posthumous autobiography, T. E. Kyei (b. 1908), who during the mid-1940s would serve as the principal research assistant on Meyer Fortes's *Ashanti Social Survey*, recalled the allure of cocoa during his childhood in Asante. As a young boy, Kyei's father had brought his family from Kwaaman to Agogo to pursue cocoa farming at the urging of Kyei's maternal grandmother. For Kyei himself, it was in Agogo while listening to his grandmother convince his father of cocoa's potential that he fully realized the crop's power as he reflected on how she emphasized "the rush of able-bodied young men as well as women of Agogo" making their way to the forests.

As Kyei narrated, it was his grandmother's wish that Kyei's father place his family's future in cocoa, "tactfully urging her son-in-law to end his long wanderings abroad so that he could stay at home and concentrate on cocoa farming which was, in her view, a sure way of safe-guarding his own future and the future of his wife and children."[42]

As was the case further south, Asante cocoa cultivation operated within a complex social and economic ecosystem. As Kyei detailed, much of Agogo's production adhered to the social and gendered expectations of male and female labor at the time, with the majority of cocoa farmers being men. Women, he recalled, thus tended to devote much of their agricultural energies to the growing of food crops, including plantains, yams, cocoyams, tomatoes, and maize, among other crops. Despite these tendencies, Kyei simultaneously stressed that cocoa production in Agogo was never an exclusively male industry. Rather, he insisted that it was one in which certain "[e]nterprising women"—often, in his memory, "elderly" and "unattached"—could also find a place. Even some women in his own family, he related, played a prominent role in the area's history of cocoa cultivation. In the case of his paternal grandmother, for instance, she had been one of the first cocoa farmers in Agogo. Moreover, Kyei continued, his grandmother had also worked to have a group of Basel missionaries establish a church in Agogo, which subsequently became a conduit for the church's elders and others to receive cocoa seeds for further cultivation.[43] In other instances, as historians Jean Allman and Victoria Tashjian note, women harnessed their positions as wives to demand that their husbands establish new cocoa farms from which they, as wives, would command an independent cut of the profit. At least in the case of one woman interviewed by Allman in the Asante town of Effiduasi, she specifically ended one of her marriages due to her husband's failure to pursue a cocoa farm on her behalf.[44]

In the old Brong Ahafo Region, women similarly played an active role in the region's cocoa industry. In contrast to Kyei's recollections for Agogo further south, anthropologist Gwendolyn Mikell argues that the Brong Ahafo female cocoa industry was not one largely defined by—to use Kyei's words—"elderly" and "unattached" women. Rather, Mikell details a vibrant history of female cocoa production in the region, focusing largely on the area surrounding Sunyani. As outlined by Mikell, rising international cocoa prices during the interwar years encouraged women's entrance into the cocoa market. Many women in turn worked both on their husbands' farms as well as acquired their own. Furthermore, Mikell notes that, within the Sunyani District specifically, approximately an eighth of all cocoa farmers were women, with "[a]n unusually high number" owning lands exceeding 200 acres. As with their male counterparts, the Sunyani District's female farmers used their profits to invest in other enterprises. Moreover, many also looked to cocoa farming as a means by which to help ensure that their daughters had access to economic independence and in turn utilized their investments to help secure their daughters' autonomy in their current and future marriages.[45]

Cocoa, Labor, and Histories of Extraction I: The Northern Territories

As farms rapidly spread throughout the Gold Coast, farmers faced the ever-present question of labor in their desires to ensure the fullest productive potential for their investments. For farmers who established farms far from their natal homes or who maintained numerous farms in a variety of different locales, the situation proved particularly acute. In many instances, family members and other relatives helped in the labor process, settling nearby to aid in clearing land, weeding, plucking ripe pods, and in the drying of beans. More broadly, however, the labor of cocoa production was a cosmopolitan affair. As anthropologist Meyer Fortes and his co-authors argued in 1947, then writing on the Asante specifically, the goal of many, if not most, cocoa farmers was to be an absentee farmer.[46] However, such ambitions were not exclusive to the Asante. As a result, much of the day-to-day labor of cocoa farming was in turn undertaken by an array of hired and contracted laborers coming from throughout the Gold Coast, Togoland, and Northern Territories as well as from as far afield as Côte d'Ivoire and Upper Volta (Burkina Faso). In Asante in particular, one 1914 colonial report emphasized that the growth of the region's cocoa industry was inextricably tied to migrant labor from contemporary Ghana's northernmost regions. In doing so, the report derisively added, "The Ashanti, never an agriculturalist, is only too pleased to pay the native of the Northern Territories from 1s. to 1s.3d. per diem, in addition to his food, in exchange for his work on the cocoa farms."[47]

The link between northern labor and Asante, however, did not begin with the rise of cocoa production in the region. Rather, it represented the shifting nature of a set of political and economic relationships forged out of the Asante expansionism of the eighteenth and nineteenth centuries. As discussed in Chapter 1, Asante's eighteenth-century expansion north of the Akan forests brought many of the region's northern savanna states within Asante's orbit. The result in many instances was the establishment of a set of tributary relationships. For instance, writing in 1819 on the Asante relationship with Dagbon, the British merchant Thomas Bowdich explained that, as it became clear that Dagbon could not defeat Asante, the King of Dagbon "prudently invited a peace" and agreed to a tributary system that allowed for both "commercial intercourse … and security."[48] For Asante, such relationships not only provided the forest state political influence over the savanna's most politically influential centralized states, but, through these relationships, the empire also gained access to trade routes leading to the West African Sahel. Likewise, at the heart of many of the northern states' tributary relationships was the supply of slaves to the forest empire, with Bowdich reporting that, at the time of his voyage, Dagbon alone was sending 500 slaves a year to Asante—a number Ivor Wilks suggests reflected an intentional governmental policy designed to reduce the number of tributary slaves coming into Asante. At other times during the nineteenth century, Wilks highlights, Asante would demand upwards of 1,500 slaves a year from Dagbon, with other savanna states such as Gonja enduring similarly onerous demands.[49]

In nineteenth-century Asante, northern slaves maintained an often-maligned position in their new homes. As several Akan proverbs suggest (e.g. "A slave does not dress like his master" and "If a slave becomes too familiar we take him to a funeral custom"), communities understood slaves as socially distinct from those who owned them.[50] In terms of labor, slaves often worked alongside those who owned them as well as with those of other classes of subject peoples tied to the slaves' owners. However, as historians T. C. McCaskie and Gareth Austin independently note, the most difficult, dangerous, and unwanted tasks tended to befall northern slaves, individuals one nineteenth-century Asantehene referred to as "stupid, and little better than beasts."[51] As Austin specifically emphasizes, Asante slave owners tended to deploy recently arrived slaves on lands viewed as intractable.[52] Likewise, McCaskie positions such undesirable labor as one of the primary social and cultural markers—others included clothing, limited access to property, and a lack of say in their genealogical future—that not only set them apart from even other non-Asante subject populations, but also opened them to further social and economic exploitation.[53] As a result, throughout much of the nineteenth century, northern slave labor represented a key feature of Asante's labor system as northern slaves helped maintain the productive capacities of an empire that, during the early decades of the century, was still growing and, in the second half, was fending off civil war and increasing colonial encroachment on its autonomy.

As the Gold Coast transitioned into the twentieth century, the centrality of northern labor in the Akan forests did not wane. In the region's gold mines, northerners supplied a steady labor pool for the various commercial mining companies seeking to exploit the region's rich mineral resources.[54] Meanwhile, in the agricultural sector, the 1908 prohibition of slavery in Asante, which broadly coincided with cocoa's rise, challenged both Asante's slaveholders and newly freed slaves to redefine their relationships with each other, especially in relation to the full exploitation of the new cash crop's wealth potential. For these former slaves, the question ultimately became that of whether they should stay in their former owners' communities or leave their property and existing social connections in search of opportunities elsewhere. As a result, some, such as a group highlighted by Kyei, used the opportunity of emancipation to abscond to Basel Mission communities, where they forged new relationships around the church.[55] Others, however, stayed. In doing so, they often worked under social arrangements and statuses that embodied the ambiguities in distinguishing between free and unfree labor.[56]

By the 1920s, a broader seasonal market for northern migrant labor had begun to develop on Asante's cocoa farms, providing many northerners access to the emerging colonial cash economy.[57] Meanwhile, in Asante, such migratory labor proved essential to the region's developing cocoa industry as the rapidly growing scale of the region's and, more broadly, the Gold Coast's cocoa trade demanded increasing amounts of unskilled labor to sustain itself. As a number of observers have noted, the exploitation of such labor helped transform Asante cocoa into one of the bedrocks of the colonial economy as a whole over the next several decades. However, at the same time, some colonial officials expressed concerns about the effects of this migration on life in both Asante and the Northern Territories. In the north specifically, they worried that it could disrupt their own developmental, commercial, and labor ambitions for the region. In 1914, for instance, one official stationed in the North-Eastern Province near the border of the contemporary North East and Upper East Regions emphasized how migration south had made labor "scarce" in the area, albeit he did predict most of those who had traveled south would return "as soon as the farming season commences."[58] The broader Northern Territories' assessment for the same year further lamented that, while there was "still an adequate supply of unskilled labour" in the region, inflationary pressures caused by the seasonal migration had conditioned northern laborers to demand greater pay upon their return home.[59]

For a colonial administration that viewed its role in the Gold Coast and elsewhere in Africa to be that of ensuring the colony's greatest productive potential on the cheap, increased labor costs represented a clear threat to its mandate. The following year, another report on the Northern Territories offered an even more pessimistic tone regarding the labor situation, arguing that it was "becoming increasingly difficult to obtain" unskilled labor in the north, at least at a rate the government deemed acceptable (6d. per diem) as "so many of our natives have realized that by going to Kumasi they can readily obtain from 1s. to 2s. per diem for their services."[60] By the late 1930s, another colonial report suggested that the trend had become the new reality, for the Gold Coast cocoa industry could not operate without such migratory labor. "There is little indigenous labour available for hire in the cocoa districts," a 1938 report on cocoa marketing explained, "and although there are now fairly large settlements of outside labourers in the districts of heavy cocoa production, farmers are dependent mainly on migrant labour which comes in from the Northern Territories, where money crops are inadequate, or from neighbouring French colonies, where money is a necessity to meet direct taxation."[61] Such a reliance on hired labor, the report thus asserted, demanded a rethinking of the popular image of the Gold Coast farmer as "a peasant cultivator who, with his own labour and the help of his family, grows his food and tends an acre or two of cocoa trees." Instead, what had developed by the 1930s in the colonial administration's eyes was an intricate labor system linking the northern savanna and the Akan forests around the individual, collective, and colonial profit potential manifested in the cocoa pod.[62] However, what the report did not recognize was that it was a labor system that, while giving the appearance of being relatively new, was one that in key ways reflected a reframing of historical, precolonial relationships between the north and the Akan forests.

Cocoa, Labor, and Histories of Extraction II: The Ewe and Togoland Diaspora

Further south and to the east, similar patterns developed with the incorporation of Ewe and Togolander labor in the southern forests' cocoa farms and, to a lesser extent, Asante's. Like with many in the north, histories of trade, warfare, and slaving marked the Ewe relationship with the major Akan states of the precolonial period.

As with other non-Akan groups, the Akan state-building wars of the eighteenth century drew the predominately Ewe polities of the eastern Volta into new types of political and economic networks in which, allied with Asante and Akwamu, the Ewe maintained a liminal space between independence and being subject to Asante suzerainty during much of the period. As a result, in contrast to Asante's subject states in the north discussed earlier, which supplied upwards of 1,500 slaves a year to the forest empire, many Ewe polities sent as few as two.[63] Meanwhile, as warfare proliferated in the Akan forests of the eighteenth century and created surpluses of slaves for export, several Ewe coastal communities developed into important slave-trading hubs during the century, feeding the Atlantic market of the western Slave Coast. In the nineteenth century following the 1807 abolition of the external slave trade, some on the Ewe coast attempted to subvert the new political and economic reality by participating in the illegal Atlantic slave trade until at least the 1860s. Later, they turned to smuggling goods into German-held Togoland. At the same time, renewed Asante expansion would unleash a new period of instability in Eweland as the region became a key wartime slaving ground for an Asante state that itself was increasingly in a state of political disarray.[64]

The lives of enslaved Ewe during the late nineteenth century in many ways mirrored those of other enslaved individuals during the period. As discussed in Chapter 1 with Aaron Kuku, enslavement brought with it a fracturing of one's social bonds, separating the enslaved from his or her family and community and often leaving one isolated and socially alienated. Enslavement and slavery were thus fundamentally traumatic processes. Furthermore, throughout the region, it was often enslaved labor that helped create and sustain the Gold Coast's transition into the era of "legitimate trade." As a slave captured by the Asante in 1870, Kuku, for his part, contributed to this new economy by aiding his master in the gathering and processing of the region's major commodities, including kola nuts and the products of oil palm trees.[65] Similarly, Yosef Kwaku Famfantor, another individual enslaved by the Asante during the early 1870s and also featured in Sandra E. Greene's collective biography of formerly enslaved Ewe, found himself separated from his family following his enslavement. Initially sent to his master's sister's home, Famfantor, after being resold to the Fante coast, traveled throughout the Gold Coast, trading goods along the coast and as far north as at least Bondoukou in northeast Côte d'Ivoire.[66] More broadly, as political scientist Paul Nugent has noted, the Asante campaign in Eweland dispersed Ewe peoples throughout the Gold Coast and Togoland, creating a diaspora that—even after emancipation— included ex-slaves trying to make a life for themselves in these new lands; returnees seeking to reconstitute their communities; and, in other instances, refugees living in diverse communities of non-Ewe peoples.[67]

As with others, the rise of cocoa ushered in new economic opportunities and challenges for many Ewe, particularly along the coast. Largely residing outside of the Gold Coast's major cocoa-growing regions, the coast east of the Volta tended to produce little to no cocoa for export, with cash-crop production in the region tending to focus on the export potential of copra. In the early 1890s, the government expressed consternation with what it viewed as the shortsightedness of many seaside communities in their perceived reluctance to advance the industry.[68] However, by 1915, the government suggested a transformation in many of these communities' thinking about copra's economic potential. In the Keta District, for instance, one agricultural official emphasized that the industry had so taken off that it had begun "to resemble the great coconut districts on the north-west and eastern shores of Ceylon." As a result, the report predicted that, with proper attention and development, copra could serve as "a valuable 'stand by' to cocoa."[69] Despite such early twentieth-century optimism and periodic spikes in copra exports, such as during World War I, copra never fully took off as a Gold Coast export commodity, at least to the levels for which the government had hoped. Furthermore, along the coast east of the Volta, the extractive trade in coconut products competed with a vibrant local market for coconut oil, while, geographer K. B. Dickson notes, producers during the period endured "coconut pests [that] were more numerous and more destructive than ever." By 1930, the quality of copra coming from the Ewe coast had so deteriorated that it had become virtually unsaleable.[70] In addition, the rise of cocoa, which predominately shipped from ports in Accra and Sekondi, weakened many of the Gold Coast's smaller ports, consolidating much of the colony's export activity; east of the Volta, only Keta's port was able to endure these pressures.[71]

As the economic situation east of the Volta became more uncertain, the promise of cocoa drew many to the new industry. To the north in the newly mandated trusteeship of British Togoland, where cocoa cultivation was on the rise, many sought to establish their own farms. As in the Gold Coast Colony, these aspiring farmers were also joined by an ethnically diverse array of Krobo, Ewe, and Akan migrant farmers. Again, much like their western counterparts, many worked together to establish companies to alleviate the capital pressures required for purchasing land. As Nugent has shown, in the eastern Volta forests, the success of Ewe cocoa cultivation can foremost be seen in the transformation of British Togoland's major urban centers, most notably Hohoe, Ho, Jasikan, and Peki. In the case of Hohoe specifically, he notes, the town's population essentially tripled between 1921 and 1931 as cocoa took off in the area, reaching a population of just under 4,000 people. More broadly, as cocoa production reached deeper into the forests of British Togoland, newly constructed roads allowed merchants to travel further into the countryside, thus catalyzing the continued extension of cocoa production even deeper into the region.[72]

Meanwhile, others turned west, working as laborers on farms in the cocoa-growing regions west of the Volta. As Polly Hill notes, in cocoa's earliest days, some of these individuals aspired eventually to own their own farms. However, as the industry matured, the likelihood of one making this transition in the Akan-dominated southern forests waned.[73] Instead, most of these migrants' relationships to cocoa became defined through their labor. So prominent were Ewe laborers on the region's cocoa farms that, in one area just north of Koforidua, Hill estimates that approximately two-thirds of the area's laborers were Ewe.[74] Likewise, in Adeiso, northwest of Accra, Daniel Boatin, who his family claimed was one of the first individuals to receive seeds from Tetteh Quarshie, maintained about twenty Ewe laborers as tenants on a large parcel of land he purchased in 1904. Furthermore, each of these laborers had established their own villages on or near the land. Like many farmers, Boatin himself never lived on the land he maintained in Adeiso. Instead, he and his wife made their permanent home in Pretu, where he had purchased his first farm and where, after serving as a "houseboy to a German at Akropong," "'he planted ... and got money.'" Thus, in order to sustain his Adeiso farm, Boatin employed his laborers on annual contracts of between £10 and £12 a year.[75]

However, through their work, Boatin's laborers not only worked the land, but they also helped establish a micro-economy built on long-standing social relationships that fundamentally complicate normative definitions of "worker" and "employer." As Boatin's nephew explained to Hill, "They [the laborers] 'plough' where he tells them."[76] Yet, for Boatin and his laborers, such work occurred within a moral economy defined by the permanence of a workforce with its own sustained connections to the land and farm. As Boatin's nephew detailed, many of those working Boatin's land had worked there for up to twenty-five years. Moreover, on the land, they grew their own food crops, most notably maize. As their landlord/employer, Boatin would claim half of his laborers' yield. Similarly, when his laborers sought to partake in palm oil and palm kernel collection, his workers again provided him with half their proceeds. They would also pay him for any trees they wished to fell, presumably for the production of palm wine. In another instance involving land owned by Boatin, Hill talked with a Ewe laborer from French Togoland who had worked there for ten years. As Hill recounted, this individual had previously worked in a corn mill in Accra before coming to work for Boatin. Like his fellow laborers, he too "grew all the usual crops," with Boatin taking "a proportion." More broadly, Boatin's workers even went so far in establishing their own community that they installed one of the farm's laborers as chief.[77]

In the case of Boatin and his laborers, it was thus the farm as a form of community—not just as a workplace—with its own values, hierarchies, networks, and expectations that mediated the relationship between Boatin and his laborers. More broadly, the depth of one's relationship to the farm was often reflected in the types of labor one conducted and especially in the compensation one received. In the Eastern Region village of Domi, for instance, the village's chief (*Odikro*) and the village's laborers—most from French Togoland, but not necessarily Ewe—each emphasized this relationship in their reflections on the village's cocoa industry.[78] The *Odikro* himself was newly arrived in the village, coming during the early 1940s from Kyebi-Apapam to serve as successor to his brother and to take over the cocoa lands his brother had established possibly as early as 1900. Speaking to Hill circa 1960, the *Odikro* had lost most of his cocoa trees to swollen shoot disease—a virus that ravaged much of the southern Gold Coast's cocoa industry during the 1940s (see Chapter 4)—over the preceding decade, plummeting his annual yields from "more than 100 loads" (6,000 lbs.) to "only 15 loads" (900 lbs.) a year. Despite this decline, the *Odikro* still employed several laborers on his farm, including those paid by piece (*nkotokuano*) and sharecroppers (*abusa*). According to Hill, in Domi, "*abusa* laborers had always helped to establish the farm originally."[79] As a result, *abusa* laborers tended to receive a third of the farm's yield at the end of the season, granting them a much more intimate stake in the success of the farm than their fellow laborers who were paid per load.[80] With the *Odikro*'s farm's decline, though, only one *abusa* worker remained, a "Frenchman"—someone from French Togoland—who had "arrived in Domi more than 18 years ago."[81]

Domi's *nkotokuano* laborers, meanwhile, maintained and protected their own unique relationship with the farms on which they worked. On the *Odikro*'s farm, for instance, a man Hill characterizes as the farm's "chief labourer" established a family for himself on the farm, bringing a wife from French Togoland. As Hill's notes explain, this man had worked for the *Odikro* for "about 20 years." He reportedly felt so bad for the *Odikro* following the collapse of his cocoa trees that, at least at the time of the *Odikro*'s interview with Hill, the man refused to work for anyone else. Presumably to honor this loyalty, the *Odikro* and his chief laborer farmed their own plots together, sharing the plots' yields. Meanwhile, other *nkotokuano* laborers in the village took on contract work, with most being from unspecified areas of French Togoland and, like the *Odikro*'s laborer, living in Domi and working for its farmers for twenty or more years. Moreover, as with the farmers themselves and *abusa* laborers, as the farms succumbed to swollen shoot during the 1940s, they too suffered. One laborer complained that on a farm, where he used to pluck up to 100 loads of cocoa a season, he was only able to pluck six. Even more dramatic, one laborer complained that his father had recently only plucked a single load on the farm on which he worked.[82]

Conclusion

By the eve of World War II, cocoa had fundamentally entrenched itself into nearly every aspect of Gold Coast life. As one Larteh farmer, Akoi Ontumi, emphasized to Hill in 1959, "Cocoa at present is our backbone." At the time of his interview with Hill, he was in the process of replanting his farm, employing up to thirteen daily laborers earning 3s. per diem at any given time.[83] As Ontumi's statement to Hill suggested, he and his colleagues had little choice but to replant their cocoa. The economic centrality of the crop to their lives was undeniable. In just over half-a-century, cocoa production had, for all intents and purposes, not only pushed to the sidelines all other Gold Coast commodities, but also displaced nearly every other major commercially driven form of export activity in the colony.

In contrast to the turn of the century, when the government was intent on experimenting with an array of potential cash crops including palm oil, copra, rubber, coffee, and others, by the 1940s, together farmers and the government had reorganized the Gold Coast economy into one beholden to the fate of cocoa. However, cocoa's importance extended far beyond the economy as it helped transform political, social, and cultural life throughout the colony. To this end, both farmers and laborers migrated deep into the colony's southern and central forests to partake in the real and anticipatory wealth that cocoa promised. Many locales in turn gained new forms of ethnic and social diversity, while others renewed and reshaped historic links of migration and labor extraction that predated colonial rule. As a result, for large numbers of Gold Coasters, cocoa consequently came to embody the future, or, as the lyrics of Fred Sarpong's popular mid-century song exclaimed: "Whatever you want to do in this world, It is with cocoa money that you do it."[84]

Chapter 4

CONDITIONS OF PROTEST:
WAR, CRISES, AND THE POLITICS OF
POSTWAR AGITATION

As cocoa came to dominate the Gold Coast scene during the first half of the twentieth century, the politics of what it meant to be a Gold Coaster shifted. At the governmental level, increasing cocoa profits—along with those of the Gold Coast's other mineral and agricultural commodities—helped to fund a range of development projects throughout the colony during the 1920s and 1930s. In the 1920s in particular, government investments resulted in an expansion of the colony's road and rail networks, the construction of the colony's first deep-water harbor in the western city of Takoradi, the establishment of Korle Bu Teaching Hospital in Accra, and the construction of what would be one of Anglophone West Africa's premier secondary schools in Achimota. In a 1924 speech in the Legislative Council, the then Gold Coast governor, Gordon Guggisberg, celebrated the compounding growth of the Gold Coast's cocoa exports over the previous years, connecting it to the colony's development agenda. In doing so, he noted that, in 1923, the colony had exported 40,000 tons more cocoa than it had in the previous year. Trade as a whole from the colony, Guggisberg added, had also grown by more than 100,000 tons.[1] For Guggisberg, the colony's economic success offered a path to a reinvented Gold Coast. It was a Gold Coast that, for him, was to blend the technology, infrastructure, education, and liberal politics of Europe with the social and cultural values of the Gold Coast's African population—an ambition that found its clearest expression in Achimota's curriculum.[2]

The onslaught of the global economic depression during the 1930s had severe repercussions on the Gold Coast government and, more importantly, on the livelihoods of the colony's peoples. From 1927 to 1930, the value of the colony's cocoa production experienced a more than 40 percent decline from a high of £11.7 million to just under £7 million. By 1934, the value of the Gold Coast's cocoa crop would plummet even further, bottoming out at just over £4 million.[3] For farmers, the effects of cocoa devaluation were devastating. For instance, during the 1927–8 fiscal year, Gold Coast farmers earned £47 per ton of cocoa produced. That price dropped to £35 during the 1929–30 fiscal year. The following year, the depression would more than halve it to £17 before it collapsed to £11 in 1933–4.[4]

The colony's cocoa farmers responded to the market contraction with a series of protests against a purchasing system that they found exploitative by periodically withholding their crops from the market during the depression years.[5] Meanwhile, inside the Gold Coast's various African-run newspapers like the Accra-based *African Morning Post*, the colony's journalists and political activists rallied behind the Gold Coast's cocoa farmers as they questioned a global market that, for African-produced goods, set the price of goods at the point of consumption and, for European-produced goods, at the point of production.[6]

The situation was similar in other industries. Cash crops like palm oil and rubber, which had been among the colony's most important exports just a few decades earlier, had all but disappeared from the Gold Coast economic stage by the early 1930s. In the case of rubber, the industry had nearly a 100 percent decline in export volume and value between 1926 and 1932. Likewise, the price paid to farmers fell by nearly 70 percent.[7] The palm oil industry followed a similar trajectory, ostensibly losing all of its value and production capacity by 1933. Like with the Gold Coast's other cash crops, the price of palm oil more than halved during the early 1930s and declined more than 75 percent from its high in 1920. Meanwhile, in the mining sector, manganese witnessed a comparable decline. Unlike the cash crops, however, manganese experienced a relatively quick rebound in production and price as, by mid-decade, the Gold Coast became the third-largest producer of the mineral in the world.[8] Among other industries to survive the depression with little to no sustained decline were the colony's gold and diamond industries, both of which had production capacities that held relatively steady through the early depression. Moreover, by 1934, gold in particular was steadily increasing in value.[9]

Largely operated via European-owned mining companies as opposed to the small-scale African-run farms that comprised many of the colony's cash-crop industries, the relative health of the colony's mining sector did not necessarily translate into a higher quality of life for the Gold Coast's African miners. Rather, as Jeff Crisp has shown, mine workers increasingly expressed their discontent with their employers through organized strikes, protesting everything from wages and long hours to rents and the racist and abusive behavior of their supervisors. Employers in turn responded to the strikes by dispatching police and other authorities to break up the disturbances. Furthermore, inside the mines themselves, workers faced increased surveillance while on the job.[10]

By the first years of World War II, the Gold Coast was thus a colony under sustained economic duress, with resonant political and social tensions accompanying the economic. This chapter interrogates the history of the Gold Coast during World War II and in the immediate postwar years. At the heart of the chapter is a reflection on the changing ways in which Gold Coasters throughout the colony understood and re-envisioned their relationships with one another, their communities, the state, and the Gold Coast itself. In doing so, it focuses on the many new challenges, opportunities, and struggles manifested by World War II and its aftermath. As such, this chapter reframes conventional narratives of mid-century Gold Coast activism and, in the postwar years specifically, those narratives' overarching focus on the politics of political organizations like the

United Gold Coast Convention (UGCC) of J. B. Danquah and Kwame Nkrumah's Convention People's Party (CPP). To this end, the chapter details how each of these iconic parties, while key to this historical moment, were part of a broader, more eclectic political atmosphere, where Gold Coasters—representing a vast array of political, ethnic, class, regional, and occupational interests—advocated for their futures and laid the groundwork for subsequent debates over the meaning of the nation and the responsibilities and promises of the state. As Chapter 5 will show, by the mid-1950s, the groundwork for these debates laid during the postwar years would be intensely debated and even violently contested as Nkrumah—then the Gold Coast's prime minister—and the British began discussions for what would become Ghana's independence.

The Gold Coast and World War II

In August 1939, the Accra-based newspaper, the *Gold Coast Independent*, advised its audience of the rising German threat to Europe. Over the previous year, Germany had occupied portions of neighboring Czechoslovakia, annexing the area into an expansionist Germany. By mid-1939, German aggression had increasingly turned to Germany's eastern border with Poland. For the *Independent*, however, the German aggression was not only a threat to Europe. Instead, it held much broader dangers for the world, potentially endangering the British Empire and specifically Britain's African colonies. Moreover, the newspaper advised its readers that those in West Africa specifically had reason for concern as the *Independent* raised the prospect of Germany aiming to reconstitute its authority over the colonial territories taken from it following World War I. Most notably, for Gold Coasters, the concern was the stability of the League of Nations Mandated Territories of British and French Togoland along the Gold Coast's eastern border.[11] In September, German forces invaded Poland and began what would become World War II. By the end of the year, the new Kumasi-based newspaper, the *Ashanti Pioneer*, would announce that Europe had gone "mad, mad with longing for blood, blood, blood." Like the *Independent*, the *Pioneer* would emphasize the global dimensions of the escalating conflict. "Some of her [Europe's] victims are European," the newspaper noted. However, it also stressed that "others are other nationalities, especially Africans."[12]

Reflections on the war dominated the Gold Coast political sphere of 1940. Inside most, if not all of the colony's major newspapers at the time, regular accounts of the events in Europe led each newspaper's pages. In both the *Gold Coast Independent* and *Ashanti Pioneer*, for instance, coverage emphasized such issues as German attempts to spread rumors and misinformation via radio broadcasts and attempts to boost the colony's patriotic spirit by celebrating the values of the British Empire.[13] From a practical point of view, for much of the first part of the year, the war was thus felt as a real, yet relatively distant threat. By mid-year, much would change as Germany invaded France in early May. In just over a month, France would fall to German forces, resulting in the establishment of a new French government allied with the Germans. What France's fall meant for the Gold Coast was a new political reality on the colony's borders as the Gold Coast was now surrounded by territories politically aligned with Germany and its fellow Axis powers. As the threat of the war reached the Gold Coast's doorstep, historian Nancy Lawler has noted, the Gold Coast and British governments were caught fundamentally unprepared. At the time, the government in London had no British troops stationed in the colony and, at best, the Gold Coast had only a limited tradition of a centralized standing military upon which to build.[14]

Similar to the situation in East Africa with the King's African Rifles (KAR), the West African military situation was one defined by small, locally based regiments of a few hundred soldiers during peacetime. However, in moments of crisis such as with World War I, conscription swelled. In East Africa, for instance, the size of the KAR would grow to nearly 32,000 soldiers during that war, with an additional "half a million African non-combatants" supporting them.[15] A similar increase occurred in the Royal West African Frontier Force (RWAFF), with more than 26,000 soldiers enlisted during WWI. The British would integrate another 42,000 West Africans into various other wartime tasks. Moreover, the Gold Coast contingent alone would comprise more than 11,000 individuals, with nearly 10,000 serving in the Gold Coast Regiment (GCR) of the RWAFF.[16] As the war concluded in 1918, the British demobilized nearly all of the RWAFF's soldiers. As a result, during the lead up to World War II, the GCR maintained about 1,200 active troops.[17]

Efforts to draw up the Gold Coast forces accelerated rapidly. By the end of 1940, the GCR alone had grown from two incomplete battalions to five, with three more projected. Furthermore, by the end of the year, only one of those battalions remained in the Gold Coast, with one stationed in the Gambia and three in East Africa.[18] As with previous wartime mobilization efforts, recruitment in the Gold Coast armed forces primarily focused on the colony's Northern Territories. A vast expanse of largely savanna comprising nearly 60 percent of contemporary Ghana's land mass, the Northern Territories had long been neglected by the colonial state as schools, roads, industries, and other social and infrastructural resources tended to go to the wealthier and more populated southern portion of the colony. For instance, as historian Lacy Ferrell has shown, the northern Gold Coast had only ten schools—all but one primary—by 1935. The dearth of schools thus required students to leave home and travel vast distances—upwards of hundreds of kilometers for some—to attend school in a process Ferrell describes as "educational migration."[19] Likewise, by as early as the 1910s, some in the colonial government had already deemed efforts to establish a viable cotton industry in the north— one presumably on par with cocoa or palm oil in the south—as unsustainable.[20] Later commentators would echo these concerns as they emphasized that cash-crop development could not occur in the north without significant infrastructural investment.[21] British district commissioner A. W. Cardinall, for his part, argued that the monetary incentives simply were not there for northern Gold Coasters to commit to such "experimental crop[s]." As he viewed it, "A benevolent despotism might succeed in an agricultural metamorphosis [of the north], democracy, benevolent or otherwise, could not."[22]

In many cases, colonial and other British officials justified their neglect of the Northern Territories due to what they pejoratively perceived as the region's unique backwardness. As one British official argued in 1926, "The people of the Northern Territories of the Gold Coast are far less developed in their organization, and far more primitive in their manners of life and customs [than their southern counterparts]." The result, the official suggested, was the need for a more flexible administrative apparatus in governing the region. In cases where there were strong centralized polities, he noted that the government strove to "recognize them." However, he argued that these polities were few and far between, thus requiring localized, administrative experimentation.[23] Other officials, likewise, reflected on what they perceived to be the differences between northern and southern Gold Coasters. Writing in a history of the RWAFF, two British officers described those of the West African savanna, including most northern Gold Coasters, as part of West Africa's "debased races," contrasting them with the "finer types" of peoples to the south.[24] To this end, officials regularly advanced ideas of northerners as embodying a distinctly martial race uniquely suited for military recruitment.[25]

Much like during World War I, the effect of the colonial administration's perceptions of northern Gold Coasters was a transformation of the region into the colony's primary recruiting grounds for the war effort. In recruitment, officials celebrated what they viewed as an eruption of patriotism in the Gold Coast's north. In the northwestern Gold Coast, for instance, colonial officials in Wala boasted about eighty individuals who had purportedly willingly and enthusiastically joined the military, an action the officials chalked up to the "spirit of adventure which animates the people of the District and also of their loyalty to the Government." The officials also noted that others committed themselves to the war effort by "increasing the production of foodstuffs." For officials, these individuals' decisions to join the war effort grew out of "indignation" at Germany's actions in starting the war and their desire to see the Germans punished.[26] Two hundred kilometers to the northeast in Navrongo, officials, likewise, celebrated recruiting successes as they emphasized that the GCR had enlisted 750 men from the district, a success that they laid at the hands of the "loyalty and enthusiasm" of the district's chiefs. Navrongo's soldiers would go on to fight with "conspicuous success and bravery in East Africa" the report continued. As a result, the officials emphasized that those in the district remained "rightly proud of their [the district's soldiers'] exploits" in the war.[27]

The reliability of the colonial administrators in Wala and Navrongo to accurately describe the intentions and emotions of those who joined the war effort should be viewed with skepticism. It is likely that some soldiers did join the GCR out of a sense of duty, loyalty, and perhaps even adventurism. However, many individuals' reasoning involved a complex nexus of local and regional power dynamics and personal decision making. Like with northern Gold Coasters' labor migration south, a lack of social mobility may have encouraged some northerners to look to the military as an opportunity for social and economic advancement.[28] Many, though, faced forced conscription as mobilization for the expanding war effort required a more stable and rapid mechanism for wartime recruitment than the apparent free will of the region's young men. As it did in Navrongo, the government leaned heavily on the region's chiefs for the conscription of most of its northern soldiers. Reflecting on his own recruitment, one former GCR soldier—Agolley Kusasi—recalled in a 1979 interview with historian David Killingray that "[t]he chief picked out some men and sent them to Bawku. ... The chief told me to go and do something there and I was put in the army."[29] As Killingray explains, the military then sent Kusasi—nineteen at the time—away for training before deploying him to Burma (Myanmar). Kusasi would not see his family again until 1946.[30]

Among those forcibly enlisted in the military, interest in military life was often weak, leading many to desert shortly after recruitment. In one late-1939 case, for instance, local Dagomba chiefs sent approximately 300 young men to the regional capital of Tamale for training. Many would abscond within days of arrival, forcing the GCR to send troops to return the deserters. As reports of the incident indicate, only 52 of the 300 soldiers would ultimately remain in the GCR.[31] In another incident in May 1940, another colonial administrator reported a case where the government convicted the Yejihene (chief of Yeji) and his elders of "habouring 12 deserters from the Regt. [GCR]." After the government captured the fugitives, the "[d]eserters were taken off to Kumasi." Just days after their capture and shipment south, the same administrator reported on his communications with the GCR about the accommodation needs of a new batch of recruits.[32] Killingray further notes that, in order to avoid possible conscription, many individuals in the Northern Territories simply refused to go to their local markets and chiefs' courts during the early years of the war.[33] Regardless, over the course of 1940, the ranks of the GCR would expand rapidly and would only continue to do so as the war effort intensified during the early 1940s as Gold Coasters became celebrated figures of the Allied cause in a number of theaters.

By mid-1940, the GCR had soldiers stationed in battlefields throughout East Africa, where Gold Coast soldiers fought Italian forces in Kenya, Somalia, Ethiopia, and elsewhere. By early 1941, the colony's troops had helped push back the Italian forces in Somalia, a victory celebrated in a number of the colony's most important newspapers. In the *Gold Coast Independent*, the newspaper's writers singled out the soldiers' accomplishments from even those of other West African troops. In doing so, the newspaper surmised that, even in reports containing generic references to West African soldiers, it was safe to assume that those celebrated were almost certainly Gold Coasters. Someday, the newspaper's writers assured their audience with pride and considerable shade, "both Sierra Leone and Nigeria will soon be in the news."[34] By the end of 1941, the Italian military had been pushed out of East Africa, securing, in Ethiopia, the reinstallation of Haile Selassie as the country's emperor. As Gold Coast soldiers helped secure victory in East Africa, attention then turned to the Asian theater as Gold Coasters like Agolley Kusasi deployed to Burma. In Burma, they joined other West African soldiers in challenging Japanese expansionism in Asia and the Pacific. As Killingray notes, British officials felt Gold Coast soldiers would be especially equipped for the Burmese campaign due to what the officials assumed to be the Gold Coasters' familiarity with living and working in heavy jungle environments. As a result, after initially serving to cut transportation paths through the jungle, by 1944, Gold Coast soldiers found themselves on the Burmese frontlines until the war's end.[35]

Meanwhile, on the home front, key aspects of Gold Coast life and infrastructure shifted along with the war effort. At home, communities mobilized around the Allied cause by holding fundraising campaigns in support of the war effort. Launched in 1940, the Spitfires Fund—the most famous of these campaigns—raised £65,000 that year and sought another £100,000 for 1941 for the purchase of the iconic aircraft. However, in 1941 alone, Gold Coasters would contribute more than £340,000 and an additional £205,000 in war bonds and savings certificates.[36] Likewise, in the western harbor city of Takoradi, the city became a key staging ground for a continent-wide transportation network ferrying Allied aircraft from Takoradi harbor to Egypt in the North African theater.[37] Furthermore, Takoradi, along with Accra, where the USA constructed a major airbase, an infusion of Allied soldiers provided a market for Gold Coast boys and young men to serve as intermediaries between the foreign soldiers and the local population. Seen by the colonial government as scourges to the social order, these so-called pilot boys, the government and others claimed, shepherded American and European soldiers, sailors, and airmen through the cities they disembarked in, guiding them through the cities' various bars and in the solicitation of prostitutes. The government also accused these pilot boys of other perceived delinquent activity such as petty theft, loitering, and gambling.[38] At the same time, popular organizations like the Boy Scouts promoted themselves as a democratic answer to the "dramatic spectacle of regimented youth of totalitarian lands."[39]

Demobilization, Swollen Shoot, and the Politics of Disillusionment

For Gold Coasters not directly involved in the war effort, World War II had similarly wide-ranging effects on the lives of the colony's peoples. Despite the Northern Territories supplying a clear majority of the GCR's troops and labor, the colonial administration only furthered its neglect of the region, with the administration engaging in what political scientist Martin Staniland described as the "purest form of indirect rule" in the Gold Coast north during the war. As such, colonial officials cut back extensively on the region's already sparse governmental infrastructure as district commissioners' visits to towns and villages became increasingly more infrequent, and local administrators were asked to do more with even less.[40] Fellow political scientist Paul Ladouceur added that much of the colonial administration's continued neglect of the region emanated from a long-standing fear of "untoward influences" from the south disturbing what the government viewed as an unstable political and social equilibrium in the region.[41] However, as one 1946 report on the far northeastern Gold Coast lamented, the lack of attention to the north ended up having unintended deleterious effects. Inefficiencies emerged in governance as the link between chiefs and colonial officials dissolved. Furthermore, wage-earning northern Gold Coasters faced inflationary pressures. At the same time, in 1945, a poor harvest in parts of the region resulted in a weakening of the region's ability to export grains between local markets and the south.[42]

Further intensifying pressures on the region during the period was the impending demobilization of troops as the war came to a close. Both from an economic and social standpoint, demobilization proved a challenge as servicemen and their families awaited the opportunity to be reunited with friends and family that most had not seen in years. As Killingray details, throughout British-held Africa, feelings of hope, excitement, and trepidation marked both soldiers' and their communities' responses to what emerged as a nearly two-year-long period of demobilization.[43] Meanwhile, in the colonial administration, officials sought to plan for how best to ensure the ex-servicemen's productive integration back into their communities. In the Mamprusi District in the colony's northeast, for instance, officials in 1947 celebrated what they interpreted as the demobilization scheme's success, highlighting what was, in their view, most ex-servicemen's ability to "settle[] back into civilian life without much difficulty."[44] Likewise, officials in the Dagomba District, where approximately 26,000 demobilized soldiers passed through the region's commercial hub of Tamale, perceived similar successes in the government efforts. In doing so, they emphasized their satisfaction with the relatively high percentage of individuals who had applied for employment who had received it and in particular the number of ex-servicemen who had returned to farming. They also highlighted what they viewed as a general "lack of crime and litigation" among the demobilized.[45]

Other officials, however, were not as enthusiastic in their assessments of the Gold Coast's demobilization. In Kete Krachi, one official complained that "there are about 200 ex-servicemen who are doing nothing." According to him, "They [the ex-servicemen] stated that they were not going to leave the town to go to the villages and farm." Instead, the official predicted that they would "in all probability drift to the South."[46] The same colonial official offered a similar appraisal of the situation in Bawku and Mongonori (Mognori), where he emphasized that there too was a "large number of ex-servicemen [who] are doing nothing." As he described, like their colleagues in Kete Krachi, many of these ex-servicemen had little interest in farming. Instead, they desired wage labor and, above that, positions as "headmen." The prospects for wage labor, however, were few, the official intimated, in part due to what he portrayed as the negative perception of the ex-servicemen's work ethic. He also complained about the ex-servicemen's supposed "squander[ing]" of their postwar benefits and savings upon their return, noting the effects of this rapid influx of ex-servicemen money into an economy the size of Bawku's—then a town of less than 7,000 people.[47]

For the ex-servicemen returning home, however, the colonial administration's lamentations regarding the economic and social decisions they were making did not necessarily reflect the circumstances to which they returned. For many northern Gold Coasters, their conscription represented a continuation of long-standing processes of northern labor migration, leading many to seek to return to their previous ways of life. Many, though, would arrive home without much monetarily to show for their years of service.[48] For the much smaller group of former soldiers who had some schooling or had training in marketable trades, their ambitions after the war appeared more varied as many sought to convert their military experience into employment in a range of trades and other businesses. Yet, even among these relatively more privileged ex-servicemen, many found themselves competing for work against individuals who had not spent the previous years away from home and the connections home afforded.[49] As a result, by the late 1940s, discontent among the colony's former soldiers had begun to rise precipitously as ex-servicemen from both the north and south increasingly felt abandoned by the British Empire for which they had fought.

Further fueling not just the ex-servicemen's, but much of the broader population's, frustrations during the period was a broader postwar economic crisis in the colony. The war's end had offered a sense of hope and opportunity. However, what its end ultimately ended up meaning for much of the colony was a period of continued constraint. Internationally, the war had shaken the foundations of Europe's two most powerful empires. France's early collapse had split its empire. In the case of the British, the war had devastated the country's economy. In Britain itself, Britons had endured years of austerity and rationing during the war. Many of these restrictions would continue long after the war's end. For instance, even as late as 1953, Britons still experienced rations on some items including butter and meat.[50] Furthermore, the government also came out of the war highly indebted to the USA. For many British politicians, the debt to the USA struck at a deeper question that linked the need to rebuild to the prospects for political stability in the postwar world. Speaking to the House of Commons in 1949, for instance, Labour Member of Parliament Harold Davies insisted that "paying for the last World War is a problem not merely for the British people, but for the entire world." Only by addressing the debt as a global problem, Davies asserted, could the world avoid what he described as "revolutionary situations."[51]

The effects of the postwar economic crisis on Britain's colonies were no less dramatic. In the Gold Coast, inflation ran rampant during the 1940s. Throughout much of the colony, food costs would more than double, while the prices of many imported goods rose even more. Some imported goods would ultimately reach more than five to eight times their prewar levels.[52] In prominent districts like Tamale, Navrongo, and North Mamprusi in the Northern Territories, inflationary pressures were even more extreme. As one 1946 Department of Agriculture report explained, prices for some food staples had recently risen to "six to seven times" their prewar levels. The price increases were so extreme, the report's author wondered how "wage earners" could subsist "on wages only 50% above prewar levels."[53] The situation only intensified as seasonal rains fell well short of expectations. As a result, in the second quarter of the year, food prices skyrocketed and shortages abounded. Farmers, who the government had encouraged to grow their farms in order to increase production, now found the expansions impossible, as, according to the Department of Agriculture, many had already twice planted fields only to see their crops die after germination. Farmers in turn sneered at continued governmental encouragement to increase production. More importantly, the shortages led to famine-like conditions with many people, "particularly children … visibly losing weight." In response, some traditional authorities sought to restrict the movement of foodstuffs in the region much to the frustration of the colonial administration.[54]

Similarly, in the cocoa-growing regions further south, many Gold Coast farmers faced existential threats to their livelihoods as increasing numbers of cocoa trees succumbed to a viral infection known as swollen shoot disease. Identified by officials in the Department of Agriculture during the mid-1930s in the colony's Eastern Province, the insect-transmitted virus decimated large swaths of the region's cocoa trees. At first causing discoloration of the tree's leaves, the virus would then cause its namesake "swollen shoot" on the plant's stems and blackened cocoa pods before eventually leading to a tree's death. Despite the disease's 1930s taxonomy, Eastern Province farmers had begun describing symptoms afflicting their trees consistent with the disease beginning by at least the early 1920s.[55] As yields from infected trees plummeted and the virus spread to increasing numbers of trees, the colonial government sought to respond to the epidemic by ordering the removal of all infected trees in 1940. However, the initial cutting campaign proved ineffective given the lag between infection and when diseased trees became symptomatic. As a result, the government responded in early 1941 by encouraging the destruction of nearby healthy trees as well as the sick. Over the course of the early 1940s, the government's response only intensified. By late 1946, the government demanded that all cocoa farmers destroy nearby healthy trees and remove them from their farms, while also hiring an array of inspectors to police compliance.[56]

Many farmers ultimately felt betrayed by the government in its efforts to control the disease's spread. As described in a report by a general manager working for the United Africa Company (UAC), one of the most important international trading firms in West Africa, officials did little to educate farmers about the need for the "Cutting Out" campaign. Furthermore, other officials—including some who served as members of the Cocoa Marketing Board—undercut the government's message by arguing that "Cutting Out is not necessary." In the confusion, farmers were generally left to fend for themselves. At the same time, a culture of corruption developed around the "cutting gangs" as some desperate farmers would agree to pay bribes of up to £20 to keep their farms from being cut. Ultimately, the report's author asserted, "No farmer has yet been convinced that Cutting Out is the only cure for Swollen Shoot, some," he continued, "were coerced into it." As a result, the hostility toward the campaign was overwhelming, leading the report's author to recommend that it be halted immediately and, "in about six months' time," have the government begin anew in trying to educate farmers about the need to restart the campaign. "[O]therwise without any doubt," the report's author predicted, "there will be bloodshed."[57]

Among farmers themselves, the effects of swollen shoot's spread throughout the Gold Coast's major cocoa-growing regions were nothing short of devastating. As discussed in Chapter 3, in the Eastern Province town of Domi, the chief watched his annual cocoa yield decline by more than 85 percent when the disease reached his farm. Those who labored on his farm had little choice but to find work elsewhere despite having lived and worked in Domi for, in some cases, more than two decades.[58] Similarly, in Mepom, another Eastern Province village between Asamankese and Nsawam, Kwao Abbey claimed that, when swollen shoot hit his farm, his yields went from 300 loads a year to 2.5. As a result of the drastic decline in the farm's profitability, Abbey requested a deduction in the £180 rent owed on the farm's land. However, Abbey never received a response from the land's "caretaker"—the chief of Mepom—and thus had to pull the money together from "various members" of his family.[59] Still another farmer, who had previously purchased a farm in Adeiso approximately 14 kilometers east of Mepom, watched his investment evaporate with swollen shoot as the disease killed off his entire farm. The Accra-born farmer would eventually join a company of prospective Ga farmers and try his hand again in 1950 on land more than 350 kilometers to the northwest in Sefwi-Wiawso.[60] Other farmers abandoned cocoa and turned toward the cultivation of local food products, an activity many considered women's work.[61] In other instances, men "dash[ed]" their stricken farms to female relatives.[62]

The Disturbances of 1948

As Gold Coasters coped with the effects of the growing economic crisis and its concomitant social upheavals during the postwar years, pressure against the colonial system as currently constructed began to grow. Most notably, in Accra, a local chief and businessman named Nii Kwabena Bonne III protested the structure of the colony's economic system. Key to Bonne's complaints was a system that privileged foreign-owned firms over local traders and businesses, allowing the firms to "fix their own prices."[63] Much of Bonne's ire was specifically directed toward the colony's Lebanese population, a decades-old community largely identified as commercial middlemen.[64] As Bonne would explain in 1948, the actions of European firms, in conjunction with the Lebanese community, collaborated to impoverish the colony's African population. "By first-hand informations [*sic*]," he asserted after undertaking his own factfinding mission, "I was able to discover that the poorer class of the villagers could not clothe themselves, and [a] majority of them went almost in rags [due to the colony's trade conditions]."[65] As a result, Bonne unleashed an anti-inflation campaign that would culminate with a national boycott commencing in January 1948.[66]

As the boycott expanded, tensions grew in the colony. In meetings with colonial officials, chiefs and other prominent Gold Coast figures emphasized the populace's dedication to the anti-inflation cause. On February 20, for instance, the Konor (king) of Manya Krobo, Nene Azzu Kate Kole, insisted to a group of colonial officials and businesspeople that the "people of the Gold Coast did not want to cause internal disorder or to upset the smooth administration of the country." However, he added that, despite the personal economic difficulties caused by the boycott, Gold Coasters were committed to seeing it through to a successful conclusion. "If a settlement is not reached," the Konor advised the officials, "we cannot forecast how long the boycott will last."[67] Furthermore, sporadic rioting and other disturbances accompanied the boycott. Likewise, xenophobic attacks on the colony's Lebanese community featured in the African-run press, with one writer in the Cape Coast-based *West African Monitor* crediting Bonne III for bringing to the colony's attention the "Syrian Menace."[68] Others made similar accusations, with Linton Val-Vannis—the founder of the Freedom Defence Society—describing the so-called Syrian menace as the source of Ghana's "blackmarkets [sic]."[69]

In the midst of the boycott, ex-servicemen associated with the recently reorganized Ex-Servicemen's Union announced plans to organize a march on the seat of the colonial government, Accra's Christiansborg Castle.[70] Among the demands issued in the ex-servicemen's petition were the government's recognition of the Union; the establishment of a cooperative relationship with the colonial government-sponsored Gold Coast Legion; the release of ex-servicemen in prison for petty offences committed abroad; increases to their pensions; an Africanization of the Gold Coast officer corps; and war service credits issued to junior sanitary inspectors, pupil nurses, and pupil dispensers (pharmacists).[71] Meanwhile, as the ex-servicemen planned their march, the leaders of the Anti-Inflation Campaign struck a deal to end the boycott on February 28, the day of the march on Christiansborg. Reports from that morning indicate that shoppers crowded Accra's major commercial sites, with activists monitoring the shops' compliance to the terms of the agreement.[72]

Around midday, crowds began convening in Accra's Old Polo Grounds and, at 3 p.m., approximately 2,000 individuals began the nearly 2.5 kilometer walk to the castle. As one observer recounted, as the crowd moved forward, they did so in an orderly fashion, singing.[73] Agitated that the marchers deviated from the agreed-upon path to the castle, the Gold Coast police tried to push the crowd back. As described by marcher Emmanuel Kpokpo Allotey, the police formed a line across the road. "We wheeled round immediately," Allotey explained, "and the police started the tear gas. … When they were using the tear gas everybody was confused."[74] In the mêlée, the Gold Coast Superintendent of Police, Colin Herbert Imray, opened fire on the crowd, killing multiple people.[75] Several others, including Allotey, who was shot in the hip, were injured.[76] Chaos then broke out. As another observer, a customs officer who at the time was drinking at a nearby bar, recounted, he and his companions heard the shots and rushed to the streets to see what was happening. They encountered a crowd scattering and shouting "'One of us has been killed.'" Next, they saw the confusion turn to anger as individuals began throwing stones. "Stones were thrown at the Y.M.C.A.," he recalled. "I saw one European whom I know, Mr. Daley, sitting in front of the Y.M.C.A., they were throwing stones, so he rushed inside and locked the doors."[77]

The response in Accra was dramatic. Gold Coasters almost immediately took to the streets to protest the police shooting, looting foreign-owned businesses. By 4:30 p.m., crowds had already ravaged the iconic Kingsway store on High Street, with another crowd—largely composed of women and children according to an assistant superintendent of police—congregating at the UAC's main warehouse. The building's main door was then set afire, dispersing the crowd. Others took to Salaga Market, looting the market and overturning at least two cars and setting aflame a third. Heavy rains quelled the crowds overnight. However, by 5 a.m. the next day, the disturbances started anew.[78] Officials received reports from European store managers and other business officials about how they feared injury in the chaos and "[a]ll European officers were warned that the Military might have to open fire on the crowds."[79] Moreover, the disturbances quickly spread to other major cities and towns. In Kumasi, stores briefly opened at 8 a.m. on March 1 before closing approximately a half-hour later as crowds gathered outside. At 9:15 a.m., crowds began throwing stones at the city's Kingsway store, breaking windows and letting people into the store. In response, the police called in the Tear Gas Squad and also attempted a baton charge. As this failed to disperse the crowd, they called for military assistance, briefly regaining control of the area by midday. Shortly thereafter, the crowds regathered and continued to "batter down doors and windows of stores." Around this time, a soldier opened fire, killing one and injuring two.[80]

In Koforidua, the situation was equally unsettling. By March 2, officials deemed the city unsafe, largely directing their concern to the white population living there. According to one report, European women had been confined to the residential area, with one house already set afire. In response, the police initiated a plan to evacuate European women and children from the city. However, as the police reports recount, the evacuation was disrupted even before it began as officials brought in to coordinate the removal encountered opposition en route to Koforidua. "When nearing Koforidua lorries began to pass our convoy containing shouting and singing people," one police official recounted. "These lorries were loaded with what was obviously loot—some of the loads being even packed on the wings of cars."[81] As the evacuation proceeded, the women and children were loaded into a caravan leaving the city. Approximately seven to ten miles outside the city, however, the caravan stopped to force several converging vehicles into the procession. Another vehicle then approached, refusing to stop. To try and stop the vehicle from purportedly ramming into the convoy, an officer opened fire on the vehicle, trying to shoot out its tires before other officers followed suit. Fleeing the bullets, the vehicle's occupants jumped from the moving lorry, with one person suffering severe injuries. That person died shortly after.[82]

The disturbances would continue through March, with reports of sporadic violence and looting featuring prominently in reports coming from inside and outside the colony. By the end of the month, the death toll from the disturbances would reach twenty-seven people, with another 237 injured.[83] In response to the events, the government turned its attention to those it viewed as the disturbances' agitators. In mid-March, the government arrested six of the newly formed United Gold Coast Convention's leaders, including longtime activist and former newspaper editor J. B. Danquah and Ghana's eventual first prime minister and president Kwame Nkrumah. Furthermore, the government cancelled an upcoming session of the Legislative Council and sought to quell reports of a potential general strike. Meanwhile, in Cape Coast, the government temporarily closed three boys' secondary schools and sent students home due to what the government described as "undisciplined behaviour" among the students. Similarly, the Department of Post-Secondary Education at Achimota College threatened to revoke the scholarships of students protesting the government's actions over the preceding month. Moreover, in an attempt to threaten the general population, the government also made it a crime to assist those against whom it had issued detention orders.[84]

Parties of Protest

The aftermath of the disturbances unleashed a torrent of political activism in the Gold Coast. Among established groups like the ARPS, which even though its influence had declined significantly from its height during the early twentieth century still had a prominent voice in the colony's political circles, many used their positions to question the government's narrative of the events and specifically the process established to investigate its actions. Writing to the commission of enquiry investigating the disturbances (the Watson Commission), Sakyi Djan of the ARPS protested what he viewed as the self-imposed limits of the enquiry. In terms of investigating the lawfulness of the officers' actions on February 28 and afterward, Djan openly questioned why the commission would rely on a coroner's report to answer such a question. "[Y]ou will I am sure appreciate the fact that such an inquest will only probe the question of whether those victims died as a result of gun shot, but not whether it was lawful for the soldirs [sic] to shoot the civilians," he asserted. "There are several of those victims who though received bullet-wounds in their bodies yet still survive." Those cases, Djan continued, would thus fall outside the scope of the investigation and the victims would have no recourse to have their voices heard.[85]

The ARPS also sought to center the colony's cocoa crisis in both official and popular accounts of the disturbances. In doing so, the ARPS aligned itself with a consortium of farmers' organizations to challenge the government's swollen shoot policies. As one letter petitioning the Watson Commission to take up the farmers' cause explained, "They [the farmers] say that, if the so-called Scientists [sic] had been working as seriously as they should, they might have been able to arrive at a better cure other than cutting out." The farmers' organizations, through the ARPS, thus called for a three-year moratorium on cutting to "watch the result" of areas already cut.[86] In addition, the ARPS submitted another report on behalf of the farmers in which they traced the current cocoa crisis back to at least 1930. The low cocoa prices of the depression, the ARPS argued, encouraged farmers to neglect their trees. Environmental challenges like low rainfall and geological events such as the 1939 earthquake further disrupted the depression-era cocoa industry. As the ARPS recounted, however, the foremost change during the 1930s was the withdrawal of governmental support and technical assistance for farmers, seen by farmers as a punishment for their protests against the collapsing cocoa prices of the era. This abdication of responsibility from the government only forced cocoa producers to further disinvest their time and labor from their farms.[87]

The ARPS's and farmers' attempts to historicize the roots of the 1948 disturbances were not unique. Several of the Gold Coast's African-run newspapers also sought to connect the disturbances to the broader history of colonialism, with some like the *West African Monitor* and the *Daily Echo* renewing postwar speculation that the government ultimately aimed to transform the Gold Coast into a white settler state. "WHITE SETTLEMENT [*sic*] in the Gold Coast is not a distant project," the *West African Monitor* predicted in March 1948, "it has been carefully planned and is now in full swing." The *Monitor* in turn continued by highlighting scientific successes in making West Africa more livable for Europeans. Most notably, the newspaper emphasized the scientists' role in "finding potent antidote [*sic*] for malaria." The recent wave of independence movements in South and Southeast Asia—both in terms of the economic consequences and the need to repatriate those former colonies' white populations—only promised to accelerate the Gold Coast's transformation into a settler state in the newspaper's reading of the events. "The plan is in operation in the Gold Coast, and so our dear native land is now slipping away into European hands," the *Monitor* warned its readers. "It is a fact. A few years more and we shall also be pushed into the interior somewhere to live in circumscribed areas and die of starvation and disease like the aborigines of Australia."[88]

Attempts to mobilize against the colonial government came from a variety of directions in 1948, including several nascent political parties that appeared in the postwar years. However, the UGCC quickly emerged as the most influential. Founded in April 1947, initially under the name of the People's National Party, the UGCC advocated for a transition to self-rule in the "shortest possible time" and the establishment of a new constitution that prioritized what the party's ostensible head, J. B. Danquah, described as a "blend [of] the old with the new, chieftaincy with democracy, the inherited culture with progressive modernism."[89] According to Danquah, the future he and the UGCC envisioned would entail "a clean break away from the memories of the old days of exploitation and imperialism, and the colonial adjective Gold Coast will give way to the substantive name of the people and country, Ghana and Ghanaland."[90]

By the end of the year, the party's growth began to garner the attention of officials in the colonial government. In a December 1947 report to the British Secretary of State, Arthur Creech Jones, Kenneth Bradley, the governor's deputy, argued that much was still not known about the UGCC's potential, yet a relative political vacuum in the Gold Coast—especially among organizations that could serve as the voice of the youth—had provided a clear opening for its growth. Bradley, for his part, remained skeptical of the UGCC's prospects. In particular, he noted that among the party's foremost aims was "to wrest power from the chiefs," leading to tensions between the UGCC and many of the colony's most important chiefs. Bradley also perceived a lack of cooperation between the UGCC and the colony's unions. Additionally, he presented the party's leadership as "discredited politicians or politicians who are out of office," arguing that what he perceived to be their diminished position "helps to explain why many of the most influential of the younger African politicians as well as those who at present are members of the various Councils and Committees of the Central Government have, so far, withheld their active support from the new party."[91]

Among the key concerns associated with the UGCC for Bradley and others in the colonial government, however, was the party's invitation of a Gold Coast activist named Kwame Nkrumah to serve as the party's general secretary.[92] Born in the far southwestern Gold Coast town of Nkroful, Nkrumah was among the first class of students invited to enroll in what would become Achimota Secondary School, graduating in 1932. In 1935, Nkrumah left for the United States, where he would attend Lincoln University and subsequently the University of Pennsylvania. In the United States, Nkrumah associated himself with an array of radical political and cultural institutions and philosophies, developing a nascent anticolonial thought that he would take to London in 1945. In London, Nkrumah joined the Trinidadian pan-Africanist George Padmore, among others, in organizing the 1945 Manchester Pan-African Congress, which called for an immediate end to colonial rule in Africa and the Caribbean. Following the Manchester Congress, Nkrumah helped found the West African National Secretariat (WANS), an organization that, among other things, sought to "combat all forms of imperialism and colonial exploitation" and secure "national unity and absolute independence for all West Africa."[93] The project the WANS imagined was also an explicitly socialist project, with one of the organization's founding members, Gold Coaster Bankole Awooner-Renner, promoting in one of the secretariat's publications the idea of a "West African Soviet Union."[94]

The colonial government looked to Nkrumah's invitation to serve in the UGCC with particular trepidation, fearing what it perceived to be Nkrumah's communist sympathies. A police report prior to his arrival noted, for instance, his role in the organization of the Manchester Congress and connections to Padmore as well as T. Ras Makonnen and Peter Abrahams, two other prominent Britain-based pan-Africanists. Furthermore, the report cited connections between Nkrumah and the British Communist Party, claiming that he sought "advice and assistance in connection with his work in organizing a West African National Congress" and that, in 1948, he had planned on attending a Communist Party School.[95] Bradley, in his report to the secretary of state, advised Creech Jones that:

> Kwame Nkrumah will arrive to find the new party of which he is to be the paid secretary still in a malleable and formative stage, impatient at being out-manoeuvred by the chiefs and other of the more responsible politicians, and the young "intelligentsia" of whom its ranks are mostly composed [of individuals] ready to accept radical ideas and to respond to the type of leadership which he may be able to provide.

Bradley predicted that, given all that he had previously heard of Nkrumah and of the "rapturous accounts of his talents," Nkrumah surely was returning to the Gold Coast with "few illusions (if any) about the messianic nature of his 'mission.'"[96]

As the riots broke out in Accra in late February, the UGCC responded with a telegram from the Convention's Working Committee arguing that "Civil Government [in the] Gold Coast [had] broken down." The Working Committee then predicted an even greater breakdown of civil order "[u]nless [the] Colonial government is changed and [a] new Government of the people and chiefs installed," which would "result in worse violent and irresponsible acts by uncontrolled people." In an effort to quell the violence, the UGCC's Working Committee insisted that the UGCC was "prepared and ready to take interim [control of the] Government."[97] Nkrumah, acting on his own, would send an additional telegram to the colonial government with accompanying copies to a range of major publications and political organizations on both sides of the Cold War divide in which he called out the police's attack on the unarmed ex-servicemen. In doing so, he emphasized that it occurred "without provocation," while also noting the violence and looting that followed. Nkrumah concluded by announcing that the "people demand selfgovernment [*sic*] immediately" and demanded the "recall [of the] governor."[98]

Shortly thereafter, the government would arrest Nkrumah, Danquah, and four other key members of the UGCC leadership. The arrests would unleash a torrent of anticolonial activism, which, over the next two years, would define the colony's political scene. Following their release, tensions would arise between Nkrumah and the other members of the so-called Big Six as Nkrumah continued to advocate for what he and, following the July 1949 formation of his own political party, the Convention People's Party (CPP), his allies described as "Self-Government Now." In contrast to the UGCC and the political parties that preceded it, the CPP represented one of the first mass political parties on the African continent. Not only did it mobilize around the abstract concept of "self-government now," it actively integrated the demands of the Gold Coast's cocoa farmers, ex-servicemen, market women, consumers, workers, students, and youth, among others into its anticolonial message. In its press, most notably the Nkrumah-founded *Accra Evening News*, the CPP would thus combine messages of self-government with regular coverage of everything from work conditions and access to employment to farmers' opposition to the Cutting Out campaign to the need to expand educational access to all Gold Coast youth, including girls.[99] Furthermore, the party took this message to villages and towns throughout the colony, drawing on the youth and market women to recruit and organize against the colonial state. As one early supporter of Nkrumah explained, even before Nkrumah's break from the UGCC, Nkrumah "realized early that there was no radio, there was no communication system, but the youth can carry information across in the most wonderful way unconscious to the youth themselves." Over the next several years, he would recruit for Nkrumah and the CPP himself, traveling from near Accra to as far as the Northern Territories.[100]

Conclusion

In late 1946, J. B. Danquah wrote a letter to a friend in Nigeria, J. F. Duncan, explaining that "I feel really guilty in a sense that there is at present no 'visible' political movement in the Gold Coast." However, Danquah noted, "There is intense political activity going on." For Danquah in 1946, defining the relationship between the intelligentsia and the colony's chiefs represented the future of African politics in the colony. He saw the path forward in forging this relationship as rocky and laden with mistrust, but necessary. This reality, he suggested, was the major limitation in pursuing "any large movement, e.g. a People's Party" in the Gold Coast.[101] Over the next four years, the political situation in the Gold Coast would shift dramatically as events locally and regionally—including demobilization, the swollen shoot crisis, rampant inflation, the police shooting in Accra, and the riots that followed—politicized the populace in ways not seen before. The rise of the CPP in particular, with its emphasis on political organization and mobilization, vastly expanded the scope of the colony's politics beyond the intelligentsia and chiefs of whom Danquah spoke. By 1950, groups including market women, ex-servicemen, students, unemployed and underemployed youth, and farmers, among others, not only became key players in the colony's politics, but, more importantly, became the foundation upon whom those politics would be built and contested in the decolonization era.

Chapter 5

STATES OF TRANSITION:
NATION AND THE POLITICS OF INDEPENDENCE
IN A DECOLONIZING GHANA

By the end of 1949, the CPP had established itself as the most dynamic voice on the Gold Coast political stage, as fissures with the UGCC increasingly weakened the Convention. At the heart of the CPP's political program was a focus on mass organization. As Kwame Nkrumah explained in the Foreword to J. Benibengor Blay's 1950 account of the 1947 Gold Coast Mine Employee's Union strike, "[o]rganization decides everything."[1] Party newspapers like the *Accra Evening News* echoed such calls with articles appealing to nearly all segments of the Gold Coast populace to mobilize and organize themselves in support of the CPP's demand for an immediate end to colonial rule. Writing in one February 1949 article, for instance, Dorothea Lokko called upon her "fellow women, mothers and daughters of Ghana ... [to] all rise up from our deep slumber, and know that we have an important part to play in the present struggle for the liberation of our country. Let us organise," she exclaimed, "and with united effort, walk side by side with men to our target which is Self-Rule."[2] From Sunyani, the capital of the contemporary Bono Region, the Brong Youths Union made a similar plea, claiming that the future of "Brongland ... depends to a greater extent on us, the few who have seen a bit of the light of modern civilisation." Like Lokko, the Brong Youths Union in turn implored "us [to] be organised now for positive action."[3]

As Nkrumah's and the CPP's influence grew, the colonial government attempted to respond by seeking to sideline Nkrumah and his party from the colony's political stage and by aligning itself with what it considered to be the colony's more tempered political voices. Most notably, these voices included the colony's chiefs and even the UGCC's leadership. In forging these relationships, the colonial government sought to embark on a set of political reforms that would open pathways for new forms of political engagement. These reforms would ultimately include the colony's first popularly contested elections in 1951. However, while more democratic on its face, the political system developed in the aftermath of the 1948 disturbances still ensured a subordinate relationship between Great Britain and Gold Coast Africans, leaving the colony's political atmosphere unsettled. As one mid-1949 Colonial Office dispatch noted, the "trend of afairs [*sic*] in the Gold Coast ... definitely causes us uneasiness." However, it predicted that the government's actions in appointing a committee to explore constitutional change within the colony would assuredly "bring things into their proper perspective, and confront the extreme political element in the Gold Coast with realities, to their consequent discredit in the eyes of public opinion."[4] For its part, the CPP responded to the proposed constitutional reforms—made public in October of that year—with hesitancy, initially refusing to support them before demanding further amendments to the proposed constitution.[5]

Despite the colonial government's predictions that the CPP's perceived obstinacy would diminish Nkrumah's and the CPP's influence in the colony, both—the party and its leader—continued their political ascent. The declaration of a general strike in January 1950, known and subsequently commemorated as "Positive Action," only further burnished the CPP's radical credentials in the public's and government's eyes. Less than two weeks after the January 8th declaration of Positive Action, the colonial government arrested Nkrumah, along with numerous other CPP activists on charges of sedition, pursuing an illegal strike, and fomentation of violence.[6] As much of the CPP's leadership sat in prison, the party's remaining leaders redoubled their mobilization efforts, turning their attention to a series of upcoming elections within the colony. Following the early November 1950 municipal elections in Kumasi, the Gold Coast's newly installed governor, Charles Arden-Clarke, wrote to the British Secretary of State, James Griffiths, to warn him that the CPP's successes in the municipal elections were not an aberration. Rather, he explained that they represented the party's "real organising capacity" and insisted that "the debâcle of the opposition was due to apathy and not (repeat not) to intimidation."[7] By the time the colony's first general election came around in February 1951, the CPP had thus built itself into a truly mass party. As a result, the CPP dominated the general election, winning thirty-four of the thirty-eight contested seats in the newly formed Legislative Assembly.[8]

The CPP's 1951 election victory culminated with Nkrumah's near immediate release from prison. As one individual who rushed to Accra's James Fort Prison to watch Nkrumah's release reminisced in 2007, on that day, "I saw whites running away for the first time."[9] Released from prison, the crowd shepherded Nkrumah to Christiansborg Castle, where he and the CPP would form their own government under the auspices of the colonial government. In this period of shared governance (dyarchy), the CPP maintained the ability to form its own cabinet, pass legislation, and negotiate on behalf of the Gold Coast people, while the British-led colonial administration maintained authority over foreign affairs and the colony's defense. In 1954 and 1956, the CPP would win two additional general election victories with relative electoral ease. The CPP's victories in these elections ultimately paved the way for Ghana's March 6, 1957 independence. Throughout this period, Nkrumah and the CPP advocated for an idea of the postcolonial Ghanaian nation that transcended the boundaries of the new Ghanaian nation-state via the broader project of African liberation. At the same time, the Nkrumah government of the 1950s and 1960s also regularly sought to exercise the force of the Ghanaian state against those who pushed back against the Nkrumah government's vision for Ghana and Africa and, perhaps even more fundamentally, what it meant to be a "Ghanaian."

This chapter details the construction of the decolonization-era Ghanaian state. In Ghana and elsewhere, decolonization represented more than a transfer of political power from the colonial administration to an African-led government. Just as importantly, it represented a deeply contested process of negotiation, redefinition, and realignment as numerous competing constituencies sought to articulate their own visions or sets of visions for the new Ghana. In the case of Nkrumah and the CPP, which dominated the Ghanaian political stage for nearly twenty years from the late 1940s to their overthrow in 1966, the new Ghanaian state was at its foundation envisioned to be pan-African both internationally and domestically. Internationally, the goal was the broader liberation and unification of the continent. Domestically, it was the creation of a new type of citizen in Ghana. This citizen was to be organized, disciplined, and dedicated to the Nkrumahist cause. To cultivate this new idea of citizenship, the Nkrumah government created a dizzying array of political and social institutions, bringing within the state's orbit everyone from school-age children to workers, farmers, civil servants, and market women, among others.[10]

For Ghanaians, the ramifications of the Nkrumahist project were many. Even as the meaning and nature of the Nkrumahist project shifted, opportunities to deviate from it increasingly became closed off as the postcolonial government used the power and mechanisms afforded by the new state to advance and even police conformance to its political vision. However, the Nkrumah government's attempted civic engineering was simultaneously done at a time when diverse groups of soon-to-be Ghanaians were articulating their own ideas of what it meant to be Ghanaian. As this chapter will show, the debates about what it meant to be Ghanaian during the decolonization era ranged from the local, regional, and ethnic to the national and continental. As such, they were multi-scalar in dimension, harkening to both the transnational rhetoric and ambitions of the Nkrumahist state and the intimacy of individual peoples' and communities' historical understandings of their pasts and senses of belonging and self. Moreover, the stakes of these debates were immense for both individuals and the government and, as subsequent chapters will show, would have resonances in the country's politics well into the twenty-first century.

Anticolonial Contestations

On July 10, 1953, Kwame Nkrumah stood before the Gold Coast Legislative Assembly and made his case for the then colony's independence. As he introduced a motion for constitutional reform, Nkrumah called upon the British to grant his "Government the power to bring to fruition the longing hopes, the ardent dreams, the fervent aspirations of the chiefs and people of our country." The previous century, Nkrumah reminded his audience, had been one marked by "alien rule." Gold Coasters, he then asserted, "with ever increasing tendency, looked to the bright and glorious day when they shall regain their ancient heritage, and once more take their place rightly as free men in the world."[11] As Nkrumah reminisced about this moment in his autobiography, he described this speech, which has come to be known as his "Motion of Destiny" speech, as a moment of exuberance. Outside the Legislative Assembly, Nkrumah recalled, crowds had gathered, proudly celebrating a key step in the colony's path to self-government.[12] Present at the Legislative Assembly, the prominent African-American journalist and novelist Richard Wright noted that, following Nkrumah's speech, "Crowds lifted the Prime Minister aloft and bore him through the grounds of the Assembly as the throngs yelled, sang, and danced. ... The sound trucks blared. Men and women ran, their hands throw [*sic*] high into the air." In sum, Wright exclaimed, "THIS WAS THE GREAT DAY."[13]

Following Nkrumah, J. A. Braimah, the CPP's Minister of Communications and Works, rose to second Nkrumah's motion before J. B. Danquah, then representing the Ghana Congress Party (GCP), stood to address the Legislative Assembly. Danquah challenged what he presented as an equivocation by the CPP regarding the question of self-government. The technical claim in Nkrumah's motion was that the British take up legislation recognizing the Gold Coast as a sovereign state. Danquah argued that, by failing to assert the Gold Coast's independence, the CPP was betraying its founding demand of "Self-Government Now." As Danquah claimed before the Legislative Assembly, the CPP government's reliance on "simple phrases like 'Self-Government Now', 'An Act of Independence' or the latest phrase 'Sovereign and Independent State'" carried little meaning. Rather, he insisted that they helped to "deceive ... [us] with words and nothing but words and," in doing so, "exchange the real substance of our struggle for a mere shadow of words—a shadow of many words." Danquah then proceeded with significant hyperbole to present the GCP as the colony's true revolutionary party, eliciting laughter and calls of condemnation.[14] Wright, for his part, mocked Danquah's speech, contrasting its "slickness" with Danquah's own "powerless[ness]." As Wright read the Gold Coast political scene, Danquah ultimately "represented nobody ... [except the] frightened elements in the community."[15]

Underlying the contrasting speeches delivered by Danquah and Nkrumah in July 1953, however, was a growing schism within the late-colonial-era Gold Coast. For much of the previous four years, the CPP and its promises of self-government had stood at the center of the colony's politics. At the heart of the CPP's anticolonial demands for "Self-Government Now" and its accompanying calls for "freedom" was more than a claim for postcolonial statehood. "Self-Government Now," instead, became a call for addressing a wide array of popular frustrations with the colonial state. In many ways, the vagueness of the phrase provided the space for a vision of the party as a place open to all Gold Coasters and their interests. As one man, M. N. Tetteh, who would eventually work his way through several levels of the CPP governmental apparatus, explained in 2008, "Nearly every average man who heard about Kwame Nkrumah ... by instantaneous emotion liked to hear the words 'the white man must go.'"[16] Meanwhile, Magnet Abenkwan, a nonagenarian farmer from Koforidua during the late 2000s, described the CPP as a party of "mainly women."[17] In doing so, she went far beyond more conventional claims that the party simply provided a place for Gold Coast women and their concerns on the Gold Coast political stage.[18] Lawrence Asamoah, also of Koforidua, seemingly also alluded to such sentiments as he recalled his mother's support for the party and its ability "to do wonders" at a time when Gold Coasters were "under whites."[19] Similar reflections of the CPP as a farmers', workers', and/or youth party have also come from individuals associated with those sectors in the decades since its formation.

What Nkrumah's speech before the Legislative Assembly aimed to do was to stake claim to the process of reframing the CPP movement away from that of resistance to that of a builder of possible futures. Key to Nkrumah's speech was the centrality of the region's many connected histories: those of European trade, slavery, and colonialism as well as those of the ancestors. The path forward, according to Nkrumah, was one of leadership—both nationally and continentally—as the envisioned Ghana provided a pathway toward a strong, independent, and collective future. As Nkrumah explained, the new Ghana was not to be a copy of Europe. Instead, it was to take from Europe and other world regions what it needed, adapting, innovating, and inventing where it saw fit. The goal, as Nkrumah alluded in his 1953 speech, as well as in others throughout the 1950s and 1960s, was thus the emergence of a new type of state and citizenry centered around a meaning of Ghanaian-ness rooted in the postcolonial nation-building process. It was also to be one shielded from what he presented as the divisive legacies of class, ethnicity, and racism.[20]

Danquah did more than try to cast Nkrumah's speech off as little more than rhetorical fluff. Instead, his speech—perhaps inadvertently—pointed to many of the challenges the CPP faced as it sought to bring its vision of the new nation into fruition. For Danquah, the project Nkrumah and the CPP envisioned for Ghana was marked by a perceived shallowness. Two years later, in a 1955 interview with the African-American sociologist St. Clair Drake, Danquah elaborated. In doing so, he complained that the CPP's nationalism was "political nationalism[,] not cultural nationalism" and that any gesture the CPP made to culture was only for show.[21] Danquah, who had written extensively about Akan tradition and beliefs and whose brother had been king of Akyem Abuakwa until his 1943 death, constructed a view of the Ghanaian that competed with the Marxist pan-African anticolonialism espoused by Nkrumah.[22] Danquah's Ghanaian nation was to be one firmly rooted in the specificities of the Gold Coast/Ghanaian past and what that past could uniquely contribute to the future. As political scientist Yaw Twumasi has detailed, Danquah had long put forth a political philosophy bound to what the Kyebi-born politician referred to as each people's "national inheritance"—a "spirit" guiding each people's unique contribution to world history. In the case of the Gold Coast/Ghana, it was in the social, moral, and spiritual power of its tradition of "elected monarchs" that Danquah understood the power of Gold Coasters' pasts and futures. The task ahead was thus that of adapting this system to modern realities.[23]

The question of history dominated what would become the anti-CPP politics of the 1950s, with fights over the past playing out in different ways in different regions of the emergent country. In the north, tensions rose over what many viewed as the CPP's complicity in exacerbating the inequities between the colony's north and south through its demands for self-government.[24] Tied to the long history of southern extraction of northern labor and the lack of colonial investment in the region discussed in previous chapters, many northern politicians called upon both the CPP and the British to slow the possible path to self-governance. As Shanni Mahama, one of the grandsons of Ya Na Mahama III of Dagbon, explained to Paul André Ladouceur in the 1970s, for many northerners, self-governance granted without consideration of the north's historic and contemporary relationship to the south represented an existential threat to the northern way of life. According to Mahama, when Nkrumah visited his grandfather in 1948, his grandfather sought to explain this position to the then-UGCC general secretary. "My grandfather told Nkrumah," Mahama recounted,

> the story of the three women who were pregnant, one at nine months, one at seven months, and the other at three months, and that of the Colony, Asante and the Northern Territories were like these three women. If they were to give birth, the woman at nine months would give birth to a child, and also the woman at seven months, but that at three months would deliver only blood and tissue. So the Colony and Asante could go ahead with independence but the North was not ready.[25]

What concerned Mahama's grandfather was the potential of subsuming the region's unique history and way of life in a new state dominated by the south. As a result, in 1954, a group of aspiring politicians—most of whom with familial connections to the region's chiefs or were chiefs themselves—formed the region's first political party, the Northern People's Party.[26] As outlined in its constitution, the aim of the party was to protect the "culture of the people of the Northern Territories (Protectorate)," increasingly integrate more northerners into the Gold Coast's governmental administration, and ensure the "vocational and cultural advancement of the population, child and adult."[27] The Mamprusi politician Mumuni Bawumia was even more direct about the party's objectives at its April launching. Speaking in Tamale, Bawumia assured his audience that the Northern People's Party supported the Gold Coast's "fight[] for freedom—freedom from an outside power." However, he continued by asserting that northerners had to also fight for "their internal freedom." Moreover, it was an act of emancipation that had to occur "now … instead of waiting to fight for it tomorrow." The success of the Northern People's Party, Bawumia further insisted, would ultimately "strengthen the unity which had existed between the people of the North and the South."[28]

Alongside the Northern People's Party, another party—the Muslim Association Party (MAP)—emerged within the so-called stranger communities (*zongos*) of Kumasi and Accra. Officially formed in early 1954, the MAP's roots dated back more than two decades with the formation of the Muslim Association in Accra. As historian Jean Allman has detailed, in the late 1930s, the Muslim Association had protested what it viewed as the malapportionment of aid following the 1939 Accra earthquake, continuing with its political advocacy through the war and early postwar years. By 1948, it would align itself with the UGCC and eventually the CPP. Key to its political demands during the late 1940s and early 1950s was an expansion of Koranic education in Accra's and Kumasi's *zongos*. However, by 1953, many in the Muslim Association began to feel betrayed by the CPP as promised educational reforms appeared stalled. As a result, the Association sought alliances with other Gold Coast opposition parties, namely Danquah's GCP. By the end of the year, the Muslim Association announced its break from the CPP as it promised to challenge the CPP in all future elections. By the time of its inauguration in early 1954, the MAP had firmly established itself as the first Gold Coast opposition party with nationwide support.[29]

Like with the Northern People's Party, the MAP focused on the CPP's alleged role in reinforcing historic inequalities within the Gold Coast. As Abdul Rahim Alawa argued in an April 1954 rally in a Kumasi sheep market, the MAP was calling on Gold Coasters to "throw off" what he described as "Black Imperialism."[30] In particular, Alawa turned his attention to the nature of CPP governance. Ever since the CPP's rise to power in 1951, those opposed to Nkrumah and his government questioned not only the efficacy of the CPP's policies, but, more importantly, they also challenged the government on whether it was pursuing these policies in good faith as accusations of an impending one-party dictatorship ran rampant in opposition circles.[31] Alawa, for his part, emphasized to the audience before him that the CPP had so mismanaged the colony that "it was therefore imperative that all should join forces together" against the Nkrumah-led party.[32] Other politicians in attendance picked up on what would also become a hallmark of the opposition's critiques of Nkrumah and the CPP throughout the 1950s and beyond—namely, the party's attacks on Gold Coast traditions, especially its chiefs, and both its and Nkrumah's supposed shallow connections to the colony's African heritage. Turning to the CPP's long-standing and widely promoted antagonism toward the colony's chiefs, another MAP politician, Alhaji Banda, argued at the same rally that Alawa spoke that "the C. P. P. had said it would drive away the Chiefs [*sic*], and sure enough they had been doing it. The M. A. P., on the other hand," he comforted his audience, "had assured the chiefs that they would make them more dignified."[33]

The invocation of the CPP's real and perceived attacks on the colony's chiefs was intentionally provocative. As historian Richard Rathbone has detailed, many in the party at the CPP's founding had hoped that a significant number of the colony's chiefs would elect to support the party, particularly in its rivalry with the UGCC.[34] However, antagonism between the CPP and the chiefs rose quickly. Inside the party-run *Accra Evening News*, for instance, the newspaper's editors regularly singled out the chiefs as not only potential threats to self-government, but, even more troubling, as both past and present agents of the colonial state. Key to the CPP's frustrations with the chiefs was the inclusion of certain chiefs to the proposed constitutional convention organized after the 1948 uprising.[35] Tensions between the CPP and the chiefs further escalated in the lead up to the 1950 Positive Action campaign as the *Evening News* openly threatened the chiefs, claiming that for "those ... who join forces with the imperialists ... there shall come a time when they will run away fast and leave their sandals behind them."[36] In subsequent years, the CPP continued to challenge the power and autonomy of the chiefs, often stripping those it deemed disloyal of their authority and replacing them with party/government-approved alternatives.[37]

However, what the MAP, Northern People's Party, and other opposition parties within the Gold Coast recognized was that, for many Gold Coasters, chiefs and the institution of chieftaincy carried meanings that extended beyond conventional party politics. Among scholars, the institution of chieftaincy has proven a perplexing historical and ethnographic problem, with many in the 1950s and 1960s predicting its inevitable demise as, according to many in this generation of scholars, Africans promised to increasingly adopt so-called modern ideas and institutions during the second half of the twentieth century.[38] Not only did the decline not happen, but, as historian Nana Arhin Brempong (Kwame Arhin) has outlined, the institution only gained in influence during the century, in part due to its distance and autonomy from the formal state apparatus.[39] Historian Olufemi Vaughan, writing on Nigerian chieftaincy politics, is even more direct. As Vaughan details, at the heart of chieftaincy's resiliency was the institution's ability to reinforce, perform, and even invent forms of belonging and shared identity. In some cases, these forms of belonging and shared identity may be alternatives to those advanced by the formal state apparatus (colonial and postcolonial), while, in others, they may intersect with and/or build upon those of the state. In either case, they harkened to pasts, traditions, values, and forms of social and cultural connection that extend beyond the presumed shallowness of party politics and parliamentary governance.[40]

On the ground, late-colonial-era Gold Coasters made similar claims against the CPP. A former pupil-teacher in what is now contemporary Ghana's Central Region, Eden Bentum Takyi-Micah took issue with the CPP's apparent disrespect for the colony's chiefs. In particular, Takyi-Micah reflected with disdain at what he understood to be the party's promise to destroy the institution. Reflecting on the claim that the party would chase away the chiefs so systematically that the chiefs would only "leave their sandals behind," Takyi-Micah proceeded to explain the importance of the chiefs to the people. As he framed the chiefs, they were more than political leaders or even cultural figures to most Ghanaians; more fundamentally, they were the "custodians of the land." At least for him, this was a reality that Nkrumah and the CPP could not understand. As a result, Takyi-Micah marked the rise of the CPP as a catalyst for a deleterious shift within the emergent country as peoples' connections to who they were and where they came from weakened. Not only did he chastise Nkrumah and the CPP for what he perceived to be a breaking of the bond between the people and their land, but he also accused both of claiming ownership over the land for themselves. The ramifications of this shift were many, he argued, among the most important being that he viewed the CPP and its various appendages as creating the conditions responsible for driving the youth from the land.[41]

Takyi-Micah in turn contrasted the theory of decolonization proffered by the CPP with an alternative history of the Gold Coast's colonial relationship with Great Britain. As Takyi-Micah interpreted this past, the colonial relationship was one in which the British created the conditions possible for the continued flourishing of the region's precolonial identities. In contrast to what he presented as the CPP's dangerous impatience, which he ultimately connected to narratives of corruption and mismanagement, the former pupil-teacher celebrated what he understood as the gradualism of Danquah and those allied with him.[42] Others tended to be somewhat more skeptical of British colonial intentions than Takyi-Micah, but many still questioned the effects of the CPP's actions and discourse on Gold Coasters' understandings of themselves and their histories. Writing, for instance, in a September 1954 leaflet announcing the formation of a new Asante opposition party—the National Liberation Movement (NLM)—the party's founders centered their calls to action on the uniqueness of the Asante past and what it meant to be Asante. In doing so, they connected the new party to an anticolonial lineage marked by the preservation of Asante-ness via the protection of the Golden Stool during the era of colonial conquest. The struggle now, the NLM claimed, was just as dire, for threats of "deceit, negligence, contempt and fear of communism" imperiled "THE GREAT ASHANTI NATION."[43]

Inside the opposition press, similar arguments would flourish throughout the mid-1950s. As one former Asante CPP member, Kofi Bour, would argue in an early 1955 edition of the *Ashanti Pioneer*, the CPP was a cancerous threat to Asante. More specifically, Bour insisted that attacks on the Golden Stool and Asantehene specifically, which he accused several prominent Asante CPP members and the *Evenings News* of doing, could not be understood as mere political maneuvering. Rather, they were existential challenges to that which made Asante, as a nation, unique. "To abuse the occupant of the Golden Stool [the Asantehene]," Bour argued, "is to abuse the Stool itself, and since the Stool is the very embodiment of the Ashanti nation, such an abuse amounts to an abuse of the whole Ashanti nation." Bour continued by asserting that those, especially certain chiefs who he described as "greedy," who failed to recognize this reality denigrated their own stools and heritages. As he viewed it, they had "sold their souls to that notorious swindler [Nkrumah] whose aim has been the utter destruction of our sacred institutions" and believed that "the dignity attached to their stools has been won through the acquisition of wealth by their illustrous [*sic*] ancestors and not by their noble acts of gallantry in the service of their nation."[44]

By early 1955, the NLM had become the most serious threat to the CPP since the Nkrumah-led party's founding in 1949. In doing so, it joined the cascade of political organizations and parties challenging the CPP on terms rooted in what they all viewed as the diverse and deep roots that constituted what it meant historically to be a Gold Coaster and a member of the many nations that composed the Gold Coast. Key to each of these parties' arguments against the CPP was the question of how these roots ought to be preserved and integrated into the decolonization and nation-building projects going forward. For each of these parties, the questions they raised flowed from deeply felt reflections on historical and contemporary constructions of identity and belonging. However, their framing of their opposition to the CPP in historical terms also extended to broader questions over resource allocation, political and economic agency, and, perhaps most importantly, legitimacy within the emerging postcolonial nation and state. As such, each party embedded within their protestations against the CPP's vision of the postcolonial nation clear claims to the sites and structures of political and economic power—the cocoa industry, urban and rural spaces, its religious institutions, so-called traditional power structures, and the past, among others—within the state.

Like many African mass parties during the 1940s and 1950s, the CPP balked at the arguments made by its opposition, viewing them as divisive and anti-modern. Adopting the language of tribalism to delegitimize these arguments, the CPP insisted that at the center of each of these largely ethnically and religiously constructed parties were ambitions to divide the colony's peoples around purportedly outmoded traditions and identities and to do so at the worst possible moment—the height of the colony's anticolonial struggle. Likely directing its attack at the MAP specifically in its 1954 general election manifesto, the CPP argued that "the formation of political parties on the basis of racialism, tribalism, and religion" was antithetical to the Gold Coast tradition of "religious tolerance."[45] Likewise, approximately a year later, the *Evening News* built upon these arguments as it extensively covered the CPP's accusations that the NLM, the Asanteman Council, and the Asantehene aimed to usurp the cause of national unity by embarking down a tribalist path. At issue for the CPP specifically was the NLM's demands for the creation of a federal constitution dividing power regionally and, by extension, roughly ethnically in the anticipated new state.[46] As one 1955 letter to the editor published by the *Ashanti Pioneer* explained, the call for federation, at least from the perspective of the NLM, was the only way to ensure the "real freedom [of] a democratic Gold Coast." Under any just system, the letter writer declared, "Ashanti must have the biggest say practicable in purely Ashanti affairs."[47]

Meanwhile, on the ground, tensions rose dramatically throughout 1955 and 1956. In Accra and Kumasi specifically, violence between the CPP and those who opposed it became a regular feature of daily life. As a result, party officials and supporters on both sides of the political divide encountered attacks from rival parties, while party offices and officials' homes were targeted for bombing. As one former CPP official reported to a committee investigating the political violence, he had "joined [the] NLM to save my life." According to him, nine men from his village sought to force his political conversion by "forc[ing] [him] to drink urine after he had been beaten up." They then "took him to a place where N. L. M. members including chiefs and elders had assembled" and demanded he join the party before making him pay £8.[48] As a result of the violence, exile communities developed in each city, with Asante CPP members seeking refuge in Accra while NLM supporters escaped to Kumasi.[49] In an attempt to assuage this violence, the colonial government responded by declaring, over the CPP's objections, the need for a new general election. Set to occur in July 1956, the new election was ostensibly to pick the government that would guide the colony to independence.

As the colony prepared for the election, the political atmosphere throughout the Gold Coast remained tense. However, as historian Jean Allman writes, the election occurred without violence.[50] Much to the disappointment of the opposition, though, the CPP handily defeated the opposition parties, garnering 71 of 104 seats in the Legislative Assembly. In doing so, the CPP swept all the seats in the Colony and gained a respectable number of seats in each of the Gold Coast's other regions.[51] Shortly thereafter, Nkrumah petitioned the British to set a date for independence, with the British establishing March 6, 1957 as the date for the transfer of power. As the CPP government undertook preparations for the country's independence, the opposition parties, especially the NLM, persisted in their resistance to CPP authority. The NLM, for its part, shifted what had previously been demands for a federal constitution to threats of secession.[52] As one individual writing in January 1957 to the *Ashanti Pioneer* put it, the Asante situation in a CPP-led Ghana was analogous to the story of the Biblical Joseph, whose close relationship with the Egyptian Pharoah resulted in the Israelites eventual enslavement. "Had the Israelites known what was to happen," the letter writer surmised, "they might have avoided it by returning to their land." He then added: "History is there to guide the paths of men. We must be warned."[53]

Independence and Definitions of Citizenship

As planned on March 6, 1957, Ghana gained its independence and became the first sub-Saharan state to emerge from European colonial rule. In Accra, the city was transformed in the lead up to the country's independence celebrations as the government planned to signal to the world the birth of a new and modern Africa. Richard Wright would ultimately refer to Ghana's independence as "a kind of pilot project of the new Africa."[54] W. E. B. Du Bois, who the US government denied a passport to attend the independence festivities, likewise, called on Ghana to "be the representative of Africa" and commissioned the new government to "lead a movement of Black men for Pan-Africanism."[55] Nkrumah, for his part, celebrated the attention Ghana received as part of its independence. As a result, as part of his famous speech during Ghana's independence celebrations, Nkrumah aimed to connect Ghana's independence to that of the rest of Africa, committing the newly formed state to the broader task of African liberation. In subsequent years, Nkrumah and his government would center this promise in their postcolonial political and social project as they committed significant resources, people, and capital to the cause of African liberation and pan-African unity. This included convening numerous conferences inside Ghana on pan-African affairs; the hosting of exiles, refugees, and freedom fighters; the offering of scholarships to African students; and the funneling of funds and arms to anticolonial and liberation movements from throughout the continent.[56] By 1960, when the South African pan-African and anti-Apartheid activist Peter Molotsi arrived in Accra, he—like many others—had come to understand Accra as "the Mecca of Pan-Africanism."[57]

However, even as the world arrived in Accra to celebrate Ghana's independence, tensions grew in the new West African state. Asante demands for secession did not subside. Rather, groups of radical Asante activists would continue to threaten the new government with violence until at least the early 1960s.[58] Furthermore, in the southeast, proponents of Ewe unification in Trans-Volta Togoland promised violence in the aftermath of independence.[59] In response, the CPP's Minister of the Interior, Ako Adjei, argued that the government had both the right and obligation to respond to this nascent insurrection with the full power of the state, for "when people resort to lawlessness the perpetrators cannot justly complain if their violence is met by violence." As a result, he advised the National Assembly that, during the first month of Ghana's independence, more than 5,000 firearms "had been seized or surrendered" in Trans-Volta Togoland and 355 people arrested, with 158 convictions.[60] As a result of the government's actions, historian Kate Skinner has shown, nearly 6,000 Ewe Ghanaians left the country for French Togoland, where they established a vibrant refugee community that would serve as an opposition in exile.[61]

As the late-colonial-era conflicts over history, belonging, and nationhood continued to simmer during the first months of independence, the necessary protocol of state-building increasingly tied these debates to new political and legal questions surrounding citizenship, nationality, resource allocation, and the stated and unstated expectations of Ghana's participatory democracy. Introduced approximately two months after independence, the Ghana Nationality and Citizenship Bill became the first, among a slate of proposed bills, aimed at defining the political and legal parameters of "Ghanaian-ness" in the new state. As Ako Adjei explained to his colleagues in the National Assembly, the need for such action was imperative to the new country's well-being, for the transition from colony to an independent state introduced a number of uncertainties about who should or could qualify as Ghanaian. Among those uncertainties included the current liminal status of "Ghanaians" under the independence agreement negotiated with the British. Since Ghanaian citizenship could not be conferred until Ghana formally existed and the institutions designed to debate and govern citizenship convened, the decolonizing people, Adjei explained, would retain their previous status under the British Nationality Act until such definitions of citizenship and nationality could be delineated. For Adjei, the passage of what would become the Ghana Nationality and Citizenship Act, 1957 thus represented "the last formal step in the independence of Ghana."[62]

During the bill's debate, conflict quickly arose over who could claim citizenship rights within the new country. In the Gold Coast, as elsewhere within the British Empire, the question of "citizenship" had long been fraught with legal and political implications tied to the colony's dependent relationship to the metropole. Gold Coasters in turn had stated and unstated obligations to the empire, most notably in terms of supplying labor, raw materials, and cash crops for the imperial market. For much of the colonial era, this discourse from the perspective of the metropole rarely, if ever, took on the language of citizenship as it would be conceived during the mid-twentieth century by African activists and intellectuals. Rather, it emphasized the distinctly hierarchical and paternalistic structure of British notions of political belonging connecting those in the colonies to the Crown. However, as discussed in Chapter 2, many Gold Coasters, along with others, also argued that the empire had obligations of its own toward its subject population. To this end, Gold Coast activists, dating back to the late nineteenth century, made regular claims for rights, recognition, and various forms of social and economic development against the Gold Coast colonial and British imperial governments. At the root of these claims was thus a recognition of a shared, albeit fundamentally unequal, sense of belonging linking the colony and the metropole together.[63]

Independence transformed these relationships. Not only did it break the Gold Coast/Ghana's dependent connection to Great Britain, but it also forced a rethinking of the relatively catholic form of "citizenship" administered under the imperial system. As outlined by Adjei in his presentation of the citizenship and nationality bill, despite the bill being modeled after the 1948 British Nationality Act, the unique nature of the Ghanaian social and historical context necessitated additional limitations on who could obtain automatic citizenship so as to ensure that citizenship could be claimed "only by persons who can be said to be of true Ghana descent."[64] As a result, for the CPP government, questions of personal history and genealogy intersected with concerns over legal and bureaucratic convention in its framing of the assembly's debates. To this end, the government argued that guaranteed birthright citizenship proved inappropriate for Ghana, asserting instead that would-be Ghanaians would need to show "Ghanaian" heritage that extended beyond at least their parents' generation regardless of whether they were born in Ghana. For these individuals, the bill promised to create alternative avenues to citizenship such as via residency and language hurdles, marriage for women, and familial descent if one parent was already considered eligible for or had received birthright citizenship.[65]

In constructing this system, the government argued that decades of colonial rule, combined with West Africa's long history of inter-regional migration, had brought large numbers of people to Ghana whose connections to the country did not carry what it implied to be the political and cultural weight of what it meant to be Ghanaian. As Adjei argued, among those born in the country but whose so-called proper Ghanaian heritage was in doubt:

> [I]n the great majority of cases, the parents of these people immigrated to this country and have stayed, with their children, only for the purposes of trade or because they have found employment here, and it cannot be said that they are of true Ghana descent, and it is not considered that their children should have the privilege of acquiring Ghanaian citizenship automatically merely because they were born in a British territory.[66]

W. Baidoe-Ansah, representing the CPP for the Western Region constituency of Eastern-Nzima Axim, added to Adjei's argument, focusing specifically on the country's Lebanese and French Togolander population. According to Baidoe-Ansah, applying birthright citizenship indiscriminately or even just among those who were born in the Gold Coast and other British colonies would weaken the country going forward. Looking at the country's aggressive development agenda, which included a radical transformation of the country's social and economic infrastructure (see Chapter 6), Baidoe-Ansah asserted that the pursuit of these goals would simply be impossible under such a citizenship model.[67]

Opposition Members of Parliament (MPs) scoffed at the government's arguments, insisting that nearly all born in the country on or before independence should be eligible for citizenship. Offinso Kwabre MP Victor Owusu, representing the NLM, opened the opposition's case against the bill. In doing so, he argued against what he presented as the unfairness of the proposed requirements. According to Owusu, "one notices that a lot of British subjects who have lived in this country for a very long time and who indeed come from various parts of West Africa are suddenly going to lose their citizenship." As a result, he proposed amending the legislation to include any British subject born on or before independence and who had a year's worth of residency be eligible for automatic citizenship. "This," he declared, "will assist to enfranchise a lot of our brethren from Gambia, Sierra Leone and Nigeria who have lived in this country for many years." To further add to this argument, Owusu also spoke to many of the MPs', including his own, class interests in ensuring that the country not become depopulated of non-"Ghanaian" West Africans. "[A] lot of our labourers and domestic servants come from Nigeria," he reminded his colleagues. Without the opportunity to secure citizenship, the Asante politician warned, many of these individuals may suddenly decide to leave the country and few outside the country may migrate to it.[68]

Even more problematic than the question of fairness for Owusu and his colleagues in the opposition, though, was how the proposed law empowered the government in new ways, which, for them, held the potential for abuse. As Owusu noted, under the proposed law, the Minister of the Interior gained near absolute discretion in adjudicating contested citizenship claims. This emphasis on ministerial discretion thus absolved the minister—in this case Adjei—of having to justify his decisions.[69] Owusu's fellow NLM MP, R. R. Amponsah, likewise, noted that, unlike in other recently decolonized countries like India, petitioners in Ghana would have no recourse in the courts.[70] MAP MP Cobina Kessie was even more direct in outlining the potentially troubling nature of this ministerial discretion. In doing so, he highlighted how the law would give the minister the power to deny citizenship for virtually any reason. "No matter what happens, whether it is made in good faith or not, once something is conceived a person can be denied the right of citizenship," the Kumasi North MP emphasized. The logical end to such a situation, Kessie continued, was a political context in which the right to citizenship could become a political loyalty test. "Who is going to decide whether such a person is disloyal or not? Who is going to be the final arbiter?," he asked. "These are the anomalies whereby the Government will be able to get rid of people who want to come into this country."[71]

Others, meanwhile, shifted the opposition discourse to that of the Nkrumah government's own stated commitment of transforming Ghana into a pan-African state. "We have all along been thinking about an African Socialist Republic," J. A. Braimah—now of the Northern People's Party—reminded his colleagues. "Why now try to make this differentiation and say that certain people should not automatically become citizens although they have stayed in this country for more than five years."[72] Responding to both Braimah and Kessie,

A. J. Dowuona-Hammond, representing the CPP, sidestepped a direct answer to Braimah's questioning of the CPP government's commitment to its pan-African rhetoric. Instead, the Awuta MP cast the question of citizenship as one of national loyalties. "We do not want somebody from Nigeria or any foreign country to apply for citizenship of Ghana just because he finds himself better off in this country," he argued, "but runs away to his home in a time of crisis. We want every person who applies for Ghana citizenship to be a person who is prepared to rise or fall with Ghana." Likewise, he rejected an earlier expressed premise that Northern French Togolanders working in Ghanaian mines or serving in the Ghanaian military should receive special treatment, for, he dismissively declared, "those people are in these employments for their daily bread and for nothing else." Their situation was clear to him—"to work somewhere for one's daily bread does not presuppose loyalty."[73]

Postcolonial Democracy and the Politics of a "Legitimate Opposition"

Approximately two months after the CPP passed the Nationality and Citizenship Act, opposition fears that the citizenship process could become politicized began to bear out as the government sought to instrumentalize the power of the state in determining who did and did not belong in the new Ghana. As a result, over the course of mid-1957, the government quickly turned its attention to groups and individuals it saw as threats to the CPP's envisioned political project. In Accra, a new Ga political movement—the Ga Shifimo Kpee—disrupted the semblance of stability the government wished to project in the capital as the Ga Shifimo Kpee sought to pressure the government over the loss of Ga lands in Accra to Akan strangers and a lack of Ga representation within the government. Further troubling the CPP was the fact that the Ga Shifimo Kpee arose within Nkrumah's own electoral constituency in the heart of the capital.[74] Likewise, in Kumasi, the government targeted two Muslim politicians—Alhaji Amadu Baba and Alhaji Larden Lalemie—associated with the MAP for deportation in July 1957. Despite claims by the men that they were both born in what was now Ghana and, in the case of Lalemie, his mother being born in Trans-Volta Togoland and Baba's in Accra, the government claimed that neither qualified as Ghanaian citizens and both had proven themselves to be—in the words of the country's soon-to-be attorney general Geoffrey Bing—"not conducive to the public good."[75] After initially running into trouble in the courts with its deportation orders, the government rushed a new deportation bill through the National Assembly, securing the men's deportations to Nigeria and unleashing a new wave of unrest in Kumasi.[76]

In addition to Baba and Lalemie, the government also successfully deported Bankole Timothy, the deputy editor of the *Daily Graphic*—the country's most prominent newspaper. Born in Sierra Leone, Timothy was one of Nkrumah's earliest biographers, publishing the first edition of his biography in 1955.[77] However, Timothy had also proven himself to be a regular and sometimes harsh critic of the government, provoking the *Evening News* to portray him as the leader of the "White Press."[78] Internationally, Timothy's deportation unleashed a wave of criticism directed at the Nkrumah government, with the London-based biweekly magazine *West Africa* noting that "it is difficult to recall a case where a journalist settled in a country, married to a local girl, and with children born there, has been deported without warning at such short notice."[79] The London-based *Daily Express*, meanwhile, quoted an unnamed Ghanaian journalist who reflected on Timothy's deportation by arguing that "[a]part from cocoa, freedom is the only exportable commodity we can boast about—and now they are stopping its production."[80] The wave of deportations did not stop with Timothy. Rather, deportation orders would come to dominate the Cabinet's agenda, with, as Richard Rathbone has tallied, the Cabinet debating more than 200 cases during the late 1950s.[81]

Inside the CPP, however, the actions it took against these individuals appeared necessary as the CPP sought to ensure the success of its vision for the security and prosperity of the newly independent state. Among the party's intellectual and political elite, decolonization represented as much a threat to this vision as it embodied the hope and elation exhibited at the country's independence celebrations. For many of them, most taking their cues from Nkrumah himself, decolonization increasingly represented the changing face of colonialism in the twentieth century. In 1963 and 1965 respectively, Nkrumah would fully articulate many of these fears in two of his most important published works: *Africa Must Unite* and *Neo-colonialism: The Last Stage of Imperialism*.[82] However, from at least the early 1950s, the CPP press had begun gesturing to such concerns as it presented the colony's increasing number of opposition parties as potential agents of the changing face of colonialism. As power increasingly shifted to the CPP, the party press suggested that the colonial system needed new ways to ensure access to, if not control over, African resources and people in the emerging postcolonial era. Exercising its long-standing practice of "divide and rule," the CPP argued, the colonial and imperial governments thus viewed these parties—with their largely ethnically and religiously based constructions—as opportunities to split the allegiances of the country's burgeoning citizenry.[83]

As tensions rose during the mid- and late-1950s, interrogations of both real and perceived threats to the new government became regular fixtures of the Ghanaian political scene. By the end of 1957, the CPP government responded by effectively dismantling all of the country's opposition parties as the passage of the Avoidance of Discrimination Act made illegal ethnically and religiously based parties. The opposition answered by consolidating into a single national opposition under the umbrella of the United Party (UP). Meanwhile, in late 1958, the government uncovered what it presented as an advanced plot to overthrow the government. The so-called Zenith Seven conspiracy—named after seven Ga opposition leaders who were among the more than three-dozen opposition figures arrested—included, according to one Ghanaian official, "evidence … [of] the manufacturing of dangerous explosives, a plot to poison certain members of the public, the assassination of three Cabinet Ministers including the Prime Minister, and a campaign of organised violence."[84] Just a few weeks later, the government discovered another plot against the government. Eventually known as the Awhaitey affair—named after Ghanaian army major Benjamin Awhaitey—this plot purportedly sought to overthrow the government and assassinate Nkrumah as he prepared to leave the country in December 1958.[85]

The cases of the Zenith Seven and especially that of the Awhaitey affair would become the first major tests of the new Preventative Detention Act (PDA). Passed several months earlier, the PDA granted the government the ability to hold perceived threats to the state in detention for up to five years without trial. Writing on the Awhaitey case approximately a decade later in his 1968 memoir, Geoffrey Bing argued that the case—specifically due to the intra-governmental nature of the alleged conspiracy—highlighted the necessity of such a juridical tool as preventative detention in dealing with what he described as "political crime" in a newly independent state. To maintain a democratic government, he suggested, all parties in the democracy had to operate in good faith. This included a commitment to the sanctity of the ballot box and acceptance of the policies and decisions of the popularly elected government regardless of one's political leanings. As a result, opposition to the government was thus to only take place via the proper institutions and protocol of the country's democratic system. Moreover, he maintained, legal mechanisms had to be put into place to prosecute those who failed to exercise such a principled view of the democratic process. However, in Ghana, he lamented how, prior to the establishment of the PDA, the criminal code that the young country had adopted from Great Britain provided the government with few tools with which to protect against an opposition unwilling to adhere to the democratic process.[86]

The CPP itself would adopt similar arguments for much of the next seven years as it maintained that the need for such political and legal tools was of particular importance in newly independent countries. By their very nature as formerly colonized territories in an international community with direct roots to capitalist imperialism, these countries were necessarily destined to face persistent threats to their sovereignty the party argued. Nkrumah himself spoke to this belief as he introduced the bill that would become the PDA to the National Assembly in July 1958. Here, he reminded his fellow MPs that, even as more African countries gained independence, Ghanaians and Africans more broadly could not forget that powerful groups inside and outside Africa were set on proving that they as Africans could not govern themselves. At its foundation then, Nkrumah held that the bill sought to ensure the future of African independence and, in Ghana, the sanctity of the country's status as an "independent democratic state," protecting it from what later would become known as the seemingly invisible threats of neocolonial subversion.[87] Over the next several years, the CPP only intensified this rhetoric as Nkrumah faced multiple additional attempts on his life and events inside and outside of Ghana betrayed what remaining faith the Ghanaian leader had in multi-party democracy. As a result, by the end of 1961, and arguably earlier, the narrative of a Ghanaian multi-party democracy would be fully subsumed as Nkrumah and the CPP formally and openly began to explore the possibilities of a so-called one-party democracy.[88]

Preventative Detention and the Powers of the Postcolonial State

In March 1959, a commission of enquiry convened to investigate the allegations against the three—Awhaitey and UP MPs R. R. Amponsah and Modesto Apaloo—accused in the Awhaitey affair published a majority report that concluded that the evidence before them had clearly demonstrated that all three had been involved in a plot to overthrow the government and assassinate Nkrumah. A minority report largely centered on the actions of Amponsah and Apaloo more broadly, but not necessarily in the Awhaitey affair.[89] Amponsah and Apaloo had each been held by the government since their initial arrest in December 1958. Each would remain in detention until Nkrumah's 1966 overthrow.[90] Awhaitey's fate proved more complicated. Extensively questioned, but not arrested after the discovery of the alleged plot, the then major suffered demotion and dismissal from the army after court martial. However, he remained free. Yet, with the majority report implicating him in the conspiracy, the government had to decide whether to issue a preventative detention order for the man at the center of the case. Coming from the military, Major-General Victor Paley—the army's General Commanding Officer—cautioned Nkrumah against issuing such an order without serious reflection, arguing that "Awhaitey is now a proven liar and is completely discredited. He will deserve to go to prison. But," the major-general asked, "is he any longer a danger and is it necessary or wise to imprison him under the Preventative Detention Act on a majority report alone?"[91] Despite Paley's hesitance, the government arrested Awhaitey shortly thereafter. He too would remain in detention until Nkrumah's overthrow.[92]

During the ensuing years, nearly every major figure in the Ghanaian opposition would succumb to detention, including Danquah who would die in prison in February 1965. Others went into exile. For instance, in 1959, the former leader of the opposition, K. A. Busia, absconded to the Netherlands where he would teach sociology at Leiden University. A year later, in a conversation with US Embassy officers in Brussels, Busia insisted that he simply could not return to Ghana if he wanted, for, if he did, he was certain to face imprisonment. As the transcript of his conversation notes, Busia "added, with a smile, that probably the present Ghanaian Government would be most happy to see him return so that they could take this action against him."[93] Furthermore, by the early 1960s, even several prominent members of the CPP who had falling outs with Nkrumah faced similar fates, with perhaps most famously K. A. Gbedemah—the architect of the CPP's 1951 electoral victory—escaping to Togo in October 1961 after denouncing Nkrumah in the National Assembly.[94] Three others—including Tawia Adamafio (one of Nkrumah's closest confidants), Ako Adjei (who initially recommended the UGCC invite Nkrumah to serve as the organization's general secretary in 1947), and Coffie Crabbe (the CPP's executive secretary)—were arrested in late 1962 following a bombing that had severely wounded Nkrumah in the northern border town of Kulungugu. The three were initially sentenced to death before Nkrumah commuted their sentences to life in prison; they too were released only after Nkrumah's overthrow.[95]

Even those not directly involved in the country's formal political and governmental apparatus endured the threat of preventative detention and other forms of governmental intimidation. In the Ashanti Region town of Jachie, for instance, one man faced the threat of detention for allegedly defaming Nkrumah and questioning the guilt of the accused in the Kulungugu bombing.[96] In another case, Leo Kalinauckas, the British-born headmaster at the Opoku Ware Secondary School in Kumasi confronted what was certainly significant pressure to let the Regional Organiser of the Ghana Young Pioneers (R. O. Frimpong-Manso) speak at his school. As the head of a Catholic school, Kalinauckas argued that, unlike internationally recognized youth organizations like the Boy Scouts, the Young Pioneers "might wreck the Christian beliefs of the students." He then went on to compare the Young Pioneers to similar youth movements in communist countries like China and Cuba. However, as the report on the incident details, Frimpong-Manso—with the power of the government behind him—then set out to convince the headmaster of the purported true mission of the Young Pioneers, namely "to train the mind, the body and the sould [sic] of the youth of Ghana to be up to their civic responsibilities and to fulfil their patriotic duty."[97] After facing sustained pressure from Frimpong-Manso over the course of two meetings, Kalinauckas eventually acquiesced and let Frimpong-Manso speak in his school.[98] Despite his submission, the government would still deport the headmaster a year later.[99]

As I have detailed elsewhere, the result of the CPP government's actions was an increasingly closed political environment in which most people opted for silence so as to not raise the government's ire.[100] As one man explained in 2008, the costs of speaking out extended beyond the individual himself or herself. Rather, whole extended families could have their lives turned upside down should one be detained by the government. Silence was simply safer.[101] For those who did engage the government, they often had little choice but to do so in a way where they performed an intricate choreography linking themselves and their desires to the political, social, and economic ambitions of the state. In most cases, this performance involved elaborate praise for Nkrumah and his pan-African and socialist vision for Ghana and Africa. In doing so, they sought to secure such things as new employment opportunities for themselves, raises in their wages, and other material and social benefits. However, engagement was nearly always a risk as personal, local, and national political alliances were constantly in flux.[102]

Conclusion

Between 1948 and 1966, when several factions in the Ghanaian military and police overthrew Nkrumah, the political atmosphere in the Gold Coast/Ghana changed dramatically. Colonial rule had given way to at first a period of shared Afro–Anglo governance and eventually independence. It is difficult to overstate the importance of Ghana's 1957 independence to the history of African decolonization and to histories of global decolonization more broadly. Ghana, in part through its status as the first sub-Saharan country to become independent from a European colonial power, marked a new beginning for not only the country, but, just as importantly, for Africa. As a result, over the course of the late 1950s and early 1960s, Ghana drew in activists and others from throughout Africa, the African Diaspora, and elsewhere to share in the experience of building a new Ghana, a new Africa, and, most ambitiously, the postcolonial world itself. However, both real and perceived threats to the new state—some often stemming from long-standing tensions over how to define what it meant to be Ghanaian and even what "Ghana" was—culminated in a political environment during the early and mid-1960s that increasingly sought to delegitimize and ultimately mute nearly all vocal opposition to the state and the so-called Nkrumahist project.

Part II

Chapter 6

THE DEVELOPMENT DILEMMA:
DECOLONIZATION AND DEBT DURING GHANA'S 1960s

In March 1964, the CPP government formally unveiled what it referred to as the country's *First Seven-Year Development Plan* (1964–71).[1] The plan came on the heels of two previous development plans launched by the Kwame Nkrumah-led government. The first of these plans, released following the CPP's rise to power, included such features as the country's intensive investment in education and promise of fee-free primary education.[2] This governmental investment in education, while controversial in how the government implemented it, resulted in a nearly threefold increase in Gold Coast primary school students between 1951 and 1959. In 1961, the government extended its commitment to fee-free education with the inclusion of the country's middle schoolers and by making both primary- and middle-school education compulsory.[3] In addition to its education program, the 1951 Development Plan included investments in everything from the colony's numerous cash crops and mineral resources to harbors, roads, and railways to a variety of manufactured goods and an array of social services.[4] Furthermore, the 1951 plan also laid the groundwork for the government's pursuit of what would become the centerpiece of Nkrumah-era development—the construction of a hydro-electric dam on the Volta River. The Volta River Project (VRP), as it came to be known, at once sought to electrify the country and create a new self-sustaining aluminum industry in the anticipated Ghana.[5]

The Second Development Plan (1959–64), introduced just days before the second anniversary of Ghana's independence, was even more ambitious. As the plan's introduction outlined, the original 1951 plan had sought to "lay[] the framework on which economic development … [could] now be built."[6] As a result, the objective going forward was now that of transforming Ghana into an African agricultural and industrial powerhouse. In doing so, the government aimed to subvert the unequal and extractive relationships that had previously connected the Gold Coast to the outside world. As discussed in previous chapters, the roots of these relationships could, in many ways, be dated as far back as the medieval and early modern gold trade. Subsequent iterations of these relationships further took shape with the slave trade and, paving the way for the colonial era, the rise of the "legitimate trade" and the Gold Coast's cash crop economy. As such, the government more than tripled its investment in agricultural and natural resources under the new plan—up from £G7,616,000 in 1951 to £G24,668,000 in 1959. Industry and trade promised similar jumps in spending, with a nearly fivefold increase during the period (£G5,548,000 to £G25,331,000). Other areas of the budget that were to witness substantial influxes of spending included electricity, communications, education, housing, health, and sanitation. In total, the 1959 plan more than doubled the country's development commitment, reaching £G250 million. On top of these commitments, the government further allocated an additional £G100 million to the VRP.[7]

By the release of the Seven-Year Development Plan, much had changed in the new country politically and economically. Decolonization had spread like a wave throughout much of the continent in the years since Ghana's independence, with South Africa, Rhodesia, and the Portuguese colonies of Mozambique, Angola, Cape Verde, and Guinea-Bissau representing the most prominent holdouts. However, the continent's transition to self-rule did not occur without tensions and contradictions. Moves by Nkrumah and other radical African political leaders for more support for the continent's liberation struggles were often met with suspicion by other politicians inside and outside of Africa, especially those in the West. Furthermore, the intrusion of Cold War politics into Africa threatened the autonomy of the continent's newly independent states, including that of Ghana. In particular, the 1961 assassination of Patrice Lumumba in the Congo reinforced to Nkrumah and those allied to him the dangers of forging their own way through an international community built upon the extractive wealth of capitalist imperialism. Both real and perceived fears of foreign, neocolonial subversion into Ghanaian affairs—bolstered by a wave of attempts on Nkrumah's life—defined much of the political atmosphere of the period.[8]

Internally and externally, the CPP government responded to the neocolonial threats it viewed as enveloping Ghana by adopting an increasingly radical tone in its approach to the country's political and economic development. Economic self-determination, which had long featured prominently in the discourse of Nkrumah and the CPP, increasingly took on new political importance during the early and mid-1960s as the Nkrumah-led government rethought its political and economic relationships to nearly all the major Western capitalist powers. Investments of Western capital, labor, and know-how into sectors such as healthcare, education, and infrastructure now all became suspect for the CPP and in turn had the potential of opening the country to external subversion. The result, the CPP argued, was at best the creation of new opportunities for stunting the country's growth and, at worst, the rise of an array of existential threats to its political and economic independence. The CPP responded by seeking to strengthen its relationship with the Eastern Bloc, importing goods, expertise, and machinery from the Soviet Union and its allies with varying degrees of success.[9] The goal, however, embedded in the Seven-Year Development Plan, along with its predecessors, was the creation of an economy that could stand on its own. This economy was to be self-sustaining, thus freeing the new Ghana from the traps posed by the rapidly changing face of Cold War-era imperialism.

This and the subsequent chapter interrogate the development and economic ambitions of the early postcolonial Ghanaian state and the realities faced by Ghanaians as they sought to make their way through the changing political and economic contexts of the post-independence era. On the ground, the radicalism of the Nkrumah era often confronted a populace demanding not necessarily the ideological socialism of the party's and government's discourse, but rather the goods, services, and opportunities necessary for them to achieve the modernizing promises independence was supposed to bring—a level of social and material uplift envisioned as raising all Ghanaians' standards of living. In this respect, Ghanaians were not alone on a continent that, during the 1960s, "everyone knew ... was 'emerging.'"[10] In Ghana specifically, the exact language of development and modernization may have shifted as subsequent governments came to power following the CPP's 1966 overthrow. However, each government faced a populace with similar expectations even as local and international political and economic realities continuously challenged and, in many cases, undermined their authority. The result was an era of widespread political and economic instability between the mid-1960s and the early 1980s. For most Ghanaians, the political instability of the period led to extensive economic insecurity as both local and international pressures forced Ghanaians to look for and establish new networks of political, social, and economic exchange inside and outside the country in order to survive.

Decolonization and Development

The CPP-led government's economic theory during the 1950s and 1960s largely derived from Nkrumah's own understanding of the political economy of colonialism. It was during his decade in the USA that Nkrumah first began to develop his theory, a process that only accelerated after his 1945 arrival in Great Britain. For Nkrumah, colonialism was necessarily an extractive system designed to excavate the wealth of colonized territories and peoples for European gain. Writing in 1947 in what would become one of his most important, yet underappreciated treatises on colonialism—a small pamphlet titled *Towards Colonial Freedom*— Nkrumah differentiated colonialism from imperialism, which he viewed as a consolidating force bringing "diverse peoples ... together by force under a common power." Colonialism, by contrast, he argued, was a process of "bind[ing]" together the colonized and the colonizer in a political system aimed at "promoting her [the colonizing country's] own economic advantages." Production, trade, and commerce in the colonial system, he asserted, were in turn all aimed at advancing the colonizing power's political and economic position at home and abroad by creating a monopoly whereby the colonized's resources and labor provided goods for the colonizer to manufacture at home and then re-market abroad.[11]

Not necessarily unique to Nkrumah, aspects of his interpretation of the colonial system had featured prominently in the works of major political and intellectual figures including V. I. Lenin, W. E. B. Du Bois, and J. A. Hobson. Furthermore, it had embedded itself in the thought of a generation of anticolonial nationalists throughout the Global South during the first half of the twentieth century.[12] In the Gold Coast/Ghana, the CPP-run press thus sought to popularize this vision of colonialism, with the *Evening News* regularly running stories outlining the reach of the colonial system into Gold Coast/Ghanaian life. In 1956, for instance, the *Evening News* argued that the all-encompassing nature of colonial exploitation had catalyzed the political conflicts that had recently engulfed the colony by catering to the development of what it referred to as the colony's "die-hard reactionaries." According to the newspaper's editors, the result was a whole segment of the population that could not "attune their mental and psychological outlook to the new largely Democratic atmosphere."[13] This was in part due to what subsequent CPP theorists, among others, would portray as Gold Coasters'/Ghanaians' "colonial mentality" as well as the "self-interest" cultivated by the colonial system.[14] In another instance, the *Evening News* emphasized the color bar in the operation of international labor. Taking on the question of labor solidarity, the newspaper highlighted the alliance between white labor and the imperial government, which, the newspaper argued, had resulted in the government's apparently more tolerant reaction to labor disputes in the metropole compared to the harsh reactions faced by the colonies' workers.[15]

The goal of Nkrumah and the CPP was ultimately the development of an economy structured around a new, Ghanaian-centered system of production and exchange. For the Nkrumah-led government, such a system represented an assertion of the new country's sovereignty. No longer was the country to be dependent on outside powers for its economic growth; rather, it was to have the power to define the terms of its economic future. The result was the government's heavy investment in infrastructure, industry, and agriculture during the 1950s and 1960s. Moreover, the rapid expansion of schools and other social services that marked the period was as much about economic sovereignty as it was about personal social mobility.[16] In addition to these projects, the government also erected new public buildings throughout a number of the emergent country's major cities, transforming these cities' civic and public life.[17] Expansions of the country's road and rail networks, meanwhile, increased mobility. Likewise, government experimentation with a range of new industries and agricultural enterprises—including tobacco-product manufacturing, sawmilling, food processing, brewing, and soap production, among others—offered the country's men and women new economic opportunities.[18] Moreover, state-run labor organizations such as the Ghana Builders (later Workers) Brigade provided Ghanaians additional pathways to both social and cultural mobility.[19]

During the mid-1950s, skyrocketing international cocoa prices, combined with widespread deficit spending, funded much of the country's investment in its development agenda. To reap the full benefits of the increasing cocoa prices, the government in 1954 established a cocoa duty limiting the price paid to the colony's cocoa farmers, raising the farmers' ire.[20] The government, for its part, argued that the duty promised to ensure that the wealth of the colony's cocoa industry contributed to all of the emergent country's development needs. As one CPP politician explained to the Legislative Assembly, the future of cocoa in the Gold Coast could not be ensured as disease threatened existing trees while countries throughout the world were looking for "a scientific way of creating a fertile land which would suit the growth of cocoa." As a result, he continued and the CPP's Minister of Finance, K. A. Gbedemah, also added, the government was only trying to protect the future of the "budding nation" by setting it on sound financial footing through the creation of a reserve fund that could finance the soon-to-be Ghana's development needs.[21] Through independence, however, the cocoa duty contributed significantly to the rising political tensions of the mid-1950s as various factions within the colony all made claims on the development funds raised by the duty, while the income from the duty itself proved highly volatile during the second half of the decade.[22]

Meanwhile, the deficit spending engaged in by the CPP raised concerns within the Ghanaian government and among those it looked to for expertise. Writing in December 1957, for instance, the future Nobel-Prize-winning economist W. Arthur Lewis reported a mixed picture for Ghana's economic prospects. Citing the "strong measures" taken by the government to quell the political violence of the previous years, the Saint Lucian economist noted a "very quiet and peaceful" political environment in the country. In his report, he also marked the recent rapid increase in cocoa prices, emphasizing that, internationally, the rise had the potential to "discourage consumption in favour of substitutes." More concerning to Lewis, though, was the effect of the government's seemingly unrestrained spending on the country's financial outlook. According to him, the government's limited revenue could not simply keep up with its expenditures.[23] Lewis was even more blunt in another report written nearly five months later. "I am appalled by the rate at which this country is heading for bankruptcy," he exclaimed,

> Ordinary expenditure has increased 60 per cent in the last four years, and is on its way up, what with military services, external broadcasting, extravagance in university expenditure, Ghana airline [*sic*] and what not. The ambitions of members of the Cabinet for Ghana's prestige expenditures grossly exceed what is appropriate to a country whose national income is only £50 per head per year. (compare U. K., £300).[24]

On top of the spending concerns, Lewis also noted the effects of the government's Africanization plan on the country's fiscal outlook. Not only were the expatriate officers who were to leave their posts in the next eighteen months set to receive generous pensions, but the loss of their expertise also foreshadowed increased inefficiencies.[25]

In general, Lewis increasingly questioned the wisdom of what he saw as the government's over-investment in large-scale development projects at the expense of smaller, more economical ones. By the late 1950s, the VRP in particular would raise his suspicions. Initially drawn into the Gold Coast government's orbit in 1954 to assess the feasibility of the project, Lewis would over time characterize it as a white elephant that only promised to sap the country's rapidly dwindling resources, while delivering only modestly in employment, industrial production, and electrification.[26] Contrasting the VRP with the development experience of Puerto Rico, which he characterized as "the most successful industrialiser of recent times," in a 1958 letter to Nkrumah, Lewis argued that the dam and specifically the hydro-electric power it promised offered little in the way of helping the country industrialize. By contrast, he emphasized that Puerto Rico had built more than 500 factories over the course of the decade without coal, oil, or hydro-electric power. "The secret to its success," he asserted, "has been a very dynamic Commissioner for Industrial Promotion"—someone he saw as absent in Ghana. As a result, he gently suggested to Nkrumah that Ghana consider forgoing the project and redirect the investment into more modest industrial pursuits, for, he proclaimed, "If we wait much longer before putting our backs into promotion, Nigeria will be getting all the potential industries."[27]

Nkrumah vehemently disagreed with Lewis's assessment. Rather, the VRP emerged as the centerpiece of his government's economic agenda. Tied to the VRP was thus an industrial vision centered on modern urban centers, new planned cities in Tema and Akosombo, electrified towns, new roads and railway networks, a new deep-sea harbor in Tema, and an ever-increasing number of factories producing Ghanaian-made goods. By 1962, the government's Minister of Industries, Krobo Edusei, thus insisted that the country was not only well on its way to turning these visions into a reality, but he also argued that the time had come for Ghanaians to commit to the government's industrial vision through their consumptive practices. "We can be and we have a right to be really proud of what we make here in Ghana," Edusei argued in the National Assembly as he unveiled a ten-point "Buy Ghana Products" program, "and it is our duty as representatives of our people in Parliament to set an example to everyone else by openly patronising our local products."[28] The *Evening News* added to Edusei's sentiments with calls on Ghanaians to "WEAR[] cloths made in Ghana. LIV[E] in houses made from local materials. SLEEP[] on beds and mattresses made in Ghana, and in the very near future RID[E] in cars, not only assembled but actually made in Ghana."[29]

The completion of the VRP for the Nkrumah-led government was to promise only more growth and the Seven-Year Development Plan was in turn devised to prepare for and reap the benefits of what the CPP assumed would be this eventuality. As Nkrumah outlined in 1965, the completion of the VRP, slated for the following year, was to mark the culmination of the developmental groundwork laid by the CPP government over the previous decade-and-a-half. Citing the country's investment in education at all levels, investments in transportation and communication infrastructure, and technical know-how, he contended that the VRP's electricity represented the final piece of Ghana's development puzzle.[30] The authors of the Seven-Year Development Plan agreed. In their draft plan, they predicted the VRP would put Ghana in the enviable position "of having a sizeable surplus of electrical energy." According to them, no other country in Africa "and probably in the world" was as well-positioned. For them, perhaps the greatest obstacle to any type of development was access to electricity, for unreliable electrical grids and electricity shortages fundamentally limited the types and scale of industrial investments possible within a given country.[31] As

NORTHERN TERRITORIES CHIEFS AND ELDERS AT THE
VOLTA RIVER PROJECT TRAVELLING EXHIBITION

Figure 6.1 Volta River Project Travelling Exhibition, *c*. 1955.

such, access to unlimited electrical power thus foretold a future absent of what many within the government believed to be the most significant constraint on the country's development and thus promised to unlock the country's true productive capabilities.[32]

The reality for most Ghanaians, however, was more mixed. For those living along the Volta River, the construction of the hydro-electric dam resulted in the flooding and resettlement of their communities. As historian Stephan Miescher has shown, many struggled in the government's newly constructed resettlement villages and became disillusioned with the government's (and subsequent governments') real and perceived inability to live up to its promises to adequately compensate those affected by the flooding.[33] Similarly, sociologist Dzodzi Tsikata has outlined the social and environmental effects of the dam's construction on communities within the Lower Volta. As a result of the creation of the massive new lake (one of the largest man-made lakes in the world), the number of Ghanaians involved in the Volta fishing industry multiplied drastically, growing from approximately 2,000 fishermen prior to the lake's flooding to 20,000 by 1969.[34] Accompanying the lake's formation, though, was also the importation of new diseases such as *bilharzia* into the region and an end to the seasonal flooding that had previously marked life along the river.[35] Even in the new planned city of Akosombo, the promises of an urban center replete with modern housing, shops, tourism, and industry gave way to racial and class inequalities associated with the dam's construction and operations. Health and sanitation issues followed as well.[36]

Furthermore, as the government ramped up its development plans during the early 1960s, it also pressured the country's industrial and agricultural laborers to rededicate themselves to their work so as to ensure ever-greater productivity. As understood by the CPP, productivity represented Ghana's escape from the constraints of the colonial economy, for it promised a self-sufficient and socialist future. Writing in the *Evening News*, for instance, one columnist describing him or herself as the "Labour Spokesman" directly connected gains in national productivity to the Seven-Year Development Plan and promises of socialist consumption. "Food, clothing, housing and the provision of material things necessary to live an ample, cultivated, and civilised life," the columnist argued, "is the object of the gigantic Seven-Year Development Plan … launched to bring the workers and their families, complete happiness and for them to enjoy maximum life."[37] In other instances, the government aimed to promote what it described as the "dignity of labour" in its efforts to increase national productivity. To do so, one government committee recommended the creation of new workers' councils to better educate the workforce, push a focus on punctuality, put an end to unscheduled time off for personal needs, and advance a nationwide public service campaign "against … lazy workers." "The intention of such a campaign," the committee argued, "should be to arouse the sense of service and responsibility of the ordinary worker and to make him give of his best."[38] Similar rhetoric pervaded the agricultural sector as well.[39]

On the ground, though, pressures to expand the country's production encountered a range of both logistical and social challenges that extended beyond the country's farmers and workers themselves. In many instances, Ghanaian industries simply did not have the capacity or tools to further expand production. In the agricultural sector, the government's network of State Farms—established in 1962—offered promises of a national transition toward mechanized farming replete with the purchase of new tractors from Eastern Bloc countries. However, these promises met a reality marked by parts shortages and breakdowns partially caused by Ghana's tropical climate.[40] Similar circumstances arose in the Ghanaian Builders/Workers Brigade. Established in 1957 as a nationwide network of work camps to alleviate youth unemployment, the Brigade engaged in a range of agricultural initiatives, along with construction and manufacturing enterprises, among other tasks. For brigaders, the Brigade experience provided them with access to meaningful wage employment, thus opening many to new opportunities for social mobility.[41] However, like with the State Farms, key to the Brigade's justification was its productive potential, most notably promoted through investments in mechanization. By the end of the Nkrumah era, the promise of mechanized agriculture had so inundated the popular consciousness that Brigade tractors, particularly those driven by women, would emerge as one of the most resilient symbols of Nkrumah-era development, with many Ghanaians continuing to reminisce about them decades later.[42] In practice, though, access to tractors in Brigade camps remained sporadic and, like in the State Farms, the Brigade found it difficult to keep many of them in operation, encouraging most brigaders to engage in more conventional, labor-intensive cultivation practices.[43]

Likewise, in the manufacturing and construction sectors, the early Nkrumah era witnessed rapid increases in the number of firms operating within the colony/ country. As one mid-century survey indicated, nearly 60 percent of the country's manufacturing and construction firms arose during the 1950s alone.[44] Even more would follow during the 1960s as the government experimented with different institutional and bureaucratic mechanisms to promote these sectors. By 1962, the two sectors would together employ more than 320,000 workers.[45] Yet, much of the country's manufacturing and construction—distinct from the government imagery of new technologically advanced factories—remained in the hands of small-scale producers, most often individually or family owned and frequently operated with unpaid family labor. Among those working in larger firms, workers often encountered employers with near monopolistic or oligarchic power in the labor market.[46] Moreover, by the late 1950s, the government had largely quelled Ghana's historically active and independent trade union movement, effectively nationalizing it in 1958 as workers increasingly endured a work culture defined by surveillance and a discursive environment that demanded ever more from them.[47] As one journalist in the state-run magazine, *The Ghanaian*, put it in 1965, workers in Ghana's emerging socialist state fundamentally had to recognize that "[f]or now in Ghana, working for the state is working for ourselves."[48]

Labor and the Nkrumahist State

Most famously dramatized in Ayi Kwei Armah's 1968 novel *The Beautyful Ones are Not Yet Born*, the social and political conditions of the Ghanaian workplace, combined with the real and perceived rise in a politics of patronage, alienated many Ghanaian workers from their work.[49] At the same time, the early 1960s witnessed a general decline in the international cocoa market. Between 1950 and 1962, for instance, the price of cocoa dropped by nearly 25 percent. Moreover, by 1962, it had plummeted approximately 60 percent below its 1954 Nkrumah-era high. Meanwhile, between 1954 and 1962, the volume of cocoa produced essentially doubled (see below).[50] For the government, the declining cocoa prices not only threatened its ambitious development agenda and escalated the country's deficit spending, but it also endangered its political legitimacy as key aspects of its governance rested on translating Ghanaian self-governance into postcolonial prosperity. As a result, in 1961, the government responded to the economic decline with calls for belt-tightening throughout the populace, with Ghanaians asked to contribute to the national budget through new taxes on consumption and, for those earning a wage, the mandatory purchase of national savings bonds. Likewise, in the agricultural sector, cocoa farmers—distinct from all other farmers—faced a new 10 percent tax on their yields.[51] By early 1965, the CPP's

Minister of Finance, K. Amoaka-Atta, ultimately identified three major challenges facing the Ghanaian economy: 1) how to sustain the level of economic and social development proposed by the Seven-Year Development Plan; 2) how to realign government expenditures from "unproductive to productive investment"; 3) how to slow the country's escalating inflation.[52]

The challenge for Ghanaians, however, was more fundamental as they sought to make their way through the rapidly changing political and economic environment in their daily and work lives. Workers and other laborers who did not fit the Nkrumah government's vision of the ideal, self-sacrificing builder of the nation regularly faced scorn and opprobrium from the government, press, and other workers. In the case of the country's drivers, for instance, historian Jennifer Hart has documented how, by as early as 1957, the government and others had targeted drivers for their perceived lack of patriotic duty stemming from the drivers' protests over increased state regulation in their work lives. As Hart explains, the drivers—all of whom came of age in a profession long known for its independence—viewed the government's interventions as both unnecessary and financially burdensome. In response to the government's actions, the drivers went on strike in August 1957. However, much to their dismay, the strike only strengthened the government's hand as the public turned on the drivers, accepting the government's portrayal of them as threats to the country's development and as key contributors to national inflation. Meanwhile, over the next several years, drivers would encounter additional challenges to the stability of their work lives. Key among these obstacles were shortages of spare parts and tires as well as a road network that, while improved by pre-Nkrumah standards, still failed to live up to the state's infrastructural promises.[53]

It is important to note that the effects of these challenges impacted a not-insignificant number of people. For instance, by 1960, approximately 60,000 Ghanaians worked in the transportation industry.[54] For these individuals, the country's infrastructural deficiencies, combined with the lack of materials necessary to properly maintain their vehicles, required them to find creative ways to stay on the road. As one driver explained to Hart in 2009, when he was a "mate" during the 1960s, he and his "master" would place the tires of six-ton vehicles over their regular tires in order to ensure they could keep their vehicles in operation. According to him, drivers had to "find our own ways and means and then do what we can do to do our work."[55] Similarly, locomotive drivers and engineers faced public, albeit likely unrealistic, threats from members of the Ghana Young Pioneers to serve as strike breakers during a 1961 strike of the Ghana Railway and Harbours Union. As one Young Pioneer, writing in October of that year, explained in the *Evening News*, "As future Nkrumaists, we unanimously condemn such actions [the strike] by a really small section of our community, including some grown-ups who should think wisely for the social and economic reconstruction of our beloved nation." To this end, the author declared that the Young Pioneers were ready to take on the work vacated by those railway and harbor workers "with imperialist, neo-colonialist or capitalist tendencies in Ghana."[56]

Workers in other industries often faced similar pressures. Recounting a 1962 episode involving workers constructing army barracks in the western town of Appremdu and the then CPP Minister of Defence, Kofi Baako, historian Nana Osei-Opare described a situation whereby the workers had been effectively abandoned by their European contractor. They in turn faced the possibility of not getting paid for the work they had completed. Moreover, most of the workers—many of whom had come with families—were not from the area. Rather, they had traveled the approximately 250 kilometers or more from their homes in the Greater Accra and Eastern Regions to Appremdu for the work. Following Baako's arrival, the workers made their case to the minister. Despite their pleas, Baako—who Osei-Opare highlights was commonly known as a hub of the Nkrumah administration's socialist thought—reacted to their plight with hostility. Instead of targeting the absentee contractor, Osei-Opare writes, Baako threatened the workers themselves by providing them with an ultimatum requiring them to return to work as part of the Workers Brigade (albeit without pay) or, if they stayed onsite, face arrest and imprisonment. What distinguished these workers' situation from that of many others during the late Nkrumah era, though, was that these particular workers sought remedy elsewhere by petitioning to the Western Regional Commissioner for relief instead of immediately acquiescing to Baako's demands.[57]

The actions taken by the workers in Appremdu were highly risky in an era when the CPP increasingly sought to dissuade dissent through arrest and detention. However, as Osei-Opare shows, these workers were not alone in turning to petitions to make their cases for better treatment and pay.[58] Many workers, though, did face detention for labor activism deemed antithetical to the interests of the state. In the midst of the 1961 Railway and Harbour Union strike, for instance, the government arrested numerous individuals involved in the strike, including most of the union's leaders. Those aligned with the strikers also faced reprisal and arrest. Among those arrested were approximately fifty United Party politicians.[59] Likewise, among mineworkers, labor scholar Jeff Crisp has argued that the period between 1961 and 1964 proved particularly "passive" in terms of rank-and-file activism in the mines, with only a few notable protests. Despite the relatively few protests of the era, the government and those in the unions aligned with it tended to react to this activism with little empathy. In the case of D. K. Foevie—the president of the government-aligned Mine Workers' Union—he responded to workers' grievances by threatening to withhold union elections and banning speech within the union in response to the threat of rank-and-file activism. By 1964, Foevie went even further as he resigned his post within the union to become Managing Director of the State Gold Mining Corporation. In doing so, he led an even deeper CPP integration into the union with the creation of a new set of committees outside the union structure to investigate worker grievances. Following this takeover, Crisp notes, workers' real wages declined significantly as the country approached inflation rates of 24 percent in 1964 while workers themselves faced stagnant wages.[60]

Military Rule and Liberalization

The February 1966 overthrow of Kwame Nkrumah shifted the government's economic policy almost overnight. Like with the parts shortages that had plagued the country's transport drivers during the Nkrumah years, numerous other industries and consumers suffered from widespread shortages of staple goods, including medical supplies, water-purification chemicals, flour, sugar, and milk, among other items. Additionally, at the time of the coup, the Ghanaian government found itself on the brink of bankruptcy, with the country's reserves unable to meet its fiscal obligations.[61] To the new military government—calling itself the National Liberation Council (NLC)—the country's economic situation was perhaps the most blatant example of what it understood to be the dangerous irresponsibility of the Nkrumah government and its commitment to state-run socialist development. Announcing in a broadcast issued just days after the coup, the NLC's chairman, J. A. Ankrah, committed to an economy driven by the private sector as well as investigations into a variety of features of the government's economic policy apparatus—most notably, taxes, licensing, and trade agreements.[62] Furthermore, the government expelled nearly all of the socialist and Eastern Bloc experts and expatriates living and working within the country.[63] The goal of the NLC, then, was an economic system that would not only be legible and favorable to its re-affirmed Western allies, but would dramatically decrease the state's role in the country's economy.

Among the NLC's first actions upon seizing power was thus the deconstruction of much of the Nkrumahist state. For the NLC, this process was as much an economic project as a political one. As a result, prominent state and parastatal organizations including the Ghana Young Pioneers, the Ghana Bureau of African Affairs, and the Kwame Nkrumah Ideological Institute, among others, were quickly shuttered and their accounts frozen pending promised audits.[64] In the case of the Ideological Institute, the result was pleas from the Institute's 474 non-political workers—"artisans, labourers, administrative staff"—for assistance in finding new areas of employment and payment of their February wages.[65] Other institutions such as the State Farms and the Ghana Workers Brigade proved more difficult to unilaterally disband. Each employed a not-insignificant number of men and women at the time of the coup. In the case of the Workers Brigade, it employed more than 25,000 individuals, with more than two-thirds primarily engaged in the agricultural sector.[66] By September 1966, the NLC stated a desire to close a dozen camps and reduce the number in the Brigade to below 20,000.[67] A similar process played out in the State Farms as, by early 1967, the NLC dismissed 10,000 workers and closed 32 farms.[68] Historian J. D. Esseks notes that these closures represented "more than a quarter" of the 105 State Farms within the country at the time of the coup.[69] Meanwhile, the NLC also sold many of Ghana's state-run factories to private-sector buyers or sought international equity investments for larger enterprises.[70]

The liberalization of the country's fiscal infrastructure following the coup was no less dramatic than the deconstruction of the political. As previously discussed, the CPP had long connected Western capitalism to the exploitation and inequities of colonial rule. The intensity of the CPP's critique of capitalist imperialism, however, escalated dramatically over the course of the 1960s as the state-run press regularly targeted the West's capitalist powers as active threats to African self-determination. For the CPP, socialism offered the only developmental path away from this threat. The NLC, though, rapidly sought to change course upon coming to power. Not only did it expel Eastern Bloc experts and expatriates, but it also aimed to shore up Western confidence in the new government. Most notably, this included the cancelation of the Nkrumah government's Seven-Year Development Plan.[71] At the same time, the government turned to the Bretton Woods institutions of the International Monetary Fund (IMF) and World Bank for assistance in addressing the country's debt. Within months, the NLC had successfully negotiated a rescheduling of a portion of the country's debt to more than a dozen Western creditor states and outlined plans for similar mediation with Eastern Bloc creditors. These stabilization efforts, the World Bank estimated, ultimately included drastic reductions in Ghana's development expenditures, turning a 1964 budget deficit of N¢165 million into a predicted N¢32 million surplus three years later.[72] Even with these initiatives, Ghana still maintained a foreign debt exceeding $439 million in 1967.[73]

Despite the challenges on the horizon, the broader Ghanaian response to the NLC's messaging was swift. Several institutions and constituencies within and adjacent to the government quickly expressed their support for the coup and the new government. Those working in the civil service, for instance, "congratulate[d] the National Liberation Council ... on the bold and timely action they have taken to rescue our beloved country from the clutches of dictatorship, nepotism, and economic chaos."[74] Similarly, the Ghana Chamber of Mines recited a litany of struggles that the mining industry faced under the CPP. "In recent years and particularly in the last few months," the Chamber argued, "our task in keeping the wheels of this great industry turning has been made so difficult, owing to the economic straits into which the country had fallen, that those wheels were slowly grinding to a halt, production lowered and in some cases ceasing altogether. As a result," it continued, "the foreign exchange earning capacity of the mines, second only to that of cocoa, has been in danger of rapidly falling, thereby further aggravating the country's economic position."[75] Likewise, the Ghana Trades Union Congress (TUC), which from the late 1950s on had been described by some as the CPP's "Political Siamese Twin[],"[76] also abandoned its Nkrumahist allegiances after the coup. In doing so, it denounced Nkrumah as "Africa's Number One dictator," while calling for his extradition and trial. Similar to the others, the TUC also praised the NLC for its "liberal and sound economic policy statement."[77]

On the ground, anti-Nkrumah and anti-CPP sentiments dominated the country's popular discourse, forcing those who had even minor connections to the previous government to go into hiding or face harassment.[78] Others openly expressed their disillusionment with the prospects of democracy.[79] Meanwhile, individuals in nearly every sector of the Ghanaian economy faced new challenges brought on by the coup and the military government's efforts. For those who had lost land to Nkrumah-era initiatives like the Builders Brigade and State Farms, the CPP's demise brought new hope about the lands' return. As a result, estranged landholders petitioned the government for their lands' return, often arguing that the Brigade had acquired the lands through illegitimate deals with local chiefs.[80] In 1967, more than a year into NLC rule, some farmers even claimed that the Brigade was still actively expanding into their lands, threatening the farmers to abandon their farms.[81] However, the NLC had little patience for such claims and tended to address them not as government matters, but as disputes between local chiefs and/ or farmers.[82] At the same time, brigaders themselves complained to the NLC about their current treatment in the organization, particularly as it pertained to pay inequities. One petitioner, describing a situation where skilled brigaders who had served the institution for upwards of five to ten years, claimed many earned as little as 65 national pesewas (N¢.65) a day. According to the petitioner, the situation was thus analogous to that of the "non-whites of South Africa."[83]

Discord spread in other employment sectors as well. In protest of what they described as abuse from their insurers, drivers again went on strike in 1967. Similar to their strike a decade earlier, the drivers' actions raised the ire of both the government and general public as the strike's effects rippled throughout the Ghanaian economy.[84] Likewise, in the mines, the late 1960s and early 1970s saw a renewal of instances of worker resistance. As Jeff Crisp has outlined, after the Nkrumah years, miners slowly returned to collective protest. However, within two years of the coup, worker activism in the mines increased dramatically, with what he described as "an explosion of protest."[85] In Tarkwa, for instance, financial insecurity within the State Gold Mining Corporation made it impossible for the Tarkwa Goldfields to pay bonuses to some workers in late 1967. Over the next ten months, labor and management found themselves in near constant conflict, including several short strikes over pay and working conditions.[86] In March 1969, another labor dispute at the Ashanti Goldfields resulted in a weeklong strike, which culminated in a riot that left three dead (two of whom were shot by police) and more than two-dozen injured.[87] In the Ghanaian labor sector writ large, political scientist Jon Kraus has traced more than 160 strikes between 1966 and 1969. The strikes in turn generated nearly 87,000 manpower days lost per year. Moreover, the number of strikes continued to accelerate during the early 1970s, with 137 recorded in 1970 and 1971 alone.[88]

Much as the CPP had done, the NLC and reorganized TUC responded to the worker strikes with little sympathy. In its newsletter, the TUC, for its part, celebrated the economic initiatives undertaken by the NLC, promoting recent pay raises and management decisions in a number of different labor sectors.[89] At the same time, it actively sought to dissuade strike actions. As the first issue of the TUC's newsletter suggested, workers had a patriotic duty to the post-coup government to avoid any such labor disruption, while a later issue added that, with some procedural amendments to the 1960 Industrial Relations Act and some better behavior from both workers and employers, Ghanaians could avoid strikes altogether.[90] The goal then for the NLC and TUC—for all intents and purposes echoing the CPP—was an economy that prioritized ever-increasing levels of productivity.[91] The effects of productivity pressures on workers was equally as demoralizing under the NLC as under the CPP. As sociologist Margaret Peil has detailed in her study of Ghanaian factory workers, the pay raises some workers received under the NLC did not go unnoticed. However, vast numbers of workers still only earned the Ghanaian minimum wage of 75 pesewas per day or N¢18–20 per month. For many families, such low wages were simply not sustainable, particularly in a context where renting a single room would consume nearly a third of their wages. Moreover, it was not uncommon for many Ghanaians to earn even less than the minimum wage. As a result, one man described to Peil his family's struggle to survive by noting that his family regularly spent more than he made on any given day.[92]

Conclusion

From the time it came into power in February 1966, the NLC had promised to transfer power back to a civilian government in the quickest possible time. A constitutional commission established in September 1966 unveiled a draft constitution to the public in 1968, with the constitution ratified in August 1969.[93] At the end of August, Ghanaians then took to the polls in the country's first competitive multi-party election in nearly a decade, electing to office the Progress Party (PP) of K. A. Busia—the former leader of the United Party. Coming into office, Busia and the PP adopted the tenuous economic situation of the NLC years. In addition to worker unrest, the country's daunting debt burden, and the continuing specter of Nkrumah—now exiled in Guinea—abroad, the PP came to power in an era of declining cocoa production. For much of the late 1950s and early 1960s, instability marked the Ghanaian cocoa industry, particularly from the perspective of farmers who endured both new forms of taxation and declining real wages. Between 1956 and 1965, for instance, inflation-adjusted prices paid to farmers collapsed by two-thirds.[94] Production through this period, though, steadily increased. For each of the last six years of Nkrumah's administration, the country produced more than 400,000 tons of cocoa, topping out in 1964–5 at more than 570,000 tons.[95] However, in 1969, the country's cocoa production plummeted to approximately 300,000 tons—a number the colonial-era Gold Coast first exceeded in 1936.[96]

The Busia government responded to the growing economic uncertainty much as the NLC had done more than three years earlier as it sought to reassure Ghana's Western allies of the country's commitment to post-Nkrumah liberalization. Looming over any attempt to rectify the country's economic situation was its remaining debt obligations, which amounted to approximately a fourth of the national budget.[97] As political scientist Eboe Hutchful has outlined, by the end of 1972, the stabilization measures previously negotiated by the NLC would expire, requiring the Ghanaian government to begin repayments on the vast majority of its debts. Prior to transferring power to the PP, the NLC had described the effects of this repayment process as unfathomable, for it would require cuts "beyond what is conceivable or humanly possible."[98] Yet, concerns remained among the country's creditors about Ghana's prospects for fulfilling its obligations, with some creditors objecting to the country's continued investments in key social services and what Hutchful classified as the "growth"-focused policies of the PP's Minister of Finance, J. H. Mensah.[99]

The tensions over Ghana's debt obligations came to a head in July 1970 as Mensah, among other Ghanaian representatives, met with many of the country's creditors in London. Speaking to the audience of creditors, Mensah outlined the country's predicament as understood by the PP. Both the NLC and the PP government had adopted what he described as "the tangled mess of incompetence and corruption" of the Nkrumah years. The progress made over the previous four years could only continue through an enduring commitment to "self-sustained growth," he argued, which would in turn shore up the country's democratic revolution and "ameliorate the immediate hardships under which the people of Ghana have lived for so many years."[100]

The Ghanaian press echoed Mensah's and the PP's arguments. In the *Daily Graphic*, for instance, journalist Cameron Duodu advised the newspaper's audience that, "[a]s expected, Ghana's Western creditors are proving difficult." According to Duodu, key to the conflict between the Ghanaian government and its creditors was the shortsighted nature with which the creditors examined the country's debt. In particular, he chastised the creditors for their emphasis on maintaining a commercial interest rate on any deferred payment. Duodu added that, even within Western countries, those countries' "super-affluent companies regard [such an interest rate] as atrociously ruinous."[101] Several days later, A. Kumor added to Duodu's sentiments, again in the *Daily Graphic*. For Kumar, key to Ghana's misfortune was that Great Britain held much of Ghana's debt. In contrast to the USA, France, or West Germany, Great Britain needed Ghanaian payments to help cover its own deficits at home. Kumar continued by characterizing the creditors' treatment of Ghana as "politically opportunistic" and prejudicial. "They," he argued, "would help a friend in need if the country being helped were also an advanced Western country, such as happened when the American Marshall Plan completely wrote off outstanding debts owed by Britain to the U. S. after the Second World War." True aid, Kumar thus lamented, only came to those that Western countries deemed as having "teeth in their foreign policy"—something Ghana lacked and for which Ghanaians suffered.[102]

Chapter 7

THE POLITICS OF PRECARITY:
DEPENDENCE AND DEVELOPMENT
DURING GHANA'S 1970s

In a series of letters to the editor published by the *Daily Graphic* in mid-July 1970 as the negotiations over Ghana's debt obligations closed, a number of Ghanaians expressed anger and dismay at the country's treatment by its creditors. Writing to the newspaper, Baffour Awuakye-Akantang II, the chief of the Eastern Region town of Akim Osarase, lamented what he perceived as the Ghanaian desire to please. As he viewed it, outsiders recognized this Ghanaian trait and regularly took advantage of it for personal gain. For him, the refusal of the country's creditors to appreciate Ghana's economic situation exemplified the unequal power dynamics created by Ghanaians' goodwill. As a result, he claimed, "The issue of foreign debts has now become a national woe. Every Kofi, Adwoa, and Yaw knows that we are drowning under a huge wave of debts. It is the talk in every village, every corner of the nation." The original sin, according to the chief, was thus the NLC's failure to "repudiate these debts" when it came to power in 1966.[1] Another letter-writer, Kwamena Anaman, meanwhile, criticized the futility of negotiating with bad-faith partners who ignored the will of Ghana's elected government, the opinions of the country's experts, and even the potential economic boom promised by "the possible discovery of oil in Ghana." Much like Awuakye-Akantang, Anaman advocated for Ghana to go it alone if the country's creditors refused to cooperate. To this end, he claimed that "there is nothing which prevents us from furthering the economic development of our own dear motherland."[2]

The options available to the PP government, however, were much more limited than the *Daily Graphic*'s readers suggested, at least from the perspective of the government. Like nearly all recently decolonized countries, Ghana relied on the international economic system in order to pursue nearly every aspect of its political and economic policy. This included everything from the enactment of its domestic agenda—such as the funding of schools, healthcare, and its infrastructure projects—to trade and access to hard currency.[3] Ghana's recent democratic transition added further difficulties for the PP. As the government reminded its creditors in a report prior to the 1970 debt negotiations, democratic governments retain their legitimacy by serving the interests of their constituencies. For much of the previous decade, Ghanaians had suffered through shortages, declining standards of living, and high levels of unemployment. By enacting its stabilization reforms following the 1966 coup, the PP government suggested, the NLC may have steadied Ghana's macro-economic environment, but, given that it was not democratically elected, it did not have the same responsibilities toward the Ghanaian populace. In short, the PP asserted, "economic progress must be made" if Ghana's democratic transition was to succeed.[4]

As a result, when the negotiations over Ghana's debt relief fell apart in July 1970, a fundamental feature of the PP government's political legitimacy also fractured. Insisting upon not just a rescheduling of the country's debt as the NLC had previously done, but rather a refinancing of it, the PP went into the negotiations demanding that Ghana's creditors fundamentally restructure the country's debt burden. In doing so, they called upon the country's creditors to waive the interest accumulated from Ghana's previous two (1966 and 1968) rescheduled payments and consolidate the debt into a single forty-year loan with a ten-year grace period.[5] However, as the PP's Minister of Finance, J. H. Mensah, sought to explain, the various parties in the negotiations failed to agree on what he and the government considered the most important issue of the discussions—the question of the accrued interest from the previous payment moratoriums. For Mensah and the PP, the future of the PP's economic agenda rested upon this concession, for the waiving of this interest promised to reduce the country's deferred debts "by about 89 million new cedis."[6] Despite Mensah's and the government's insistence on the centrality of this position to the future of the Ghanaian economy, the country's creditors refused to concede. Mensah, seeking to reassure the international community on Ghana's credit-worthiness, thus left the conference with little choice but to affirm that the country would abide by its current obligations. However, he insisted, it would do so "under protest."[7]

The refusal of Ghana's Western creditors to accept the PP government's vision for the country's economic future not only undermined the political and economic legitimacy of the PP, but would also have ramifications that would continue to destabilize the country through the 1970s and beyond as the quality of the country's political and economic sovereignty came into question. During this time, Ghana's political and economic decisions were not entirely its own. Rather, the Ghanaian government and Ghanaians themselves encountered a wide array of external actors who sought to pressure, if not, in some cases, coerce the West African state into a set of political and economic policies aimed at serving the norms and expectations of global capital over those of Ghanaians and their government. In response, much of the political debate during the period sought to address the effects of this power imbalance on the country and, even more importantly, on the lives of Ghanaians. In doing so, Ghanaians from a wide range of backgrounds positioned themselves as the restorers of the country's political and economic sovereignty during the period through the continued language of development. Development talk, as such, became synonymous with sovereignty talk. Moreover, such debates took place at every level of Ghanaian politics—local, national, and international— and gave voice to the people's expectations for the future. However, the failure of the country's various governments to reclaim this lost sovereignty did not simply undermine the governments' popular legitimacy, but, in many ways, buttressed their political and economic instability.

This chapter thus traces the discourses of development deployed by Ghanaians through the 1970s. Aspects of these debates began as early as the 1969 election, which brought K. A. Busia and the PP to power, as both major parties during the election—the PP and K. A. Gbedemah's National Alliance of Liberals (NAL)—invoked the connection between the country's political and economic sovereignty to its democratic future. Moreover, upon coming to power in 1969, the PP sought to center the quest for economic sovereignty in the promise of the country's rural and agricultural sectors, at least rhetorically. This shift away from the cities, however, not only centered the production capacity and interests of Ghana's farmers, but, in doing so, also revived the broader question of who was and was not a Ghanaian. The failure of the 1970 debt negotiations, coupled with a devaluation of the cedi in 1971, undermined the legitimacy of the PP, leading to its overthrow in early 1972 in a military coup led by I. K. Acheampong. The Acheampong government that followed echoed its predecessor's quest for Ghanaian political and economic sovereignty. Yet, it did so by repudiating much of the country's debt while embarking upon a campaign of national self-sufficiency that centered not just agricultural production, but the growing of everyday staple crops. A palace coup in July 1978 would ultimately lead to Acheampong's collapse. Following another coup in June 1979, Ghana's new head of state, Flight Lieutenant Jerry John Rawlings, ordered Acheampong's, his successor Fred Akuffo's, and five others' executions.

The Progress Party and Ghana's Second Republic

The 1969 election had been one in which the country's economic future featured prominently. Following the May 1969 legalization of political parties in Ghana, more than a dozen parties formed to contest the election anticipated for later that year. As Dennis Austin notes, only five parties would survive to actually contest the election and, of those, two—Busia's Progress Party and Gbedemah's National Alliance of Liberals—quickly came to dominate the political scene.[8] Gbedemah—who had previously served as the CPP's Minister of Finance, among other ministerial roles, and had been one of Nkrumah's most important advisors prior to his 1961 exile—faced the burden of Nkrumah's legacy during the campaign. As a result, Gbedemah, not surprisingly, regularly denounced Nkrumah during campaign events and to the press, even going so far as to call him a "tyrant" and "murderer" during one July 1969 interview.[9] In contrast to the CPP, Gbedemah asserted, the NAL was a party that "believe[d] in a free, democratic government, a free political system, where people can join any political party which appeals to them." In its economic policy, Gbedemah, likewise, attempted to distinguish the NAL from the CPP as he emphasized the new party's commitment to the equitable distribution of state resources throughout Ghanaian society. "Everyone should have the opportunity to use their talents to their best advantage, to the benefit of the State and the People," he argued. "This system will assure that there is a basis for democracy, where the people have an alternative choice."[10]

In outlining the NAL's economic program, Gbedemah promised a restoration of the personal and national wealth created through the country's productive capacity. Speaking, for instance, in June 1969 at the opening of a Sunyani branch of the NAL, Gbedemah tacitly echoed aspects of the CPP's old calls for collective mobilization in his assessment of the country's economic situation. Ghana's "plight," as he described it, required all Ghanaians to "act promptly to salvage the situation" and marshal "all the country's resources that had been dormant in order to raise productivity at home and also to expand as rapidly as possible all the export potentials." The NAL, for its part, promised to aid in this process by "revolutionis[ing] the country's agriculture, expand[ing] the scope of medical services, develop[ing] traditional medicine, and mount[ing] a realistic rural housing scheme."[11] Other NAL candidates reiterated these sentiments. For instance, in the Dangbe-Shai constituency east of Accra, J. T. Ofei pledged that the NAL would usher in such a dramatic transformation of the Ghanaian economy "that the people would never think of giving their votes to any other party for a long time to come."[12] The Manya constituency's NAL candidate, E. R. T. Madjitey, meanwhile, pledged to Ghana's working peoples that, with a NAL victory, Ghanaians would be assured not just jobs, but employment in fields of work for which they were trained.[13]

The Progress Party made similar promises of a Ghanaian economic renaissance in its campaign messaging. In a mid-July rally in the coastal town of Apam, Busia highlighted the disconnect between the country's current economic reality and the wealth of the country's vast resources. For him, like many Ghanaians, the economics of the late 1960s represented a betrayal of the people by the country's previous leaders.[14] As a result, in what could be read as an indirect reference to Gbedemah, who throughout the campaign faced legal challenges connected to his time in Nkrumah's government, Busia argued that "Ghana could easily overcome her suffering if selfless and dedicated persons were voted into power."[15] Busia took the issue on even more directly in a subsequent rally in Akosombo as he insisted that "Ghanaians would be labouring under serious misapprehension and fatal disregard for the lesson in the past years if they voted unscrupulous politicians into power again." As Busia saw it, the actions of those in the Nkrumah government had so sullied what it meant to be Ghanaian that those Ghanaians who traveled outside the country had become embarrassed to acknowledge their heritage. Such sentiments, he claimed, would have been unheard of prior to Nkrumah's rule.[16]

For Busia and the PP, Ghana's economic future was thus tied to the quality of the democracy that emerged out of the new civilian government. The foremost crime of the Nkrumah administration, members of the PP, among others, argued, was its perceived dictatorial tendencies. As discussed in Chapter 5, accusations of a Nkrumah-led dictatorship had haunted the CPP since its earliest days, but only accelerated as the CPP consolidated power during the 1950s and 1960s through the enactment of the Preventative Detention Act, the centralization of civic organizations, and eventually the establishment of the one-party state.

By subverting the parliamentary democracy established at independence, the argument went, Nkrumah and the CPP had not only weakened the connection between the people and their government, but had breached the social contract forged through the creation of the new state. In particular, the PP and others condemned what they perceived to have been the rampant corruption of the Nkrumah administration. This corruption, they suggested, had robbed Ghanaians of the country's national wealth by transferring it into the hands of individuals affiliated with the CPP.[17] Key to the PP's vision for the country, then, was a political and economic future rooted in the flourishing of the country's newly re-established democratic institutions and the good faith of its politicians. As the PP's Oheneba Kow Richardson advised an audience in Awutu, party members should be eager to criticize the party when it makes mistakes and they should also refrain from offering politicians money, for each corrupt act would only weaken the country, breed distrust, and weaken the country's democracy.[18]

In August 1969, when the Progress Party won at the polls, what most surprised those observing Ghana's politics was the magnitude of the PP's victory, with the *Daily Graphic* describing the election as a "landslide" on par with the CPP's past triumphs.[19] In the National Assembly, for instance, the PP won 105 of the assembly's seats, including all of the seats in the Ashanti, Brong Ahafo, and Central Regions and just under 60 percent of the total vote. The NAL, by contrast, gained 29 seats and earned 30 percent of the vote, with the rest going to minor parties.[20]

In office, the PP quickly trained its attention on the country's economic troubles. On the ground, the NLC's post-coup austerity had left much of the Ghanaian economy reeling as, even in the days immediately following the election, strike threats and worker unrest accompanied reports of the post-election transition in Ghana's newspapers. In one instance, police arrested forty-eight striking rubber workers in the Western Region town of Abura.[21] Three days later, the *Daily Graphic* reported on another disturbance in Sekondi and Takoradi, where approximately 500 city council employees threatened to strike if the government failed to re-align their salaries in accordance with a recent government report.[22] The new government responded to the discontent by promising an economic program focused on responsible growth. As J. H. Mensah would describe throughout much of 1969 and 1970, Ghana's economic future demanded a shift away from the austerity measures that had defined the post-coup era. Instead, the new government had the responsibility of seeking economic growth opportunities without incurring the unsustainable debt it attributed to the Nkrumah government.[23] In the new government's political theory, this economic program fundamentally required a rejection of the socialist politics of the Nkrumah era, relying instead on an ethos of capitalist individualism. Thus, gone were the days of massive industrial development and large-scale investment in public sector development initiatives. Rather, the PP promised to exploit the country's current productive capacity to its fullest.[24]

The shift away from large-scale development schemes coincided with a similar move from a focus on the country's urban centers toward its rural and agricultural sectors. As noted in Chapter 6, the Nkrumah government had dedicated extensive resources to the modernization of Ghana's major cities, with the construction of new international hotels, government buildings, factories, and other major infrastructural initiatives. Similarly, as discussed in that chapter, in the cases of Tema and Akosombo, the government, for all intents and purposes, went so far as to create whole new cities laid atop of or nearby pre-existing communities. However, from the perspective of the Progress Party, along with many other Ghanaians, the seeming urban focus of the previous civilian government proved misguided in that it overlooked the needs and interests of most Ghanaians and the foremost sites of Ghana's wealth. As one letter-writer advised the *Daily Graphic's* readers in October 1969, "Ghana is predominately an agricultural country and the Government should give agriculture top priority." The letter-writer in turn called for a governmental commitment to "profitable investment in agriculture."[25] Of particular concern to this letter-writer was the issue of cocoa, which he reminded the newspaper's readers stood at the foundation of the country's economic past and future. At least according to him, the country's governments had for too long ignored this reality and abused the goodwill of Ghana's cocoa farmers, resulting in unemployment and the smuggling of Ghanaian cocoa out of the country in search of higher prices.[26] Accompanying the letter-writer's call was a similar plea from the country's cocoa farmers themselves.[27]

Busia, among others in the PP government and the outgoing NLC, seemingly agreed with the letter-writer's assessment regarding what the new government's priorities should be. One day after the *Daily Graphic* published both appeals, Lt. Col. Akwasi Afrifa, representing the former NLC leaders in the new Presidential Commission, affirmed a three-year floor of N¢8 per load for the country's cocoa producers, assuring them a baseline price regardless of the international market.[28] In doing so, the government sought to blunt the potential for extending the longstanding tensions that plagued relations between Ghana's cocoa producers and the country's previous governments. Moreover, Afrifa also committed the new government to a further review of the country's cocoa industry.[29] As noted in Chapter 6, Afrifa's announcement came on the heels of one of the weakest years in Ghanaian cocoa production since independence. It also came at a time when NLC attempts to stem inflation in the country resulted in stagnating prices paid to Ghana's cocoa producers. As the bi-weekly *West Africa* noted in September 1969, the woes of the country's cocoa farmers were real and widely felt as they received a fixed price that, in real terms, was lower than that offered by the Nkrumah government a decade earlier.[30] Beyond the cocoa industry, the incoming government also pledged a set of additional rural investments that included an expansion of rural electrification, a new bus service, greater access to clean water, and a new network of healthcare facilities that would reach "every village and hamlet."[31]

The press's response to the government's priorities was initially one of general support. In the *Daily Graphic*, reports and editorials after the election praised the PP as a model of good governance. In particular, comparisons to the Nkrumah government featured prominently in the newspaper, with one writer juxtaposing the lost exuberance of 1957 to the promise of the Second Republic.[32] Another writer emphasized the challenges facing the government in the north, which it attributed to neglect from the Nkrumah administration. Focusing specifically on the Northern Region's new regional chairman, J. A. Braimah, the *Daily Graphic's* correspondent outlined a range of challenges facing Braimah as it labeled him and, by extension, the PP government as "daring" in their desire to tackle the region's most persistent problems.[33] A few days later, the *Daily Graphic* added to its piece on Braimah with another that followed the government's Minister of Social and Rural Development, Akumfi Ameyaw Munufie, on his tour of the north. This largely photographic essay highlighted the minister's visits to a Walewale water supply station, meeting with Braimah, and greeting the Ya-Na in Yendi.[34]

Accompanying the PP government's commitment to the country's rural and agricultural development, however, was a nativist politics that culminated in a mid-November announcement that the government would enforce Ghana's 1963 Aliens Act. In this announcement, the government ordered that all non-Ghanaians residing in the country provide the appropriate paperwork within two weeks to prove they were legally living and working in the country or leave the country. The initial order provided the vague justification that the government simply desired to uphold the country's immigration laws.[35] In a December PP rally in Accra, John Agyekum Kufuor—then Ministerial Secretary to the Ministry of External Affairs and, decades later, the second president of Ghana's Fourth Republic—reiterated the government's stated rationale for the order.[36] However, Kwaku Baah—the Ministerial Secretary to the Ministry of the Interior—at the same event went even further in his explanation of the order. According to him, the need for the order was simply a matter of resources, for "[w]e cannot afford to feed other mouths when ours are not fed."[37] Speaking before the National Assembly, also in December 1969, Baah similarly insisted that, going forward, the government would only approve those immigrants who could verify that they had "a job awaiting" them.[38] Additional justifications for the order included governmental attempts to thwart such scourges on Ghanaian social and economic life as petty crime and smuggling.[39]

During the 1960 census, more than 800,000 foreign-born West Africans resided in the country.[40] For those there at the time of the expulsion order, the PP government destabilized their lives overnight. In the north, where many immigrants lived and worked as traders, the order resulted in a mass exodus as families uprooted themselves in order to comply. As anthropologist J. S. Eades describes in his 1994 book on Tamale's Yoruba community, when he first arrived in the city in August 1969, Yoruba traders comprised more than a third of the traders in the city's central market. The vast majority of these traders came from four Nigerian towns (Ogbomosho, Igboho, Shaki, and Igbetti) and numbered just over 2,000. By the end of the year, he recalled, "that community had ceased to exist."[41] In the case of one of his research participants, Alhaji Lasisi, a middle-aged cloth seller from Igbetti, the order disrupted nearly every aspect of his life. At the time of the order, he had owned two houses and rented out twenty rooms between them. Like many in Ghana, the economic situation following the 1966 coup had weakened his financial position, which had grown considerably during the 1950s and early 1960s. Despite his declining business, he was still able to secure approximately N¢100 a month through rent. When the government announced the quit order, Lasisi tried to get around expulsion by hiring a Dagomba woman to claim she was his mother, allowing him Ghanaian citizenship. Despite successfully attaining citizenship, Lasisi, like nearly all other Tamale Yoruba, ultimately left Ghana and returned to Nigeria.[42]

Historian Rashid Olaniyi recounts similar stories of immigrant innovation and devastation following the expulsion order. Among those he interviewed, he found two main groups of immigrants—ones that had lived in Ghana since the 1920s and a second that was born in Ghana prior to independence. For those born in Ghana, citizenship still eluded them given Ghana's qualified absence of birthright citizenship. Among those Olaniyi interviewed, it was the sheer abruptness of the order that caused the most pain and uncertainty. Overnight, they needed to secure money for travel, requiring many to liquidate their possessions at absurdly low prices. Likewise, others had land and specifically cocoa farms confiscated and portions of their savings expropriated. Meanwhile, many of those with Ghanaian wives and children had to leave their families behind. Those who wished to stay had to confirm that they would withhold their children from school and that they worked or would begin working as farmers or laborers. According to Olaniyi, the order proved so draconian that it led some immigrants to suicide.[43]

Those who illegally remained in the country after the two-week leave period faced arrest and deportation as the police searched markets, tro-tro stations, and other public venues for undocumented individuals.[44] As one official statement explained, the government's actions were necessary for the "protection" and "proper treatment" of the undocumented.[45] To this end, the government advised all immigrants to work only with proper embassy or "accredited immigration" officials. Likewise, the government condemned vigilante attempts to assist the police in identifying undocumented individuals.[46] The government reaffirmed its condemnation of vigilantism on December 9th after reports surfaced of violence against undocumented agricultural workers.[47] In other instances, undocumented traders in the Upper Region (contemporary Upper East) town of Sandema had their shops ransacked. As reported by the *Daily Graphic*, the looting resulted in "pandemonium as the aliens made efforts to protect themselves and their wares." The looting had ramifications in other nearby towns too. In both Bolgatanga and Navrongo, many immigrant traders simply refused to open their shops following the Sandema incident.[48] Contested reports of undocumented individuals themselves looting in places like Tema further stoked tensions between Ghanaians and non-Ghanaians during the exodus.[49]

Meanwhile, en route to their home countries, Ghana's West African refugees endured a cascade of political, economic, and personal hardships. In the December 5th edition of the Lagos-based *Daily Times*, for instance, journalist Chinaka Fynecontry reported that the quit order had stranded more than a thousand Nigerians in the Togolese capital of Lomé. According to Fynecontry, once out of Ghana, most of these individuals could not find transport across Togo and Dahomey (Benin).[50] Olaniyi, likewise, recounted that, even within Ghana, drivers extorted Nigerians seeking to leave the country by charging fares of at least 300 percent the standard rate, forcing many to make the trek by foot.[51] In another story, the *Daily Times* detailed the plight of another thousand Nigerians residing in Accra's jails, with "many more" imprisoned elsewhere in the country.[52] Additionally, it described a scene in Accra at the Nigerian High Commission where "[s]everal hundred Nigerians—mainly women and children—were squatting … cooking and feeding their babies while the garages overflowed with baggage."[53] The plight of the Nigerian refugees grew even more dire following a mid-December coup in Dahomey, closing the Nigeria–Dahomey border and leaving refugees stranded. As one individual quoted by the *Daily Times* decried in frustration, "Why should this happen when we are only a few yards from our country?"[54] Another individual who had been in Ghana for nearly two decades, angerly professed that he would "never spend one shilling to travel out of Nigeria again."[55]

Even more devastating, numerous deaths accompanied the exodus. On December 7, 1969, at least twenty from Niger died in a lorry crash upon their exit from Ghana.[56] Another crash killed two women and three children making their way through Dahomey toward the Nigerian border.[57] Twenty-seven more from Niger died in a crash in northern Dahomey in mid-December, while still another incident—this time in the Ghanaian border town of Aflao—killed an elderly Nigerian man and injured at least eighteen others.[58] Meanwhile, according to Nigerians arriving in Lagos in late December, ten others—most of whom children—died in Ghanaian refugee camps as they awaited transport out of Ghana, with exposure killing eight more stranded at Tema Harbour.[59] As a result, as the year came to a close, the *Daily Times* outwardly condemned the Busia government's actions during the expulsion, arguing in an editorial headline that the quit order and the deaths that ensued had resulted in "a case for Ghana to answer." The newspaper acknowledged that the Ghanaian government had the right to exercise the order, but that the only responsible and ethical way to have done so was to "ensure that these unfortunate victims of circumstance received all available care and treatment compatible with human dignity till the last moment of their departure from Ghana."[60]

Expulsion and Devaluation

By mid-1970, the devastation wrought by the expulsion order was felt throughout West Africa. At the Ghana/Togo border, an estimated 50,000 people crossed into Togo during the first two weeks following the order. Additional estimates suggest between 150,000 and 175,000 West Africans left Ghana by the end of April, with the Nigerian High Commission putting the number of Nigerians at 140,000 by June.[61] Frustration broke out throughout the region as refugees sought to adapt to the new realities they faced in their home countries. In one of her accounts of the episode, sociologist Margaret Peil emphasizes the experience of one man from Upper Volta (Burkina Faso), Amadu Moshie, who had no family or social connections in the Sahelian country and thus found it impossible to survive, let alone make a life for himself, there. Moshie thus sought to return to Ghana. Arrested and then prosecuted in Sunyani, Moshie faced a three-month prison term for his return before re-deportation.[62] As he told the court, he had little choice but to return to Ghana, for "there was not [as] much food there [in Upper Volta] for me to eat as in Ghana."[63] Meanwhile, Ghanaians expressed their own frustrations with the government's actions, as nativist complaints that the government was not taking strong enough action in implementing the order made their way into the country's newspapers.[64]

After six months of deportations, it was becoming increasingly clear that many of the objectives that the government had laid out rationalizing the order were not coming to fruition. Among the most prominent justifications for the order were claims that the deportations would help alleviate unemployment within the country. A perennial problem since well before independence, the compliance order did little to rectify Ghana's unemployment crisis. As Peil notes, to stave off economic chaos, the government had permitted non-Ghanaians working in essential fields (some levels of government, the cocoa industry, docks, mines, and certain corporations) to remain, ensuring that those jobs did not open up. However, most non-Ghanaians in Ghana were self-employed as traders or craftsmen and therefore did not possess conventionally fillable jobs.[65] Peil similarly observes that, in the country's major cities, the order created a hole in those cities' markets as it left more than 4,000 market stalls vacant. The process to fill these vacancies proved fraught, with "at least 24,000 women" seeking to take them over. In Accra, Peil argues, accusations of corruption dominated the re-allocation process, with the already prosperous claiming many.[66] Meanwhile, in Kumasi, anthropologist Gracia Clark recounts how the compliance order re-oriented Kumasi's commercial culture. In doing so, it forced Hausa, Yoruba, and Lebanese traders to sell their shops, allowing others to purchase the shops on the cheap.[67]

In other areas of the country, the order had equally mixed results. Among the foreign-owned transport companies forced to close due to the order, few had Ghanaian-owned alternatives replace them.[68] Even in areas of the economy purportedly protected from the compliance order, such as the cocoa industry, the order had deleterious effects. In the case of cocoa specifically, labor became hard to find.[69] Many who had previously worked on Ghanaian cocoa farms migrated to other West African countries, specifically Côte d'Ivoire, and, as Paul Nugent notes, it was many of these refugees who helped develop that country's cocoa industry.[70] Gwendolyn Mikell similarly highlights the rising costs of labor in the cocoa industry caused by the order. The result was a situation whereby many farmers—particularly poorer farmers and women—resorted to working on wealthier producers' farms to make ends meet.[71] At the same time as labor difficulties plagued the cocoa industry, Busia's biographer Kwaku Danso-Boafo recounts, additional labor shortages in the sanitation sector plagued Ghana's cities. According to Danso-Boafo, all of this upheaval ultimately netted just 5,000 Ghanaian jobs.[72]

Meanwhile, still haunting the PP government was the country's debt burden and the negotiations over its restructuring. The collapse of those negotiations left the government with few alternatives in pursuing the economic recovery it had promised during its election campaign a year earlier. Additional negotiations would continue throughout the year, with little progress toward a resolution. The debt crisis would only intensify over the course of 1971. By November, the government acted by delinking the cedi with the pound sterling and tying it to the US dollar. In this transition, the official exchange rate remained at N¢1.00=US$.98. Yet, by the end of the year, the government found itself faced with little choice but to devalue the currency. As a result, in late December, it announced a 44 percent devaluation of the cedi, establishing a new exchange rate at N¢1.00=US$.55 or US$1= N¢1.82.[73] Busia justified the government's actions by arguing that, without devaluation, the country would have faced wide-ranging shortages on imported goods.[74] The *Daily Graphic*, for its part, celebrated the devaluation, arguing in a frontpage headline that it put Ghana on a path "towards a free economy." According to the newspaper's editors, devaluation gave the government space to "liberalise further the economy of Ghana," correct the national balance sheets, raise cocoa prices, enact wage hikes for workers, and alleviate the conditions of the impoverished.[75] The result, however, was rapid inflation and, within days, Busia announced "hard times ahead."[76] Busia's government would not last another month as a military coup led by I. K. Acheampong overthrew the civilian government on January 13, 1972.

Yentua ("We Will Not Pay") and the Politics of Self-Reliance

The *Daily Graphic* announced the coup the following day. Speaking over the radio, Acheampong connected the failures of the Busia-led government to that of Nkrumah's overthrow nearly six years earlier. According to Acheampong, the armed forces—through the actions of the NLC in handing over power in 1969—had shown that they could responsibly right the ship of state following civilian mismanagement. Given that the PP government had followed in the CPP's footsteps, he continued, the military had to act. Much as the NLC and its civilian successor had previously done in regards to Nkrumah and the CPP, Acheampong accused the PP government of betraying the constitution, of rampant corruption and mismanagement, and of general incompetence. "[W]e, in the Armed Forces," he thus asserted, "have once again decided to take over the reins of Government to save Busia from total disgrace, from committing further blunders and to prevent him from totally collapsing the country before he runs away to enjoy the huge fortune he has acquired outside the country." Going forward, Acheampong promised to re-introduce key Nkrumah-era development initiatives such as the State Farms and Workers Brigade. He also vowed to review the cedi's recent devaluation and the Alien Compliance Order.[77]

Four days later, Acheampong, speaking as chairman of the newly formed National Redemption Council (NRC), further tied the coup to the country's economic conditions by announcing that the NRC had "declare[d] total war on the economy."[78] For those aligned with the NRC, Busia and his government had proven themselves to be cowards through their economic policy. In particular, the NRC accused the Busia government of a general lack of honesty when speaking to the Ghanaian people about the dire state of the economy. From Acheampong's perspective, not only was this weakness dishonest, it was also disqualifying. In contrast, he argued that the military was uniquely adept at taking on crises, including the economic crisis. "We are soldiers," he reminded the country. "We know when we are dealing with crisis situations, and that is action." This "action" could be understood as both the overthrowing of Busia's government and the promised response to the country's economic troubles. Acheampong then added that, for the military, "No sacrifice will be too great for us in this gigantic task." To this end, the new head of state committed Ghana to a path toward "self-reliance."[79]

A conceptually broad term, "self-reliance" harkened to a political ideology centered on narratives of both struggle and accomplishment. As Acheampong explained during his 1972 Easter broadcast, the country faced no easy answers to its current economic struggles. Instead, he warned Ghanaians to prepare for further hardships ahead. However, he also insisted that, through both the marshaling of the country's human and natural resources and "a spirit of realism, hard work, and sacrifice," Ghanaians could forge a path out of their current troubled state.[80] The 1972 *Charter of the National Redemption Council* further articulated the meaning of "self-reliance" under the NRC.[81] Here, self-reliance entailed more than Ghana's economic transformation; it required a re-orienting of what it meant to be Ghanaian. Ghanaians had to see themselves as a unique people capable of transforming themselves and the nation simultaneously. This transformation— in many ways echoing the Nkrumahist decolonization language of the previous decade[82]—was to be systematic and complete, altering how Ghanaians understood who they were, their relationships with one another, as well as those with the outside world. It was in this re-orientation of the Ghanaian self (the "January 13 Man") that Acheampong and the NRC envisioned a renaissance—a restoration that was fundamentally Ghanaian driven and Ghanaian created.[83]

The most prominent expression of the NRC's emphasis on "self-reliance" came with the February 1972 launch of "Operation Feed Yourself" (OFY). Following in the wake of both the Busia government's faltered development agenda and the mixed results of Nkrumah's agricultural initiatives, OFY sought to reframe the role of Ghanaian agricultural development in the country's broader political and economic policy by celebrating in a reciprocal relationship between *Ghanaian* production and *Ghanaian* consumption. From the perspective of the NRC, which adopted a martial tone in nearly all of its economic pronouncements, the country's economic troubles rested in the lost autonomy that came from Ghana's seeming dependence on international markets. An over-reliance on imported goods ranging from various commercial products (automobiles, mechanical parts, appliances) to everyday staples (basic foodstuffs) thus left the country beholden to external pressures in ways that undermined its sovereignty. Key to the NRC's economic program was thus a re-assertion of Ghanaian sovereignty by tying the country's consumptive practices to what Ghanaians themselves could and did produce. At the same time, it also envisioned OFY as a means by which to alleviate regional inequalities through new systems of resource allocation.[84]

In practice, OFY resulted in an ambitious and sustained investment in Ghanaian agricultural production. As political scientist Emmanuel Hansen has outlined, the NRC divided the country into agricultural zones, with key food crops promoted within these specific zones. In contrast to the more than century-old focus on cash crops, the crops promoted by OFY were food items grown for local consumption—maize, plantains, cassava, yams, and millet, among several others.[85] Hansen adds that the government heavily promoted the program on television, radio, and in other forms of mass media. Furthermore, state institutions such as prisons, schools, and sectors of the armed forces, along with some private businesses, established their own agricultural wings to grow these food crops. Meanwhile, in the country's cities and towns, backyard gardening also became a popular pastime as a result of the OFY campaign.[86] Moreover, in some locales, OFY irrigation projects sought to combat the effects of a drying and unstable local climate. In one Volta resettlement village, historian Stephan Miescher notes, such investments allowed farmers to reliably grow vegetables including tomatoes, onions, and peppers.[87]

The effects of OFY in the north were equally dramatic. Eliding much of the 1960s and 1970s together in their recollections, residents of the northern Mamprusi town of Kpasenkpe spoke of the period as the "time of Agric," referring to the possibilities created by the government's investments in food production. Reflecting on accounts of these experiences, historian Alice Wiemers emphasizes the transformative nature that new investments in plows, fertilizer, and seeds had on the town. For some, access to plows and fertilizer specifically not only provided them opportunities to increase production, but allowed them to also experiment with new crops. Others gained access to increased job prospects due to the effects of these implements on the town's labor market.[88] John Dramani Mahama, reflecting on his own family's agricultural experiences during OFY, recounted how his father's (Emmanuel Adama Mahama) rice farm and rice mill prospered under Acheampong. Of particular benefit to the elder Mahama was the government's ban on rice imports, freeing him and others of outside competition. According to the younger Mahama, the result was a "revitali[zation]" of his father's rice interests.[89]

Looking beyond the experiential level, the national statistics for Ghanaian food production during the first years of OFY bear out much of this anecdotal data.[90] Naomi Chazan notes an overall growth rate of more than 18 percent between 1972 and 1974 for Ghanaian agricultural and livestock production. Rice production specifically increased by nearly six times its 1971 levels by 1972. Maize witnessed a similar growth, with farmers' crops reaching levels approximately eight times their Busia-era equivalents.[91] The numbers for several less high-profile crops were just as impressive. In the program's first year alone, cassava, groundnuts, millet, and vegetables all showed production numbers that exceeded the government's marks by double digits. It was only rice and plantain production that failed to meet the government's ambitious targets. Yet, as Maxwell Owusu highlights, in the case of rice specifically, the NRC had asked farmers to increase their yields by 44 percent during OFY's first year, with the farmers only falling short by 8 percent.[92]

OFY's February 1972 launch came in the midst of a nearly simultaneous shift in Ghana's fiscal policy. Beginning on February 5th with an announcement that the new government aimed to nullify Busia's 1971 currency devaluation and renounce some of Ghana's debt, the Acheampong government argued that both personal and national economic security trumped vague democratic abstractions such as "One Man One Vote." The principle for the new NRC's chairman had to be "One Man One Bread."[93] Referencing the intended revaluation of the currency, which realigned the cedi to the dollar at N¢1=US$.78,[94] Acheampong promised lower prices in the country's markets, combating the rapid inflation that followed the devaluation. Furthermore, Acheampong reminded the country's businesses of their obligation to ensure that consumers enjoyed the "full benefit of this revaluation."[95] In terms of the country's external debts, the government announced that it was undertaking a review of all foreign contracts executed prior to Nkrumah's 1966 overthrow, arguing that any contract signed in which evidence of "fraud, corruption, and other illegality" is present would be repudiated. With immediate effect, Acheampong canceled the contracts with four foreign companies, totaling $94.4 million. In addition, the government renounced a third of the principal owed to suppliers, the interest accrued during the post-Nkrumah payment moratoriums ($72 million), laid out new conditions for contractors to request payments, and asserted that the government would not pay "any debt arising from any suppliers' credit for the next 10 years."[96]

Acheampong justified the NRC's actions as a restoration of the country's and each Ghanaian's sovereignty. "We cannot expect to be bailed out by some miraculous intervention or the generosity of other countries," he explained in a broadcast announcing the changes to the country's fiscal policy. "What we are declaring to the whole world now," he continued, "is that we have the will-power and the human and material resources to be self-reliant. ... We cannot as a nation continue to be buffeted by forces which we are powerless to control."[97] Two days later, Acheampong was even more direct as he attacked the economic policies of the Busia government for the PP's rhetorical commitment to democratic governance in a context of growing inequality. "A Government which operates on the basis of One Man Ten Bread for the broad masses of the people is unjust," he declared, and "unjust rulers do not deserve to be sustained by any theoretical conceptions of democracy. As you all know, Dead Men have use for only one type of Box—*not* the ballot box."[98] Busia and his government, Acheampong added, had thus turned Ghana into a "Beggar Nation" as democratic niceties and an expressed commitment to *laissez-faire* capitalism underpinned a "Busian concept of social justice" that resulted in "the contraction of the areas of happiness and the corresponding expansion of the scales of poverty."[99]

Shortages and the Limits of Self-Reliance

By the mid-1970s, however, the initial successes and popular praise of the NRC's economic policies had begun to wane as a cascading wave of political and economic phenomena challenged the NRC's ambitions. Explaining the country's changing fortunes during the time, economist Douglas Rimmer suggested that, in many ways, the NRC—rebranded as the Supreme Military Council (SMC) in late 1975—had gotten lucky with OFY's early successes. As he viewed the program, OFY had benefited from an initial push in productivity and a period of fortuitous weather, variables of success unlikely to continue in perpetuity.[100] Chazan echoed Rimmer in her assessment. For her, the NRC's/SMC's economic policy represented a house of cards as pervasive corruption, rampant inflation (exceeding 50 percent by 1976),[101] declining productivity, and widespread shortages not only threatened economic progress, but also undermined the legitimacy of many of the government's political and moral arguments. The government in turn responded to the country's economic fortunes with what Chazan presents as at best band-aids— appointments that had little influence, political education campaigns, and the scapegoating of key players in the everyday economy.[102] Meanwhile, a prominent critic of the NRC/SMC, Mike Oquaye—who decades later would become Speaker of the Ghanaian Parliament—accused the government of outright malice and incompetence. The result, according to him, was a period of sustained hardship marked by widespread shortages.[103]

The implications of Ghana's declining economic fortunes during the mid- and late 1970s reached deep into Ghanaian daily life. The hardships caused by the country's shortages and escalating inflation exacerbated what the NRC/SMC had already viewed as Ghanaians' troublesome trend toward the hoarding and smuggling of goods. At the time of the January 13th coup, Acheampong and the NRC attributed these acts to the failures of Busia-era economic policies and especially the currency devaluation.[104] Both rhetorically and in the execution of state power, the government embarked on an all-out assault on these assumed unpatriotic and anti-consumer behaviors. By mid-decade, though, the practice had only expanded, with Ghanaians hoarding goods out of fear that they would not become available again. As political scientist Paul Nugent explains, a "dialectical relationship" emerged in the Ghanaian economy as a black market developed to get around the NRC's newly imposed price controls. As a result, people stockpiled key goods that could disappear from the market, while traders refused to sell certain items in hopes that prices would rise. The crisis was only compounded by the ability of those in the military government to use their positions to gain access to certain goods and sell them for a profit.[105] By the end of the decade, Nugent adds, many goods had come to lose their use-value. Instead, their utility was only in their ability to be held until they could be passed on for profit.[106]

Traders thus emerged as key governmental scapegoats, often receiving stiff punishments for accusations of anti-consumer actions. In 1974, for instance, Acheampong advised the public that those convicted of hoarding and price gouging, among other offences, would not face a fine for their actions. Rather, they would "go to prison 'straight away.'" Justifying the government's actions, the Ghanaian head of state insisted that such actions were necessary to ensure the January 13 Revolution's success. Even more ominously, Acheampong—reiterating previous calls for public incrimination—seemingly deputized the public in "smok[ing] out" those allegedly involved in anti-consumer sales practices as a way to help "rid ourselves of these evil people."[107] Three years later, the NRC renewed calls to "expose profiteers" following a recent increase in wages within the country. Speaking in Winneba, Colonel Parker H. S. Yarney advised workers to "be on the alert" as the so-called profiteers aimed to undermine the government's efforts "to put more money in their [the workers'] pockets" by illegally raising the prices of key goods.[108] For Acheampong specifically, the issues surrounding these presumed anti-consumer sales practices were simple; it was an attack on the revolution he and the NRC/SMC envisioned for the country. As a result, he ultimately demanded that all Ghanaians ask themselves: "How do we help the nation if we decide to sell goods at high prices which can only make our fellow Ghanaians the poorer; and if they are poor, can they assist in the community services which we all need?"[109]

However, the situation from the perspective of Ghana's traders and consumers alike was fundamentally more complicated. As anthropologist Gracia Clark explains, the legal and illegal markets for goods operated symbiotically and thus could not be easily separated as goods flowed from one "market" to the other. The ramifications of this system, though, were not equally felt. As noted, those most likely to have access to the legal market were those with connections to the government or large firms. When certain goods on the legal market became available to the general public, long "often violent lines" emerged, excluding large swaths of the population—the ill, elderly, self-employed, and rural population—from potentially gaining access.[110] As one individual, C. K. Abroso, writing in a letter to the editor of the *Daily Graphic*, complained in April 1975, a battery shortage had a particularly deleterious impact on the rural blind like him. In specific, he complained that the battery shortage had cut him off from the country's news, for his radio had now become obsolete and, given that Ghana's newspapers did not publish in braille, he had no other options available to him for accessing the news.[111]

Abroso's frustrations were also felt by others. Again referencing battery shortages, another letter-writer, E. K. Amoako-Anane, described the situation in the classical economic terms of supply and demand. According to the Yeji letter-writer, the shortages necessarily pushed the batteries' real price (50 pesewas) to approximately double the control prices of 22 and 27 pesewas. Amoako-Anane further adds that it was hard to find batteries at even the inflated real price. For him, the difficulties caused by the shortage were most acutely felt at night as he could no longer use his "torchlight." As a result, Amoako-Anane concluded his letter by asking manufacturers for clarity on why the shortages exist and when they may be alleviated.[112] Likewise, accompanying Amoako-Anane's letter, another letter-writer, St. John Clottey, wrote on what he viewed as the deficiencies in the country's meat production and specifically the government agencies responsible for promoting it. As Clottey understood the country's meat industry, Ghana's inability to transition to self-reliance in meat production had forced the country to depend upon shortage-inducing imports. In many ways echoing the objectives of OFY, Clottey thus called upon the government to invest more heavily in pathways toward self-sufficiency through research into the cross-breeding of cattle.[113]

Among sellers, discontent also abounded. Not only were they scapegoated as criminals for their attempts to adapt to the country's unstable economic environment, but the uncertainty around access to goods upended generational hierarchies within many markets. As Clark explains in her analysis of the Kumasi market, older women with limited connections to goods in short supply often found themselves having to turn to younger intermediaries for their wares. Dissatisfied with their dislocation from the centers of market power, many older traders began to stereotype their younger colleagues by claiming that the younger women had only achieved their connections by exploiting their sexuality.[114] Meanwhile, in Accra, historian Claire Robertson similarly notes how the government regularly put the city's traders in precarious situations. In one example, she recounts how, in 1976, the government demanded all traders purchase their kiosks from the government, charging a price that only the wealthiest could afford. Later, the government then turned around and announced that all kiosks be abolished.[115] The situation for Accra's traders would only deteriorate further as the decade came to a close following Acheampong's overthrow in 1978 and that of his successor, Fred Akuffo, a year later when soldiers from Jerry John Rawlings's Armed Forces Revolutionary Council looted and razed Accra's Makola No. 1 Market.[116]

Conclusion

In his 2012 memoir, *My First Coup d'Etat*, John Dramani Mahama recalled the rollercoaster of Ghana's 1970s. Reminiscing on a letter his father had once written to Acheampong, Mahama recounted how his father had advised the Ghanaian head of state "to leave ... when the applause is loudest."[117] The consequences of Acheampong's failure to heed the elder Mahama's advice proved catastrophic for him and others in the NRC/SMC. Yet, they embody the instability manifested in Ghana's immediate post-Nkrumah history as multiple governments not only aimed to re-orient the country's political and economic policies following Nkrumah, but also to re-assert a sovereignty seemingly lost by the decisions of the Nkrumah era. Debt stood at the center of much of this debate. At its most basic level, it constrained the ambitions of multiple governments by making them beholden to the whims of a collection of external lenders. For the PP and Kofi Busia in particular, Ghana's debt burden weakened the country's democratic possibilities by stunting its ability to live up to its political and developmental promises. For their part, Acheampong and the NRC/SMC aimed to reclaim this lost sovereignty as they overthrew Busia and his government and sought to construct a society built upon Ghanaian self-reliance. However, as would occur with many of the initiatives of the 1970s, the results of the NRC's/SMC's efforts were far from clear cut. Early successes in national productivity eventually gave way to insecurity, forcing Ghanaians to adapt to continued shortages, inflation, and a political system in constant flux.

Chapter 8

SITES OF UPHEAVAL:
THE RAWLINGS REVOLUTION AND THE
COMING NEOLIBERAL AGE

In an address outlining the reasons for I. K. Acheampong's July 1978 removal from power, Ghana's new head of state, Lieutenant-General Fred Akuffo, explained that the move was necessary due to Acheampong's failure to take the advice of other members of the SMC. As Akuffo advised the public, by the end of Acheampong's tenure, he had turned the operations of the Ghanaian government into "a one-man show." Going forward, the new head of state—like nearly all of his predecessors— promised to tackle the country's dire economic situation and particularly its long-standing troubles with inflation. Again, like his predecessors, Akuffo argued that the path forward required a commitment to increased production. Akuffo also committed the government to taking on such plagues on national budgeting as tax evasion and excessive government spending on what he described as unnecessary or wasteful government projects. Akuffo then concluded by warning his audience that "[t]he measures we propose to adopt may be harsh, but they must be endured if we should weather the storm." He similarly advised those listening that "[t]hese are hard times which demand frugality on the part of all Ghanaians."[1] The result of these sacrifices, Akuffo announced, would be Ghana's planned transition back to civilian, democratic governance the following year.[2]

Akuffo's government would not survive that full year. On June 4, 1979, Flight Lieutenant Jerry John Rawlings announced on Radio Ghana the end of Akuffo's government. Rawlings, who that day was to report for court martial, accused Ghana's military officers of "ruin[ing] this country." Ghana's uncorrupted officers, he insisted, thus had a "duty [to] save … her."[3] An announcer on Radio Ghana was even more blunt as he accused the officers under Akyeampong and Akuffo of "seven years of hypocrisy and corruption."[4] The first weeks of Rawlings and his newly formed Armed Forces Revolutionary Council (AFRC) proved tumultuous, culminating in the June 26th execution of three former Ghanaian heads of state— Acheampong, Akuffo, and A. K. Afrifa of the National Liberation Council—plus four others. As historian Abena Ampofoa Asare has shown, the AFRC justified its actions by claiming that, unlike with Ghana's previous coups, the AFRC did not overthrow a constitutional government, but instead removed a government ruling by force. The former AFRC spokesman Osahene Boakye Gyan also insisted that the violence of the AFRC remained focused on bad actors within the Ghanaian armed forces, not the citizenry. Asare, however, contrasts Boakye Gyan's statements with accounts of "market women flogged in public, families separated by imprisonment and exile, and men made to stare at the sun or frog-jump in the noonday heat."[5]

Shortly after coming to power and in the midst of the violence it portrayed as Ghana's "house cleaning,"[6] the AFRC announced that it would allow the country's previously scheduled elections to take place as planned on June 18th, with the second round occurring on July 9th. After the vote, Hilla Limann—a relatively unknown diplomat representing the People's National Party (PNP)—won handily over long-time politician Victor Owusu and the Popular Front Party (PFP). Proclaiming the PNP as an heir to Kwame Nkrumah's CPP, one of the PNP's founders, Kofi Batsa—who two decades earlier had edited the Nkrumah-era ideological newspaper, *The Spark*—presented the PNP's ambitions as those of adapting Nkrumahism to the realities of Ghana's transition into the 1980s. Most notably, according to Batsa, this included a revival of Nkrumah-era ideals of social and economic sovereignty in tackling the country's economic troubles.[7] As such, the PNP often highlighted the shared populist commitments between the PNP and the long-defunct CPP.[8] However, in the lead up to the actual votes in June and July, the PNP increasingly emphasized more general claims of good governance, economic revival, and a commitment to constitutionalism.[9]

As Limann rose to power after the election, though, the fate of him and his government remained tethered to his immediate predecessor. Even at Limann's September inauguration, Rawlings raised the possibility of upending the new civilian government should it not live up to the expectations laid out through the AFRC's house cleaning. In doing so, Rawlings suggested that the decision to turn over power to Limann's government was not clearcut, for much still needed to be done in ridding the country of its bad actors. However, he reaffirmed his confidence that the transfer of power was the right decision by predicting that "we shall never regret our decision to go back to the barracks."[10]

Just over two years later, though, Rawlings re-asserted himself on the Ghanaian political stage by overthrowing Limann and re-establishing Ghanaian military rule. As he took power, Rawlings described the PNP as "a pack of criminals" and promised a "holy war" that would transform "the socio-economic structure of Ghanaian society."[11] Immediately following the coup, the new government thus arrested prominent PNP members, including Limann.[12] Meanwhile, calls to support the Rawlings revolution came quickly from key segments of the Ghanaian political class. As one PFP parliamentarian explained after the coup, "[E]ven if the revolution had been initiated by any person it should be supported by Ghanaians because the country needed such a revolution for a total economic and political liberation." Rawlings and his allies, he continued, "have not set the clock back because if the take-over had not happened 'people would have eaten themselves up within one year.'"[13]

This chapter traces Ghanaians' experiences under Rawlings and the Provisional National Defence Council (PNDC) in the aftermath of the December 31st Revolution. The tumult of the 1970s did not cease as Rawlings and the PNDC forced their way back on to the Ghanaian political stage with renewed promises of populist revolution. Instead, much of the Rawlings era marked a continuing sense of social and economic instability. Colliding with international power inequities, Rawlings's government faced a cascade of challenges seemingly all converging during the new government's first years. These included one of the worst droughts in Gold Coast/Ghanaian modern history, a wave of bush fires that ravaged the countryside, a refugee crisis caused by Nigeria's expulsion of illegal West African migrants, an accompanying food crisis, and the implementation of a World Bank and International Monetary Fund-supported Economic Recovery Programme. Rawlings's and the PNDC's actions during these early years of PNDC governance would set the stage for the gradual emergence of Ghana's neoliberal age during the 1980s and early 1990s. As Ghanaians adjusted to neoliberalism's introduction into their country, they encountered an evolving set of political and economic realities that juxtaposed a withdrawal of the state from key segments of the Ghanaian economy and weakening of the assumed state-citizenry social contract with a stabilizing, growth-oriented, yet increasingly unequal national economy.

Revolution and the Promises of Grassroots Democracy

As he returned to power during the last moments of 1981, Rawlings renewed his promises of a revolution—a term that, by the 1980s, had seduced many a Ghanaian politician. Speaking in a radio broadcast on the day of the coup, Rawlings insisted that what had occurred was "not a coup." Instead, he asserted, "I ask for nothing less than a revolution. Something that would transform the social and economic order of this country." As he continued, Rawlings went on to insist that the Limann government had nothing to show for its time in power, "but repression."[14] Rawlings next invoked the question of human rights, yet shifted the concept's meaning outside of its conventional usages in international law. In doing so, the new head of state argued that it was only during the time of the AFRC that Ghanaians "realised human rights," for it was only then when "the masses of this country felt that they could be a part of the decision-making process of this country."[15] The next steps for the country, he further argued, were thus up to the people. The soldiers had sacrificed and it was now the people's job to forge the path forward. "I therefore leave it up to you," he announced to his radio audience, "to marshal yourselves, to harness your might so we can protect the intellectual, and physical power of this country, Ghana."[16]

Over the next couple of weeks, Rawlings further made his case for the military's return to power and his vision for Ghana. As he explained to a group of journalists on January 18th, what he perceived as his need to return to power came not with enthusiasm, but instead with disappointment. He then reiterated his belief in the democratic process. However, he suggested that it would have been inappropriate to have blind faith in electoral democracy. Democracy equally depended on the ability of the elected to govern with "effectiveness" in order for it to maintain its legitimacy. To wit, Rawlings insisted that the PNP government had "acted outside the bounds of normal democratic politics" and erased what Rawlings portrayed as the anti-corruption and good governance gains initiated by the AFRC.[17] Here, Rawlings was building upon remarks he had previously laid out in the week following the coup, where he criticized those who had denounced him and the PNDC for overthrowing the PNP government. These "people," he asserted, "have argued that however badly the Government was going, let there be no coup, no military intervention since we have seen what previous military regimes have done to the economy and to the people of this country. Let the existing authorities provide the remedy." However, Rawlings maintained that those who made such denunciations were the same people who had caused many of Ghana's current problems.[18]

The question of corruption stood at the center of Rawlings's interpretation of Ghana's political and economic troubles. As Rawlings outlined in January 1982, corruption had become "so pervasive and deep-seated" that the country had little hope for being able to operate properly, "let alone ... change," without its "elimination." Accordingly, he asserted that its persistence and the inhospitable political, social, and economic environment it created weakened Ghana by restraining the country's "reservoir of talent and intellect."[19] A little over a year later during Ghana's twenty-sixth anniversary celebrations, Rawlings, likewise, reflected on what he saw as having been lost during Ghana's first quarter-century of self-rule. "I am sure that the earlier fighters for freedom," he explained, "did not seek to replace colonialism with political and economic irresponsibility, moral decay, and a spiritual blackout. There is no doubt that they realised the potential of the people of this country." Many governments had attempted to "put Ghana back on track and realise those aspirations of our fore-runners." However, he continued, all had failed until the AFRC and then the December 31st Revolution. What distinguished the Rawlings-era revolution from those of its predecessors, the Ghanaian head of state proposed, was its attempted restructuring of the people's relationship to the state.[20]

At the center of this re-envisioned civic relationship were so-called People's Defence Committees (PDCs) and Workers' Defence Committees (WDCs)[21]—later renamed "Committees for the Defence of the Revolution." According to Zaya Yeebo—a member of the leftist June 4th Movement (JFM) and, for a time, a minister in the PNDC—the P/WDCs had their origins in the September 1981 issue of the JFM's mouthpiece, the *Workers Banner*, where the JFM rejected the productivity pushes of Ghana's previous governments. Instead, the JFM asserted that Ghana's future prosperity would "be decided principally by who effectively wields state power."[22] As outlined in the *Workers Banner*, the path forward thus necessitated the formation of small citizens' committees populating nearly every aspect of Ghanaian civic life. Through these committees, Ghanaians would be able to "debate national issues and take decisions affecting the lives of the ordinary people." The committees were therefore to "represent the highest form of democracy—grassroots democracy—because through them all the people will participate in taking vital decisions and in running the country."[23]

In the creation of the P/WDCs, the PNDC government, at least rhetorically, adopted the JFM's emphasis on the centrality of direct or "grassroots" democracy to the revolution. As political scientist Paul Nugent has described, part of the emphasis on direct democracy stemmed from a general distrust of other democratic models, including parliamentary and electoral, which tended to promote oligarchic power.[24] Speaking in late 1983, for instance, Rawlings sought to historicize the power inequities embedded in representative forms of democratic governance. In doing so, he linked these inequities to colonial-era tendencies toward governmental centralization. In both the colonial and postcolonial eras, the Gold Coast's and Ghana's governments betrayed their civic obligations by wresting decision-making authority away from the populace and thus alienating the people from their government. The effects of such a tendency, Rawlings recounted, were wide-ranging as, in the case of Ghana's rural–urban divide, it encouraged rural Ghanaians to leave their homes and communities for the real and perceived benefits of greater access to the locus of Ghanaian political and economic power— its cities.[25]

The P/WDCs were thus to provide a practical and conceptual alternative to the imported and, one could argue, imposed representative democratic models of Ghana's recent past. In practice, though, the operations of the defense committees proved more complicated. The ease by which communities, workplaces, and other entities could form P/WDCs meant that the number of defense committees grew rapidly during the 1980s. In Accra alone, more than 1,200 P/WDCs dotted the city by the end of 1982, according to Mike Oquaye. By 1988, Oquaye similarly highlighted that the nationwide number had exceeded 10,000.[26] Meanwhile, in the P/WDCs' operations, the PNDC ceded to the defense committees a wide-ranging mandate with both delineated and undelineated powers. For instance, in taking up the revolutionary call of stabilizing the national economy, the defense committees promoted the collective initiatives of several communal labor projects, including communal farming. As Nugent notes, in rural communities, the revenue garnered through the sale of communally produced goods funded local infrastructure projects like the construction and maintenance of healthcare centers and schools. Nugent also explains that the defense committees offered an alternative to what many in the PNDC perceived to be Ghana's flawed bureaucratic state, with its history of red tape and both petty and systemic corruption.[27]

In addition to its economic and (anti)-bureaucratic objectives, Ghana's defense committees aimed to oversee Ghanaians' maintenance of the revolutionary ideals. In doing so, some P/WDCs took on an extra-judicial role, policing and punishing citizens for their failures to uphold a respective defense committee's interpretation of what it meant to live a revolutionary life. As anthropologist Deborah Pellow depicted in 1983, the result was often a culture of fear and reporting in many communities. "While the PDC activists did not carry guns," Pellow reported, "many people feared them, because they went on rampage as a group, acting on vague rumors that those in power had stolen from them in times past."[28] Oquaye, meanwhile, reflected on a nihilistic attitude among many associated with P/WDCs.[29] For Oquaye, the most dangerous consequence of the defense committees, though, was their "dichotomisation of the society into friends and enemies." What emerged, at least in his interpretation, was a binary marked by "a pantheon of saints (PDCs and people) and devils (citizens)." Key to this binary was thus a political and social environment that allowed for the physical abuse of those deemed insufficiently revolutionary and the cultivation of a simmering, constant fear.[30]

Drought, Fire, and Environmental Crisis

The challenges facing Ghana that the PNDC aimed to rectify were long-standing and familiar. As noted, at the core of the Rawlings government's justifications for the December 31st coup was the Limann government's real and perceived corruption and incompetence. If the 1979 revolution was to "clean house" and make way for a new civilian government, the 1981 coup was a concession to how deep-rooted the issues plaguing Ghana's political and economic landscape appeared to be. As Rawlings explained in a July 1982 broadcast, the expectation following the 1979 transfer of power was that the new civilian government would "bring some measure of sanity into the economy." The to-do list the AFRC provided Limann was long and complicated: "check inflation, balance our budget, reduce our public debts, both domestic and foreign, bring prices down to the level at which the mass of our people can afford, reduce our balance of payments, deficits and end the rampant speculation and the general privatisation of government property and the political corruption and moral decay which prevailed in the country." As Rawlings would argue during the broadcast, not only had the Limann government failed to rein in many of these threats to Ghanaians' economic wellbeing, but, in many cases, it had further exacerbated Ghana's problems as it oversaw a country with closed credit lines, decreasing levels of productivity in key industries, and food shortages.[31] A year later, the World Bank painted a similarly dim picture of the Ghanaian economic situation. Outlining Ghana's travails, one report unequivocally described the situation since 1980 as "a bad situation [that] has become critical."[32]

On the ground, meanwhile, Ghanaians continued to feel the pressures of nearly two decades of tumult. In the early 1980s, environmental concerns induced additional stresses on Ghanaian life as seasonal rains failed throughout much of the country, leading to drought and the collapse of many food crops. Like much of the West African savanna, Ghana's northernmost regions have historically proven particularly susceptible to the dangers of irregular rainfalls. As historian Holger Weiss has outlined, during the early twentieth century, concerns over periodic droughts and food shortages featured prominently in colonial reflections on the Gold Coast's Northern Territories.[33] Irregular rainfall patterns returned at various times during the 1940s and 1950s, with their concomitant food insecurity and higher prices.[34] However, periodic rainfall shortages have not been the purview of the north alone, with Accra receiving just over a third of its expected rainfall in 1926. Its rainfall numbers were nearly as bad in 1920 and 1946 respectively. Even the Gold Coast's southwest—the colony's rainiest region—endured occasional droughts. For instance, in 1919 and 1920, the coastal town of Axim received only 66 percent and 75 percent of its expected annual rainfall.[35]

As discussed in the previous chapter, favorable weather conditions during the early 1970s helped to catalyze many of the initial successes of the Acheampong government's marquee agricultural program, Operation Feed Yourself. By the mid- to late 1970s, those conditions had largely shifted. In the country's two geographical extremes of Navrongo and Accra, for example, both localities suffered from significantly reduced rainfall numbers, with Navrongo receiving only about 80 percent of its normal rainfall totals during 1975 and Accra 70 percent. Axim, for its part, received just under 90 percent. Looking at northern and southern Ghana more broadly, geographer E. Ofori-Sarpong notes, deficits of this magnitude were not anomalies. The effect was often severe reductions in crop yields and, in the north in particular, contested reports of famine.[36]

The climatic situation during the early 1980s proved even more catastrophic. Beginning in 1981, rainfall levels began to decline not only in Ghana, but throughout much of Africa, with the West African Sahel coming to endure some of the worst of the impending drought. For instance, as the drought peaked in countries like Mauritania and Mali in 1982 and 1983, the water shortage left nomadic families reeling, killing off their cattle and stripping them of their wealth. Attempting to flee the devastation, many became refugees further south.[37] By mid-decade, even the region's most prominent river—the Niger—flowed at, according to one commentator, "little more than a trickle."[38] Other regional rivers faced a similar fate, transforming the region's social and economic life.[39] Outside the West African Sahel, Ethiopia joined the Sahel as the international face of the continent's drought as a devastating famine struck the northeast African country, with estimates of up to half-a-million dead.[40] Further south, much of eastern and southern Africa also faced rainfall shortages during the period.[41]

In Ghana, 1981 saw rainfall shortages in all administrative regions, with much of the country receiving approximately 20–30 percent less precipitation than normal.[42] During the following year, conditions continued to deteriorate as nearly the entirety of the country suffered from a lack of rain. Among the worst-hit parts of the country was the central forests, where Kumasi received just 60 percent of its expected rainfall and Ejura 71 percent.[43] The country's rainfall bottomed out in 1983. Of the sixteen weather stations examined by Ofori-Sarpong, only one—Kete-Krachi—reported more than 70 percent of its anticipated rainfall. Meanwhile, coastal cities experienced some of the lowest rainfall levels. Takoradi, for its part, received just 39 percent of its average—the lowest of the stations surveyed by Ofori-Sarpong—and Accra 42 percent. Further north, the situation was only slightly better as each of the central forest stations recorded deficits of 60–70 percent, on par with those of Ghana's extreme north and east.[44] In addition to low rainfall totals, the rain that did come proved erratically timed. In one of the most extreme examples—Bole in contemporary Ghana's Savannah Region—the city's residents endured approximately 50 percent less rainfall than expected in July and August, which, with September, represented the height of the area's rainy season. However, in December, as the city's residents prepared for the Harmattan, the skies opened and the city reported more than 4.5 times the rainfall expected for the month.[45]

Agricultural production declined precipitously due to the drought. In some regions, major crops in 1983 yielded just half of what they did during the previous year. More broadly, plantain production suffered the most among Ghana's major food crops during the 1983 growing season, yielding just 23 percent of the crop it did in 1982. Compared to a decade earlier, agricultural production of food crops during 1983 equaled just 64 percent of those at the outset of OFY in 1972. Similarly, prices for food crops soared between 1982 and 1983, with the cost of maize more than tripling and cassava more than doubling. Rice, sorghum, and yams all almost doubled in price as well.[46] Likewise, Gwendolyn Mikell reports that Ghanaians with livestock and poultry struggled to keep their animals alive. Moreover, even some wealthy city-dwellers, she notes, found it difficult to meet their nutritional needs during the drought.[47] In fact, a general tendency toward relatively steadier food supplies in certain rural areas led some urban-dwellers to send their children to stay with extended families.[48] However, even in rural areas, a lack of adequate nutrition resulted in threats of *kwashiorkor* and emigration out of other rural communities as Ghanaians searched for greater food security.[49] Meanwhile, those who could turned to bushmeat and wild plants for their nutritional needs, which they combined with mixed farming techniques.[50]

Accompanying the drought not only in Ghana, but also in neighboring countries including Togo and Côte d'Ivoire, was an outbreak of bush fires that ravaged communities, farms, and the countryside. In the case of one rice farm near Kintampo, one farming association lost nearly 90 percent of its 80.9-hectare farm.[51] In another instance, the *People's Daily Graphic* reported on a bush fire that destroyed half of a 500-hectare rubber plantation in Akyem Manso. The same report noted another Eastern Region community that suffered the loss of ten cocoa farms to bush fires and another community endured the destruction of an educational facility.[52] Just north of Kumasi, another set of fires destroyed 30,000 tons of cocoa. As the *People's Daily Graphic* also noted, this area additionally provided much of the food consumed by Kumasi's residents. Many of those affected in turn decided to harvest early out of fear that their crops would rot, while also asking the government to provide relief in the form of food, farming implements, fertilizer, and seedlings in order to "save the people from the threat of famine."[53] Nearly simultaneously, bush fires to the west in the Sefwi-Wiawso district similarly threatened food supplies on their way to coastal markets as the fires burned down three bridges in the area.[54]

In addition to their prevalence, what distinguished 1983's bush fires from previous fires was how they transcended the country's climatic zones. In specific, one United Nations Food and Agriculture Organization report emphasized, the combination of extensive drought and wind during that year's Harmattan created a set of conditions that uniquely opened Ghana's tropical zones to such devastation.[55] In the state-controlled press, the government and others in positions of authority responded to the fires by blaming farmers for the blazes through the farmers' use of fire to help clear fields for agricultural production, a practice widely utilized in West Africa.[56] Isolating out the Talensi in contemporary Ghana's Upper East Region, for instance, one *People's Daily Graphic* column seemingly blamed Talensi chiefs for continuing to propagate the idea that the annual bush burning was a customary practice necessary to pay respect to Talensi gods. "Whether it [bush burning] is a custom or a necessary farming process," the newspaper argued, "the indiscriminate aspect of it is now one of the worst social habits of the people." Moreover, the newspaper continued, it was "responsible for the fast deterioration of all the renewable natural resources—the soil, water, natural vegetation, and wildlife—in Ghana."[57]

Other columns, reports, and editorials in the *People's Daily Graphic* struck a similar tone. Writing in February 1983, journalist P. Ossei-Wusu, likewise, lamented the vast destruction caused by the fires, while emphasizing what he characterized as the human-made nature of the devastation. "It must be pointed out," Ossei-Wusu argued, "that bush fires can be started by natural phenomena such as lightening [*sic*]. But human beings are undoubtedly the chief culprits. Lightening [*sic*] occurs only during the rainy season whilst all major fire outbreaks occur in the dry season." Accidents may have been the cause of many fires, he conceded. However, he also claimed that many Ghanaians, out of jealousy for others' successes, purposefully started many of the destructive fires. Among other groups, Ossei-Wusu isolated out the P/WDCs as playing a leading role in helping educate the population about the dangers of fire.[58] In a similar vein, another *People's Daily Graphic* column, while reporting on suspected arson on five oil palm plantations, acknowledged the utility of bush burning as an agricultural practice. However, the *People's Daily Graphic* suggested that, given the extent of the devastation during the first half of 1983, something was amiss. As interpreted

Figure 8.1 Truckloads of Ghanaian refugees expelled by Nigeria as illegal aliens cross the Nigeria–Benin border at Seme, Nigeria, January 1983.

by the newspaper, many of the fires were most likely the work of those aiming to thwart the revolution. Much like Ossei-Wusu, the newspaper's editors thus called upon the P/WDCs to help remedy the situation. In this case, though, they demanded the P/WDCs take on a law enforcement role by helping "bring to book people who cause bush fires indiscriminately."[59]

"Ghana Go Home"[60]

In January 1983, the Nigerian government exacerbated the pain in Ghana caused by drought, bush fires, and accompanying food shortages as it announced the expulsion of an estimated two- to three-million individuals living and working in Nigeria illegally, an estimated million of whom were Ghanaian.[61] Over the previous decade, Nigeria's oil boom had transformed the West African state, which, just years earlier, had represented to the international community the political and economic turmoil of the African postcolonial state.[62] As the oil boom took hold during the mid-1970s and buoyed by the free-movement provisions of the recently created Economic Community of West African States (ECOWAS), large numbers of West African migrants entered Nigeria in search of work and economic security. Among Ghanaians in particular during the early 1980s, its West African neighbor represented a future of wealth and luxury. Juxtaposing the then current state of Ghana with that of Nigeria, future Ghanaian president John Dramani Mahama, who moved to Nigeria after his father's 1982 exile from Ghana, wrote in his memoir of a Nigeria glistening with modern and impressive infrastructure, shops with well-stocked shelves, and new cars. He compared this to the barren shelves and "rickety" cars that marked a Ghana that "had hit rock bottom." As a result, Mahama matter-of-factly declared that, by the early 1980s, Ghana's decay had led many to "vote[] with their feet and [leave] the country ... [taking] along ... their talents."[63]

On January 17, 1983, when the Nigerian government announced the quit order, giving those illegally in the country two weeks to leave, the government's justifications for the order echoed those given by Kofi Busia's government more than a decade earlier. Like Busia's government, Shehu Shagari's Nigerian government cited crime and jobs as the key motivators for the order. As the Nigerian Minister of Internal Affairs Alhaji Ali Baba explained while unveiling the order, the Nigerian government—like all governments—had a responsibility to protect the interests and security of its citizenry. As a result, it had no choice but to act on what it perceived to be the escalating number of non-Nigerians "found on our streets roaming about without any feasible means of livelihood."[64] Supporting the order, the Lagos-based *Daily Times* applauded the government's actions, arguing that "Unfortunately for Nigeria most citizens of the poverty-stricken ECOWAS nations see the 'oil-rich' Nigeria as a country whose land is flowing with milk and honey." As it continued, the newspaper's editorial team echoed the government by insisting that many, especially women, "had no decent and respectable means of livelihood" and therefore "contaminat[ed] the moral fabric of the Nigerian society."[65]

Meanwhile, inside Nigeria, the order came on the heels of public discontent connected to a turn in the country's economic fortunes. By the early 1980s, the widespread prosperity that had marked the oil boom of the mid-1970s had begun to wane, with the international price of oil weakening considerably by the decade's end. It would continue to fall through the mid-1980s.[66] To this end, nearly simultaneously with the announcement of the quit order, officials in the Nigerian business community were promising the public that "We Can Survive Recession."[67] What Nigeria's weakening economic situation would mean for Nigerians was therefore a seemingly sudden contraction of government spending, rapidly increasing public debt, and, in 1982, the introduction of austerity measures.[68] The result was rising inflation and joblessness, leading many to strike, smuggle goods out of Nigeria, and demand delinquent payments from the government for work completed.[69]

At the same time, a series of violent religious riots broke out in Nigeria's north. The most prominent episode occurred in Kano in late December 1980. Associated with a Cameroonian mallam named Marwa, the so-called Maitatsine riots killed at least 5,000 people.[70] Marwa's Cameroonian origins, as well as the perception that non-Nigerians dominated the movement, helped buttress anti-immigrant sentiments.[71] Such feelings spread as subsequent riots swept through several other northern Nigerian localities. The government, for its part, aimed to take advantage of these sentiments, with Alhaji Ali Baba referencing them in both his initial announcement of the quit order and again on February 14th.[72] Speaking in his February 14th address, the minister emphasized that "the central figure in these violent religious episodes, Maitatsine, was an alien." For this reason, Alhaji Ali Baba argued that the government had to act. "No responsible government," he asserted, "can fold its arms and allow such [an] unwholesome development to plague the Nation; hence the decision to require illegal aliens to leave the country within 14 days."[73] Accompanying this violence, many southern cities were also beset with rising crime rates, which both the Nigerian public and government tended to attribute to non-Nigerians.[74]

Just as it had been for the West Africans expelled from Ghana in 1969, the Nigerian quit order almost overnight upended people's lives as they prepared to leave their homes and return to their respective countries. The situation for Ghanaians in Nigeria proved particularly fraught. By far the largest number of those ordered to leave, Ghanaians faced an array of political and logistical hurdles during their exodus. At the most basic level, Ghanaians returning via land encountered closed borders. Long-standing political tensions between Ghana and Togo had regularly resulted in border closures. On the Ghanaian side, concerns over smuggling and political subversion had precipitated many of these closures, with numerous Ghanaian governments dating back to Nkrumah's fearing that Togo had become a safe haven for dissidents. However, of even more immediate concern when Rawlings announced the border's closure in September 1982 were concerns over smuggling.[75] Yet, for the Ghanaian refugees attempting to return, the border closures not only blocked their access to Ghana, but also created a bottleneck along the region's other frontiers as the governments of Togo and Benin closed their borders as well to stem the tide of refugees returning through their countries. In doing so, they argued that it would be improper to keep their borders open to Ghanaians travelling through if the Ghanaian government could not guarantee the refugees would be let into Ghana.[76]

The effect on Ghanaians seeking to cross the land borders of these West African countries was harrowing. For nearly two weeks, refugees seeking to return to Ghana congregated at the frontiers awaiting permission to move, garnering international attention. As political scientist Olajide Aluko has outlined, the international press was scathing in its response to the emerging crisis as newspapers and magazines in Great Britain, the USA, France, and Germany, to name a few, accused the Nigerian government of creating a humanitarian disaster.[77] The Nigerian government, through Alhaji Ali Baba, responded by denouncing the Western media coverage as imperialist and in turn presenting the coverage as illegitimate and wrongheaded. Likewise, the Nigerian government argued that the humanitarian crisis developing along the West African frontiers could be easily rectified if the Ghanaian government would simply open its land borders.[78] Ghanaian refugees, meanwhile, faced an uncertain voyage marked by fears of possible extortion, xenophobic harassment, illness, and a loss of personal and economic security. As the *People's Daily Graphic* reported, among the first returnees to arrive back in the country, nearly three-dozen suffered from an array of illnesses and most exhaustion.[79] One man, speaking to the newspaper, explained that, for Ghanaians in Nigeria, the distinction between living legally and illegally did not matter, for all Ghanaians endured threats of robbery and physical violence. Even after leaving Nigeria, he recounted, Ghanaians were not safe as he recalled beatings by Togolese soldiers and the deaths of "at least three of our people."[80]

The Ghanaian government's response to the developing crisis tied the re-integration process into its revolutionary discourse. For their part, Rawlings and parts of the Ghanaian press characterized the expulsion as an attempt to destabilize the PNDC government, noting the previously cordial relations between Shagari and Limann.[81] At the same time, the press and the government developed a concerted campaign to prepare the public for the impending arrivals. For instance, in one highly nuanced *People's Daily Graphic* column, journalist George Yankah provided the newspaper's readers with a concise history of Ghanaians' recent migrations to Nigeria. Emphasizing both Ghana's recent economic troubles and the relative prosperity coming from Nigeria's oil boom, Yankah juxtaposed the sense of possibility and accomplishment that turned the "trickles" into "a flood" of Ghanaian migrants during the late 1970s with the loss, uncertainty, and havoc in Ghana caused by those who left. In doing so, he recounted tales of teachers and other professionals who left their jobs without notice. He even accused some teachers of having family members collect their wages after leaving. Despite these harms and lingering hard feelings, as Yankah's headline "Countrymen, Welcome" indicates, the journalist utilized his column to call for an orderly process welcoming the returnees back into Ghanaian life. "There is no place like home," he concluded, "however bad it is." Yet, he added, the path forward must entail a plan for "the home-comers ... [to] contribute their quota to the struggle for national reconstruction."[82]

The government largely echoed Yankah in its rhetorical response to the emerging refugee crisis. Speaking, for instance, in Kumasi in January 1983, Rawlings openly welcomed Ghana's returnees home while asking the country's chiefs for assistance in their resettlement. In his request, he encouraged the chiefs to provide those returning with land "so that they can contribute their quota to the development of the country."[83] Likewise, in early February, the PNDC instructed the Ministry of Labour and Social Welfare to turn its attention to the anticipated unemployment emergency caused by the quit order while echoing Rawlings's language that such efforts were essential to the advancement of the December 31st Revolution.[84] One official in Brong Ahafo was even bolder as he presented the "rehabilitation of deportees ... as a national obligation." For him, like Rawlings, a return to the land and specifically farming proved key to the returnees' successful re-integration into Ghanaian society.[85]

The focus on agriculture served multiple purposes. The fears of urban unemployment that had long troubled Gold Coast/Ghanaian governments not only arose again, but, as the instructions to the Ministry of Labour and Social Welfare suggest, intensified at the prospect of an estimated million Ghanaians returning home over a fortnight. In his column, Yankah relatively bluntly suggested that the returnees should not expect a place for themselves in the country's cities, for severe shortages of work and goods already plagued these locales. For those with rural roots, Yankah was frank; they were not welcome in Ghana's cities. Not only would they cause "congestion," he speculated, but they could also turn the revolutionary clock backwards to a time when "day-light robberies, pick-pocketing and bag snatching were common features in the cities."[86] In this respect, Yankah seemingly accepted the Shagari government's justifications for the quit order by casting at least some of Ghana's returnees as criminals. However, in the case of the Ghanaian professionals returning, Yankah was similarly ambivalent as to where they should end up. Most notably, his ambivalence is exemplified in the time he spent in his column detailing how, in his view, these individuals had previously used their privileged positions to abandon and weaken Ghana. For this reason, he questioned the extent to which the government should help secure employment for these returnees, with many, if not most, presumably aiming to return to Ghana's cities. Yankah did all this while still premising his piece on the belief that Ghanaians should welcome the returnees home so that they could commit themselves to the revolutionary cause.[87]

In another forum published in early February, the *People's Daily Graphic* added to Yankah's skepticism about the potential for the returnees' urban resettlement. "For deportees to swarm towns and cities," Egya Kwamena-Johnson argued in the newspaper's "Farmers' Forum," "would simply mean nothing but perpetuation of the suffering they went through. A deportee may gain a salaried job in town, but to secure one's food and better life by getting involved in farming is much better. We cannot eat money."[88] Underpinning Kwamena-Johnson's analysis was what he described as Ghana's "twin problem" of unemployment and food shortages. A commitment to integrating the returnees into the agricultural sector promised to alleviate both problems, the columnist predicted. Foremost, he noted, farmers in the south had spent the previous few years complaining about a labor shortage. As such, he asserted, "These farmers should hire as many deportees as they can. And the deportees should allow themselves to be hired, at least as an immediate temporary measure." Moreover, Kwamena-Johnson advised, in an environment where there were not many options available to people, agricultural labor provided one of the clearest pathways to eventual self-employment.[89]

Both Yankah's and Kwamena-Johnson's arguments tended to align with the government's own prioritization of agricultural labor, care for the environment, and productivity in the midst of Ghana's growing food emergency. In a late February speech in the Western Region town of Agona Swedru, Rawlings acknowledged the crisis developing in the country. In doing so, he positioned Ghana's declining food production alongside the need to feed what he initially estimated to be up to one-and-a-half million additional mouths and a set of consumer habits that, according to him, privileged indulgences (e.g. "fashion dresses, lip sticks, new watches, hats, [and] nice scented soaps") over national necessities (tractors, farming implements, and school books).[90] In this particular speech, one directed at an audience composed of supporters of the Ghana Federation of Agricultural Cooperatives, Rawlings praised the cooperative model of farming by arguing that it helped to re-orient people's base, individualistic interests toward the collective good.[91] Meanwhile, in another speech given on December 30, 1983 at the University of Ghana, Rawlings emphasized the centrality of the environment to the December 31st Revolution. Many of Ghana's current problems, he announced, stemmed from what he described as Ghanaians' lack of respect for the environment as individuals purportedly pursued "selfish and corrupt" interests and thus left the environment to be "thoughtlessly exploited." Key to the revolution's success then, Rawlings exhorted, was the quest for "harmony" in humankind's relationship with the natural world. This quest fundamentally entailed centering the health of the land and environment in the country's productive and specifically agricultural advancement.[92]

Ghana's returnees had a clear role to play in Rawlings's and the PNDC's envisioned agricultural and environmental renaissance. Throughout the first half of 1983, numerous newspaper reports highlighted the returnees' integration into the Rawlings-era nation-building agenda. Among the so-called returnee rehabilitation projects celebrated by newspapers like the *People's Daily Graphic* were those of 400 resettled Ghanaians in the Eastern Region town of Akyem Tafo who engaged in several building and road construction projects designed to make food more accessible. As one of the spokespeople for the returnees stressed to the newspaper, those involved were simply "using their skills for the development of the area."[93] In another story, the *People's Daily Graphic* touted the efforts of another 100 returnees engaged in a communal labor project in Akyem Manso—another Eastern Region town—where returnees cleared land and cared for the town's sanitation needs. In addition, the returnees operated a three-hectare maize farm. The returnees had even grander ambitions for this farm, one of the resettled Ghanaians implied as he asserted that only a shortage of seed limited the farm's growth.[94] Other reports promoted the returnees' contributions to fishing, the excavation of riverbeds for sources of water, and a whole range of farming activities.[95]

The government's and press's efforts to celebrate the returnees' contributions to the PNDC's envisioned revolutionary project, however, did not quell the anger and frustration created by the Nigerian quit order as the broader public contemplated the effects of the massive resettlement effort on their own daily lives. In the initial stages of the resettlement, some called for retribution against the Nigerian government. This included demands that the Ghanaian government announce the expulsion of non-Ghanaians living in Ghana. According to one individual writing into the *People's Daily Graphic* from the Apam Secondary School, such an action was a national imperative "because we cannot continue to feed other nationals plus ourselves."[96] In terms similar to Yankah discussed earlier, this letter-writer and others also accused the returnees of criminal activities and long-maligned anti-consumerist activities like smuggling.[97] Periodic reports in the press of such behaviors likely buttressed these sentiments.[98] Others, meanwhile, looked to the government and international aid earmarked for the returnees and demanded that the aid be distributed equally among all Ghanaians regardless of returnee status. One Volta Region letter-writer was even more blunt about what he saw as the unfairness of the situation. From his perspective, it was "quite unjustified" to reserve this aid for those who had abandoned the country during hard times.[99]

Economic Recovery and the Dawn of Ghanaian Neoliberalism

By the end of 1983, the intersecting challenges of drought, bush fires, and the Nigerian quit order had added a deeper sense of urgency to what Rawlings and his government recognized as an already critical situation. In their rhetoric, Rawlings, the PNDC, and the Ghanaian press thus continued to advance a language of self-sufficiency in their sketches of Ghana's path toward political and economic stability, if not prosperity. Touting both the actions of returnees engaged in self-help and other productive enterprises, along with the foresight of the PNDC government in the creation of the P/WDCs, the *People's Daily Graphic* insisted that even more needed to be done to mobilize the population. "There are young people who are genuinely interested in farming or in some other productive ventures," the newspaper's editors argued. The fortunate among them had access to land; however, the editors insinuated, that would not be enough. Rather, success depended on greater governmental investment to connect a populace ready to serve Ghana with the resources needed to do so. "Abundant labour is ready to be organised," the *People's Daily Graphic* asserted, "and no time could be better than now."[100]

In the eyes of the government, the democratic decentralization that had marked the creation of the P/WDCs provided the clearest path forward. Not only did it theoretically promise to bring everyday decision-making to the citizenry, it also aligned closely with the developing values of a changing international political economy. At the heart of this new political economy was a focus on an ever-more limited role for government in both the people's and the state's economic life. As historian Frank Gerits has outlined, Ghana's economic thinkers adapted to this emerging reality with an economic program that emphasized what Gerits calls "anticolonial capitalism." As he detailed, this idea of anticolonial capitalism continued to allow Rawlings and the PNDC to project themselves and the Ghanaian state as a whole as vehemently anticolonial—radicals set on continuing to advance the seemingly stalled project of complete African independence.[101] For his part, Rawlings exemplified this anti-imperial mode of political presentation as he continuously invoked the language of anticolonialism in his critiques of the international community.[102] What distinguished Rawlings and the PNDC from much of the previous generation of African radicals, including Nkrumah, Julius Nyerere, and Sékou Touré, if one extrapolates from Gerits's work, was their ambivalence toward a socialist worldview. Instead, Rawlings-era development and, most importantly, the PNDC's attempts to break the cycle of Ghanaian economic upheaval centered on an embrace of the market-oriented economics of the emergent neoliberal capitalist system.[103]

The international shift from state-centered development economics, which in leftist states took shape in the language of socialism and in the West in the deficit-spending of Keynesian economics, to the celebration of the decentralized market destabilized the economic models of multiple generations of economic thinkers in both the Global South and North. Developing out of an intellectual tradition tied to the so-called Chicago and Austrian schools of economics, this market-based political economy found its initial foothold in Latin America during the 1970s.[104] Reaganism's and Thatcherism's ascent in the 1980s not only helped legitimize the neoliberal economic vision, but also helped transform it into what would become the foundational global economic ideology of the next three-plus decades.[105] At its core, neoliberalism gave moral authority to the power of the market, while maligning state intrusions into the ethereal decision-making process of markets themselves. In practice, for governments, this meant a multi-decade process of what economist David Harvey describes as "creative destruction." This destruction included the complicated tasks of governmental disinvestment in social services like healthcare and education, the removal of tariffs and other supposed impediments on the free market, the lowering of certain taxes, and the creation of new markets when and where they already did not exist.[106]

As Gerits argues in his discussion of anticolonial capitalism, Ghana's economic thinkers during the 1980s viewed market-based economics as a pathway out of the corruption that had marked the first decades of Ghanaian self-rule and away from the supposed failures of dependency theory in explaining the country's developmental stagnation.[107] In policy terms, the PNDC began shifting toward a market-based economic philosophy early within its tenure as the government's Minister of Finance and Economic Planning, Kwesi Botchwey, put the public on notice of a major shift in the government's economic planning on December 30, 1982. As Botchwey explained in a speech reproduced in parts over the course of a week in the *People's Daily Graphic*, the PNDC's new economic plan would bring to

Ghana a new commitment to efficiency, realism, and collaboration.[108] To this end, Botchwey catered to his audience by reassuring it that Ghanaians could take solace in knowing that many of their struggles were not Ghana-specific. Rather, they were universal and many even afflicted the presumed more developed countries of the Global North. What did strain Ghana uniquely, though, he continued, was a history of imbalance in the economy, which discouraged local production and incentivized a brain drain that depleted the country of its skilled labor. In rectifying these imbalances, Botchwey thus called for an economic re-alignment that—as would be common globally—promised reforms of Ghana's tax, banking, trade, budget, and insurance policies; the enactment of stricter regulations on state enterprises and the dismantling of some; the re-organization of the country's transportation sector; and the easing of regulatory constraints on the flow of capital.[109]

The budget that the government released in April 1983 thus unleashed the dramatic transformation of the Ghanaian economy that Botchwey had promised months earlier. Guided by pressures from the IMF and World Bank and promoted as an Economic Recovery Programme (ERP), the budget aimed to move away from deficits via greater fiscal discipline in government policies.[110] This was to begin with a focus on taxation, particularly in terms of who and what was taxed as well as the establishment of a more efficient system for tax collection. It also outlined changes to the country's income tax and rent tax structure. Likewise, trade policy saw the introduction of a surcharge and bonus system designed to, as framed by Nugent, stealthily weaken the cedi against the dollar without formally devaluing it.[111] In addition, the budget dropped many import duties, introduced a higher schedule for a number of government fees, and instituted a dramatic increase in healthcare costs. In the case of healthcare specifically, the costs of certain medical visits and procedures in turn rose ten to twenty times their earlier levels at their most extreme.[112] Additional new government receipts were to come from new surcharges on travel, private education, and oil consumption, among others. In total, Botchwey outlined a plan that the government predicted would nearly quadruple its year-end receipts over those of the previous year, with the country's cumulative receipts anticipated to lead to a balanced budget.[113]

As the budget went into effect, prices rose dramatically throughout the country and, despite its best efforts, the government still found it necessary to devalue the cedi in October 1983. Furthermore, when it did devalue it, it did so on a scale previously unseen as the cedi's strength against the dollar collapsed by more than 1,000 percent.[114] The government added to the currency uncertainty as it introduced new higher denomination bank notes in November. Recognizing the potential for public unease, the PNDC spent much of the month using the *People's Daily Graphic* to gain the public's confidence in the new notes.[115] Now pegged at GH¢30 to US$1, the cedi would weaken further over the course of the ERP, with the PNDC introducing currency auctions within the central bank. By the end of the decade, the cedi's value would ultimately collapse to GH¢289 to US$1, a more than 10,400 percent change from its 1983 fixed value.[116] Meanwhile, for most Ghanaians, the costs of key social services and utilities rose exponentially over the first years of the ERP, with the London-based magazine *West Africa* citing water and electricity prices rising 150 percent and "up to 1,000%" respectively.[117] Additionally, by 1990, the effects of economic neo-liberalization on labor relations had resulted in the loss of up to 150,000 jobs. By 1992, that number would rise to 200,000.[118] Despite these repercussions, Botchwey defended the ERP. He insisted that, given Ghana's economic state at the beginning of the program, the "only pragmatic questions" to be asked were what sacrifices needed to be made and how could they be targeted as much as possible to the "parasitic elements" of the economy.[119]

Conclusion

In 1986, as he released the PNDC's budget statement, Botchwey praised the PNDC government for the successful conclusion of the ERP's first phase. The next phase was to shift the ERP's priorities toward questions of reforms in the "social sectors, agriculture, and rural development." Moreover, he insisted that the governmental focus throughout this new phase could not waver. In fact, if anything, it had to intensify. In doing so, Botchwey called for the marshaling of "substantially increased resources through stepped-up revenue collection, the elimination of wasteful and unproductive public expenditure, and an incomes policy that not only provides incentives for work but also strikes the right balance between current consumption and investment, between what we consume today and what we save for development and growth in the future."[120] Later that year, Rawlings himself highlighted what he viewed as the ERP's successes during a broadcast on the fifth anniversary of the December 31st Revolution. In doing so, he cited a "seven-fold" increase in the price of cocoa under the PNDC, praised the government for its disciplined monetary policy, condemned corruption in certain areas of the government, and celebrated the PNDC's ability to successfully negotiate with the Bretton Woods institutions and other international organizations.[121]

Coming out of the crises of 1983, along with the almost two-decade-long period of political and economic instability that preceded them, it is difficult to argue that many of the ERP's macroeconomic achievements were not impressive. Among the key ambitions of the ERP was macroeconomic growth. By 1991, the Ghanaian economy averaged 5–6 percent growth per year, a number almost triple that of the rest of the continent.[122] It also led to a period between 1983 and 1993 in which the government produced a cumulative surplus.[123] Critics, however, noted the extreme costs of the economic retrenchment on the population and the public's dissatisfaction with it, combined with the PNDC's repressive practices.[124] Others argued that the government with its economic policy had all but abandoned those upon whose labor and wealth the country had long been built, namely its farmers. Speaking to this sentiment, historian and politician A. Adu Boahen emphasized the low prices paid to the country's cocoa farmers specifically—at least when compared to the international cocoa price—and the rapidly increasing costs of insecticides and farm machinery, rising 400 percent and 460 percent respectively. The foremost sin, according to Boahen, though, was the PNDC government's apparent abandonment of these farmers and their needs in favor of the anti-subsidy preferences of the World Bank, the IMF, and those who shared those institutions' economic worldview.[125] Meanwhile, as farmers, workers, and others endured the effects of Ghana's economic liberalization during the 1980s, an equally dramatic shift came to the country's politics in 1992 when the government accepted a referendum on a new constitution that would open the Ghanaian political sphere to competitive elections for the first time since 1979.

CONCLUSION:
THE CONTINGENT FUTURES OF GHANA'S
FOURTH REPUBLIC

In March 1992, on the eve of the thirty-fifth anniversary of Ghana's independence, Jerry John Rawlings explained to the public that Ghana was ready to begin the next phase of its political transformation. As he outlined for his audience, the December 31st Revolution was the catalyst of Ghana's transition to a "true democracy" as it opened the space for "the meaningful participation of all Ghanaians in the structures and practice of government."[1] In order to get to the point Ghana was at in March 1992, Rawlings advised, Ghana had to first stabilize its economy. The success of the ERP during the previous decade had thus opened up new possibilities for Ghana's political future according to the PNDC chairman. As a result, he announced a national referendum, which would take place in late April on a new constitution with a multi-party democracy as its cornerstone. To this end, Rawlings also reported that, by the end of May, political parties would again be legal. Even more importantly, he announced that presidential elections would take place on November 3rd and parliamentary elections on December 8th. The culmination of Ghana's transition to a multi-party democracy would be on January 7, 1993 as Ghanaians inaugurated the birth of the country's Fourth Republic.[2]

In the months following Rawlings's broadcast, a flurry of activity marked the Ghanaian political scene. On April 28th, Ghanaians overwhelmingly supported the referendum on the new constitution.[3] A little over a month later, on June 2nd, the Danquah–Busia Club—a politically focused organization founded a year earlier—launched the New Patriotic Party (NPP). Key among the NPP's founding objectives was a commitment to many of the pillars of the liberal democratic tradition: multi-party democracy; freedom of speech, religion, and association; and fidelity to the rule of law.[4] Shortly after the NPP's inauguration, on June 11th, a rally in Accra culminated in the formation of what would become Ghana's second major political party—the National Democratic Congress (NDC). History featured prominently in the event launching the NDC as the chairman of the party's organizing committee, Issifu Ali, emphasized Ghanaians' need to learn from the past as the country moved forward. Likewise, Ali—in an homage to the PNDC and the ERP—insisted on the need for Ghanaians to build upon the country's recent economic progress during its transition to the Fourth Republic. According to Ali, the NDC sought to be "for all Ghanaians who believed in setting a sound and sustainable economic and political agenda which is both pragmatic and realistic."[5] In August, the NPP would name the prominent University of Ghana historian A. Adu Boahen as its flagbearer in the upcoming presidential election, with the NDC naming Rawlings to the head of its ticket shortly thereafter.[6]

During the campaign, the two major parties built upon the priorities outlined in their founding. Newspaper advertisements for the NDC, for instance, celebrated the party's linkages to the PNDC, promoting the military government's achievements over its decade in power. "For the first time since we attained political independence as a Nation," one advert touted, "we have experienced a decade of uninterrupted common purpose, and we are all witnesses to what has been achieved."[7] Meanwhile, Kow Nkensen Arkaah, the NDC's vice-presidential candidate, evoked a deeper historical reference when campaigning for Rawlings and the party as he tied Rawlings's legacy to that of Kwame Nkrumah. According to Arkaah, who had helped found the Nkrumahist-influenced National Convention Party (NCP) that had recently allied with the NDC—"Chairman Rawlings was a true Nkrumahist." To buttress his arguably dubious claims of Rawlings's Nkrumahist predilections, Arkaah cited the recent construction of the Kwame Nkrumah Mausoleum in Accra. As such, Arkaah claimed that, as president, Rawlings would not align with "any group of people who were poised on destroying the achievement of Dr. Kwame Nkrumah."[8] Boahen and the NPP, for their part, emphasized the break with military governance in their presidential campaign.[9] In addition, the NPP sought to remind the Ghanaian public of the PNDC's history of state violence. In particular, one party advertisement addressed to Ghana's women rekindled the memory of the PNDC's treatment of market women during the Rawlings government's first years and, even more recently, the public canings of women that had occurred in 1991.[10]

On the day of the election, the *People's Daily Graphic* predicted a "massive turn-out."[11] The next day, the newspaper confirmed its prediction bore out as it reported on long queues forming as early as 4:00 and 5:00 a.m. in some polling sites. Despite the queues, the newspaper reported that the voting proceeded relatively smoothly, with only minor incidents and disruptions.[12] As the vote came in, Rawlings jumped to an early lead. By November 5th, as Boahen failed to close the gap, the *People's Daily Graphic* began contemplating the possibility that Rawlings might avoid a runoff.[13] The following day, the newspaper heralded Rawlings's victory.[14] The NPP, along with two other smaller parties, responded to the news with accusations of "widespread abuses, fraud and rigging of the election results." As evidence, they cited the discovery of ballots in Kumasi trash heaps. Further inflaming the post-election tensions, armed men disrupted the parties' press conference where they were announcing their objections to the results. The men then began arresting the parties' supporters. As recounted by the *People's Daily Graphic*, the supporters answered by "demand[ing] to be killed amid singing of party songs" before the men ultimately released them.[15]

The NDC's response to the opposing parties' accusations was one of incredulity. Rawlings, for his part, rejected the parties' allegations and called for them to join him in pursuit of a better Ghana.[16] Similarly, prominent editorials and columns in the *People's Daily Graphic* cited the confidence of international observers in the vote's results, thus insisting that, until proven otherwise via the legal system, the election should be considered valid. Failure to do so, one columnist suggested, could "plunge[] the country into a Liberian, Ethiopian, Somalian, Angolan, or Ugandan type of armed conflict" due to the actions of certain "misguided political activists."[17] Such calls, whether from Rawlings and the NDC or the press, would ultimately go unheeded as the opposing parties, led by the NPP, promised to boycott the following month's parliamentary elections. As the NPP would assert in a post-election report entitled *The Stolen Verdict*, the election was "a sorry tale ... in which virtually all known electoral offences were committed to ensure the success of the PNDC agenda—the transformation of Chairman Rawlings into President Rawlings." As a result, the NPP insisted that the election was at its core illegitimate, as would be any attempted democratic activity until "a level playing field" could be ensured.[18] In a similar vein, Adu Boahen, reflecting on the election in 1995, further added that it would have been irresponsible to accept the results if the "*Ghanaian public*" did not, just as it would have been foolish for the NPP to contest the parliamentary elections knowing that their results would also likely be rigged.[19]

As the major parties fought over the election results, tensions grew on the ground. Almost immediately after the election, the government instituted a curfew in Kumasi, a NPP stronghold.[20] On November 4th, policemen in Accra raided a NPP office, arresting three and shooting another.[21] Nearly a week later, the *People's Daily Graphic* reported on the abduction of a Takoradi NDC official, Alhaji Imoro Adam, from his shop in the Western Region city. Adam's abductors would beat him, pour petrol on him, and set him on fire. After the assault, Adam would lie in Accra's 37 Military Hospital in critical condition.[22] He would eventually die of his injuries in London.[23] Shortly after Adam's attack, the *People's Daily Graphic* published an article in which figures in the NDC and two allied parties—the NCP and the Egle Party—called for the arming of their members in order to protect themselves from the NPP's supporters. The parties' statement in support of this outfitting asserted that the violence that had followed the election was the result of "a small clique of desperate men in the NPP who want to plunge the country into chaos and civil war as a result of their defeat at the polls."[24] The next day, the NDC leadership denounced the newspaper's account of the statement, arguing that it had no previous knowledge of the call to arms.[25] By November 16th, with the post-election unrest still brewing, the government promised not to declare a state of emergency.[26]

As November came to an end, the Interim National Electoral Commission (INEC) announced that it planned to move the date of the parliamentary elections to December 22nd. At the same time, the government amended part of the Electoral Law so that individuals could stand as independent candidates.[27] In early December, the INEC again revised the date of the poll, moving it back to December 29th.[28] The changes had little effect on the NPP-led boycott. When the parliamentary elections occurred at the end of December, the NDC and its allies dominated. The NDC alone would control 190 of 200 seats, with candidates from its allied parties winning nearly all the remaining constituencies.[29] As 1992 turned into 1993, Rawlings opened the new year by declaring that the transition to the Fourth Republic would simply be a new phase in the revolution he started a decade earlier. "Continuity," he explained, however, "does not mean doing the same thing unchanged. To us, it means continuing a dynamic and logical process of change based on sound principle of social justice, responsibility, and respect for the basic rights of the moral, material, and spiritual growth of the people."[30] Just under a week later, Rawlings, dressed in Kente, ushered in the birth of Ghana's Fourth Republic. In his speech, he again tied the Fourth Republic to the successes of the December 31st Revolution.[31]

Neoliberal Openings and Closings

The Fourth Republic's inauguration in many ways marked both a break and a continuance in Ghana's modern history. At the political level, Rawlings's election represented the most clearcut continuity in Ghana's recent past. Rawlings would win re-election in 1996. Thus, when he left office in January 2001, he had completed just over nineteen years as Ghana's head of state, exceeding the fifteen years (1951–66) Nkrumah had served atop the Gold Coast/Ghanaian political system several decades earlier. Moreover, many of the political, economic, and social challenges that had long-afflicted the Gold Coast/Ghana would persist not only under Rawlings as president, but also his successors. Economically, inflation and unemployment—the most pervasive threats to Ghanaian economic well-being over the past century—would continue to frustrate the Ghanaian people and the country's economy for much of the next three decades. At the same time, among the most visible effects of the post-ERP neo-liberalization of the Ghanaian economy has been an ever-widening level of economic inequality in the country. In 2016, for instance, the *Review of African Political Economy* described Ghana as "The 'Rising Star' of Inequality" in Africa. In doing so, it juxtaposed the impressive macroeconomic successes of the previous two-plus decades with the large number of Ghanaians living on what was then less than GH¢8 per day (approximately US$2).[32]

Persistent questions surrounding the need for debt relief and currency depreciation have also plagued Ghana's Fourth Republic governments. In the first three decades of the Fourth Republic, Ghana's governments would on multiple occasions seek relief from the IMF and World Bank as fluctuations in the national and international macroeconomic climate threatened the country's economic stability. In 2001, for instance, as the NPP's John Agyeman Kufuor explained his government's decision to enter the IMF's and World Bank's Heavily Indebted Poor Countries (HIPC) Initiative, which aimed to alleviate qualifying countries' debt burdens, the then Ghanaian president bluntly asserted, "Man must be practical, so we took HIPC as a reality and must work to turn the situation round."[33] A little more than a decade later, in March 2014, John Dramani Mahama, who served as Ghana's president during one of the country's most devastating electricity shortages, cited increasing budget deficits, inflation, rising interest rates, and debt as threats to Ghana's economic future. Like Kufuor, Mahama contended that the government would have to make difficult choices to right the country's economy.[34] Three months later, the *Ghanaian Chronicle* announced: "Ghana Heads Back to HIPC."[35] Most recently, Nana Akufo-Addo's decision in 2022 to turn to the IMF in the midst of a rapidly escalating inflation crisis led to political upheaval, with traders, workers, activists, and others questioning the government's motives and competency.[36]

The economic challenges that have persisted during Ghana's neoliberal age are juxtaposed with the political changes ushered in by the Fourth Republic. By far, the most important achievement of the 1992 constitution has been the sense of democratic stability the Fourth Republic has instilled in Ghana's political system, breaking a decades-long cycle of military intervention in Ghanaian politics. As a result, since 1992, Ghana has successfully held seven additional multi-party elections, with multiple transfers of power between the NPP and NDC. Internationally, there are few things for which Ghana is more celebrated than this electoral stability. In early 2017, for instance, the Nigerian-British journalist, Onyekachi Wambu, described Ghana as the "exemplar of citizen democracy," a country whose successes were "defying entrenched notions of Africa's failures with democracy." Citing the democratic weaknesses of the USA following Donald Trump's 2016 electoral victory, Wambu argued that Western countries like the USA—the assumed global "democratic exemplar"—had a lot to learn from Ghana. What Ghana offered, according to Wambu, was an electoral system with established rules, a stable state ideology, and a "tamed" army. For him, the result was a context where the newly elected Nana Akufo-Addo could "talk about the citizen taking centre stage, with an attempt to again define and codify freedom and justice, and what it truly means to be a Ghanaian citizen."[37]

Others have been equally effusive in their praise of contemporary Ghana's democracy. Nearly a decade before Wambu, Canadian journalist Susan Mohammad described Ghana as "[a] beacon of democratic hope for Africa." This time contrasting the recent election of the NDC's John Atta Mills, who narrowly defeated Akufo-Addo, with the quality of democratic participation in Cameroon during that country's most recent election, Mohammad argued that Ghana stood apart from the "democratic pretenders" that surrounded it.[38] In a similar vein, the Senegalese journalist Adama Gaye expressed the hope that extended throughout the continent in a 2001 article celebrating John Agyekum Kufuor's election and, more importantly, Ghana's first peaceful transfer of power between its two major political parties. "Africa badly needs such victories," Gaye argued. In an era of significant upheaval throughout Africa, Gaye asserted, Rawlings built the path to this peaceful transfer of power as he understood "the changing times" of the early 1990s and, in Gaye's words, "fostered the growth of an honest opposition." As the Senegalese journalist closed his piece, though, he warned his readers that elections were not enough; the people needed to see the "dividends of democracy," for "[p]overty can only kill that hope."[39]

The economic challenges that have haunted Ghana's Fourth Republic and its seeming electoral stability do more than paint a Janus-faced picture of the country during the late twentieth and early twenty-first centuries. In fact, their relationship could be understood as reciprocal, feeding off each other as the Ghanaian state and populace negotiate Ghana's place in a post-Cold War world constructed around the celebration of the free market and the lore of the ballot box. What this post-Cold War world has excised from at least elite discussions of political economy has been the nuance of political and economic possibilities beyond the opening of markets and the quadrennial act of voting. Or, to reiterate Gaye's 2001 warning: "Poverty can only kill that [democratic] hope."[40] Back in the 1970s during the era of the National Redemption Council, I. K. Acheampong offered an even more blunt critique of the fetishization of the ballot box. For him, the preoccupation with the ballot box often came at the expense of governmental and international commitments to ensuring people had enough to survive. As noted in Chapter 7, he went so far as to even ridicule the idea of "One Man One Vote." Alternatively, he declared an adherence to the principle of "One Man One Bread."[41]

Acheampong was clearly no democrat, nor should his government be held as a model of good governance, human rights, or most forms of popular participation. But what Acheampong recognized—and Rawlings in different ways a decade later—was the shallowness of an imported, Western-oriented democratic model that minimized the necessity of structural transformation in addressing the immediate needs of the Ghanaian populace. Rawlings, in theory and—to an extent—in action, went even further than Acheampong with his vision of a people's democracy in the immediate aftermath of the 1981 coup. Pushed even more systematically by the June 4th Movement, this idea of a people's democracy sought to center the material wants and needs of the populace over what many construed as the performative political abstractions of Western democratic models. Even before Rawlings and Acheampong, Nkrumah grappled with similar tensions as he, the Convention People's Party, and many African anticolonial radicals of his generation promoted ideas of one-party democracy in Ghana and Africa more broadly. Nkrumah's and his government's frustrations with the parliamentary system Ghana adopted at independence began early in Ghana's post-independence history as numerous party- and state-run publications sought to articulate not only the perceived limitations of multi-party democracy in an African postcolonial setting, but, even more importantly, the possibilities of other models.[42] To further ground such arguments, some in Nkrumah's government advocated for Ghana's *asafo* companies to serve as more culturally organic democratic models for the future, while others, echoing the socialist rhetoric of the state, promoted an idea of democracy presented as a "dictatorship of the proletariat over the bourgeoisie."[43]

At the core of this reflection on the political alternatives offered by Nkrumah, Acheampong, and Rawlings is not an argument that any of these figures, nor their governments, offered truer or better democratic models than those of the contemporary moment. As Abena Ampofoa Asare has meticulously detailed, Ghana's postcolonial history is littered with the abuses of all of Ghana's mid- to late twentieth-century governments—abuses that more than anything highlight the gap between these governments' rhetoric and their actions.[44] However, their political experiments—and arguably even those of the governments of Kofi Busia and the National Liberation Council—in rethinking the structure of political and economic development offer a lens into deeper meditations on how to make sense of what Ghana was/is. Central to any reflection on Ghana itself is the country's position in an international community built from the realities and legacies of the Atlantic slave trade and European colonialism. As discussed in this book's first chapter, the idea of the Gold Coast itself, which, at independence, became Ghana, had its origins in the perspectival geographic shift from the African interior to the Atlantic. This shift, while never complete, re-oriented the people and region toward an emergent international sphere increasingly defined by the extractive values of European capitalism. Continentwide, this process—as scholars ranging from W. E. B. Du Bois to Walter Rodney to, most recently, Howard French, among others have shown—is at the center of the creation of the modern world.[45]

In Ghana, as elsewhere, the construction of the modern world of the past five centuries introduced new values, religions, systems of governance and trade, and much more. It was not a totalizing experience and most people selectively adapted many of these new features to their lives as they saw fit. However, global power relations shifted over these centuries as well, gradually closing off possibilities and opportunities for many throughout what would become Ghana as it would for others throughout Africa. Through personal and collective innovation, many responded with a creative array of direct and indirect attacks on the systems, values, beliefs, administrators, and promoters of what grew to be a fundamentally anti-Black and anti-African modern world. In the nineteenth-century Gold Coast, this process played out, among other places, in the vibrant nationalist debates of the colony's African-owned newspapers. Aspects of these debates would carry on well into the twentieth century. Likewise, cocoa farmers and others protested what they viewed as the exploitative colonial pricing practices of the interwar years by withholding their crops from the market. And most dramatically, by the end of the Second World War, groups of Gold Coasters would take to the streets of the colony's cities and towns to protest the colonial system. By the end of the decade, the call from inside one of the continent's first mass political parties had grown into a demand for "Self-Government Now."

When Nkrumah returned to the Gold Coast in 1947 from a decade-plus abroad, he committed himself to the organization of the populace around this message of self-government. However, he and those around him envisioned more. They foremost aimed to restructure the international community in a way that centered the values, experiences, needs, and desires of formerly colonized peoples the world over and in Africa specifically. In the 1950s and 1960s, this quest transformed Ghana into one of the foremost centers of global anticolonial activism, a legacy— most recently exhibited by Ghana's so-called Year of Return in 2019, where thousands from the diaspora converged on Ghana to remember those lost in the slave trade on the trade's 400th anniversary—that still draws countless numbers to the country in person and in spirit. More fundamentally, at least to Ghana's own national history, this quest has featured prominently and, for some, maybe even haunted the country over its more than sixty-year postcolonial history as it has taken different iterations, been repurposed, silenced, abandoned, rediscovered, and redefined in the form of rhetoric, policy, ideology, and lived experience by now several generations of Ghanaians and their governments. Additionally, its overt and covert presence in the country's civic culture has on multiple occasions forced complicated reflections on what it means to be "Ghanaian" as Ghanaians and their governments grappled with tensions over nativism, family connections, political and economic upheaval, and Ghana's deep history of pan-African activism. As a result, by the time Rawlings put Ghana on the path to first economic and then political neo-liberalization and the contingent futures embedded within these decisions, the question became and continues to be: what does full Ghanaian self-determination look like and, maybe even more importantly, what pathways are there in Ghana for a deeper, richer sense of social democracy and prosperity in the twenty-first-century world?

Ghanaian Pasts and Futures

This book opened with a reflection on the 2007 Ghana@50 celebrations. As discussed, among the many challenges faced by the festivities' organizers were those of how best to commemorate the Ghanaian past and tell a history that encompassed the hopes, ambitions, and contradictions of this past. More than fifteen years later, Ghanaians and their leaders are continuing in this task. As Carola Lentz has shown with Ghana's 60th anniversary celebrations, debates, contestations, and performances of nation and history featured prominently in those commemorations as well.[46] However, such events are only one facet of these debates. At the time of writing, Ghana is in the midst of some of the most challenging economic times of the past several decades. The lingering effects of Covid-19—not just health, but also social and economic—along with the 2022 Russian invasion of Ukraine, has inflation running rampant. Likewise, for a period in 2022, Ghana had the world's worst-performing currency as the cedi collapsed.[47] Furthermore, in late 2022, Ghana halted payments on some of its debt obligations, sending the country into default.[48] What this has meant for most Ghanaians has been devastating. As writer Adwoa Preiman detailed in a series of tweets in November 2022, the economics of daily life simply no longer worked. Food, water, and transport prices in Accra specifically had all increased to the extent that it had become impossible to survive. "The mental toll on their [Accra's residents] health and just quality of life in general is horrible to watch," she lamented. "Accra is uninhabitable for regular Ghanaians."[49]

In the midst of this upheaval, Ghanaians have taken to the streets, radio, press, and internet to protest the country's current state. Taking aim at seeming governmental prestige projects like the currently under construction National Cathedral, which President Nana Akufo-Addo unveiled following Ghana's 60th anniversary celebrations, Ghanaians have countered the government's own historical messages celebrating a specific form of national unity with their own visions of Ghana that demand more from the government.[50] What this "more" has meant has been wide-ranging. They have demanded more in the form of social and economic support and, even more fundamentally, more in terms of the shared sacrifices and benefits of Ghana's participatory democracy. As one group, "Arise Ghana," argued in a mid-2022 press release, Ghana was "on the verge of becoming a failed state" as the government looked on helplessly while Ghanaians suffered and those in the government allegedly engaged in various forms of fraud and corruption.[51] As supporters of Arise Ghana took to the streets in mid-2022 to air their grievances, the government responded en force, tear gassing protesters and arresting twenty-nine following one June rally.[52]

At the heart of the Arise Ghana protests, among others like it, that have dotted the contemporary Ghanaian political landscape are continuations and reformulations of many of the debates, fights, and struggles discussed in this book. To wit, they are fundamentally assertions of what it means to be Ghanaian at a moment when such senses of self and belonging under the Fourth Republic appear hollow. As such, the protesters are seeking to answer the questions laid out above: what pathways are there toward a more fulfilling democracy? In doing so, they stand on the shoulders of the activists, intellectuals, farmers, traders, and others before them—pushing for a yet unrealized Ghana that not only breaks from the uncertainty and contradictions of the past, but also allows for the fullest expression, celebration, and realization of their and Ghana's potential.

NOTES

Introduction

1 "Ghana@50 Cost US$60m and Still Owes," *Ghana Business News*, January 23, 2009, https://www.ghanabusinessnews.com/2009/01/23/ghana-50-spends-60m-and-still-owes/ (accessed January 3, 2022).

2 For eyewitness reflections on the festivities, see Carola Lentz and Jan Budniok, "Ghana@50: Celebrating the Nation: An Account from Accra," *Africa Spectrum* 42, no. 3 (2007): 531–41; Carola Lentz, "Ghana@50: Celebrating the Nation, Debating the Nation," *Cahiers d'Etudes Africaines* 211 (2013): 519–46; Paul Schauert, *Staging Ghana: Artistry and Nationalism in State Dance Ensembles* (Bloomington, IN: Indiana University Press, 2015), 184–92.

3 See, for instance, the file folder in The National Archives of the United Kingdom, Dominions Office 201/40, "Ghanaian Independence: Correspondence and Papers, 1956–1957." See also Mary E. Montgomery, "The Eyes of the World Were Watching: Ghana, Great Britain, and the United States, 1957–1966" (PhD diss., College Park, MD: University of Maryland, 2004), 36–48.

4 Russell Warren Howe, "Gold Coast into Ghana," *Phylon Quarterly* 18, no. 2 (1957): 155.

5 "We Salute Ghana," *Crisis* (March 1957).

6 Kwame Nkrumah, speech at the independence of Ghana, March 6, 1957, excerpted in Kwame Nkrumah, *I Speak of Freedom: A Statement of African Ideology* (New York: Frederick A. Praeger, 1961), 107.

7 Julius Nyerere, speech at the 40th Anniversary of the Independence of Ghana, March 6, 1997, excerpted in Godfrey Mwakikagile, *Life Under Nyerere*, 2nd ed. (Dar es Salaam: New Africa, 2006), 100.

8 For a broader discussion of Ghanaians' interactions with the Nkrumah government, see Jeffrey S. Ahlman, *Living with Nkrumahism: Nation, State, and Pan-Africanism in Ghana* (Athens, OH: Ohio University Press, 2017).

9 Lentz, "Ghana@50," 519–46.

10 Ibid. Lentz examines the variety of ways in which these ideas were performed via the Ghana@50 celebrations.

11 Jane Burbank and Frederick Cooper, *Empires in World History: Power and the Politics of Difference* (Princeton, NJ: Princeton University Press, 2010), 413–42.

12 "New Names for Old Ones," *Evening News*, October 24, 1956. On the symbols of the Ghanaian nation-state, see Harcourt Fuller, *Building the Ghanaian Nation-State: Kwame Nkrumah's Symbolic Nationalism* (New York: Palgrave Macmillan, 2014).

13 Catherine Cole, *Ghana's Concert Party Theatre* (Bloomington, IN: Indiana University Press, 2001), 133–58; Nate Plageman, *Highlife Saturday Night: Popular Music and Social Change in Urban Ghana* (Bloomington, IN: Indiana University Press, 2012), 147–82; Schauert, *Staging Ghana*, 39–77.

14 Robert L. Tignor, *W. Arthur Lewis and the Birth of Development Economics* (Princeton, NJ: Princeton University Press, 2006), 112.

15   For the most succinct account of Ghana's cocoa revolution, see Gwendolyn Mikell, *Cocoa and Chaos in Ghana* (Washington, DC: Howard University Press, 1992 [1989]).

16   J. F. Ade Ajayi, "The Continuity of African Institutions under Colonialism," in *Emerging Themes of African History: Proceedings of the International Congress of African Historians held at University College, Dar es Salaam, October 1965*, ed. Terence Ranger (Dar es Salaam: East African Publishing House, 1968), 194.

17   In the literature on the Gold Coast/Ghana, for instance, such arguments date to some of the earliest decolonization-era works on the country's politics; see, for instance, David Apter, *The Gold Coast in Transition* (Princeton, NJ: Princeton University Press, 1955).

18   Mahmood Mamdani, *Citizen and Subject: Contemporary Africa and the Legacy of Late Colonialism* (Princeton, NJ: Princeton University Press, 1996).

19   See, for instance, Stephen Ellis, "Writing Histories of Contemporary Africa," *Journal of African History* 43, no. 1 (2002): 1–26.

20   Ludewig Ferdinand Rømer, *A Reliable Account of the Coast of Guinea (1760)*, trans. and ed. Selena Axelrod Winsnes (Oxford: Oxford University Press, 2000), 34–5.

21   Ivor Wilks, *Forests of Gold: Essays on the Akan and the Kingdom of Asante* (Athens, OH: Ohio University Press, 1993), 95–6.

22   "Interview with Odefo Boa Amponsem III, Denkyirahene, 4th May, 1970 at Aponsem Ahenfie, Jukwa," in *UNESCO Research Project on Oral Traditions: Denkyira*, no. 2 [collected and compiled by K. Y. Daaku] (Legon: Institute of African Studies, University of Ghana, 1970), 15–16; Otumfuo Nana Agyeman Prempeh I, *"The History of Ashanti Kings and the Whole Country Itself" and Other Writings*, eds. A. Adu Boahen, Emmanuel Akyeampong, Nancy Lawler, T. C. McCaskie, and Ivor Wilks (Oxford: Oxford University Press, 2008), 85–7.

23   Perhaps the historian most attuned to such perspectives is Kwasi Konadu; most recently, see Kwasi Konadu, *Our Own Way in This Part of the World: Biography of an African Community, Culture, and Nation* (Durham, NC: Duke University Press, 2019).

24   Kwame Anthony Appiah, *In My Father's House: Africa in the Philosophy of Culture* (Oxford: Oxford University Press, 1992).

25   Eric Hobsbawm and Terence Ranger, eds., *The Invention of Tradition* (Cambridge: Cambridge University Press, 1983).

26   See, for instance, Carola Lentz, *Ethnicity and the Making of History in Northern Ghana* (Edinburgh: Edinburgh University Press, 2006); Benjamin Talton, *Politics of Social Change: The Konkomba Struggle for Political Equality* (New York: Palgrave Macmillan, 2010).

27   Although among his later works, yet most succinct on the subject, see, for instance, Basil Davidson, *The Black Man's Burden: Africa and the Curse of the Nation-State* (New York: Three Rivers, 1992). More recently, in his history of Uganda, Richard Reid opens with the provocative question of whether "*Uganda*, as a national entity, has a history." Reid's point is not a denial of Ugandan history. Instead, it is an acknowledgment of the diversity of histories that comprise the Ugandan past; see Richard J. Reid, *A History of Modern Uganda* (Cambridge: Cambridge University Press, 2017), 1–14, quote on 1. Emphasis in original. Wale Adebanwi makes a similar point in reference to Nigeria, with a particular focus on the power of narrative; see Wale Adebanwi, *Nation as Grand Narrative: The Nigerian Press and the Politics of Meaning* (Rochester, NY: University of Rochester Press, 2016), 12–20.

28   Kwame Nkrumah, *Neo-Colonialism: The Last Stage of Imperialism* (London: Thomas Nelson and Sons, 1965), 25.

29 Kwame Nkrumah, *Africa Must Unite* (London: Panaf, 1963), 174.
30 Others who put forward similar ideas, albeit with different intentions, areas of focus, or framing mechanisms, include Frantz Fanon and Walter Rodney. See, for instance, Frantz Fanon, *The Wretched of the Earth*, trans. Constance Farrington (New York: Grove, [1961] 1963); Walter Rodney, *How Europe Underdeveloped Africa*, 2nd ed. (Washington, DC: Howard University Press, [1972] 1982).
31 Davidson, *The Black Man's Burden*, 10, 52–73.
32 See, for instance, Paul Nugent, *Boundaries, Communities and State-Making in West Africa: The Centrality of the Margins* (Cambridge: Cambridge University Press, 2019). In the Ghanaian context, perhaps the most famous example of colonial bisection is the case of the Ewe following the establishment of British and French Togoland.
33 Crawford Young, *The Politics of Cultural Pluralism* (Madison, WI: University of Wisconsin Press, 1976), 93, 163–372.
34 Crawford Young, *The African Colonial State in Comparative Perspective* (New Haven, CT: Yale University Press, 1994), 9–10, 283.
35 No work better reflects on the complicated legacies of the exercise of Ghanaian state power than Abena Ampofoa Asare, *Truth Without Reconciliation: A Human Rights History of Ghana* (Philadelphia, PA: University of Pennsylvania Press, 2018).
36 Government of Ghana, Ghana Statistical Service, *Ghana 2021 Population and Housing Census: General Report, Volume 3A: Population of Regions and Districts* (Accra: Ghana Statistical Service, 2021), 2.
37 Anthony D. Smith, *National Identity* (Las Vegas, NV: University of Nevada Press, 1991), 15.
38 Benedict Anderson, *Imagined Communities: Reflections on the Origin and Spread of Nationalism*, rev. ed. (New York: Verso, [1983] 1991).
39 Partha Chatterjee, *Nationalist Thought and the Colonial World: A Derivative Discourse* (Minneapolis, MN: University of Minnesota Press, 1993); Partha Chatterjee, *The Nation and Its Fragments: Colonial and Postcolonial Histories* (Princeton, NJ: Princeton University Press, 1993); Elleni Centime Zeleke, *Ethiopia in Theory: Revolution and Knowledge Production, 1964–2016* (Chicago, IL: Haymarket, 2019).
40 Jean Marie Allman, *The Quills of the Porcupine: Asante Nationalism in an Emergent Ghana* (Madison, WI: University of Wisconsin Press, 1993), 9–13, 15, 199n49. Allman derived the quote from Wole Soyinka. Among the works she cites as offering a particularly Eurocentric definition of the nation and nationalism is E. J. Hobsbawm, *Nations and Nationalism since 1780: Programme, Myth, Reality* (Cambridge: Cambridge University Press, 1990).

Chapter 1

1 Richard Wright, *Black Power: A Record of Reactions in a Land of Pathos* (New York: Harper and Brothers, 1954), 37.
2 Wright, *Black Power*, 37. On the practice or lack thereof of "silent trade" in West Africa, see P. F. de Moraes Farias, "Silent Trade: Myth and Historical Evidence," *History in Africa* 1 (1974): 9–24.
3 Wright, *Black Power*, 43.
4 Ibid., 43–6, quote on 44.
5 Ibid., 12.

6   See Saidiya Hartman, *Lose Your Mother: A Journey along the Atlantic Slave Route* (New York: Farrar, Straus and Giroux, 2007).

7   On the castles and forts, see Edmund Abaka, *House of Slaves and "Door of No Return": Gold Coast/Ghana Slave Forts, Castles & Dungeons, and the Atlantic Slave Trade* (Trenton, NJ: Africa World, 2012).

8   Johan Conrad Busch's Journal for the period February 2 to May 13, 1681, in *Danish Sources for the History of Ghana, 1657-1754*, vol. 1, ed. Ole Justesen and trans. James Manley (Copenhagen: Det Kongelige Danske Videnskabernes Selskab, 2005), 70. The king eventually settled for say, brandy, and gunpowder.

9   William Bosman, *A New and Accurate Description of the Coast of Guinea divided into the Gold, the Slave, and Ivory Coasts* (London: Ballantyne Books, [1705] 1907), 39-41, quote on 40.

10 Most notably, see Walter Rodney, *How Europe Underdeveloped Africa*, rev. ed. (Washington, DC: Howard University Press, [1972] 1982), esp. 75-146. For Rodney's analysis of the Gold Coast, see Walter Rodney, "Gold and Slaves on the Gold Coast," *Transactions of the Historical Society of Ghana* 10 (1969): 13-28. Among the most recent scholars to make a similar argument is Howard French, *Born in Blackness: Africa, Africans, and the Making of the Modern World, 1471 to the Second World War* (New York: Liveright, 2021).

11 For a brief survey of the late-medieval global trading networks, see Eric R. Wolf, *Europe and the People without History* (Berkeley, CA: University of California Press, 1982), 24-58. See also Janet Abu-Lughod, *Before European Hegemony: The World System A. D. 1250-1350* (Oxford: Oxford University Press, 1989).

12 Ira M. Lapidus, *A History of Islamic Societies*, 2nd ed. (Cambridge: Cambridge University Press, [1988] 2002), 250-8.

13 Al-Fazārī quoted in Nehemia Levtzion, *Ancient Ghana and Mali* (New York: Africana Publishing, [1973] 1980), 3.

14 Abū ʿUbayd ʿAbd Allāh b. ʿAbd al-ʿAzīz al-Bakrī, in *Corpus of Early Arabic Sources for West African History*, eds. Nehemia Levtzion and J. F. P. Hopkins and trans. J. F. P. Hopkins (Cambridge: Cambridge University Press, 1981), 80, 81.

15 Ibn Faḍl Allāh al-ʿUmarī, in *Corpus of Early Arabic Sources for West African History*, 270-1. See also Howard French's discussion of Mansa Musa's *hajj*; French, *Born in Blackness*, 28-35.

16 Merrick Posnansky, "Aspects of Early West African Trade," *World Archaeology* 6, no. 2 (1973): 154-6; Merrick Posnansky, "The Archaeological Foundations of the History of Ghana," in *Proceedings of the Seminar on Ghanaian Historiography and Historical Research: 20th-22nd May, 1976*, ed. J. O. Hunwick (Legon: Department of History, University of Ghana, 1977), 11.

17 Ivor Wilks, "The Juula and the Expansion of Islam into the Forest," in *The History of Islam in Africa*, eds. Nehemia Levtzion and Randall L. Pouwels (Athens, OH: Ohio University Press, 2000), 94.

18 Ivor Wilks, "The Northern Factor in Ashanti History: Begho and the Mande," *Journal of African History* 2, no. 1 (1961): 29-30.

19 Nehemia Levtzion, *Muslims and Chiefs in West Africa: A Study of Islam in the Middle Volta Basin in the Pre-Colonial Period* (Oxford: Oxford University Press, 1968), xiv-xv.

20 Wilks, "The Northern Factor in Ashanti History," 30-2.

21 For a bibliographic survey of the region's Islamization, see Holger Weiss, "Variations in the Colonial Representation of Islam and Muslims in Northern Ghana, ca. 1900–1930," *Journal of Muslim Minority Affairs* 25, no. 1 (2005): 74, 88n4.

22 Wilks, "The Northern Question in Ashanti History," 32–4; Ivor Wilks, *Forests of Gold: Essays on the Akan and the Kingdom of Asante* (Athens, OH: Ohio University Press, 1993), 4–8.

23 Duarte Pacheco Pereira, *Esmeraldo de Situ Orbis*, ed. and trans. George H. T. Kimble (London: The Hakluyt Society, 1936), 116–17.

24 Wright, *Black Power*, 37.

25 Toby Green, *A Fistful of Shells: West Africa from the Rise of the Slave Trade to the Age of Revolution* (London: Penguin, 2020), 116.

26 For a more extensive recent account of Elmina, see French, *Born in Blackness*.

27 Pacheco Pereira, *Esmeraldo de Situ Orbis*, 120.

28 Wilks, *Forests of Gold*, 5.

29 John Vogt, *Portuguese Rule on the Gold Coast, 1469–1682* (Athens, GA: University of Georgia Press, 1979), 170–204.

30 Abaka, *House of Slaves and "Door of No Return"*, 230–1.

31 Gérard Chouin and Christopher R. DeCorse, "Prelude to the Atlantic Trade: New Perspectives on Southern Ghana's Pre-Atlantic History (800–1500)," *Journal of African History* 51, no. 2 (2010): 123–45.

32 Among the many places Wilks articulates this theory, see Ivor Wilks, "The Forest and the Twis," *Transactions of the Historical Society of Ghana*, new series 8 (2004): 1–81 and, with a more Asante-centered perspective, Wilks, *Forest of Gold*, 1–126. For recent challenges to Wilks, see Gérard Chouin, "The 'Big Bang' Theory Reconsidered: Framing Early Ghanaian History," *Transactions of the Historical Society of Ghana*, new series 14 (2012): 13–40; Mariano Pavanello, "Foragers or Cultivators?: A Discussion of Wilks's 'Big Bang' Theory of Akan History," *Journal of West African History* 1, no. 2 (2015): 1–26.

33 Wilks, "The Forest and the Twis."

34 John Parker, *Making the Town: Ga State and Society in Early Colonial Accra* (Portsmouth, NH: Heinemann, 2000), 8–16.

35 James Anquandah, "The People of Ghana: Their Origins and Culture," *Transactions of the Historical Society of Ghana*, new series 15 (2013): 10.

36 Interview with Kodwo Ngwando III, Opanyin Antwi, Opanyin Antwi, and Opanyin Kwamina Nyan, Simbew, Central Region, [circa 1974], in *Oral Traditions of Fante States: Edina (Elmina)*, collected and compiled by John Kofi Fynn (Legon: Institute of African Studies, University of Ghana, 1974), 56. Opanyin Antwi is speaking here.

37 Ibid., 57. Fynn does not denote the speaker, but suggests a shift by indicating "another speaker."

38 "Interview with Odefo Boa Amponsem III, Denkyirahene, 4th May, 1970 at Aponsem Ahenfie, Jukwa," in *UNESCO Research Project on Oral Traditions: Denkyira*, no. 2, [collected and compiled by K. Y. Daaku] (Legon: Institute of African Studies, University of Ghana, 1970), 15, 16.

39 Osei Agyeman Prempeh II, quoted in T. C. McCaskie, "Asante Origins, Egypt, and the Near East: An Idea and Its History," in *Recasting the Past: History Writing and Political Work in Modern Africa*, eds. Derek R. Peterson and Giacomo Macola (Athens, OH: Ohio University Press, 2009), 137.

40 McCaskie, "Asante Origins, Egypt, and the Near East," 137–8.

41 Interview with Nana Akumfi Ameyaw, Takyiman, October 18, 1970, in D. M. Warren and K. O. Brempong, *Techiman Traditional State, Part 1: Traditional and Stool Histories* (Legon: Institute of African Studies, University of Ghana, 1971), 72. See also interview with Nana Kwakye Ameyaw, reproduced in Kwame Arhin, "Bono-Manso and Techiman," in *A Profile of Bong Kyempim: Essays on the Archeology, History, Language, and Politics of the Brong People*, ed. Kwame Arhin (Legon: Institute of African Studies, University of Ghana, 1979), 49.

42 Interview with Nana Akumfi Ameyaw, Takyiman, October 18, 1970, in D. M. Warren and K. O. Brempong, *Techiman Traditional State, Part 1: Traditional and Stool Histories*, 71.

43 On Akwamu, see Ivor Wilks, *Akwamu 1640–1750: A Study of the Rise and Fall of a West African Empire* (Trondheim: Department of History, Norwegian University of Science and Technology, 2001).

44 T. C. McCaskie, "Denkyira in the Making of Asante, c. 1660–1720," *Journal of African History* 48, no. 1 (2007): 1.

45 Bosman, *A New and Accurate Description of the Gulf of Guinea divided into the Gold, the Slave, and Ivory Coasts*, 72–3.

46 Governor Nicolay Fensman, Christiansborg, Daybook, October 14, 1688, in *Danish Sources for the History of Ghana, 1657–1754*, vol. 1, 92.

47 Bosman, *A New and Accurate Description of the Gulf of Guinea divided into the Gold, the Slave, and Ivory Coasts*, 74.

48 Ludewig Ferdinand Rømer, *A Reliable Account of the Coast of Guinea (1760)*, trans. and ed. Selena Axelrod Winsnes (Oxford: Oxford University Press, 2000), 201.

49 Governor Joost Platfues et. al. [J. Platfues, L. F. Römer, Carl Engman, P. Houed, and M. Svane] to the Directors of the West India and Guinea Company, Copenhagen, November 26, 1749, in *Danish Sources for the History of Ghana, 1657-1754*, vol. 2, 775–6.

50 "Interview with Odefo Boa Amponsem III, Denkyirahene, 4th May, 1970 at Aponsem Ahenfie, Jukwa," in *UNESCO Research Project on Oral Traditions: Denkyira*, 15.

51 Kwasi Konadu, *The Akan Diaspora in the Americas* (Oxford: Oxford University Press, 2010), 42.

52 "Interview with Odefo Boa Amponsem III, Denkyirahene, 4th May, 1970 at Aponsem Ahenfie, Jukwa," in *UNESCO Research Project on Oral Traditions: Denkyira*, 16.

53 Ibid., 16–17; McCaskie, "Denkyira in the Making of Asante," 3.

54 Interview with Adwoa Mansa, Brenu-Akyinmu, Central Region, [circa 1974], in *Oral Traditions of Fante States: Edina (Elmina)*, collected and compiled by John Kofi Fynn (Legon: Institute of African Studies, University of Ghana, 1974), 40.

55 Ray A. Kea, *Settlements, Trade, and Polities in the Seventeenth-Century Gold Coast* (Baltimore, MD: Johns Hopkins University Press, 1982), 58.

56 Harvey M. Feinberg, "Africans and Europeans in West Africa: Elminans and Dutchman on the Gold Coast during the Eighteenth Century," *Transactions of the American Philosophical Society* 79, no. 7 (1989): 29.

57 Sowande' Mustakeem, *Slavery at Sea: Terror, Sex, and Sickness in the Middle Passage* (Urbana, IL: University of Illinois Press, 2016), 7.

58 "Embarked/Disembarked, Ten-Year Period, 1501–1807" in *Voyages: The Trans-Atlantic Slave Trade Database*, http://www.slavevoyages.org/estimates/4AOLMghB. (accessed January 7, 2023). On the acceleration of the Gold Coast Atlantic slave trade, see Rebecca Shumway, *The Fante and the Transatlantic Slave Trade* (Rochester, NY: University of Rochester Press, 2011), 47–51.

59 Osei Bonsu, quoted in Ivor Wilks, *Asante in the Nineteenth Century: The Structure and Evolution of a Political Order* (Cambridge: Cambridge University Press, [1975] 1989), 177.

60 Interview with Adwoa Mansa, in *Oral Traditions of Fante States: Edina (Elmina)*, 40. Mansa was approximately 90 years old when interviewed by Fynn.

61 On Anomabo, see Shumway, *The Fante and the Transatlantic Slave Trade*, esp. 71–3 and, more broadly, Randy J. Sparks, *Where the Negroes are Masters: An African Port in the Era of the Slave Trade* (Cambridge, MA: Harvard University Press, 2014).

62 Bosman, *A New and Accurate Description of the Gulf of Guinea divided into the Gold, the Slave, and Ivory Coasts*, 183.

63 John Hippisley, *Essays: I. On the Populousness* [sic] *of Africa; II. On the Trade at the Forts on the Gold Coast; III. On the Necessity of Erecting a Fort at Cape Appolonia* (London: T. Lownds, 1764), 11–12.

64 Interview with Adwoa Mansa, in *Oral Traditions of Fante States: Edina (Elmina)*, 40.

65 Interview with Nana Amoaben Kwasu II, Kwame Arkful, Nana Owusu, Opanin Tweneboah, Kwadwo Seenye, Kwasi Afoakwa, and J. K. Nkrumah, Kyekyewere-Nyameso, Central Region, September 22, 1969, in *UNESCO Research Project on Oral Traditions: Denkyira*, 161.

66 Interview with Nana Kofi Gyeabour, Akua Ame, Kwame Annokorang, Kofi Sem, Kwabena Okyere, Kofi Boadi, and Kofi Mensah, Ayanfuri, Central Region, September 20, 1969, in *UNESCO Research Project on Oral Traditions: Denkyira*, 103.

67 Interview with Nana Afrifaa, Baffour Adjei, Ofori Kuma, Nana Ankapong II, Nana Kwasi Nksansah, Kwame Adiyia, Oheneba Kwabena Dakwa, Okyeame Yaw Mensah, Okyeame Kwasi Nkansa, Yaw Bimpeh, Kofi Abankoro, Aboagye Agyemang, Nnipa Adjei, Kwabena Dapaa, Opanin Sarpong, Baffour Nuamah, Boama Kwadjo, Nana Sanaahene, Kwabena Banahene, and Nana Buaben, Dompoase, Ashanti Region, [July–August 1969?], in *Oral Traditions of Adanse*, collected and compiled by K. Y. Daaku (Legon: Institute of African Studies, University of Ghana, 1969), 57.

68 In West Africa more broadly, exceptions most famously include Olaudah Equiano, *The Life of Olaudah Equiano; or Gustavus Vassa, the African*, 2nd ed. (London: T. Wilkins, 1789).

69 See, for instance, Sandra E. Greene's foundational *West African Narratives of Slavery: Texts from Late Nineteenth- and Early Twentieth-Century Ghana* (Bloomington, IN: Indiana University Press, 2011), which, through the reproduction of three former slaves' accounts of their enslavement (including that of Aaron Kuku discussed below), offers one of the richest and most easily accessible sources for understanding life while enslaved in the Gold Coast.

70 Aaron Kuku, "The Life History of Evangelist Aaron Kuku from His Own Oral Account Written Down by Rev. S. Quist in Palime, September 1929," trans. Paul Agbedor and eds. Sandra E. Greene and Kodjopa Attoh, reproduced in Greene, *West African Narratives of Slavery*, 52–68, quotes on 52. See also Greene's analysis of Kuku's autobiography; Greene, *West African Narratives of Slavery*, 21–46.

71 Ibid., 57.

72 Ibid., 65.

73 Ibid., 68–74.

74 William St. Clair, *The Grand Slave Emporium: Cape Coast Castle and the British Slave Trade* (London: Profile Books, 2006), 146–60; Rebecca Shumway, "Castle Slaves of the Eighteenth-Century Gold Coast (Ghana)," *Slavery & Abolition* 35, no. 1 (2014): 90–4. See also Pernille Ipsen, *Daughters of the Trade: Atlantic Slavers and Interracial Marriage on the Gold Coast* (Philadelphia, PA: University of Pennsylvania Press, 2015).

75 Greene, *West African Narratives of Slavery*, 89 and more broadly 86–92. See also Trevor R. Getz and Liz Clarke, *Abina and the Important Men: A Graphic History*, 2nd ed. (Oxford: Oxford University Press, 2015); Trevor R. Getz and Lindsay Ehrisman, "The Marriages of Abina Mansah: Escaping the Boundaries of 'Slavery' as a Category of Historical Analysis," *Journal of West African History* 1, no. 1 (2015): 93–118.

76 Paul E. Lovejoy, *Transformations in Slavery: A History of Slavery in Africa*, 3rd ed. (Cambridge: Cambridge University Press, 2012), 63–4. For a summary of the operation of the gendered markets of the domestic and international slave trades, see Patrick Manning, *Slavery and African Life: Occidental, Oriental, and African Slave Trades* (Cambridge: Cambridge University Press, 1990), 98–9.

77 Manning, *Slavery and African Life*, 55–6, 132–3.

78 See, by way of comparison, Frederick Cooper, *Plantation Slavery on the East Coast of Africa* (Portsmouth, NH: Heinemann, [1977] 1997); Mohammed Bashir Salau, *Plantation Slavery in the Sokoto Caliphate: A Historical and Comparative Study* (Rochester, NY: University of Rochester Press, 2018).

79 A. G. Hopkins, *An Economic History of West Africa* (New York: Columbia University Press, 1973), 125–6.

80 Hopkins, *An Economic History of West Africa*, 128–9; Patrick Manning, "Slaves, Palm Oil, and Political Power on the West African Coast," *African Historical Studies* 2, no. 2 (1969): 280. On palm oil more broadly, see Jonathan E. Robins, *Oil Palm: A Global History* (Chapel Hill, NC: University of North Carolina Press, 2021).

81 K. Dike Nworah, "The Politics of Lever's West African Concessions, 1907–1913," *International Journal of African Historical Studies* 5, no. 2 (1972): 248; Hopkins, *An Economic History of West Africa*, 129.

82 Wilks, *Asante in the Nineteenth Century*, 177–9.

83 Ibid.; Kwame Arhin, "Aspects of the Ashanti Trade in the Nineteenth Century," *Africa* 40, no. 4 (1970): 363–73.

84 Edmund Abaka, *"Kola is God's Gift": Agricultural Production, Export Initiatives, and the Kola Industry of Asante and the Gold Coast, c. 1820–1950* (Athens, OH: Ohio University Press, 2005), ix–x, 4–5, 108–23.

85 Wilks, *Asante in the Nineteenth Century*, 178–9.

86 Edward Carstensen, "The Palm Oil Trade: Proposal for Danish Participation in the Trade," Chief Fort Christiansborg, December 15, 1843, in Edward Carstensen, *Closing the Books: Governor Edward Carstensen on Danish Guinea, 1842–1850*, trans. Tove Storsveen (Legon: Sub-Saharan Publishers, 2010), 63–5.

87 Martin Lynn, *Commerce and Economic Change in West Africa: The Palm Oil Trade in the Nineteenth Century* (Cambridge: Cambridge University Press, 1997), 141–4.

88 For a summary of the peace terms, see G. E. Metcalfe, *Maclean of the Gold Coast: The Life and Times of George Maclean, 1801–1847* (London: Oxford University Press, 1962), 81, 80–97.

89 W. Walton Claridge, *A History of the Gold Coast and Ashanti from the Earliest Times to the Commencement of the Twentieth Century*, vol. 2 (London: John Murray, 1915), 175–6.

90 This is actually Claridge's point as he emphasizes the extension of British legal powers between the signing and the twentieth century.

91 David Kimble, *A Political History of Ghana: The Rise of Gold Coast Nationalism, 1850–1928* (Oxford: Clarendon, 1963), 410–11.

92 Claridge, *A History of the Gold Coast and Ashanti from the Earliest Times to the Commencement of the Twentieth Century*, vol. 2, 29–43.

93 James Y. Ackah, "Kaku Ackah and the Split of Nzema" (MA thesis, University of Ghana, Legon, 1965), 150–88; Pierluigi Valsecchi, "The 'True Nzema': A Layered Identity," *Africa* 71, no. 3 (2001): 406.

94 Wilks, *Asante in the Nineteenth Century*, 512–13.

95 Rodney, "Gold and Slaves on the Gold Coast," 27.

Chapter 2

1 Most famously, see Walter Rodney, *How Europe Underdeveloped Africa*, rev. ed. (Washington, DC: Howard University Press, [1972] 1982), esp. 147–281.

2 Numerous chapters emphasize such themes. For just one example, see S. R. B. Attoh Ahuma, *The Gold Coast Nation and National Consciousness* (Liverpool: D. Marples, 1911), 37–42.

3 Ibid., 1.

4 Ibid., 1, 2. Emphasis in original.

5 Ibid., vii.

6 Michel R. Doortmont, *The Pen-Pictures of Modern Africans and African Celebrities by Charles Francis Hutchinson: A Collective Biography of Elite Society in the Gold Coast Colony* (Leiden: Brill, 2005), 110.

7 Ibid., 110–11; Magnus J. Sampson, *Makers of Modern Ghana*, vol. 1 (Accra: Anowuo Educational Publications, [1937] 1969), 75–9.

8 Sampson, *Makers of Modern Ghana*, vol. 1, 76.

9 Government of the Gold Coast, *Blue Book, 1850* (London: Her Majesty's Stationery Office, 1850), 84–5, 94.

10 Sampson, *Makers of Modern Ghana*, vol. 1, 75.

11 Doortmont, *The Pen-Pictures of Modern Africans and African Celebrities by Charles Francis Hutchinson*, 111.

12 Africanus B. Horton, *Letters on the Political Condition of the Gold Coast since the Exchange of Territory between the English and the Dutch Government, on January 1, 1868 together with a Short Account of the Ashantee War, 1863–4, and the Awoonah War, 1886* (London: Frank Cass, [1870] 1970), 18.

13 On the legal process establishing Gold Coast colonial rule, see F. A. R. Bennion, *The Constitutional Law of Ghana* (London: Butterworth and Co., 1962), 4–25.

14 "Exploration and Civilisation of Africa: Public Meeting in Glasgow," *Glasgow Herald*, November 11, 1876.

15 A. W. L. Hemming, Head of the Africa Department, Colonial Office, 1880, reproduced in Thora Williamson, *Gold Coast Diaries: Chronicles of Political Officers in West Africa, 1900–1919*, ed. Anthony Kirk-Greene (London: Radcliffe Press, 2000), 18.

16 "Elmina and the Other Late Dutch Possessions of the Gold Coast, Now Under the British Flag," *African Times*, May 23, 1872.

17 "Petition of 10 Dec. 1871, to States General of the Netherlands from Inhabitants of Elmina," quoted in David Kimble, *A Political History of Ghana: The Rise of Gold Coast Nationalism, 1850–1928* (Oxford: Clarendon Press, 1963), 411. On the British military response that followed Elmina's residents' protests, see Chapter 1.

18 Earl of Kimberly, *House of Lords Debates*, February 17, 1876, vol. 227, col. 395.

19 "An Interesting Extract from a Letter Dated 'Cape Coast, Sept. 10th, 1821,'" *The Royal Gazette and Sierra Leone Advertisers*, October 13, 1821.

20   Kimble, *A Political History of Ghana*, 141–2.
21   H. St. G. Ord to H. Labouchere, London, May 16, 1856, in *Great Britain and Ghana: Documents of Ghana History, 1807–1957*, ed. G. E. Metcalfe (Edinburgh: Thomas Nelson and Sons, 1964), 255–6.
22   Bennion, *The Constitutional Law of Ghana*, 11–12 and, more broadly, Kimble, *A Political History of Ghana*, 172–91.
23   Petition of Cape Coast Chiefs, May 18, 1887, in *Great Britain and Ghana*, 430.
24   G. A. Robertson, *Notes on Africa: Particularly Those Parts which are Situated between Cape Verd [sic] and the River Congo; Containing Sketches of the Geographical Situation—the Manners and Customs—the Trade, Commerce, and Manufactures—and the Government and Policy of the Various Nations in This Extensive Tract; Also a View of Their Capabilities for the Reception of Civilization; With Hints for the Melioration of the Whole African Population* ([Boston, MA]: Adamant Media, [1819] 2007), 219–20, 221–3.
25   John Parker, *Making the Town: Ga State and Society in Early Colonial Accra* (Portsmouth, NH: Heinemann, 2001), 17–25.
26   Carl Christian Reindorf, *History of the Gold Coast and Asante: Based on Traditions and Historical Facts Comprising a Period of More than Three Centuries from about 1500 to 1860* (Basel: Printed by Author, 1895), 329.
27   Ibid., 334, 340.
28   Parker, *Making the Town*, xvii.
29   Earl of Carnarvon, *House of Lords Debates*, May 12, 1874, vol. 219, cols. 160–62. Portions of the Earl of Carnarvon's speech are reproduced in *Great Britain and Ghana*, 365–6.
30   Government of the Gold Coast, *Colonial Reports—Annual: Gold Coast: Report for 1901* (London: His Majesty's Stationery Office, 1902), 17.
31   Parker, *Making the Town*, 118–23.
32   T. E. Fells, Western Frontier, Preventative Service Diary, February 15, 1900, reproduced in *Gold Coast Diaries*, 38–9.
33   H. W. Thomas, Diary, December 8, 1915, reproduced in *Gold Coast Diaries*, 105.
34   Public Records and Archives Administration Department-Accra, Administrative Files 11/1/1, D.C. Axim to C.S. Accra, August 22, 1902.
35   Pierluigi Valsecchi, "The 'True Nzema': A Layered Identity," *Africa* 71, no. 3 (2001): 409–10.
36   H. T. Ussher to Sir Michael Edward Hicks-Beach, Accra, May 10, 1880, in *Great Britain and Ghana*, 399–400.
37   "The Representation of the People," *Gold Coast Leader*, September 15, 1906.
38   Quow Tamfu, "The Gold Coast and Public Opinion," *Gold Coast Echo*, November 5, 1888.
39   An Old Man, "The Sovereignty of Cape Coast," *Gold Coast Echo*, October 9, 1888. The author of this piece spells Aggery's name "Aggrey." Scholarly convention spells it as "Aggery." On Aggery more broadly, see Kimble, *A Political History of Ghana*, 201–20; John K. Osei-Tutu, "Contesting British Sovereignty in Cape Coast, Ghana: Insights from King John Aggery's Correspondences, 1865–72," *Transactions of the Historical Society of Ghana*, new series 7 (2003): 231–51.
40   Roger S. Gocking, *Facing Two Ways: Ghana's Coastal Communities under Colonial Law* (Lanham, MD: University Press of America, 1999), 88. See also Stephanie Newell, Introduction to A. Native, *Marita: or the Folly of Love* (Leiden: Brill, 2002), 4–7.
41   Newell, Introduction to *Marita*, 4–7, quote on 6.

42 Ibid., 7, 10, quote on 10.
43 *Gold Coast News*, April 15, 1885.
44 Editorial Notes, *Gold Coast Leader*, July 1, 1905.
45 Dick Carnis, "The Marriage Ordinance, 1884," *Gold Coast Leader*, August 5, 1905. As Stephanie Newell notes, "Dick Carnis" was a popularly used Gold Coast pseudonym; Newell, introduction to *Marita*, 26–7.
46 J. E. Casely Hayford, *Gold Coast Institutions: With Thoughts upon a Healthy Imperial Policy for the Gold Coast and Ashanti* (London: Sweet and Maxwell, 1903), ix.
47 Carnis, "The Marriage Ordinance, 1884," *Gold Coast Leader*, August 5, 1905.
48 John Mensah Sarbah, *Fanti Customary Laws: A Brief Introduction to the Principles of the Native Laws and Customs of the Fanti and Akan Districts of the Gold Coast, with a Report of Some Cases thereon Decided in the Law Courts* (London: W. Clowes and Sons, [1897] 1904); John Mensah Sarbah, *Fanti National Constitution: A Short Treatise on the Constitution and Government of the Fanti, Asanti [sic], and Other Akan Tribes of West Africa together with a Brief Account of the Discovery of the Gold Coast by Portuguese Navigators; A Short Narrative of Early English Voyages; and a Study of the Rise of British Gold Coast Jurisdictions, etc.*, 2nd ed. (London: Frank Cass, [1906] 1968).
49 Kobina Sekyi, *The Blinkards: A Comedy and the Anglo-Fanti: A Short Story* (Accra: Readwide Publications, [1915] 1997), 173. See also Catherine M. Cole, *Ghana's Concert Party Theatre* (Bloomington, IN: Indiana University Press, 2001), 56–63.
50 Jonathan Schneer, *London 1900: The Imperial Metropolis* (New Haven, CT: Yale University Press, 1999), 3–14.
51 Hakim Adi, *West Africans in Britain, 1900–1960: Nationalism, Pan-Africanism, and Communism* (London: Lawrence and Wishart, 1998), 9–13; Schneer, *London 1990*, 203–4. More broadly on the history of Black Britain, see Hakim Adi, *African and Caribbean People in Britain: A History* (London: Allen Lane, 2022).
52 University of Massachusetts Amherst Libraries (hereafter cited as UMASS Amherst Libraries), Special Collections and University Archives (hereafter cited as SCUA), W.E.B. Du Bois Papers (MS 312) (hereafter cited as Du Bois Papers), Pan-African Association, "Report of the Pan-African Conference, Held on the 23rd, 24th, and 25th July, 1900, at Westminster Town Hall, Westminster, S.W." (typescript). See also Adi, *African and Caribbean People in Britain*, 209–11.
53 Immanuel Geiss, *The Pan-African Movement: A History of Pan-Africanism in America, Europe, and Africa*, trans. Ann Keep (New York: Africana, [1968] 1974), 182. On Accra's Brazilian returnee community, see Kwame Essien, *Brazilian-African Diaspora in Ghana: The Tabom, Slavery, Dissonance of Memory, Identity, and Locating Home* (East Lansing, MI: Michigan State University Press, 2016).
54 "The African Association," *Gold Coast Chronicle*, September 10–20, 1898.
55 P. O. Gray, "The Pan-African Conference," *New Africa* 2, no. 5 (1900): 5.
56 *Gold Coast Aborigines*, August 31, 1900, quoted in S. K. B. Asante, "The Neglected Aspects of the Activities of the Gold Coast Aborigines Rights Protection Society," *Phylon* 36, no. 1 (1975): 33.
57 Asante, "The Neglected Aspects of the Activities of the Gold Coast Aborigines Rights Protection Society," 33.
58 J. E. Casely Hayford, *Ethiopia Unbound: Studies in Race Emancipation*, 2nd ed. (London: Frank Cass, 1969 [1911]), 182–97. On *Ethiopia Unbound*, see Jeanne-Marie Jackson, *The African Novel of Ideas: Philosophy and Individualism in the Age of Global Writing* (Princeton, NJ: Princeton University Press, 2021).

59   J. E. Casely Hayford, "Introduction," in [Edward Wilmot Blyden], *Africa and the Africans: Proceedings on the Occasion of a Banquet Given at the Holborn Restaurant, August 15th 1903 to Edward W. Blyden LL.D. by West Africans in London* (London: C. M. Phillips, 1903), 13. On Blyden and his legacy, see Harry N. K. Odamtten, *Edward W. Blyden's Intellectual Transformations: Afropublicanism, Pan-Africanism, Islam, and the Indigenous West African Church* (East Lansing, MI: Michigan State University Press, 2019).

60   Kimble, *A Political History of Ghana*, 374–89.

61   UMASS Amherst Libraries, SCUA, Du Bois Papers, J. E. Casely Hayford to W.E.B. Du Bois, Sekondi, March 29, 1919.

62   UMASS Amherst Libraries, SCUA, Du Bois Papers, J. E. Casely Hayford to W.E.B. Du Bois, Dulwich West, UK, December 29, 1920.

63   Alexander Walters, *My Life and Work* (New York: Fleming H. Revell, [1917]), 166.

64   Sandra E. Greene, *West African Narratives of Slavery: Texts from Late Nineteenth- and Early Twentieth-Century Ghana* (Bloomington, IN: Indiana University Press, 2011), 154–5, 193–9, 205–11. For Greene's reproduction of the oral traditions, see Ibid., 213–21.

Chapter 3

1   Samuel Crowther, quoted in *A Quarterly Token for Juvenile Subscribers: A Gift from the Church Missionary Society* 7 (October 1857): 7. This issue is compiled with other issues of *The Church Missionary Quarterly Token: 1856–1865* (London: Church Missionary Society, 1856–1865).

2   Government of the Gold Coast, *Annual Report for 1896*, no. 220 (London: Her Majesty's Stationery Office, 1897), 10.

3   Dennis Kemp, *Nine Years at the Gold Coast* (London: Macmillan, 1898), 18.

4   Food and Agriculture Organization of the United Nations, FAOSTAT Statistics Database ([Rome?]: Food and Agriculture Organization, 2018), http://www.fao.org/faostat/en/?#data/QC (accessed March 30, 2018).

5   "Tetteh Quarshie and the Cocoa Industry," *West African Review* (July 1951), 744–5. Also spelled "Quashie" by some. Sources conflict between 1878 and 1879 regarding Quarshie's return to the Gold Coast.

6   I. K. Sundiata, "Prelude to Scandal: Liberia and Fernando Po, 1880–1930," *Journal of African History* 15, no. 1 (1974): 98, 100.

7   "Tetteh Quarshie and the Cocoa Industry," *West African Review* (July 1951).

8   Ibid.; David Kimble, *A Political History of Ghana: The Rise of Gold Coast Nationalism, 1850–1928* (Oxford: Clarendon, 1963), 33. The *West African Review* also notes the possibility of some earlier unsuccessful attempts.

9   Polly Hill, *Migrant Cocoa-Farmers of Southern Ghana: A Study in Rural Capitalism* (Cambridge: Cambridge University Press, [1963] 1970), 172–3.

10   Government of the Gold Coast, *Annual Report for 1902*, no. 397 (London: His Majesty's Stationery Office, 1903), 23.

11   Edward J. Organ, *The Gold Coast Cocoa Industry & Its Recent Developments: A Paper Read at the Exhibition of Rubber, Other Tropical Products & Allied Industries, June 1921* (n.p.: Bourneville Works, 1921), 2–3.

12 "Cocoa and Palm Oil Production in the Gold Coast and Southern Nigeria," *African Mail*, December 31, 1909.

13 Government of the Gold Coast, *Her Majesty's Colonial Possessions: Gold Coast: Economic Agriculture on the Gold Coast, 1889*, no. 110 (London: Her Majesty's Stationery Office, 1890), 31–2.

14 Government of the Gold Coast, *Annual Report for 1901*, no. 375 (London: Her Majesty's Stationery Office, 1902), 21.

15 Raymond Dumett, "The Rubber Trade of the Gold Coast and Asante in the Nineteenth Century: African Innovation and Market Responsiveness," *Journal of African History* 12, no. 1 (1971): 86. For an insightful history of the Gold Coast/Ghanaian rubber industry, see Keri Grace Lambert, "Elastic Allegiances: Rubber, Development, and the Production of Sovereignties in Ghana, 1880–2017" (PhD diss., New Haven, CT: Yale University, 2019).

16 Government of the Gold Coast, *Her Majesty's Colonial Possessions: Gold Coast: Economic Agriculture on the Gold Coast, 1889*, 24.

17 Interview with Joseph Kwabena Kwateng, Opayin Yaw Nkua, Okyeame Atta Kwabena, Stephen Kojo Bie, and Nana Kwam Adu (chief of Bodi), Bodi, Western Region, in *UNESCO Research Project on Oral Tradition, No. 4, Part II: Sefwi-Wiawso*, collected and compiled by K.Y. Daaku (Legon: Institute of African Studies, 1974), 87.

18 H. N. Thompson, *Gold Coast: Report on Forests*, no. 66 (London: His Majesty's Stationery Office, 1910), 192.

19 Ibid., 156. On Thompson's general outlook regarding Gold Coast agriculture and forestry, see Timothy Vilgiate, "Forestry and the 'World on Paper': Ideas of Science and Resistance to Forest Reservation on the Gold Coast in the Early Twentieth Century," *Ghana Studies* 23 (2020): 10–11.

20 Government of the Gold Coast, *Her Majesty's Colonial Possessions: Gold Coast: Economic Agriculture on the Gold Coast, 1889*, 29.

21 "Cocoa," *Gold Coast Express*, July 20, 1897.

22 "Gold Coast Cocoa," *African Mail*, May 29, 1908.

23 "Hints on Cocoa Cultivation," *African Mail*, July 30, 1909.

24 "Gold Coast Cocoa Cultivation," *African Mail*, February 28, 1908.

25 "Cocoa Industry," *West African Mail*, August 10, 1906.

26 "The Quality of Gold Coast Cocoa: A German View," *African Mail*, April 21, 1911.

27 "Cocoa: Observations by Dr. Gruner in the Aburi District, Gold Coast Colony," *West African Mail*, October 28, 1904.

28 "Cocoa Ousting Palms in the Gold Coast," *African Mail*, September 10, 1915.

29 Northwestern University Libraries (hereafter cited as NUL), Melville J. Herskovits Library of African Studies (hereafter cited as Herskovits Library), Polly Hill Papers (hereafter cited as Hill Papers), Box 2, Folder 5, "Ofori Jyawu, aged 76, living at Aburi-Obodang, Retired Agricultural Man," Aburi, n.d.

30 NUL, Herskovits Library, Hill Papers, Box 2, Folder 5, "James Dei (elderly)—'plantation officer,'" Aburi, n.d.

31 NUL, Herskovits Library, Hill Papers, Box 2, Folder 5, "Moses Addo (born 1886)," Konkonuru, February 27, 1959.

32 NUL, Herskovits Library, Hill Papers, Box 2, Folder 5, "Kwame Appiah (Aku House)—old man, perhaps 75–80," Aburi, n.d.

33 NUL, Herskovits, Library, Hill Papers, Box 2, Folder 5, "Mr. E. E. Tham—born 1889," Aburi, n.d.

34 Hill, *Migrant Cocoa-Farmers of Southern Ghana*, 39, more broadly 38–54.

35 NUL, Herskovits Library, Hill Papers, Box 5, Folder 3, "Okyeame Kofi Darko (very old), Calls himself a 'money lender,'" Akropong, n.d. It appears that, when Hill interviewed Darko, only one of Darko's remaining twenty-two lands (Teprimang) still produced cocoa.

36 NUL, Herskovits Library, Hill Papers, Box 5, Folder 3, "Opanyin [Kwaku] Ntow (very old)," Akropong, [1959].

37 Hill, *Migrant Cocoa-Farmers of Southern Ghana*, 13–14, 178–92. On rural capitalism, see Polly Hill, *Studies in Rural Capitalism in West Africa* (Cambridge: Cambridge University Press, 1970).

38 NUL, Herskovits Library, Hill Papers, Box 3, Folder 2, "KWABENA KUMI—or rather his widow," Mamfe(?), n.d. Hill does not provide Kumi's widow's name.

39 NUL, Herskovits Library, Hill Papers, Box 3, Folder 2, "Obeng Kwadjo, January or February, 1960." Hill published a short profile of Kwadjo in Hill, *Migrant-Cocoa Farmers of Southern Ghana*, 207. He is "Mamfe, No. 5." Hill did not interview Kwadjo directly since he had died approximately twenty years earlier. Rather, she learned of him via his daughters.

40 Following a 2018 referendum creating six new Ghanaian regions, the government divided the Brong Ahafo Region into the Bono, Bono East, and Ahafo Regions.

41 Jean Allman and Victoria Tashjian, *"I Will Not Eat Stone": A Women's History of Colonial Asante* (Portsmouth, NH: Heinemann, 2000), 3.

42 T. E. Kyei, *Our Days Dwindle: Memories of My Childhood Days in Asante*, ed. Jean Allman (Portsmouth, NH: Heinemann, 2001), 11.

43 Ibid., 25–6.

44 Allman and Tashjian, *"I Will Not Eat Stone,"* 158.

45 Gwendolyn Mikell, *Cocoa and Chaos in Ghana* (Washington, DC: Howard University Press, 1992 [1989]), 101–5, quote on 103. Polly Hill found similar women's participation in cocoa farming in Akyem Abuakwa; see NUL, Herskovits Library, Hill Papers, Box 6, Folder 6, Polly Hill, "The Cocoa Farmers of Asafo and Maase (Akim Abuakwa): With Special Reference to the Position of Women" ([Legon]: Economics Research Division, University College of Ghana, 1959).

46 M. Fortes, R. W. Steel, and P. Ady, "Ashanti Survey, 1945–46: An Experiment in Social Research," *Geographical Journal* 110, no. 4/6 (1947): 165.

47 Government of the Gold Coast, *Colonial Reports—Annual: Northern Territories of the Gold Coast: Report for 1913*, no. 807 (London: His Majesty's Stationery Office, 1914), 5.

48 T. Edward Bowdich, *Mission from Cape Coast Castle to Ashantee, with a Descriptive Account of that Kingdom* (London: Griffith & Farran, 1873 [1819]), 186.

49 Ibid., 268–9; Ivor Wilks, *Asante in the Nineteenth Century: The Structure and Evolution of a Political Order* (Cambridge: Cambridge University Press, 1989 [1975]), 66.

50 Peggy Appiah, Kwame Anthony Appiah, and Ivor Agyeman-Duah, *Bu Me Bɛ: Proverbs of the Akan* (Oxfordshire, UK: Ayebia Clarke, 2007), 97.

51 Asantehene Kwaku Dua Panin, 1841, quoted in T. C. McCaskie, *State and Society in Pre-Colonial Asante* (Cambridge: Cambridge University Press, 1995), 96.

52 Gareth Austin, *Labour, Land and Capital in Ghana: From Slavery to Free Labour in Asante, 1807–1956* (Rochester, NY: University of Rochester Press, 2005), 120.

53 McCaskie, *State and Society in Pre-Colonial Asante*, 96–9.

54 Roger G. Thomas, "Forced Labour in British West Africa: The Case of the Northern Territories of the Gold Coast, 1906–1927," *Journal of African History* 14, no. 1 (1973): 79–103.

55   Kyei, *Our Days Dwindle*, 106.

56   Austin, *Labour, Land and Capital in Ghana*, 242–3.

57   Ibid., 243; Jean Allman and John Parker, *Tongnaab: The History of a West African God* (Bloomington, IN: Indiana University Press, 2005), 93.

58   Provincial Commissioner, North-Eastern Province, quoted in Government of the Gold Coast, *Colonial Reports—Annual: Northern Territories of the Gold Coast: Report for 1913*, no. 807 (London: His Majesty's Stationery Office, 1914), 28.

59   Government of the Gold Coast, *Colonial Reports—Annual: Northern Territories of the Gold Coast: Report for 1913*, 28.

60   Government of the Gold Coast, *Colonial Reports—Annual: Northern Territories of the Gold Coast: Report for 1914*, no. 863 (London: His Majesty's Stationery Office, 1915), 28.

61   Secretary of State for the Colonies, *Report of the Commission on the Marketing of West African Cocoa* (London: His Majesty's Stationery Office, 1938), 20.

62   Ibid., 19–20.

63   Wilks, *Asante in the Nineteenth Century*, 66, 68, 210–11; Lynne Brydon, "Constructing Avatime: Questions of History and Identity in a West African Polity, c. 1690s to the Twentieth Century," *Journal of African History* 49, no. 1 (2008): 26, 23–42 more broadly.

64   For a rich survey of nineteenth-century coastal Ewe history, see Emmanuel Kwaku Akyeampong, *Between the Sea & the Lagoon: An Eco-Social History of the Anlo of Southern Ghana c. 1850 to Recent Times* (Athens, OH: Ohio University Press, 2001), esp. 49–74.

65   Aaron Kuku, "The Life History of Evangelist Aaron Kuku from His Own Oral Account Written Down by Rev. S. Quist in Palime, September 1929," trans. Paul Agbedor and eds. Sandra E. Greene and Kodjopa Attoh, reproduced in Sandra E. Greene, *West African Narratives of Slavery: Texts from Late Nineteenth- and Early Twentieth-Century Ghana* (Bloomington, IN: Indiana University Press, 2011), 54, 55.

66   G. K. Tsekpo, "Yosef Famfantor," trans. Kodjopa Attoh with Kenneth Krieger and ed. Sandra E. Greene, reproduced in Greene, *West African Narratives of Slavery*, 126–8. For Greene's analysis of Famfantor, see ibid., 92–102.

67   Paul Nugent, "A Regional Melting Pot: The Ewe and Their Neighbours in the Ghana-Togo Borderlands," in *The Ewe of Togo and Benin*, ed. Benjamin Lawrance (Accra: Woeli, 2005), 31.

68   Government of the Gold Coast, *Further Reports Relative to Economic Agriculture on the Gold Coast*, no. 1 (London: Her Majesty's Stationery Office, 1891), 9–10.

69   Government of the Gold Coast, *Annual Report for 1914*, no. 859 (London: Her Majesty's Stationery Office, 1915), 21.

70   K. B. Dickson, "Development of the Copra Industry in Ghana," *Journal of Tropical Geography* 19 (1964): 29.

71   Akyeampong, *Between the Sea & Lagoon*, 79.

72   Paul Nugent, *Smugglers, Secessionists, & Loyal Citizens on the Ghana-Togo Frontier: The Lie of the Borderlands since 1914* (Athens, OH: Ohio University Press, 2002), 50–61.

73   Hill, *Migrant Cocoa-Farmers of Southern Ghana*, 190.

74   Polly Hill, *The Gold Coast Cocoa Farmer: A Preliminary Survey* (Oxford: Oxford University Press, 1956), 24.

75   NUL, Herskovits Library, Hill Papers, Box 5, Folder 3, "Interview with Opanyin BIRIKORANG, relative to Ofei Ampofo of Akropong, Adeiso on January 26th, 1960."

76 Ibid.

77 Ibid.

78 NUL, Herskovits Library, Hill Papers, Box 5, Folder 5, "Notes on Labourers at Domi," Domi, n.d. Hill does not note the ethnicity of the *Odikro*'s laborers from French Togoland.

79 NUL, Herskovits Library, Hill Papers, Box 5, Folder 5, "The ODIKRO of Domi," Domi, n.d.

80 Hill, *The Gold Coast Cocoa Farmer*, 8–39.

81 NUL, Herskovits Library, Hill Papers, Box 5, Folder 5, "The ODIKRO of Domi," Domi, n.d.

82 NUL, Herskovits Library, Hill Papers, Box 5, Folder 5, "Notes on Labourers at Domi," Domi, n.d.

83 NUL, Herskovits Library, Box 5, Folder 3, "Visit to Bepoase, April 13th, 1959."

84 Fred Sarpong, untitled song written in Twi, reproduced in Dennis Austin, *Politics in Ghana, 1946–1960* (London: Oxford University Press, 1964), 275. It is also reproduced in Allman and Tashjian, *"I Will Not Eat Stone,"* 3.

Chapter 4

1 Frederick Gordon Guggisberg, "Governor's Address to Legislative Council, 6 March 1957," in *Great Britain and Ghana: Documents of Ghana History, 1807–1957*, ed. G. E. Metcalfe (London: Thomas Nelson and Sons, 1964), 594–6.

2 Cati Coe, "Educating an African Leadership: Achimota and the Teaching of African Culture in the Gold Coast," *Africa Today* 49, no. 3 (2002): esp. 27–8.

3 Polly Hill, *The Gold Coast Cocoa Farmer: A Preliminary Survey* (London: Oxford University Press, 1956), 132; G. B. Kay, ed., *The Political Economy of Colonialism in Ghana: Documents and Statistics, 1900–1960* (Aldershot, UK: Gregg Revivals, 1992), 334–5.

4 Hill, *The Gold Coast Farmer*, 133.

5 Gareth Austin, "Capitalists and Chiefs in the Cocoa Hold-Ups in South Asante, 1927–1938," *International Journal of African Historical Studies* 21, no. 1 (1988): 53–95.

6 "Farmers and Cocoa (1)," *African Morning Post*, October 1, 1937.

7 Kay, *The Political Economy of Colonialism in Ghana*, 334–9; Keri Grace Lambert, "Elastic Allegiances: Rubber, Development, and the Production of Sovereignties in Ghana, 1880–2017" (PhD diss., New Haven, CT: Yale University, 2019), 112–13.

8 Kay, *The Political Economy of Colonialism in Ghana*, 334–9; Raymond Dumett, "Africa's Strategic Minerals during the Second World War," *Journal of African History* 26, no. 4 (1985): 400.

9 Kay, *The Political Economy of Colonialism in Ghana*, 334–9.

10 Jeff Crisp, *The Story of an African Working Class: Ghanaian Miners' Struggles, 1870–1980* (London: Zed Books, 1984), 56–69, see esp. 58–9.

11 Wendell Patrick Holbrook, "The Impact of the Second World War on the Gold Coast: 1939–1945" (PhD diss., Princeton, NJ: Princeton University, 1978), 44–6.

12 "Europe is Mad," *Ashanti Pioneer*, December 4, 1939.

13 Holbrook, "The Impact of the Second World War on the Gold Coast," 102–3, 107–8.

14 Nancy Ellen Lawler, *Soldiers, Airmen, Spies, and Whisperers: The Gold Coast in World War II* (Athens, OH: Ohio University Press, 2002), 25.

15 Timothy H. Parsons, *The African Rank-and-File: Social Implications of Colonial Military Service in the King's African Rifles, 1902–1964* (Portsmouth, NH: Heinemann, 1999), 2.

16 David Killingray, "Repercussions of World War I in the Gold Coast," *Journal of African History* 19, no. 1 (1978): 46.

17 Lawler, *Soldiers, Airmen, Spies, and Whisperers*, 31.

18 Ibid., 37.

19 Lacy Ferrell, "'We Were Mixed with All Types': Educational Migration in the Northern Territories of Colonial Ghana," in *Children on the Move: Past & Present Experiences of Migration*, eds. Elodie Razy and Marie Rodet (Rochester, NY: Boydell & Brewer, 2016), 147, 141–58. Ferrell uses the example of former Ghanaian president John Dramani Mahama's father, who traveled approximately 200 kilometers, to illustrate her point. On Mahama's discussion of his father's "educational migration," see John Dramani Mahama, *My First Coup d'Etat: And Other True Stories from the Lost Decades of Africa* (New York: Bloomsbury, 2012), 30–1.

20 Government of the Gold Coast, *Colonial Reports—Annual: Northern Territories of the Gold Coast: Report for 1914*, no. 863 (London: His Majesty's Stationery Office, 1915), 4.

21 [W. G. A. Ormsby-Gore,] "Report by the Hon. W. G. A. Ormsby-Gore, M. P. (Parliamentary Under-Secretary of State for the Colonies), on his Visit to West Africa during the Year 1926" (London: His Majesty's Stationery Office, 1926), 139.

22 A. W. Cardinall, District Commissioner, September 4, 1919, reproduced in Thora Williamson, *Gold Coast Diaries: Chronicles of Political Officers in West Africa, 1900–1919*, ed. Anthony Kirk-Greene (London: Radcliffe Press, 2000), 320–1.

23 [Ormsby-Gore], "Report by the Hon. W. G. A. Ormsby-Gore, M.P. (Parliamentary Under-Secretary of State for the Colonies), on his Visit to West Africa during the Year 1926," 21, 138.

24 Col. A. Haywood and Brig. F. A. S. Clarke, *The History of the Royal West African Frontier Force* (Aldershot, UK: Gale & Polden, 1964), 11. Also, quoted in Lawler, *Soldiers, Airmen, Spies, and Whisperers*, 29.

25 Lawler, *Soldiers, Airmen, Spies, and Whisperers*, 29. See also David Killingray with Martin Plaut, *Fighting for Britain: African Soldiers in the Second World War* (Rochester, NY: Boydell & Brewer, 2010), 40–3.

26 British Library, Endangered Archive Programme [hereafter cited as EAP] 541/1/2/74, A. F. Kerr (Ag District Commissioner), "Northern Territories of the Gold Coast Annual Report: Wala, 1939–40," Wa, Northern Territories, April 23, 1939, https://eap.bl.uk/archive-file/EAP541-1-2-74#?c=0&m=0&s=0&cv=8&xywh=-413%2C0%2C4281%2C5184&r=180 (accessed January 15, 2023), original location Public Records and Archives Administration Department (hereafter cited as PRAAD)-Tamale, Northern Region Archives (hereafter cited as NRG) 8/2/86. This EAP collection contains documents from PRAAD-Tamale. Both the EAP and PRAAD-Tamale numbering systems are included when possible.

27 British Library, EAP 541/1/3/98, E. W. Ellison (District Commissioner), "Annual Report on Navrongo District for the Year 1940–1941," Navrongo, Northern Territories, May 26, 1942, https://eap.bl.uk/archive-file/EAP541-1-3-98#?c=0&m=0&s=0&cv=1&xywh=-2114%2C0%2C7682%2C5183 (accessed January 15, 2023), original location PRAAD-Tamale, NRG 8/3/105.

28 Killingray with Plaut, *Fighting for Britain*, 39. Killingray and Plaut note that access to greater social mobility was especially the case for peacetime recruiting.

29 Agolley Kusasi, interview with David Killingray, May 5, 1979, quoted in Ibid., 35.

30 Killingray with Plaut, *Fighting for Britain*, 35.

31 Martin Staniland, *The Lions of Dagbon: Political Change in Northern Ghana* (Cambridge: Cambridge University Press, [1975] 2008), 210n52.

32 British Library, EAP 541/1/4/92, J. K. G. Syme, "Informal Diary—Gonja District, May 1942, Mr. J. K. G. Syme, D. C. Gonja," May 21, 1942, May 25, 1942, and May 28, 1942, https://eap.bl.uk/archive-file/EAP541-1-4-92#?c=0&m=0&s=0&cv=158&xywh=0%2C-2114%2C5183%2C7682&r=90 (accessed January 15, 2023), original location not included.

33 Killingray with Plaut, *Fighting for Britain*, 35.

34 "Mogadischio Captured by West African Troops: Italian Somaliland Campaign Reaching Final Stages," *Gold Coast Independent*, March 1, 1941. See also "African War News: Gold Coast Troops Capture Italian Town," *Gold Coast Independent*, February 22, 1941; "War News: Exploits of Gold Coast and South African Troops," *Gold Coast Independent*, March 1, 1941.

35 Killingray with Plaut, *Fighting for Britain*, 147–51.

36 Lawler, *Soldiers, Airmen, Spies, and Whisperers*, 188.

37 Ibid., 39–80; Deborah Wing Ray, "The Takoradi Route: Roosevelt's Prewar Venture beyond the Western Hemisphere," *Journal of American History* 62, no. 2 (1975): 340–58.

38 K. A. Busia, *Report on a Social Survey of Sekondi-Takoradi* (London: Crown Agents for the Colonies, 1950), 96–100. On inter-racial prostitution during the war, see Carina Ray, "World War II and the Sex Trade in British West Africa," in *Africa and World War II*, eds. Judith A. Byfield, Carolyn A. Brown, Timothy Parsons, and Ahmad Alawad Sikainga (Cambridge: Cambridge University Press, 2015), 339–56.

39 PRAAD-Cape Coast, Administrative Files 23/1/469, Chief Scout Commissioner to All District Commissioners, "1939 Jamboree Programme, Plans and Policies," [1939?].

40 Staniland, *The Lions of Dagbon*, 115.

41 Paul André Ladouceur, *Chiefs and Politicians: The Politics of Regionalism in Northern Ghana* (London: Longman, 1979), 71.

42 British Library, EAP 541/1/3/121, G. Hall, "Report on the Mamprusi District for the Quarter Ending 31st December 1945," Gambaga, February 15, 1946, https://eap.bl.uk/archive-file/EAP541-1-3-121#?c=0&m=0&s=0&cv=1&xywh=-2114%2C0%2C7682%2C5183 (accessed January 15, 2023), original location PRAAD-Tamale, NRG 8/3/129.

43 Killingray with Plaut, *Fighting for Britain*, 188–90.

44 British Library, EAP 541/1/3/121, Hall, "Report on the Mamprusi District for the Quarter Ending 31st December 1945."

45 British Library, EAP 541/1/3/133, "Appendix I: Annual Report on the Western Sub-District of the Dagomba District for the Year, 1946–1947," appendix to "Annual Report, Dagomba District, 1946–1947," Yendi, June 20, 1947, http://eap.bl.uk/archive-file/EAP541-1-3-133#?c=0&m=0&s=0&cv=23&xywh=-2541%2C-293%2C8536%2C5760&r=0 (accessed January 15, 2023), original location PRAAD-Tamale, NRG 8/3/141.

46 British Library, EAP 541/1/3/117, "Labour Officer's Report on Conditions Affecting Labour in the N. T.s.," [1947], http://eap.bl.uk/archive-file/EAP541-1-3-117#?c=0&m=0&s=0&cv=2&xywh=-2114%2C0%2C7682%2C5183 (accessed January 15, 2023), original location PRAAD-Tamale, NRG 8/3/124.

47 Ibid.; Government of the Gold Coast, Census Office, *Census of Population, 1948: Reports and Tables* (Accra: Government Printing Department, 1950), 338.

48 David Killingray, "Soldiers, Ex-Servicemen, and Politics in the Gold Coast," *Journal of Modern African Studies* 21, no. 3 (1983): 529.

49 Adrienne M. Israel, "Ex-Servicemen at the Crossroads: Protest and Politics in Post-War Ghana," *Journal of Modern African Studies* 30, no. 2 (1992): 361–62.

50 "Lingering Rations," *Times of London*, October 9, 1953.

51 Harold Davies, *House of Commons Debates*, November 22, 1949, col. 289, https://hansard.parliament.uk/Commons/1949-11-22/debates/e50f16de-a973-4b7d-a23b-937c8419b00d/WarDebts?highlight=debt%20united%20states#contribution-21c6b7ae-cea2-409c-b5fd-0e71b48c9ba2 (accessed January 15, 2023).

52 Colonial Office, *Report of the Commission of Enquiry into Disturbances in the Gold Coast, 1948* (London: His Majesty's Stationery Office, 1948), 38–9.

53 British Library, EAP 541/1/3/270, J. D. Broatch, "Department of Agriculture, Northern Territories: Quarterly Report January–March 1946," April 23, 1946, https://eap.bl.uk/archive-file/EAP541-1-3-270#?c=0&m=0&s=0&cv=38&xywh=599%2C412%2C3151%2C1736 (accessed January 15, 2023), original location PRAAD-Tamale, NRG 8/3/299.

54 British Library, EAP 541/1/3/270, J. D. Broatch, "Department of Agriculture, Northern Territories: Quarterly Report April–June 1946," July 20, 1946, https://eap.bl.uk/archive-file/EAP541-1-3-270#?c=0&m=0&s=0&cv=44&xywh=-2114%2C565%2C7682%2C5183 (accessed January 15, 2023), original location PRAAD-Tamale, NRG 8/3/299.

55 Francis Danquah, *Cocoa Disease and Politics in Ghana, 1909–1966* (New York: Peter Lang, 1995), 60–9.

56 Ibid., 65–6, 89.

57 The National Archives—United Kingdom (hereafter cited as TNAUK), Colonial Office (hereafter cited as CO) 964/2, P. H. Fitzgerald to United Africa Company, Gold Coast Department (London), Accra, April 11, 1948.

58 Northwestern University Libraries (hereafter cited as NUL), Melville J. Herskovits Library of African Studies (hereafter cited as Herskovits Library), Polly Hill Papers (hereafter cited as Hill Papers), Box 5, Folder 5, "The ODIKRO of Domi," Domi, n.d.

59 NUL, Herskovits Library, Hill Papers, Box 3, Folder 2, [Polly Hill], "Interview with KWAO ABBEY, nephew of Pobi, at Mepom, 28th March 1958."

60 NUL, Herskovits Library, Hill Papers, Box 6, Folder 2, Polly Hill, *An Economic Survey of Cocoa Farmers in Sefwi-Wiawso* (Legon: University College of Ghana, Economics Research Division, July 1957), 13.

61 NUL, Herskovits Library, Hill Papers, Box 6, Folder 6, Polly Hill, *The Acquisition of Land by Aburi Cocoa Farmers* (Legon: University College of Ghana, Economics Research Division, July 1959), 35–6.

62 NUL, Herskovits Library, Hill Papers, Box 5, Folder 4, [Polly Hill], "General Notes on interview with 14 ASAFO WOMEN in the Chief's house on May 8th, 1959."

63 Nii Kwabena Bonne III, *Milestones in the History of the Gold Coast: Autobiography of Nii Kwabena Bonne III, Osu Alata Mantse, also Nana Owusu Akenten III, Oyokohene of Techiman, Ashanti* (n.p.: Diplomatist, n.d.), 64. See also Dennis Austin, *Politics in Ghana, 1946–1960* (London: Oxford University Press, 1964), 71–4.

64 On the Gold Coast's/Ghana's Lebanese community, see Emmanuel Akyeampong, "Race, Identity, and Citizenship in Black Africa: The Case of the Lebanese in Ghana," *Africa* 76, no. 3 (2006): 303–20; Isaac Xerxes Malki, "Productive Aliens: Economic Planning and the Lebanese in Ghana, c. 1930–1972," *Mashriq & Mahjar* 1, no. 1 (2013): 85–114.

65 TNAUK, CO 964/15, Nii Bonne III to Secretary, Watson Commission, April 30, 1948.

66 Austin, *Politics in Ghana*, 71. For Bonne's account of the boycott, see Bonne III, *Milestones in the History of the Gold Coast*, 63–88.

67 TNAUK, CO 964/25, Nene Azzu Kate Kole in "Note of a Meeting held in the Colonial Secretary's Office at 10 a.m. on the 20th of February, 1948, to Discuss the Trade Boycott," The Secretariat, February 20, 1948.

68 TNAUK, CO 964/5, Appendix D, Atipe, "The Syrian Menace," *West African Monitor*, February 6, 1948. "Syrian" served as a catchall term for individuals of numerous nationalities—the majority of whom came from what would become Lebanon; Malki, "Productive Aliens," 87–8.

69 TNAUK, CO 964/15, L. Val-Vannis, "Statement by L. Val-Vannis before the Watson Commission of Enquiry," appendix to A. Okyere to Secretary, Watson Commission, April 30, 1948. On the interconnectedness of Ghanaian consumer politics as exemplified by the boycott and the history of decolonization, see Bianca Murillo, *Market Encounters: Consumer Cultures in Twentieth-Century Ghana* (Athens, OH: Ohio University Press, 2017), 1–4.

70 As Killingray notes, the Ex-serviceman's Union was founded in 1920 and went through several reforms and splits during the 1920s and 1930s; Killingray, "Soldiers, Ex-Servicemen, and Politics in the Gold Coast," 529.

71 TNAUK, CO 964/9, "Petition Addressed to H.E. the Governor, Handed in at the Secretariat at 2.50 P. M. on 28th February by Mr. B. E. A. Tamakloe and Five Others."

72 TNAUK, CO 964/11, "Disturbances—Summary of Events."

73 TNAUK, CO 964/26, Testimony of Ebenezer Horatio Ashley, April 13, 1948, in Gold Coast Colony, Commission of Enquiry.

74 TNAUK, CO 964/26, Testimony of Emmanuel Kpokpo Allotey, April 13, 1948, in Gold Coast Colony, Commission of Enquiry.

75 The Watson Commission recorded two deaths as a result of the police shootings, whereas Ghanaian popular memory holds three dead; see Colonial Office, *Report of the Commission of Enquiry*, 10–14; Austin, *Politics in Ghana*, 74; Enoch Darfah Frimpong, "Busts of February 28 Victims," *Graphic Online*, February 28, 2013, https://www.graphic.com.gh/features/features/busts-of-february-28-victims.html (accessed January 15, 2023). I thank Edem Adotey for highlighting this discrepancy.

76 TNAUK, CO 964/26, Testimony of Emmanuel Kpokpo Allotey, April 13, 1948, in Gold Coast Colony, Commission of Enquiry.

77 TNAUK, CO 964/26, Testimony of Victor Hutchinson, April 13, 1948, in Gold Coast Colony, Commission of Enquiry.

78 TNAUK, CO 964/11, W. R. Reeve, "Statement by Mr. W. R. Reeve, Asst. Superintendent of Police, Accra," n.d.

79 TNAUK, CO 964/11, F. J. Hockley, "Statement by Mr. F. J. Hockley, Asst. Superintendent of Police, Accra," n.d.

80 TNAUK, CO 964/11, Superintendent of Police, Ashanti, "Disturbances in Ashanti, 1.3.48-31.3.48."

81 TNAUK, CO 964/11, Capt. R. W. H. Ballantine, "Statement of R. W. H. Ballatine, C. B. E., Commissioner of Police," Accra, April 16, 1948.

82 Ibid.; TNAUK, CO 964/11, Commissioner, The Gold Coast Police, "Note for Information of Commission of Enquiry, Relative to Shooting Incident at Koforidua, on 2nd March 1948"; TNAUK, CO 964/11, Beeton, "Incident which Occurred on the Tafo-Koforidua Road, March 2nd, 1948."

83 TNAUK, CO 964/2, "Table A: Casualties Occurring during the Disturbances," n.d.

84 TNAUK, CO 964/4, "The Measures Taken by Government to Prevent the Further Spread of Disturbances and to Restore Law and Order," n.d.

85 TNAUK, CO 964/21, S. Sakyi Djan to Aitikin [*sic*] Watson, Commission of Enquiry, Accra, May 8, 1948.

86 TNAUK, CO 964/21, S. Sakyi Djan to The Secretary, The Commission of Enquiry (1948), Accra, April 26, 1948.

87 TNAUK, CO 964/21, S. Sakyi Djan, "The Gold Coast Farmers' Grievances Presented by the Farmers' Committee of British West Africa and Their Allied Bodies," Accra, April 26, 1948.

88 TNAUK, CO 964/5, Appendix D: Racial Issues: I. Enoch, "Gold Coast Slipping Away," *West African Monitor*, March 2, 1948. Fears of the Gold Coast becoming a white settler state were not new to the colony's newspapers, but were a feature of the postwar coverage of British colonialism; see, for instance, TNAUK, CO 964/5, Appendix D: Racial Issues: "Next Hoppingground [*sic*] for White Domination West Africa—The Melting Pot of British Imperialism and Colonial Exploitation," *Ashanti Pioneer*, June 9, 1947; TNAUK, CO 964/5, Appendix D: Racial Issues: "Invasion for the Gold Coast," *Daily Echo*, June 24, 1947.

89 TNAUK, CO 964/7, "The People's National Party," May 26, 1947; TNAUK, CO 964/7, J. B. Danquah, "Outline of a Constitution for Ghanaland," Accra, April 16, 1947.

90 TNAUK, CO 964/7, J. B. Danquah, "Outline of a Constitution for Ghanaland," Accra, April 16, 1947.

91 TNAUK, CO 964/7, Kenneth Bradley to Arthur Creech Jones, Accra, December 12, 1947.

92 For a brief biography of Kwame Nkrumah, see Jeffrey S. Ahlman, *Kwame Nkrumah: Visions of Liberation* (Athens, OH: Ohio University Press, 2021).

93 Yale University Beinecke Rare Book and Manuscript Library, Richard Wright Papers, Box 133, Folder 1986, I. T. A. Wallace-Johnson and Kwame Nkrumah, "Aims and Objects of the West African National Secretariat," n.d.

94 Bankole Awooner-Renner, *West African Soviet Union* (London: WANS, 1946). See also Hakim Adi, *West Africans in Britain, 1900–1960: Nationalism, Pan-Africanism, and Communism* (London: Lawrence and Wishart, 1998), 129–31.

95 TNAUK, CO 964/7, R. W. H. Ballantine to Commissioner, Sierra Leone Police, "Francis Nwia-Kofie Nkrumah alias F. N. Kwame Nkrumah," Accra, December 9, 1947.

96 TNAUK, CO 964/7, Kenneth Bradley to Arthur Creech Jones, Accra, December 12, 1947.

97 TNAUK, CO 964/25, UGCC Working Committee telegram, February 29, 1948, quoted in "Brief Narrative of Events from the 17th February, 1948 to the 13th March, 1948." An incomplete version of the telegram can also be found in TNAUK, CO 964/24, "Text of the Cablegram Despatched to the Secretary of State for the Colonies," *National Bulletin*, March 5, 1948 and an incomplete, marked draft in TNAUK, CO 964/24, United Gold Coast Convention to [Secretary of State for the Colonies], [February 29, 1948].

98 TNAUK, CO 964/24, Kwame Nkrumah to Secretary of State for the Colonies, Saltpond, n.d.

99 "Gov't and Female Education," *Evening News*, December 4, 1948; "Local Government," *Evening News*, December 4, 1948; "Cocoa Research," *Evening News*, December 20, 1948; "Gold Coast Education Department," *Evening News*, January 8, 1949; Trade Unionist, "Workers Forum: The Mine-Workers Plight (3)," September 16, 1949; "Accra Diary," *Evening News*, June 1, 1950.

100 Interview: M. N. Tetteh, Accra, March 8, 2008.

101 TNAUK, CO 964/24, [J. B. Danquah] to J. F. Duncan, December 13, 1946.

Chapter 5

1 Kwame Nkrumah, "Foreword" to J. Benibengor Blay, *Gold Coast Mines Employees' Union* (Ilfracombe, UK: Arthur H. Stockwell, 1950), 9.
2 Dorothea Lokko, "The Women's Part," *Evening News*, February 26, 1949.
3 Brong Youths Union, "An Open Letter to Brongs Everywhere," *Evening News*, May 11, 1949.
4 "A. Creech Jones to T. R. O. Mangin, May 24, 1949," in *Ghana*, vol. 1, pt. 1, of *British Documents on the End of the Empire*, ser. B, ed. Richard Rathbone (London: Her Majesty's Stationery Office, 1992), 134–5.
5 Dennis Austin, *Politics in Ghana, 1946–1960* (London: Oxford University Press, 1964), 86–90.
6 Ibid., 90;"Introduction," in *Ghana*, vol. 1, pt. 1, liv., ed. Rathbone; Foreign Office Research Department Memorandum, "A Survey of Communism in Africa," June 1950, in *Ghana*, vol. 1, pt. 1, 273, ed. Rathbone; Oliver Lyttelton, "Amendment of Gold Coast Constitution," Cabinet Memorandum, February 9, 1952, in *Ghana*, vol. 1, pt. 1, 373, ed. Rathbone.
7 "Charles Arden-Clarke to James Griffiths," November 2, 1950, in *Ghana*, vol. 1, pt. 1, 275, ed. Rathbone.
8 Austin, *Politics in Ghana*, 87–91, 103, 141.
9 Interview with Ben A. Nikoi-Oltai, Accra, November 28, 2007.
10 The attempted realization of this new type of citizenship and the experiences of those who directly and indirectly engaged with them is the subject of my first book; Jeffrey S. Ahlman, *Living with Nkrumahism: Nation, State, and Pan-Africanism in Ghana* (Athens, OH: Ohio University Press, 2017).
11 Kwame Nkrumah, in Government of the Gold Coast, Legislative Assembly, *Legislative Assembly Debates*, July 10, 1953, issue 2, col. 263.
12 Kwame Nkrumah, *Ghana: The Autobiography of Kwame Nkrumah* (Edinburgh: Thomas Nelson and Sons, 1957), 187–8.
13 Yale University Beinecke Rare Book and Manuscript Library (hereafter cited as Beinecke Library), Richard Wright Papers (hereafter cited as Wright Papers), Box 22, Folder 342, Richard Wright, Travel Journal, July 10, 1953. Emphasis in original.
14 J. B. Danquah, in Government of the Gold Coast, Legislative Assembly, *Legislative Assembly Debates*, July 10, 1953, issue 2, cols. 285–303, quotes on 287.
15 Beinecke Library, Wright Papers, Wright, Travel Journal, July 10, 1953.
16 Interview: M. N. Tetteh, Accra, March 8, 2008.
17 Interview: Magnet Abenkwan, Koforidua, May 26, 2008.
18 The CPP was not alone among African parties strongly influenced, if not dominated, by women, as numerous scholars have shown. Most recently, see Jacqueline-Bethel Tchouta Mougoué, *Gender, Separatist Politics, and Embodied Nationalism in Cameroon* (Ann Arbor, MI: University of Michigan Press, 2019); Judith W. Byfield, *The Great Upheaval: Women and Nation in Postwar Nigeria* (Athens, OH: Ohio University Press, 2021).
19 Interview: Lawrence Asamoah, Koforidua, May 26, 2008. Tetteh, Abenkwan, and Asamoah—like many Ghanaians—all use Nkrumah and the CPP interchangeably in their descriptions of decolonization-era Gold Coast politics, a feature of Ghanaian political discourse that Nkrumah and the CPP themselves helped cultivate.
20 Kwame Nkrumah, in Government of the Gold Coast, Legislative Assembly, *Legislative Assembly Debates*, July 10, 1953, issue 2, cols. 274–5.

21 New York Public Library, Schomburg Center for Research in Black Culture, St. Clair Drake Papers, Box 66, Folder 1, St. Clair Drake interview with J. B. Danquah (notes), February 1, 1955. See also Ahlman, *Living with Nkrumahism*, 70.

22 Among Danquah's relevant works, see J. B. Danquah, *Gold Coast: Akan Laws and Customs and the Akim Abuakwa Constitution* (London: George Routledge & Sons, 1928); J. B. Danquah, *The Akan Doctrine of God: A Fragment of Gold Coast Ethics and Religion* (London: Lutterworth Press, 1944).

23 Yaw Twumasi, "J. B. Danquah: Towards an Understanding of the Social and Political Ideas of a Ghanaian Nationalist and Politician," *African Affairs* 77, no. 306 (1978): 83–8, quotes on 83, 85.

24 Paul André Ladouceur, *Chiefs and Politicians: The Politics of Regionalism in Northern Ghana* (New York: Longman, 1979), 90–6.

25 Shanni Mahama, interview with Paul André Ladouceur, n.d., in Ladouceur, *Chiefs and Politicians*, 92.

26 In order to avoid confusion with the New Patriotic Party, established in 1992 and abbreviated as NPP in multiple chapters, this book will not abbreviate Northern People's Party.

27 Northern People's Party, *The Constitution* (1954), in Commonwealth Political Ephemera from the Institute of Commonwealth Studies, University of London, Phase I: Africa, Part 4: Ghana, PP7, Fiche 10.

28 Mumumi Bawumia paraphrased in Kofi Ahorsey, "N. P. P. Has been Launched," *Daily Graphic*, April 15, 1954.

29 Jean Allman, "'Hewers of Wood, Carriers of Water': Islam, Class, and Politics on the Eve of Ghana's Independence," *African Studies Review* 34, no. 2 (1990): 2, 5–11.

30 Abdul Rahim Alawa, quoted in "M. A. P. Not for Muslims Alone," *Ashanti Pioneer*, April 27, 1954.

31 See, for instance, Jean Marie Allman, *The Quills of the Porcupine: Asante Nationalism in an Emergent Ghana* (Madison, WI: University of Wisconsin Press, 1992), 33–6.

32 Alawa, quoted in "M. A. P. Not for Muslims Alone," *Ashanti Pioneer*, April 27, 1954.

33 Alhaji Banda, quoted in Ibid.

34 Richard Rathbone, *Nkrumah & the Chiefs: The Politics of Chieftaincy in Ghana, 1951–60* (Athens, OH: Ohio University Press, 2000), 22.

35 On the CPP's treatment of the chiefs in the *Evening News*, see, for instance, Kofi Aboagye, "Chiefs, and Sages! Shy in Slumber?," *Evening News*, July 22, 1949; "I am Fed Up with the African Imperialists," *Evening News*, October 6, 1949; George Padmore, "African Chiefs Instruments of British Colonial Rule, Says Fabian Colonial Bureau Report," *Evening News*, June 1, 1950.

36 Editorial, *Evening News*, January 5, 1950, quoted in Rathbone, *Nkrumah & the Chiefs*, 22. Throughout Ghana, sandals are key symbols of chieftaincy as an institution.

37 Broadly, on the relationship between the CPP and the chiefs, see Rathbone, *Nkrumah & the Chiefs*.

38 For a concise historiographical survey of how the 1950s and 1960s generation of scholars shaped academic understandings of chieftaincy, see Olufemi Vaughan, *Nigerian Chiefs: Traditional Power in Modern Politics, 1890s–1990s* (Rochester, NY: University of Rochester Press, 2000), 3–13.

39 Nana Arhin Brempong (Kwame Arhin), "Chieftaincy, An Overview," in *Chieftaincy in Ghana: Culture, Governance, and Development*, eds. Irene K. Odotei and Albert K. Awedoba (Accra: Sub-Saharan Publishers, 2006), 27, 36–40.

40 Vaughan, *Nigerian Chiefs*, esp. 6–7, 210–17.

41 Interview: Eden Bentum Takyi-Micah, Accra, May 10, 2008. For more on Takyi-Micah, specifically on his interpretation of the effects Nkrumah and CPP governance had on Ghanaian life, see Ahlman, *Living with Nkrumahism*, 107, 110–11.

42 Interview: Eden Bentum Takyi-Micah, Accra, March 17, 2008 and May 10, 2008.

43 National Liberation Movement, Leaflet, September 19, 1954, reproduced in Allman, *The Quills of the Porcupine*, 19. Emphasis in original.

44 Kofi Bour, "Attacks on Asantehene," *Ashanti Pioneer*, February 5, 1955.

45 National Executive of the Convention People's Party, *Manifesto for the General Election, 1954* (Accra: National Executive of the Convention People's Party, 1954), 7, in Ivor Wilks-Phyllis Ferguson Collection of Materials on Ghana (hereafter cited as Wilks-Ferguson Collection), Reel 1.

46 In August 1955 alone, the articles included "Asantehene Desecrates Golden Stool," *Evening News*, August 3, 1955; George Padmore, "Ashanti Tribalists Can't Holdup Independence," *Evening News*, August 4, 1955; W. S. Johnson, "Asanteman Council Has Failed," *Evening News*, August 9, 1955; Mena Mesi, "Will Asantehene Leave Jantuah Alone?," *Evening News*, August 11, 1955; George Padmore, "Tribalist Aristocrats and Feudalist Chiefs Resent Rule of Common People," *Evening News*, August 16, 1955; "Asantehene: From Grace to Grass," *Evening News*, August 16, 1955; Mabel Dove, "Golden Stool: Kwame Nkrumah Greater than Okomfo Anokye," *Evening News*, August 25, 1955; "Tribal Autocracy Opposed to Parliamentary Democracy," *Evening News*, August 26, 1955.

47 Halidu Asante Kramo, "Federation," *Ashanti Pioneer*, January 15, 1955.

48 "'I Joined the NLM to Save my Life'—Man Tells Quist Inquiry," *Daily Graphic*, July 27, 1957.

49 Allman, *The Quills of the Porcupine*, 51–83; Ahlman, *Living with Nkrumahism*, 76–7.

50 Allman, *The Quills of the Porcupine*, 152.

51 Ibid.; Austin, *Politics in Ghana*, 354. The CPP won 57 percent of the overall vote.

52 On the threats of Asante secession, see Allman, *The Quills of the Porcupine*, 162–75.

53 Akwasi Bosumtwi, "Ashanti's Future," *Ashanti Pioneer*, January 4, 1957.

54 Beinecke Library, Wright Papers, Box 5, Folder 81, Richard Wright, "The Birth of a Man and the Birth of a Nation," unpublished ms. [1957?].

55 University of Massachusetts Amherst Libraries, Special Collections and University Archives, W. E. B. Du Bois Papers (MS 312), W. E. B. Du Bois to Kwame Nkrumah, Brooklyn, 1957.

56 Much of my previous work has explored the Nkrumah-led postcolonial government's pan-African initiatives. Most succinctly, see Ahlman, *Kwame Nkrumah*, 88–138. See also Matteo Grilli, *Nkrumaism and African Nationalism: Ghana's Pan-African Foreign Policy in the Age of Decolonization* (New York: Palgrave Macmillan, 2018).

57 Peter Molotsi, quoted in Luli Callinicos, *Oliver Tambo: Beyond the Engeli Mountains* (Cape Town: David Philip Publishers, 2004), 264.

58 Ashanti Command to Kwame Nkrumah, "The Unknown Warriors," Kumasi, July 26, 1962, in Wilks-Ferguson Collection, Reel 1. See also Allman, *The Quills of the Porcupine*, 184–92.

59 On the politics of Ewe unification, see D. E. K. Amenumey, *The Ewe Unification Movement: A Political History* (Accra: Ghana Universities Press, 1989), esp. 270–7; Kate Skinner, *The Fruits of Freedom in British Togoland: Literacy, Politics and Nationalism, 1914-2014* (Cambridge: Cambridge University Press, 2015), 122–67.

60 Ako Adjei, Government of Ghana, National Assembly, *Parliamentary Debates*, ser. 1, May 1, 1957, cols. 127–8. Also referenced and quoted, along with the Ashanti Command, in Ahlman, *Living with Nkrumahism*, 87.

61 Skinner, *The Fruits of Freedom in British Togoland*, 170 and, more broadly, 168–207.

62 Ako Adjei, in Government of Ghana, National Assembly, *Parliamentary Debates*, April 30, 1957, ser. 1, vol. 6, cols. 61–2, quote on 61.

63 On the question of British imperial citizenship, see Daniel Gorman, *Imperial Citizenship: Empire and the Question of Belonging* (Manchester: Manchester University Press, 2006); Frederick Cooper, *Citizenship, Inequality, and Difference: Historical Perspectives* (Princeton, NJ: Princeton University Press, 2018), 54–62, 96–104.

64 Adjei, in Government of Ghana, National Assembly, *Parliamentary Debates*, ser. 1, April 30, 1957, col. 64.

65 Ibid., cols. 64–7.

66 Ibid., col. 64.

67 W. Baidoe-Ansah, in Government of Ghana, National Assembly, *Parliamentary Debates*, ser. 1, April 30, 1957, vol. 6, col. 73.

68 Victor Owusu, in Government of Ghana, National Assembly, *Parliamentary Debates*, ser. 1, April 30, 1957, vol. 6, cols. 68–70.

69 Ibid., cols. 69–73.

70 R. R. Amponsah, in Government of Ghana, National Assembly, *Parliamentary Debates*, ser. 1, April 30, 1957, vol. 6, cols. 76–7.

71 Cobina Kessie, in Government of Ghana, National Assembly, *Parliamentary Debates*, ser. 1, April 30, 1957, vol. 6, col. 83.

72 J. A. Braimah, in Government of Ghana, National Assembly, *Parliamentary Debates*, ser. 1, April 30, 1957, vol. 6, col. 82.

73 A. J. Dowuona-Hammond, in Government of Ghana, National Assembly, *Parliamentary Debates*, ser. 1, April 30, 1957, vol. 6, col. 87.

74 S. S. Quarcoopome, "Urbanisation, Land Alienation and Politics in Accra," *Research Review NS* 8, nos. 1 and 2 (1992): 47–50.

75 "Two Challenge Deportation Orders," *Daily Graphic*, August 1, 1957; Geoffrey Bing, quoted in R. A. Lomotey, "Two Alhajis Refused Bail," *Daily Graphic*, August 19, 1957.

76 "Deportation Cases—PM Speaks on Today's New Bill," *Daily Graphic*, August 22, 1957; "Govt Introduces New Bill on Deportations," *Daily Graphic*, August 23, 1957; Austin, *Politics in Ghana*, 377n18.

77 Bankole Timothy, *Kwame Nkrumah: His Rise to Power* (London: George Allen & Unwin, 1955).

78 "Bankole Timothy Sacked from Ghana: Deportation Orders against Two Others," *Evening News*, August 1, 1957.

79 "The Ghana Deportations," *West Africa*, August 10, 1957.

80 "British Press on the Deportations," *Daily Graphic*, August 2, 1957.

81 Rathbone, *Nkrumah & the Chiefs*, 103–4.

82 Kwame Nkrumah, *Africa Must Unite* (London: Panaf, 1963); Kwame Nkrumah, *Neo-colonialism: The Last Stage of Imperialism* (London: Thomas Nelson, 1965).

83 This reading of the Gold Coast/Ghanaian decolonization-era political scene arguably underpins the political philosophy of the *Evening News* in the 1950s and well into the 1960s, especially when read cumulatively. For some representative articles highlighting different aspects of this political viewpoint, see "Ban the MAP!," *Evening News*, June 19, 1954; "NLM is Doomed," *Evening News*, June 24, 1955; "Remnants of Imperialism," April 14, 1956.

84 Edward Asafu-Adjaye quoted in "High Commissioner Broadcasts on Ghana Arrest—Statement on B. B. C.," *Ghana Today*, November 26, 1958.

85 On the Awhaitey affair, see Jeffrey S. Ahlman, "'The Strange Case of Major Awhaitey':
    Conspiracy, Testimonial Evidence, and Narratives of Nation in Ghana's Postcolonial
    Democracy," *International Journal of African Historical Studies* 50, no. 2 (2017):
    225–49.

86 Geoffrey Bing, *Reap the Whirlwind: An Account of Kwame Nkrumah's Ghana from
    1950 to 1966* (London: MacGibbon and Kee, 1968), 244, 246. Bing carries these
    arguments much further in the government's statement on the findings of the
    commission of enquiry established to investigate the Awhaitey affair, of which he
    was the primary author; Government of Ghana, *Statement by the Government on
    the Report of the Commission Appointed to Enquire into the Matters Disclosed at the
    Trial of Captain Benjamin Awhaitey before a Court-Martial, and the Surrounding
    Circumstances* (Accra: Government Printer, 1959).

87 Kwame Nkrumah, in Government of Ghana, National Assembly, *Parliamentary
    Debates*, ser. 1, July 14, 1958, vol. 11, cols. 407, 410–11.

88 On the process by which the CPP began to argue for a one-party democracy and
    the use of preventative detention in it, see Ahlman, *Living with Nkrumahism*,
    esp. 148–203.

89 Government of Ghana, *Report of the Commission Appointed under the Commission
    of Enquiry Ordinance (CAP. 249): Enquiry into Matters Disclosed at the Trial of
    Captain Benjamin Awhaitey held on the 20th and 21st [sic] January, 1959, before a
    Court Martial Convened at Giffard Camp, Accra, and the Surrounding Circumstances*
    (Accra: Government Printer, 1959), 4–6, 26–7, 43–6.

90 "Ex-Detainee," *West Africa*, August 14, 1966; Howard University Moorland-Spingarn
    Research Center, Manuscript Division, Kwame Nkrumah Papers, Box 154-39, Folder
    1, interview by unknown with Modesto Apaloo, July 1969. The CPP government also
    submitted an extradition request to the Togolese government in an effort to detain
    a fourth individual involved in the case, John Kodjo Mensah Anthony who at the
    time resided in Togo and was Apaloo's half-brother; Public Records and Archives
    Administration Department (hereafter cited as PRAAD)-Accra, Record Group
    (hereafter cited as RG) 17/1/154 (Special Collections [hereafter cited as SC]/Bureau of
    African Affairs [hereafter cited as BAA]/108), Kwame Nkrumah to Sylvanus Olympio,
    Accra, June 5, 1959; PRAAD-Accra, RG 17/1/154 (SC/BAA/108), Sylvanus Olympio
    to Kwame Nkrumah, Lomé, June 14, 1959; PRAAD-Accra, RG 17/1/154 (SC/
    BAA/108), Kwame Nkrumah to Sylvanus Olympio, Accra, June 18, 1959.

91 PRAAD-Accra, RG 17/1/154 (SC/BAA/108), Victor Paley to Kwame Nkrumah,
    Accra, May 27, 1959.

92 "Detention Orders in Ghana," *Times of London*, June 6, 1959; "Awhaitey Detained,"
    Daily Graphic, June 6, 1959.

93 Memorandum of Conversation between K. A. Busia, Stanley M. Cleveland, and
    Robert A. Cleveland, Brussels, December 12, 1960, appendix to Amembassy
    BRUSSELS to Department of State, Washington, February 17, 1961, "Conversation
    with K. A. Busia," in John F. Kennedy National Security Files, Africa: National
    Security Files, 1961–1963 (Frederick, MD: University Publications of America, 1987),
    First Supplement, Reel 1.

94 Austin, *Politics in Ghana*, 406–7.

95 "All Five to Die for Treason," *Daily Graphic*, February 9, 1965; Kwame Nkrumah,
    Republic of Ghana, National Assembly, *Parliamentary Debates*, ser. 1, March 26, 1965,
    vol. 38, col. 1529; Ahlman, *Living with Nkrumahism*, 199–200.

96 Ahlman, *Living with Nkrumahism*, 189, 192–6.

97 PRAAD-Kumasi, Ashanti Regional Archives (hereafter cited as ARG) 17/1/18,
    "Meeting held between the Regional Organiser, Ghana Young Pioneers, Ashanti,
    Comrade R. O. Frimpong-Manso and the Headmaster of Opoku Ware Secondary
    School, Mr. Kalinauckas, on Thursday 11th January, 1962 at the Headmaster's Office
    at Opoku Ware Secondary School."
98 PRAAD-Kumasi, ARG 17/1/18, "Minutes of Discussions between Comrade
    R. O. Frimpong-Manso, Ashanti Regional Organiser of the Ghana Young Pioneers
    and Mr. Lawrence Kalinauckas, Headmaster of the Opoku Ware Secondary School,
    Kumasi, at the Headmaster's Office on Wednesday 17th, January 1962."
99 Rodney Nkrumah-Boateng, *Swords and Crosses: The Story of Opoku Ware School,
    1952-2012* (n.p.: Opoku Ware Old Boys Association, n.d.), 38–9.
100 Ahlman, *Living with Nkrumahism*, 140–1, 190.
101 Interview: N. Sifah, Accra, February 16, 2008.
102 Ahlman, *Living with Nkrumahism*, 179–87.

Chapter 6

1   "Seven-Year Development Plan to be Inaugurated: Dawn of the Socialist Paradise,"
    Evening News, March 10, 1964.
2   Government of the Gold Coast, *The Development Plan, 1951: Being a Plan for the
    Economic and Social Development of the Gold Coast as Approved by the Legislative
    Assembly, September 1951* (Accra: Government Printing Department, 1951), 17–18.
    See also Government of the Gold Coast, *Accelerated Development Plan for Education,
    1951* (Accra: Government Printer, 1951).
3   Betty Stein George, *Education in Ghana* (Washington, DC: Government Printing
    Office, 1976), 43, 47.
4   Government of the Gold Coast, *The Development Plan, 1951*.
5   Ibid., 2. On the Volta River Project, see Stephan F. Miescher, *A Dam for Africa:
    Akosombo Stories from Ghana* (Bloomington, IN: Indiana University Press, 2022).
6   Government of Ghana, *Second Development Plan, 1959-64* (Accra: Government
    Printer, 1959), 1.
7   Ibid.
8   The themes of this paragraph are more fully examined in Jeffrey S. Ahlman, *Living
    with Nkrumahism: Nation, State, and Pan-Africanism* (Athens, OH: Ohio University
    Press, 2017), 115–211.
9   For a concise survey of the "uneasy" relationship between Ghana and the Soviet
    Union during the Nkrumah years, see Nana Osei-Opare, "Uneasy Comrades:
    Postcolonial Statecraft, Race, and Citizenship, Ghana-Soviet Relations, 1957–1966,"
    Journal of West African History 5, no. 2 (2019): 85–112. See also Alessandro Iandolo,
    Arrested Development: The Soviet Union in Ghana, Guinea, and Mali, 1955-1968
    (Ithaca, NY: Cornell University Press, 2022).
10 James Ferguson, *Expectations of Modernity: Myths and Meaning of Urban Life on the
    Zambian Copperbelt* (Berkeley, CA: University of California Press, 1999), 1.
11 Kwame Nkrumah, *Towards Colonial Freedom: Africa in the Struggle Against World
    Imperialism* (London: Farleigh, 1947), 9–10.
12 Ahlman, *Living with Nkrumahism*, 35–9. This model for theorizing colonialism
    continued to be influential throughout the twentieth century, as seen in the
    study of Africa with Walter Rodney's *How Europe Underdeveloped Africa*, 2nd ed.
    (Washington, DC: Howard University Press, [1972] 1982).

13 "Remnants of Imperialism," *Evening News*, April 14, 1956.
14 Ibid.; Howard University Moorland-Spingarn Research Center (hereafter cited as MSRC), Manuscript Division, Kwame Nkrumah Papers (hereafter cited as Nkrumah Papers, Box 154-38, Folder 80, Afari-Gyan, "The Task of Mental Decolonisation," n.d. On Afari-Gyan's "mental decolonisation," see also Frank Gerits, "The Ideological Scramble for Africa: The US, Ghanaian, French, and British Competition for Africa's Future, 1953–1963" (PhD diss., Florence, Italy: European University Institute, 2014), 117–18.
15 "Colonialism and Strikes," *Evening News*, October 28, 1949. Du Bois also made a similar argument nearly a half-century earlier; W. E. B. Du Bois, "The African Roots of the War," in *W. E. B. Du Bois: A Reader*, ed. David Levering Lewis (New York: Owl Books, 1995), 642–51; originally published in *Atlantic Monthly* 115, no. 5 (May 1915): 707–14.
16 On the broader relationship between development and education in Ghana and neighboring Côte d'Ivoire, see Elisa Sophie Prosperetti, "Every Available Penny: Expectations, Education, and Development in Postcolonial West Africa" (PhD diss., Princeton, NJ: Princeton University, 2020).
17 Janet Berry Hess, "Imagining Architecture: The Structure of Nationalism in Accra, Ghana," *Africa Today* 47, no. 2 (2000): 35–58; Nate Plageman, "'Accra is Changing, Isn't It?': Urban Infrastructure, Independence, and Nation in the Gold Coast's *Daily Graphic*, 1954–57," *International Journal of African Historical Studies* 43, no. 1 (2010): 137–59; Ahlman, *Living with Nkrumahism*, 52–73.
18 Government of Ghana, *Second Development Plan*, 21.
19 Jeffrey S. Ahlman, "A New Type of Citizen: Youth, Gender, and Generation in the Ghanaian Builders Brigade," *Journal of African History* 53, no. 1 (2012): 87–105.
20 Björn Beckman, *Organising the Farmers: Cocoa Politics and National Development in Ghana* (Uppsala: The Scandinavian Institute of African Studies, 1976), 65–9; Jean Marie Allman, *The Quills of the Porcupine: Asante Nationalism in an Emergent Ghana* (Madison, WI: University of Wisconsin Press, 1993), 26–40.
21 S. G. Nimako and K. A. Gbedemah, cited in "Cocoa Ordinance to be Amended," *Daily Graphic*, August 14, 1954.
22 Beckman, *Organising the Farmers*, 194–8; Allman, *The Quills of the Porcupine*, 26–40.
23 Princeton University Archives (hereafter cited as PUA), W. Arthur Lewis Papers (hereafter cited as Lewis Papers), Box 21, Folder 6, Economic Adviser to Ghana (W. Arthur Lewis), Report No. 1, December 7, 1957.
24 PUA, Lewis Papers, Box 21, Folder 6, Economic Adviser (W. Arthur Lewis) to Prime Minister (Kwame Nkrumah), March 28, 1958.
25 PUA, Lewis Papers, Box 21, Folder 6, Economic Adviser to Ghana (W. Arthur Lewis), Report No. 1, December 7, 1957.
26 See his assessments in PUA, Lewis Papers, Box 21, Folder 11, W. A. Lewis, "Economic and Financial Aspects of the Volta River Project," September 8, 1954; PUA, Lewis Papers, Box 21, Folder 7, Economic Adviser (W. Arthur Lewis), "The Second Development Plan: The Size of the Programme," July 7, 1958. Lewis eventually became firmly against the VRP, see Robert L. Tignor, *W. Arthur Lewis and the Birth of Development Economics* (Princeton, NJ: Princeton University Press, 2006), 199–201.
27 PUA, Lewis Papers, Box 10, Folder 3, Economic Adviser (W. Arthur Lewis) to Kwame Nkrumah, October 31, 1958. Emphasis in original.
28 Krobo Edusei, quoted in "The Signal for Industrial Expansion," *Evening News*, February 12, 1962; Krobo Edusei, in Republic of Ghana, National Assembly, *Parliamentary Debates*, ser. 1, February 6, 1962, vol. 26, col. 199.

29 "The Signal for Industrial Expansion," *Evening News*, February 12, 1962.

30 Yale University Library (hereafter cited as YUL), Manuscripts and Archives, Ghana Collection (MS 1519), Box 1, Folder 10, Kwame Nkrumah, in "Sessional Address delivered by President Nkrumah to the Ghana National Assembly on January 12th, 1965/Budget Statement presented to Parliament by Mr. K. Amoako-Atta, Minister of Finance, on January 21st, 1965," supplement to *Ghana Today*, January 27, 1965.

31 Public Records and Archives Administration Department (hereafter cited as PRAAD)-Accra, Record Group (hereafter cited as RG), RG 8/2/863, Office of the Planning Commission, *First Seven-Year Development Plan*, March 1963, Chapter 2, pages 1–2, quote on 1.

32 On the enduring nature of the promise of electrification, see Stephan F. Miescher, "The Akosombo Dam and the Quest for Rural Electrification in Ghana," in *Electric Worlds/Mondes électriques: Creations, Circulations, Tensions, Transitions (19th-21st C.)*, eds. Alain Beltran, Léonard Laborie, Pierre Lantheir, and Stéphanie Le Gallic (Brussels: Peter Lang, 2016), 317–42.

33 Stephan F. Miescher, "'No One Should be Worse Off': The Akosombo Dam, Modernization, and the Experience of Resettlement in Ghana," in *Modernization as Spectacle in Africa*, eds. Peter J. Bloom, Takyiwaa Manuh, and Stephan F. Miescher (Bloomington, IN: Indiana University Press, 2014), 187–98; Miescher, *A Dam for Africa*, 195–245, 277–356.

34 Dzodzi Tsikata, *Living in the Shadow of Large Dams: Long Term Responses of Downstream and Lakeside Communities of Ghana's Volta River Project* (Leiden: Brill, 2006), 116.

35 Ibid., 115–26.

36 Stephan F. Miescher, "Building the City of the Future: Visions and Experiences of Modernity in Ghana's Akosombo Township," *Journal of African History* 53, no. 3 (2012): 376–81; Miescher, *A Dam for Africa*, 246–73.

37 "Workers' New Role is to Increase Production," *Evening News*, March 24, 1964.

38 PRAAD-Accra, Administrative Files 13/2/78, Minister of Labour and Co-Operatives, "Report of the Productivity and Anti-Laziness Committee," Cabinet Memorandum with appendix, January 10, 1961.

39 See, for instance, "Farmers Pledge to Increase Productivity," *Evening News*, May 12, 1964; PRAAD-Sunyani, Brong Ahafo Archives 3/1/29, "Programme of Work for the Year 1965 by Comrade P. A. C. Atuahene, Party Regional Education Secretary, Sunyani, Brong/Ahafo Region." More broadly, see Ahlman, *Living with Nkrumahism*, 115–47.

40 Keri Lambert, "'It's All Work and Happiness on the Farms': Agricultural Development between the Blocs in Nkrumah's Ghana," *Journal of African History* 60, no. 1 (2019): 34–7.

41 Ahlman, "A New Type of Citizen," 93–102; Ahlman, *Living with Nkrumahism*, 93–6.

42 Ahlman, *Living with Nkrumahism*, 95.

43 PRAAD-Accra, RG 14/1/1, "Note of a Meeting Held in the Ministry of Agriculture," Minutes, February 27, 1958; PRAAD-Accra, RG 14/1/15, Gersbacher, "Report on Ghana Workers Brigade/Foundation and Development," [1965?].

44 Tony Killick, "Manufacturing and Construction," in *A Study of Contemporary Ghana, volume I: The Economy of Ghana*, eds. Walter Birmingham, I. Neustadt, and E. N. Omaboe (London: George Allen & Unwin, 1966), 288.

45 Republic of Ghana, *1962 Industrial Census Report, Volume I: Industry (Mining and Quarrying, Manufacturing, Construction, Electricity, Gas, and Steam)* (Accra: Central Bureau of Statistics, 1965), xxiv.

46 Killick, "Manufacturing and Construction," 275–6, 279–80, 287.

47 Douglas Rimmer, "New Industrial Relations in Ghana," *Industrial and Labor Relations Review* 14, no. 2 (1961): 206–26; Richard Jeffries, *Class, Power, and Ideology in Ghana: The Railwaymen of Sekondi* (Cambridge: Cambridge University Press, 1978), 71–107; Jeff Crisp, *The Story of an African Working Class: Ghanaian Miners' Struggles, 1870–1980* (London: Zed Books, 1984), 125–49; Ahlman, *Living with Nkrumahism*, 115–47, 160–75.

48 E. B. Mac-Hardjor, "Increased Productivity: What It Means for Our Prosperity," *Ghanaian*, January 1965.

49 Ayi Kwei Armah, *The Beautyful Ones are Not Yet Born* (Boston, MA: Houghton Mifflin, 1968).

50 Tony Killick, "External Trade," in *A Study of Contemporary Ghana, volume I: The Economy of Ghana*, eds. Walter Birmingham, I. Neustadt, and E. N. Omaboe (London: George Allen & Unwin, 1966), 348.

51 Beckman, *Organising the Farmers*, 207; St. Clair Drake and Leslie Alexander Lacy, "Government versus the Unions: The Sekondi-Takoradi Strike, 1961," in *Politics in Africa: Seven Cases*, ed. Gwendolen Carter (New York: Harcourt, Brace & World, 1966), 73 87; Ahlman, *Living with Nkrumahism*, 134–9.

52 YUL, Manuscripts and Archives, Ghana Collection (MS 1519), Box 1, Folder 10, K. Amoaka-Atta, in "Sessional Address delivered by President Nkrumah to the Ghana National Assembly on January 12th, 1965/Budget Statement presented to Parliament by Mr. K. Amoako-Atta, Minister of Finance, on January 21st, 1965," supplement to *Ghana Today*, January 27, 1965.

53 Jennifer Hart, *Ghana on the Go: African Mobility in the Age of Motor Transportation* (Bloomington, IN: Indiana University Press, 2016), 124–30.

54 John C. Caldwell, *African Rural-Urban Migration: The Movement to Ghana's Towns* (New York: Columbia University Press, 1969), 137–8.

55 Anon, Circle Odawna Driver, Accra, August 27, 2009, interview with Jennifer Hart, quoted in Hart, *Ghana on the Go*, 130.

56 Isaac Kojo Nkrumah Buaful, "Pioneers Ready to be Trained as Loco Drivers & Engineers," *Evening News*, 14 October 1961.

57 Nana Osei-Opare, "'If You Trouble a Hungry Snake, You Will Force It to Bite You': Rethinking Postcolonial African Archival Pessimism, Worker Discontent, and Petition Writing in Ghana, 1957–66," *Journal of African History* 62, no. 1 (2021): 59–60.

58 Ibid., 59–78.

59 Drake and Lacy, "Government versus the Unions," 105; Jeffries, *Class, Power, and Ideology in Ghana*, 99–100.

60 Crisp, *The Story of an African Working Class*, 134, 136–9.

61 J. D. Esseks, "Economic Policies," in *Politicians and Soldiers in Ghana, 1966–1972*, eds. Dennis Austin and Robin Luckham (London: Frank Cass, 1975), 37–39.

62 [J. A. Ankrah], "Broadcast by the Chairman of the National Liberation Council on Wednesday, 2nd March 1966," in Government of Ghana, National Liberation Council, *Rebuilding the National Economy* (Accra: Ministry of Information, 1966), 1–7.

63 Esseks, "Economic Policies," 43; Osei-Opare, "Uneasy Comrades," 103–4.

64 PRAAD-Accra, RG 3/5/1636, Office of the NLC, "Special Audit Investigations Ordered by the National Liberation Council," April 19, 1966.

65 PRAAD-Accra, RG 3/5/1636, E. K. Acquah, F. A. Dontoh, and B. K. Hanson to NLC, Winneba, March 4, 1966; Gerardo Serra and Frank Gerits, "The Politics of Socialist Education in Ghana: The Kwame Nkrumah Ideological Institute, 1961-6," *Journal of African History* 60, no. 3 (2019): 426–7.

66   PRAAD-Accra, RG 14/1/15, Workers Brigade—Notes Taken at a Meeting in the
     Principal Assistant Secretary's Office—Ministry of Defence," Minutes, March 14, 1966.
67   PRAAD-Accra, RG 14/1/15, P. Laryea to Principal Secretary, Ministry of Defence,
     "The Re-Organisation and the Strength of the Workers Brigade," Accra, September
     14, 1966. A year later, the NLC's Chief of Defence Staff, A. K. Ocran, noted a further
     decrease in the size of the Brigade down to 18,000, albeit with an apparent increase
     in the number of camps to 78. This number was up from the 52 near the time of
     Nkrumah's overthrow; PRAAD-Accra, RG 14/1/16, Major-General A. K. Ocran,
     "Address on the Occasion of the Sector Supervisor's Conference," Accra, April 5, 1967.
     See also, PRAAD-Accra, 14/1/15, Gersbacher, "Report on Ghana Workers Brigade/
     Foundation and Development," [1965?].
68   Esseks, "Economic Policies," 45–6; Lambert, "'It's All Work and Happiness on the
     Farms,'" 42–3.
69   Esseks, "Economic Policies," 45–6.
70   Ibid., 46. However, even some NLC-era reports acknowledged that, at least after 1963,
     most of Ghana's state enterprises were profitable; see PRAAD-Cape Coast, RG 1/8/28,
     H. P. Nelson, introduction to *A Report on the Administration and Operation of State
     Enterprises under the Work Schedule of the State Enterprises Secretariat for the Period
     1964–65* (December 1, 1966).
71   [Ankrah], "Broadcast by the Chairman of the National Liberation Council on
     Wednesday, 2nd March 1966," 5.
72   International Bank for Reconstruction and Development [World Bank], International
     Development Association, Africa Department, *Stabilization and Development in
     Ghana*, Report No. AF-57a, March 14, 1967, ix–xi. See also Esseks, "Economic
     Policies," 43–4. On February 17, 1967, the Ghanaian government issued a new
     currency—the New Cedi (N¢)—which it pegged at N¢.71=$1. In July 1967, the
     government would devalue the New Cedi to N¢1.02=$1.
73   World Bank, *Stabilization and Development in Ghana*, 75.
74   MSRC, Manuscript Division, Nkrumah Papers, Box 154-39, Folder 10, Civil Service
     Statement in Embassy of the Republic of Ghana (Moscow), "Messages of Support for
     the National Liberation Council," 1966.
75   MSRC, Manuscript Division, Nkrumah Papers, Box 154-39, Folder 10, Ghana
     Chamber of Mines Statement in Embassy of the Republic of Ghana (Moscow),
     "Messages of Support for the National Liberation Council," 1966.
76   E. A. Cowan, *Evolution of Trade Unionism in Ghana* (Accra: Ghana Trades Union
     Congress, [1960?]), 91–111.
77   MSRC, Manuscript Division, Nkrumah Papers, Box 154-39, Folder 10, Ghana
     Trades Union Congress Statement in Embassy of the Republic of Ghana (Moscow),
     "Messages of Support for the National Liberation Council," 1966.
78   See, for instance, Lawrence Bessah's case in Ahlman, *Living with Nkrumahism*,
     196–7, 206.
79   Public Records and Archives Administration Department—Sekondi, Western
     Regional Archives 24/2/4, D. J. Buahin to Secretary of the National Liberation
     Council, Sunyani, April 23, 1966.
80   PRAAD-Accra, RG 14/1/60, K. Acheampong to Commanding Officer, Workers
     Brigade, "Acquisition of Site at New Edubiase," Kumasi, March 21, 1966; PRAAD-
     Accra, RG 14/1/60, Kwasi Adomah to Secretary, National Liberation Council,
     "The Humble Petition of Chief Kwasi Adomah Aduanahene of Kwamang-Ashanti,
     Sheweth," Kumasi, September 17, 1966.

81 PRAAD-Accra, RG 14/1/60, Kwaku Mensah to Chairman, National Liberation Council, "Petition of Kwaku Mensah of Bimma, Against the Mampong/Ashanti Workers Brigade," Nsuta-Ashanti, September 27, 1967; PRAAD-Accra, RG 14/1/60, Yaw Barimah to Chairman, National Liberation Council, "The Complaint of Yaw Barimah of Bimma, Near Nsuta-Ashanti," Nsuta-Ashanti, September 28, 1967; PRAAD-Accra, RG 14/1/60, Kwame Boadi to Chairman, National Liberation Council, "A Complaint Against the Members of the Workers Brigade," Nsuta-Ashanti, September [27/28?], 1967.

82 PRAAD-Accra, RG 14/1/60, P. Laryea to Principal Secretary of the Ministry of Defence, "Land for Workers Brigade, Kwamang Ashanti," Accra, October 24, 1966; PRAAD-Accra, RG 14/1/60, J. E. S. de Graft-Hayford to Principal Secretary, Ministry of Defence, "Petition of Yaw Barimah and Three Others against Dispossession of Their Farm Lands," Accra, December 14, 1967.

83 PRAAD-Accra, RG 14/1/60, A Citizen to Chairman, Expediting Committee, "Complaint about Pay Anomalies in the Workers Brigade," Omankope, May 20, 1968.

84 Hart, *Ghana on the Go*, 130–2.

85 Crisp, *The Story of an African Working Class*, 150–1.

86 Jeff Crisp, "Union Atrophy and Worker Revolt: Labour Protest at Tarkwa Goldfields, Ghana, 1968–1969," *Canadian Journal of African Studies* 13, no. 1/2 (1979): 267–70.

87 Crisp, *The Story of an African Working Class*, 151.

88 Jon Kraus, "Strikes and Labour Power in Ghana," *Development and Change* 10 (1979): 265.

89 "Radio Workers To Get Pay Increases," *Ghana Workers' Bulletin*, January 7, 1967; "Hats Off to Them!!," *Ghana Workers Bulletin*, April 6, 1968; "Workers to Get Bonus," *Ghana Workers Bulletin*, April 6, 1968.

90 "T. U. C. Will Not Encourage Strikes," *Ghana Workers' Bulletin*, January 7, 1967; Nee Amarh Amartey, "Recent Strikes—Some of the Causes," *Ghana Workers' Bulletin*, April 1969.

91 Margaret Peil, *The Ghanaian Factory Worker: Industrial Man in Africa* (Cambridge: Cambridge University Press, 1972), 221.

92 Ibid., 87.

93 Robin Luckham, "The Constitutional Commission 1966–69," in *Politicians and Soldiers in Ghana, 1966–1972*, eds. Dennis Austin and Robin Luckham (London: Frank Cass, 1975), 64.

94 Beckman, *Organising the Farmers*, 222.

95 Ibid., 279.

96 Noami Chazan, *An Anatomy of Ghanaian Politics: Managing Political Recession, 1969–1982* (Boulder, CO: Westview Press, 1983), 159; Polly Hill, *The Gold Coast Cocoa Farmer: A Preliminary Survey* (Oxford: Oxford University Press, 1956), 132.

97 David Goldsworthy, "Ghana's Second Republic: A Post-Mortem," *African Affairs* 72, no. 286 (1973): 10.

98 National Liberation Council, quoted in Eboe Hutchful, "International Debt Renegotiation: Ghana's Experiences," *Africa Development* 9, no. 2 (1984): 17.

99 Hutchful, "International Debt Renegotiation," 18–19, 21–23.

100 J. H. Mensah, speech excerpted in "Proceedings of the Ghana Debt Conference, Marlborough House, London, 7–11 July 1970, record of the opening session, 7 July 1970," in Eboe Hutchful, *The IMF and Ghana: The Confidential Record* (London: Zed Books, 1987), 259, 263.

101 Cameron Duodu, "Ghana's Case for Debt Relief," *Daily Graphic*, July 10, 1970.

102 A. Kumar, "Lessons of the Abortive Talks," *Daily Graphic*, July 20, 1970.

Chapter 7

1 Baffour Awuakye-Akantang II, letter to the editor included in "What Our Readers Say about Ghana's Debts," *Daily Graphic*, July 18, 1970.
2 Kwamena Anaman, letter to the editor included in "What Our Readers Say about Ghana's Debts," *Daily Graphic*, July 18, 1970.
3 See, for instance, the assessment of the Ghanaian economy and government in Princeton University Archives, W. Arthur Lewis Papers, Box 20, Folder 10, International Monetary Fund, "Ghana Aid Meeting," Palais d'UNESCO, Paris, February 20–2, 1968.
4 [Government of Ghana], *Ghana's External Debt Problem: Its Nature and Solution: Submitted by the Government of Ghana to the Creditor Countries* (April 1970), 6, more broadly 1–14.
5 Ibid., 67–9; "Mensah: We'll Operate Pact under Protest," *Daily Graphic*, July 13, 1970.
6 J.H. Mensah, quoted in "Mensah: We'll Operate Pact under Protest."
7 Ibid.
8 Dennis Austin, *Ghana Observed: Essays on the Politics of a West African Republic* (Manchester: Manchester University Press, 1976), 135–6.
9 Howard University Moorland-Spingarn Research Center, Manuscript Division, Kwame Nkrumah Papers, Box 154-39, Folder 13, Interview with Mr. Gbedemah, July 1969.
10 Ibid.
11 K. A. Gbedemah, reported in "Political Roundup," *Daily Graphic*, July 1, 1969.
12 J. T. Ofei, reported in "Political Roundup," *Daily Graphic*, August 25, 1969.
13 E. R. T. Madjitey, reported in "Political Roundup," *Daily Graphic*, August 28, 1969.
14 K. A. Busia, reported in "Political Roundup," *Daily Graphic*, July 10, 1969. See also interviews with Eden Bentum Takyi-Micah, Accra, March 17, 2008 and May 10, 2008.
15 Busia, reported in "Political Roundup," *Daily Graphic*, July 10, 1969.
16 Busia, reported in "Political Roundup," *Daily Graphic*, July 14, 1969.
17 See, for instance, E. T. Assimeh, reported in "Political Roundup," *Daily Graphic*, July 9, 1969.
18 Oheneba Kow Richardson, reported in "Political Roundup," July 8, 1969.
19 "Landslide Victory for Progress Party," *Daily Graphic*, September 1, 1969; "The People Have Spoken," *Daily Graphic*, September 1, 1969.
20 Austin, *Ghana Observed*, 130–1.
21 S. N. Essien, "Police Arrest 48 Strikers," *Daily Graphic*, September 5, 1969.
22 S. N. Essien, "Workers Threaten to Strike," *Daily Graphic*, September 8, 1969.
23 See, for instance, "2-Year Development Plan," *Daily Graphic*, September 24, 1969.
24 [Ghana Public Relations Department], *Second Milestone: A Record of Achievements of the Progress Party Government since It Came to Power Two Years Ago: October 1st, 1969–October 1st, 1971* (Accra: Ghana Public Relations Department, 1971), 1.
25 I. M. Otu Addo, "These Pressing Problems," *Daily Graphic*, October 2, 1969. Emphasis in original.
26 Ibid.
27 "Farmers' Appeal," *Daily Graphic*, October 2, 1969.
28 "Cocoa Price Won't Be Cut," *Daily Graphic*, October 3, 1969. Afrifa's declaration essentially confirmed a previously announced July 1969 increase in the producer from the N¢7 price established a year earlier; Douglas Rimmer, *Staying Poor: Ghana's Political Economy, 1950–1990* (Oxford: Pergamon, 1992), 112.

29 "Cocoa Price Won't Be Cut," *Daily Graphic*, October 3, 1969.

30 "Wages and Cocoa," *West Africa*, September 13, 1969.

31 "Power for Rural Areas Next Year," *Daily Graphic*, September 11, 1969; "Govt Plans Rural Bus Service," *Daily Graphic*, September 15, 1969; S. N. Essien, "NC 8M Water Project for Rural Arears [*sic*]," *Daily Graphic*, September 18, 1969; P. Peregrino-Peters, "Good Health! New Govt Pledges Nation-Wide Crash Plan," *Daily Graphic*, September 19, 1969.

32 Frank Achampong, "A Chance Never to be Forgotten," *Daily Graphic*, October 2, 1969.

33 Iddrissu Seini, "The Problems are Many, the Challenge is Great," *Daily Graphic*, October 28, 1969.

34 "Munufie in the North," *Daily Graphic*, November 5, 1969.

35 "'No Permit' Aliens to Quit," *Daily Graphic*, November 19, 1969.

36 J. A. Kufuor, reported in "Policy on Aliens Explained," *Daily Graphic*, December 13, 1969.

37 Kwaku Baah, reported in "Policy on Aliens Explained," *Daily Graphic*, December 13, 1969. Also quoted in Margaret Peil, "The Expulsion of West African Aliens," *Journal of Modern African Studies* 9, no. 2 (1971): 209–10.

38 Kwaku Baah, in Republic of Ghana, National Assembly, *Parliamentary Debates*, ser. 2, December 4, 1969, vol. 1, col. 315.

39 Johnson Olaosebikan Aremu and Adeyinka Theresa Ajayi, "Expulsion of Nigerian Immigrant Community from Ghana in 1969: Causes and Impact," *Developing Country Studies* 5, no. 10 (2014): 177.

40 Margaret Peil, "Ghana's Aliens," *International Migration Review* 8, no. 3 (1974): 369. Peil notes that the number is likely an undercount since the government undertook the census when seasonal migrants would have returned to their home communities.

41 J. S. Eades, *Strangers and Traders: Yoruba Migrants, Markets, and the State in Northern Ghana* (Trenton, NJ: Africa World, 1994), 1, 80–1.

42 Ibid., 85–91, 171–72.

43 Rashid Olaniyi, "The 1969 Ghana Exodus: Memory and Reminiscences of Yoruba Migrants," unpublished ms. (n.d.), 6–7, 18–19. See also Peil, "The Expulsion of West African Aliens," 225.

44 "Police to Comb for Defaulters," *Daily Graphic*, December 3, 1969; "Police to Intensify Hunt for Aliens," *Daily Graphic*, December 18, 1969. For a case study of the threats posed to immigrants in Kumasi specifically, see Nana Osei Quarshie, "Mass Expulsion as Internal Exclusion: Police Raids and the Imprisonment of West African Immigrants in Ghana, 1969–1974," in *Confinement, Punishment, and Prisons in Africa*, eds. Marie Morelle, Frédéric Le Marcis, and Julia Hornberger (London: Hurst, 2021), 40–55.

45 Government Statement, quoted in "Police to Comb for Defaulters," *Daily Graphic*, December 3, 1969.

46 "Police to Comb for Defaulters," *Daily Graphic*, December 3, 1969.

47 "Do Not Molest Aliens—Ministry," *Daily Graphic*, December 9, 1969.

48 "Aliens Looted at Sandema," *Daily Graphic*, December 4, 1969.

49 "Aliens Loot at Tema?," *Daily Graphic*, December 18, 1969; S. Sam Arthur, "Aliens Loot?," *Daily Graphic*, December 23, 1969.

50 Chinaka Fynecontry, "1,000 Nigerians Stranded in Lome," *Daily Times*, December 5, 1969.

51 Olaniyi, "The 1969 Ghana Exodus," 18–19; Andrew Obimah, "Nigerians Trek Home from Ghana," *Daily Times*, December 13, 1969.

52 "1,000 Nigerians in Accra Prison," *Daily Times*, December 7, 1969; "Govt to Probe Ghana Incident," *West African Pilot*, December 8, 1969. By early January, the *West African Pilot* reported upwards of 20,000 Nigerians imprisoned in Ghana; "8 Nigerians Died in Ghana Again," *West African Pilot*, January 3, 1970.

53 "1,000 Nigerians in Accra Prison," *Daily Times*, December 7, 1969.

54 Unnamed individual quoted in Idowu Sobowale, "Nigerian Refugees Shut Out at Border," *Daily Times*, December 11, 1969.

55 Tijani Oyebanji quoted in Sobowale, "Nigerian Refugees Shut Out at Border," *Daily Times*, December 11, 1969. Also quoted in Olaniyi, "The 1969 Ghana Exodus," 20.

56 "20 Refugees from Ghana Killed in a Crash," *Daily Times*, December 10, 1969.

57 "Five More Die in Crash on Way Home from Ghana," *Daily Times*, December 12, 1969.

58 "27 More Refugees Die as Lorry Overturns," *Daily Times*, December 17, 1969; "Nigerian, 63, Killed on Ghana Border," *Daily Times*, December 27, 1969.

59 "10 Nigerians Dead in Refugee Camps," *Daily Times*, December 29, 1969; "8 Nigerians Died in Ghana Again," *West African Pilot*, January 3, 1970. See also Olaniyi, "The 1969 Ghana Exodus," 19.

60 "A Case for Ghana to Answer," *Daily Times*, December 30, 1969.

61 Peil, "The Expulsion of West African Aliens," 225–6.

62 Ibid., 225; "Hungry Alien Back to Ghana," *Daily Graphic*, July 17, 1970.

63 Amadu Moshie, quoted in "Hungry Alien Back to Ghana," *Daily Graphic*, July 17, 1970.

64 See, for instance, J. C. Ashiley, "Aliens," *Daily Graphic*, July 17, 1970.

65 Peil, "The Expulsion of West African Aliens," 226.

66 Ibid., 226–7; Claire C. Robertson, *Sharing the Same Bowl: A Socioeconomic History of Women and Class in Accra, Ghana* (Ann Arbor, MI: University of Michigan Press, 1984), 102n82.

67 Gracia Clark, *Onions are My Husband: Survival and Accumulation by West African Market Women* (Chicago, IL: University of Chicago Press, 1994), 120–1.

68 Jennifer Hart, *Ghana on the Go: African Mobility in the Age of Motor Transportation* (Bloomington, IN: Indiana University Press, 2016), 134.

69 Kwaku Danso-Boafo, *The Political Biography of Dr. Kofi Abrefa Busia* (Accra: Ghana Universities Press, 1996), 105. See also Nana Osei Quarshie, "Cocoa and Compliance: How Exemptions Made Mass Expulsion in Ghana, 1969–1972," unpublished ms.

70 Paul Nugent, *Boundaries, Communities and State-Making in West Africa: The Centrality of the Margins* (Cambridge: Cambridge University Press, 2019), 440.

71 Gwendolyn Mikell, *Cocoa and Chaos in Ghana* (Washington, DC: Howard University Press, 1992), 194.

72 Danso-Boafo, *The Political Biography of Dr. Kofi Abrefa Busia*, 105.

73 "Towards a Free Economy," *Daily Graphic*, December 29, 1971; Dzodzi Tsikata, *Living in the Shadow of Large Dams: Long Term Responses of Downstream and Lakeside Communities of Ghana's Volta River Project* (Leiden: Brill, 2006), xvii. Economists A. D. Amargquaye Laryea and Bernardin Senadza calculated an 80 percent devaluation when accounting for changes in the US dollar; A. D. Amarguaye Laryea and Bernardin Senadza, "Trade and Exchange Rate Policies since Independence and Prospects for the Future," in *The Economy of Ghana Sixty Years after Independence*, eds. Ernest Aryeetey and Ravi Kanbur (Oxford: Oxford University Press, 2017), 108.

74 Mike Oquaye, *Politics in Ghana (1972–1979)* (Accra: Tornado Publications, 1980), 6.

75 "Towards a Free Economy," *Daily Graphic*, December 29, 1971.

76 Laryea and Senadza, "Trade and Exchange Rate Policies since Independence and Prospects for the Future," 108; "P. M. Warns of Hard Times Ahead," *Daily Graphic*, January 1, 1972.

77 I. K. Acheampong, radio address partially reproduced in "COUP!: Army Takes Over," *Daily Graphic*, January 14, 1972. See also Oquaye, *Politics in Ghana (1972–1979)*, 7–8.

78 Eben Quarcoo, "Economy: N. R. C. Declares Total War," *Daily Graphic*, January 18, 1972.

79 I. K. Acheampong, quoted in Eben Quarcoo, "Economy: N. R. C. Declares Total War," *Daily Graphic*, January 18, 1972.

80 I. K. Acheampong, Easter broadcast reproduced in "Let's Work with Spirit of Unity," *Daily Graphic*, April 3, 1972.

81 I. K. Acheampong, introduction to National Redemption Council, *The Charter of the National Redemption Council* ([Accra]: The Council, [1972]), 1–3. See also Naomi Chazan, *An Anatomy of Ghanaian Politics: Managing Political Recession, 1969–1982* (Boulder, CO: Westview, 1983), 129.

82 Maxwell Owusu makes a direct connection between the NRC's focus on "self-reliance" and aspects of Nkrumahism; Maxwell Owusu, "Economic Nationalism, Pan-Africanism, and the Military: Ghana's National Redemption Council," *Africa Today* 22, no. 1 (1975): 47–8.

83 Acheampong, introduction to National Redemption Council, *The Charter of the National Redemption Council*, 3.

84 Chazan, *An Anatomy of Ghanaian Politics*, 163.

85 Emmanuel Hansen, "Public Policy and the Food Question in Ghana," *Africa Development/Afrique et Développement* 6, no. 3 (1981): 109; Janet Girdner, Victor Olorunsola, Myrna Froning, and Emmanuel Hansen, "Ghana's Agricultural Food Policy: Operation Feed Yourself," *Food Policy* 5, no. 1 (1980): 15–17.

86 Hansen, "Public Policy and the Food Question in Ghana," 109; Owusu, "Economic Nationalism, Pan-Africanism, and the Military," 42–3.

87 Stephan F. Miescher, "Ghana's Akosombo Dam, Volta Lake Fisheries, & Climate Change," *Daedalus* 150, no. 4 (2021): 130.

88 Alice Wiemers, *Village Work: Development and Rural Statecraft in Twentieth-Century Ghana* (Athens, OH: Ohio University Press, 2021), 96, 101–3.

89 John Dramani Mahama, *My First Coup d'Etat: and Other True Stories from the Lost Decades of Africa* (New York: Bloomsbury, 2012), 164–6.

90 There are some important caveats. As one survey of rice producers notes, many new rice farmers had notable connections to the military, civil service, or other state agencies. In other locales, the integration of peasant farmers into the NRC's revived state farms proved limited; Nugent, *Boundaries, Communities and State-Making in West Africa*, 445–6. Nugent largely relies on the analysis of Piet Konings, *The State and Rural Class Formation in Ghana: A Comparative Analysis* (London: KPI, 1986), 186–7.

91 Chazan, *An Anatomy of Ghanaian Politics*, 168.

92 Owusu, "Economic Nationalism, Pan-Africanism, and the Military," 43.

93 I. K. Acheampong, "Address by Col. I. K. Acheampong, Chairman of the National Redemption Council and Commissioner for Finance, Economic Planning and Defence, to the Staff of the Ministry of Finance and Economic Planning on Monday, February 7, 1972," in Col. I. K. Acheampong, *Speeches and Interviews* (n.p.: n.d.), 29.

94 Tsikata, *Living in the Shadow of Large Dams*, xvii.

95 I. K. Acheampong, "Radio and Television Broadcast to the Nation by Colonel I. K. Acheampong, Chairman of the National Redemption Council, on the Devaluation and the External Debts, on Saturday, 5th February 1972," in Col. I. K. Acheampong, *Speeches and Interviews* (n.p.: n.d.), 21.

96 Ibid., 25–7, quote on 26.

97 Ibid., 27.

98 Acheampong, "Address by Col. I. K. Acheampong, Chairman of the National Redemption Council and Commissioner for Finance, Economic Planning and Defence, to the Staff of the Ministry of Finance and Economic Planning on Monday, February 7, 1972," in Acheampong, *Speeches and Interviews*, 29.

99 Ibid., 32.

100 Rimmer, *Staying Poor*, 135.

101 "Ghana's Inflation," *West Africa*, August 30, 1976.

102 Chazan, *An Anatomy of Ghanaian Politics*, 163–70.

103 Oquaye, *Politics in Ghana (1972–1979)*, 27.

104 See, for instance, "Essential Goods-Prices Slashed," *Daily Graphic*, January 21, 1972; "Acheampong Speaks to Nation," *Daily Graphic*, January 21, 1972.

105 Nugent, *Boundaries, Communities and State-Making in West Africa*, 455.

106 Nugent recounts what he presents as an apocryphal story of a woman who had bought tinned sardines, only to find that they had spoiled. Upon returning the sardines, the seller told the woman that she was not supposed to eat them, but instead find someone else to sell them to; Nugent, *Boundaries, Communities and State-Making in West Africa*, 456–7.

107 Acheampong quoted in Iddrisu Seini, "No Fine for Profiteers Says Kutu," *Daily Graphic*, February 18, 1974. Acheampong had been making similar calls since the first year of the NRC government; see "Expose Hoarders: Acheampong Tells Kwahu Traders," *Daily Graphic*, December 30, 1972.

108 Col. Parker H. S. Yarney, speech reported on in "'Expose Profiteers,'" *Daily Graphic*, July 4, 1977.

109 Gen. I. K. Acheampong, quoted in "Gen. Acheampong Tells Ghanaians … Away with Greed," *Daily Graphic*, April 4, 1977.

110 Clark, *Onions are My Husband*, 377–8.

111 C. K. Abroso, "Where Are All the Dry Batteries?," *Daily Graphic*, April 8, 1975.

112 E. K. Amoako-Anane, "Batteries," *Daily Graphic*, April 3, 1975.

113 St. John Clottey, "Shortage of Meat," *Daily Graphic*, April 3, 1975.

114 Clark, *Onions are My Husband*, 378–9.

115 Robertson, *Sharing the Same Bowl*, 244.

116 Ibid.; Gracia Clark, "Gender and Profiteering: Ghana's Market Women as Devoted Mothers and 'Human Vampire Bats,'" in *"Wicked Women" and the Reconfiguration of Gender in Africa*, eds. Dorothy L. Hodgson and Sheryl A. McCurdy (Portsmouth, NH: Heinemann, 2001), 294–7.

117 Emmanuel Adama Mahama, quoted in John Dramani Mahama, *My First Coup d'Etat*, 167.

Chapter 8

1 Fred Akuffo, statement reproduced in "Gen. Akuffo's Policy Statement," *Daily Graphic*, July 11, 1978. See also "Production Level to be Stepped Up," *Daily Graphic*, July 11, 1978.

2 "SMC to Hand Over on July 1, 1979," *Daily Graphic*, July 11, 1978.

3 "We are For Total Justice … Says Rawlings," *Daily Graphic*, June 6, 1979.

4 "Accra at Standstill," *Daily Graphic*, June 5, 1979.

5 Abena Ampofoa Asare, *Truth without Reconciliation: A Human Rights History of Ghana* (Philadelphia, PA: University of Pennsylvania Press, 2018), 61–2.

6 Barbara E. Okeke, *4 June: A Revolution Betrayed* (Enugu, Nigeria: Ikenga, 1982), 63–82.

7 Kofi Batsa, *The Spark: Times Behind Me: From Kwame Nkrumah to Hilla Limann* (London: Rex Collings, 1985), 50, and, more broadly, on the recruitment of Limann and the PNP campaign, 49–58. Mike Oquaye, for his part, describes the PNP as an "off-shoot" of the CPP; Mike Oquaye, *Politics in Ghana (1972–1979)* (Accra: Tornado Publications, 1980), 164.

8 See, for instance, George Naykene, "PNP Will Ensure Total Harmony," *Daily Graphic*, May 2, 1979; "The People Matter—PNP," *Daily Graphic*, May 21, 1979; Charles Torkonoo, "PNP: We Won't Repeat Past Mistakes," *Daily Graphic*, June 23, 1979.

9 See, for instance, "We All Belong to One Big Family," *Daily Graphic*, June 25, 1979; "We Need an Honest President," *Daily Graphic*, June 30, 1979; Kwamena Amponsah, "Democracy Must be Protected—PNP," *Daily Graphic*, July 4, 1979; "PNP We are on the Move," *Daily Graphic*, July 4, 1979; "Ghana Will Recover Lost Image—PNP," *Daily Graphic*, July 5, 1979; "Let's End Petty Bickerings—PNP," *Daily Graphic*, July 7, 1979. A notable exception is Torkonoo, "PNP."

10 Jerry John Rawlings, quoted in "Don't Pursue Self-Interest, Says Rawlings," *Daily Graphic*, September 25, 1979.

11 Jerry John Rawlings, paraphrased and quoted in "Holy War Declared," *Daily Graphic*, January 1, 1982.

12 "3 PNP Men Grabbed," *Daily Graphic*, January 2, 1982; "Limann Arrested," *Daily Graphic*, January 5, 1982.

13 Nana Mfum Baafour Sarpong II, paraphrased and quoted in "Support the Revolution," *Daily Graphic*, January 2, 1982.

14 Jerry John Rawlings, Radio Broadcast to the Nation on Thursday, December 31, 1981, reproduced in Jerry John Rawlings, *A Revolutionary Journey: Selected Speeches of Flt-Lt. Jerry John Rawlings, Chairman of the PNDC, December 31, 1981–December 31, 1982*, vol. 1 (Accra: Information Services Department, n.d.), 1.

15 Ibid.

16 Ibid., 2.

17 Jerry John Rawlings, Introductory Statement at a Press Briefing for Local and Foreign Journalists, January 18, 1982, reproduced in Rawlings, *A Revolutionary Journey*, 14–15, quote on 14.

18 Rawlings, Radio and Television Broadcast to the Nation, reproduced in Rawlings, *A Revolutionary Journey*, 4.

19 Rawlings, Introductory Statement at a Press Briefing for Local and Foreign Journalists, January 18, 1982, reproduced in Rawlings, *A Revolutionary Journey*, 14–15, quotes on 14.

20 Jerry John Rawlings, Radio and Television Broadcast to the Nation, March 6, 1983, reproduced in Jerry John Rawlings, *Forging Ahead: Selected Speeches of Flt-Lt. Jerry John Rawlings, Chairman of the Provisional National Defence Council—January 1st 1983–December 31st 1983*, vol. 2 (Accra: Information Services Department, n.d.), 8.

21 Most references to the PDCs and WDCs in this chapter will combine the two with the acronym P/WDCs.

22 *Workers Banner*, September 1981, quoted in Zaya Yeebo, "Ghana: Defence Committees and the Class Struggle," *Review of African Political Economy* 32 (1985): 66. In practice, however, the PNDC quickly abandoned the JFM's reticence with productivity discourse, eventually embracing it fully.

23 *Workers Banner*, September 1981, quoted in Yeebo, "Ghana: Defence Committees and the Class Struggle," 66. For Yeebo's broader reflections on the P/WDCs, see Yeebo, "Ghana," 64–72; Zaya Yeebo, *Ghana, the Struggle for Popular Power: Rawlings, Saviour or Demagogue* (London: New Beacon Books, 1991), esp. 64–95. In addition, see Mike Oquaye's extensive analysis of P/WDCs; Mike Oquaye, *Politics in Ghana, 1982–1992: Rawlings, Revolution, and Populist Democracy* (Accra: Tornado Publications, 2004), 143–238.

24 Paul Nugent, *Big Men, Small Boys, and Politics in Ghana: Power, Ideology, and the Burden of History, 1982–1994* (Accra: Asempa Publishers, 1995), 46–56. As referenced in Chapter 5, Ghanaian distrust of parliamentary democracy dates back to at least the Nkrumah era.

25 Jerry John Rawlings, Address at the Fifth Annual Delegates Conference of the National Association of Local Councils held at Greenhill on Tuesday, November 29, 1983, in Rawlings, *Forging Ahead*, 45–9. The ideas Rawlings espouses here are similar to the power structures articulated approximately a decade later by political scientist Mahmood Mamdani in *Citizen and Subject: Contemporary Africa and the Legacy of Late Colonialism* (Princeton, NJ: Princeton University Press, 1996).

26 Oquaye, *Politics in Ghana, 1982–1992*, 152.

27 Nugent, *Big Men, Small Boys, and Politics in Ghana*, 51–3.

28 Deborah Pellow, "Coping Responses to Revolution in Ghana," *Cultures et développement: Revue Internationale des Sciences du Développement* 15, no. 1 (1983): 15. Also quoted in Oquaye, *Politics in Ghana, 1982–1992*, 153.

29 Oquaye, *Politics in Ghana, 1982–1992*, 152.

30 Ibid., 152–3. More broadly, see A. Adu Boahen, *The Ghanaian Sphinx: Reflections on the Contemporary History of Ghana, 1972–1987* (Accra: Sankofa Educational, 1992), 31–54.

31 Jerry John Rawlings, Radio and Television Broadcast, July 29, 1982, in Rawlings, *A Revolutionary Journey*, 41, 43–4, quote on 41.

32 World Bank, *Ghana Policies and Program for Adjustment, Volume I: The Main Report*, Report no. 4702-GH, October 3, 1983, ii.

33 Holger Weiss, "Crop Failures, Food Shortages, and Colonial Famine Relief Policies in the Northern Territories of the Gold Coast," *Ghana Studies* 6 (2003): 5–58.

34 Jeff Grischow and Holger Weiss, "Colonial Famine Relief and Development Policies: Towards an Environmental History of Northern Ghana," *Global Environment* 4, no. 7/8 (2011): 82–92.

35 E. Ofori-Sarpong, "The 1981–1983 Drought in Ghana," *Singapore Journal of Tropical Geography* 7, no. 2 (1986): 116.

36 E. Ofori-Sarpong, "Impact of Drought in Ghana and Upper Volta (1970–1977)," Climatological Research Paper No. 1 (Legon: Department of Geography, University of Ghana, 1980): 3, 13–16.

37 Jonathan Derrick, "West Africa's Worst Year of Famine," *African Affairs* 83, no. 332 (1984): 283.

38 A. T. Grove, "The State of Africa in the 1980s," *The Geographical Journal* 152, no. 2 (1986): 193.

39 Derrick, "West Africa's Worst Year of Famine," 283.

40 Donald Crummey, *Farming and Famine: Landscape Vulnerability in Northeast Ethiopia, 1889-1991*, ed. James McCann (Madison, WI: University of Wisconsin Press, 2018), 51.

41 Michael T. Kaufman, "A Parched Land, Desperately Needs Food," *New York Times*, October 14, 1983.

42 Ofori-Sarpong, "The 1981-1983 Drought in Ghana," 116.

43 Ibid., 116-17.

44 Ibid., 116-17.

45 Ibid., 117-19.

46 Chih Ming Tan and Marc Rockmore, "Famine in Ghana and Its Impact," in *Handbook of Famine, Starvation, and Nutrient Deprivation*, eds. V. R. Preedy and V. B. Patel (Cham, Switzerland: Springer Nature Switzerland, 2019), 34.

47 Gwendolyn Mikell, *Cocoa and Chaos in Ghana* (Washington, DC: Howard University Press, 1992), 217.

48 Gracia Clark, *Onions are My Husband: Survival and Accumulation by West African Market Women* (Chicago, IL: University of Chicago Press, 1994), 242-3.

49 "Infant Mortality on the Rise," *People's Daily Graphic*, March 11, 1983; Mikell, *Cocoa and Chaos in Ghana*, 217.

50 George J. S. Dei, "Coping with the Effects of the 1982-1983 Drought in Ghana: The View from the Village," *Africa Development/Afrique et Développement* 13, no. 1 (1988): 112-14.

51 "Rice Farm Destroyed," *People's Daily Graphic*, January 7, 1983.

52 "Bush Fire Destroys Rubber Farm at Akim Manso," *People's Daily Graphic*, February 21, 1983.

53 Yaw Boadu-Ayeboafo, "Fire Destroys Farms," *People's Daily Graphic*, March 7, 1983.

54 Fufi Mensah, "Bush Fire Destroys Bridges at Sefwi-Wiawso," *People's Daily Graphic*, March 10, 1983.

55 Food and Agriculture Organization, *The State of Food and Agriculture 1983* (Rome: Food and Agriculture Organization of the United Nations, 1984), 53-4.

56 Derrick, "West Africa's Worst Year of Famine," 286. On the very long history of bush burning to clear land in what is now contemporary Ghana, see Mariano Pavanello, "Foragers or Cultivators? A Discussion of Wilks's 'Big Bang' Theory of Akan History," *Journal of West African History* 1, no. 2 (2015): 1-26.

57 "Indiscriminate Burning of Bushes Must be Checked," *People's Daily Graphic*, January 15, 1983.

58 P. Ossei-Wusu, "Burning Our Food Away … Let's Stop Bush Fires," *People's Daily Graphic*, February 10, 1983.

59 "Checking Indiscriminate Bush Burning," *People's Daily Graphic*, February 7, 1983. See also "Saboteurs Destroy Oil Plantations," *People's Daily Graphic*, February 7, 1983.

60 Popular slogan. Also expressed as "Ghana Must Go," as most recently referenced in Samuel Fury Childs Daly, "Ghana Must Go: Nativism and the Politics of Expulsion in West Africa, 1969-1985," *Past & Present* (2022), https://doi.org/10.1093/pastj/gtac006.

61 Olajide Aluko, "The Expulsion of Illegal Aliens from Nigeria: A Study of Nigeria's Decision-Making," *African Affairs* 84, no. 337 (1985): 541, 542.

62 For a brief overview of Nigeria's 1970's oil boom, see Toyin Falola and Matthew M. Heaton, *A History of Nigeria* (Cambridge: Cambridge University Press, 2008), 181-208.

63 John Dramani Mahama, *My First Coup d'Etat and Other True Stories from the Lost Decades of Africa* (New York: Bloomsbury, 2012), 245, 251. See also Daly, "Ghana

Must Go." Mahama's father, Emmanuel Adama Mahama, had been a member of Hilla
Limann's government. Following the 1981 coup, he fled to Côte d'Ivoire; see Mahama,
My First Coup d'Etat, 230–9.

64   Alhaji Ali Baba, "Address of Alhaji Ali Baba, Minister of Internal Affairs, on Aliens
Residing in Nigeria and Registration of ECOWAS, Chad, and Cameroun Citizens, on
Monday, 17th January 1983," in Nigeria, Federal Ministry of Internal Affairs, *Illegal
Immigrants* ([Lagos?]: External Publicity Division Department, 1983), 1. See also
Nwachukwu Ezem, "All Aliens Ordered to Leave," *Daily Times*, January 18, 1983.
For perhaps the most complete, near contemporaneous analysis of the Nigerian
government's decision-making process, see Aluko, "The Expulsion of Illegal Aliens
from Nigeria," 539–60 and, more recently, Daly, "Ghana Must Go."

65   "Illegal Aliens Must Go," *Daily Times*, January 20, 1983.

66   Kingsley Moghalu and Nonso Obikili, "Fiscal Policy during Boom and Bust," in *The
Oxford Handbook of Nigerian Politics*, eds. A. Carl Levan and Patrick Ukata (Oxford:
Oxford University Press, 2018), 495–6.

67   Christopher Kolade, quoted in "We Can Survive Recession," *Daily Times*, January 18,
1983.

68   Peter Lewis, "Nigeria's Petroleum Booms: A Changing Political Economy," in *The
Oxford Handbook of Nigerian Politics*, 509–10.

69   Falola and Heaton, *A History of Nigeria*, 204.

70   Toyin Falola, *Violence in Nigeria: The Crisis of Religious Politics and Secular Ideologies*
(Rochester, NY: University of Rochester Press, 1998), 137–8, 141. Falola notes
several names for Marwa, including "Maitatsine" as an alias and the name of Marwa's
movement. For Falola's broader discussion of the Maitatsine movement, see Falola,
Violence in Nigeria, 137–62. See also Olafemi Vaughan, *Religion and the Making of
Nigeria* (Durham, NC: Duke University Press, 2016), 124–6.

71   As Falola notes, most who took part in the Maitatsine movement were Nigerian,
including 815 of the 1,000 arrested; Falola, *Violence in Nigeria*, 159.

72   Alhaji Ali Baba, "Address of Alhaji Ali Baba, Minister of Internal Affairs, on Aliens
Residing in Nigeria and Registration of ECOWAS, Chad, and Cameroun Citizens,
on Monday, 17th January 1983" and "Address of Alhaji Ali Baba, Minister of Internal
Affairs, on Aliens Residing in Nigeria and Registration of ECOWAS, Chad, and
Cameroun Citizens, on Monday, 14th February 1983," in Nigeria, Federal Ministry of
Internal Affairs, *Illegal Immigrants* ([Lagos?]: External Publicity Division Department,
1983), 1, 10.

73   Alhaji Ali Baba, "Address of Alhaji Ali Baba, Minister of Internal Affairs, on Aliens
Residing in Nigeria and Registration of ECOWAS, Chad, and Cameroun Citizens, on
Monday, 14th February 1983," in Nigeria, Federal Ministry of Internal Affairs, *Illegal
Immigrants*, 10. Also quoted in Roger Gravil, "The Nigerian Aliens Expulsion Order
of 1983," *African Affairs* 84, no. 337 (1985): 534.

74   On Nigeria's rising crime rates, see Gravil, "The Nigerian Aliens Expulsion Order of
1983," 532–4; Aluko, "The Expulsion of Illegal Aliens from Nigeria," 539–40; Daly,
"Ghana Must Go." Gravil and Aluko, for their part, are both highly skeptical of the
government's efforts to pin Nigeria's rising crime rate on its non-Nigerian population.

75   Gravil, "The Nigerian Aliens Expulsion Order of 1983," 526; Lynne Brydon,
"Ghanaian Responses to the 1983 Nigerian Expulsions," *African Affairs* 84, no. 337
(1985): 567; Nugent, *Boundaries, Communities and State-Making in West Africa*, 459.

76   Brydon, "Ghanaian Responses to the 1983 Nigerian Expulsions," 571. For a detailed
perspective of a Ghanaian expelled from Nigeria, which includes a rich reading of the

political and social context in both Ghana and Nigeria, see Kwaku Addo, *Illegal Aliens on the Run* (Cape Coast: Catholic Mission Press, 2000).

77 Aluko, "The Expulsion of Illegal Aliens from Nigeria," 541–3.

78 Alhaji Ali Baba, "Address of Alhaji Ali Baba, Minister of Internal Affairs, on Aliens Residing in Nigerian and Registration of ECOWAS, Chad, and Cameroun Citizens, on Monday, 14th February 1983," in Nigeria, Federal Ministry of Internal Affairs, *Illegal Immigrants*, 14–15.

79 Lloyd Evans, "Serious Ailments on 30 Deportees," *People's Daily Graphic*, January 25, 1983; Stephen Kofi Akordor, "Deportees Leave for Homes," *People's Daily Graphic*, January 26, 1983. There were nearly 2,000 refugees in this first group of arrivals.

80 Bismark Nkansa Berempong, quoted in Akordor, "Deportees Leave for Homes."

81 Aluko, "The Expulsion of Illegal Aliens from Nigeria," 542–3. As Daly notes, some in the Nigerian government mocked Rawlings's and his government's "'pet ideas' and 'irrelevant political theorizing,'" while Yeebo recounts how some Ghanaians feared a Nigerian-supported invasion in support of the PNP; Daly, "Ghana Must Go"; Yeebo, *Ghana, the Struggle for Popular Power*, 49.

82 George Yankah, "Countrymen, Welcome," *People's Daily Graphic*, January 26, 1983.

83 Rawlings paraphrased in Albert Sam, "Release Land to Deportees … Rawlings Urges Chiefs," *People's Daily Graphic*, January 29, 1983.

84 Yaw Boadu Ayeboafo, "Help the Deported Find Jobs … Labour Centres Urged," *People's Daily Graphic*, February 3, 1983.

85 K. K. Kwayie, paraphrased in C. S. Buabeng, "'Resettling Compatriots is National Obligation,'" *People's Daily Graphic*, February 2, 1983.

86 Yankah, "Countrymen, Welcome."

87 Ibid.

88 Egya Kwamena-Johnson, "Deportees and Farming," *People's Daily Graphic*, February 5, 1985.

89 Ibid.

90 Jerry John Rawlings, speech excerpted in "A Call to Increase Agricultural Production," *People's Daily Graphic*, February 21, 1983. In this speech, Rawlings places the number of returnees at an estimated 1.5 million and one million in different places. The one million figure is in the continuation of the excerpt published in Jerry John Rawlings, "Call to Increase Agric Produce," *People's Daily Graphic*, February 23, 1983. Most sources estimate the number of Ghanaians returning at approximately one million.

91 Rawlings, "Call to Increase Agric Produce."

92 Jerry John Rawlings, "Address at the Opening of the 35th Annual New Year School at the University of Ghana, Legon, on Friday, December 30, 1983," reproduced in Rawlings, *Forging Ahead*, 60–4, quotes on 60 and 62.

93 "Returnees Start Development Projects at Akyem Tafo," *People's Daily Graphic*, April 21, 1983.

94 Samuel Kyei-Boateng, "Returnees Offer Communal Labour," *People's Daily Graphic*, June 7, 1983.

95 See, for instance, "Deportees to Farm," *People's Daily Graphic*, February 8, 1983; "Workers, Returnees Dig for Water … at Baafrikrom," *People's Daily Graphic*, February 26, 1983; Yaw Boadu-Ayeboafo, "10 Clear Land for Farming," *People's Daily Graphic*, March 1, 1983; "Returnees Buy Fishing Equipment," *People's Daily Graphic*, March 31, 1983; J. W. Ocran, "Assin Foso Returnees Farm," *People's Daily Graphic*, June 11, 1983; "Korle-Gonno Returnees Go to the Land," *People's Daily Graphic*, June 11, 1983.

96 Nana Compori, "Should We React?," *People's Daily Graphic*, January 29, 1983.

97 Ibid.; Innocent E. Nyenku, "But Returnees Must Behave," *People's Daily Graphic*, February 14, 1983.

98 See, for instance, Kwamena Apponsah, "Deportees May Disturb Peace If ...," *People's Daily Graphic*, February 3, 1983; "Three Deportees Arrested," *People's Daily Graphic*, February 26, 1983; Yaw Barimah, "Returnee Curfew Breakers Assault 2 Public Officers," *People's Daily Graphic*, June 25, 1983. See also Addo, *Illegal Aliens on the Run*, 159–60.

99 E. L. Adazi, "Returnees and Relief Aid," *People's Daily Graphic*, April 18, 1983.

100 "Only Self-Reliance Can Save Ghana," *People's Daily Graphic*, June 7, 1983.

101 Frank Gerits, "Anticolonial Capitalism: How Ghana Came to Embrace Market-Led Development Theory (the 1970s–1990s)," *Southern Journal of Contemporary History* 47, no. 1 (2022): 4–26.

102 See, for instance, Jerry John Rawlings, "Address to Members of Greater Accra Zonal WDCs on Friday, November 12, 1982," reproduced in Rawlings, *A Revolutionary Journey*, 76–9; Jerry John Rawlings, "Battle Against Neo-Colonialism," September 30, 1983, reproduced in Rawlings, *Forging Ahead*, 18.

103 Gerits, "Anticolonial Capitalism." It is important to note that Rawlings's embrace of market-oriented economics did not go uncontested within the PNDC. Rather, it alienated many radical thinkers and activists within the government. See, for instance, the sense of betrayal reflected in Zaya Yeebo's analysis of Rawlings and the PNDC in Yeebo, *Ghana, the Struggle for Popular Power*.

104 For a rich intellectual history on global neoliberalism, see Quinn Slobodian, *Globalists: The End of Empire and the Birth of Neoliberalism* (Cambridge, MA: Harvard University Press, 2018).

105 Broadly, see David Harvey, *A Brief History of Neoliberalism* (Oxford: Oxford University Press, 2005). For Ghana, see Lloyd G. Adu Amoah, "Six Decades of Ghanaian Statecraft and Asia Relations: Strategies, Strains, and Successes," in *Politics, Governance, and Development in Ghana*, ed. Joseph R. A. Ayee (Lanham, MD: Lexington Books, 2019), 160.

106 Harvey, *A Brief History of Neoliberalism*, 1–3, quote on 3.

107 Gerits, "Anticolonial Capitalism," 10–20.

108 Kwesi Botchwey, speech reproduced in "Building a Better Ghana—The 4-Year Economic Programme (1)," *People's Daily Graphic*, January 10, 1983.

109 Ibid.; Kwesi Botchwey, speech reproduced in "Building a Better Ghana—The 4-Year Economic Programme (2)," *People's Daily Graphic*, January 11, 1983; Kwesi Botchwey, speech reproduced in "Building a Better Ghana—The 4-Year Economic Programme (3)," *People's Daily Graphic*, January 12, 1983; Kwesi Botchwey, speech reproduced in "Building a Better Ghana—The 4-Year Economic Programme (4)," *People's Daily Graphic*, January 13, 1983; Kwesi Botchwey, speech reproduced in "Building a Better Ghana—The 4-Year Economic Programme (5)," *People's Daily Graphic*, January 14, 1983; Kwesi Botchwey, speech reproduced in "Building a Better Ghana—The 4-Year Economic Programme (6)," *People's Daily Graphic*, January 15, 1983. See also Paul Nugent's discussion of Botchwey's speech: Nugent, *Big Men, Small Boys, and Politics in Ghana*, 109–10.

110 Kwesi Botchwey, *Summary of P.N.D.C.'s Budget Statement and Economic Policy for 1983* ([n.p., 1983]). The ERP was broken into two parts during the 1980s, with ERP-1 focused on 1983–6 and ERP-2, 1987–9. For a succinct statement on the objectives of the ERP, see Kwasi Anyemedu, "The Economic Policies of the PNDC," in *Ghana under the PNDC*, ed. E. Gyimah-Boadi (Dakar: CODESRIA, 1993), 19–20.

111 Nugent, *Big Men, Small Boys, and Politics in Ghana*, 112. Here, Nugent builds his analysis around similar accounts in Jeffrey I. Herbst, *The Politics of Reform, 1982–1991* (Berkeley, CA: University of California Press, 1993), 43–5.

112 Botchwey, *Summary of P.N.D.C.'s Budget Statement and Economic Policy for 1983*, 14. The non-Ghanaian consultation fee rose to 50 times its previous level.

113 Ibid., 19.

114 Nugent, *Big Men, Small Boys, and Politics in Ghana*, 112; Herbst, *The Politics of Reform*, 44.

115 C. S. Buabeng, "New Notes to be Introduced," *People's Daily Graphic*, November 9, 1983; Zenobia Ofori-Dankwa, "New Notes Introduced," *People's Daily Graphic*, November 15, 1983; "The ¢50 Note Debate and All," *People's Daily Graphic*, November 18, 1983; "New Currency—Public Warned Against Cheating," *People's Daily Graphic*, November 28, 1983.

116 Anyemedu, "The Economic Policies of the PNDC," 20-1; Nugent, *Big Men, Small Boys, and Politics in Ghana*, 112. The GH¢ is part of the same "series" (1967–2007) as the N¢ in the cedi's history, namely the "Second Cedi."

117 *West Africa*, January 13, 1986, quoted in Kwamina Panford, *IMF—World Bank and Labor's Burden in Africa: Ghana's Experience* (London: Praeger, 2001), 58.

118 Kwame Boafo-Arthur, "Ghana: Structural Adjustment, Democratization, and the Politics of Continuity," *African Studies Review* 42, no. 2 (1999): 51.

119 Kwesi Botchwey, quoted in *West Africa*, January 13, 1986, in Panford, *IMF—World Bank and Labor's Burden in Africa*, 58.

120 Kwesi Botchwey, introduction to Provisional National Defence Council, *The P.N.D.C. Budget Statement and Economic Policy for 1986* (Accra: Ghana Publishing Corporation, 1986), 1.

121 Jerry John Rawlings, "Nation-wide Radio and Television Broadcast by the Chairman of the PNDC, Flt-Lt. J. J. Rawlings on the Occasion of the 5th Anniversary of the 31st December Revolution, December 31, 1986," in Jerry John Rawlings, *The New Momentum: Speeches of the Chairman of the PNDC, Flt-Lt. J. J. Rawlings, during the Fifth Anniversary Celebration of the 31st December Revolution* ([Accra]: Information Services Department, 1987), 9–12, quote on 9.

122 Herbst, *The Politics of Reform*, 154. Herbst, for his part, argues that, with 5–6 percent growth, the Ghanaian economy may have actually underperformed its potential.

123 Charles D. Jebuni and Abena D. Oduro, "Structural Adjustment Programme and the Transition to Democracy," in *Ghana: Transition to Democracy*, ed. Kwame A. Ninsin (Dakar: CODESRIA, 1998), 45.

124 Ibid., 46.

125 Boahen, *The Ghanaian Sphinx*, 49–50.

Conclusion

1 [Jerry John Rawlings], in Republic of Ghana, *Guidelines for Ghana's Return to Constitutional Rule: Nationwide Broadcast by the Head of State and Chairman of the PNDC, Flt.-Lt. Jerry John Rawlings, on the Eve of the 35th Independence Anniversary, 5th March, 1992* (Accra: Information Services Department, 1992), 2–3.

2 Ibid., 1–6.

3 Lloyd Evans and Joe Okyere, "Massive 'Yes' Vote Recorded Nation-wide," *People's Daily Graphic*, May 2, 1992.

4 Mike Atiadevey, "New Patriotic Party Launched," *People's Daily Graphic*, June 3, 1992. On the founding of the NPP, see Kantinka K. Donkoh Fordwor, *The Danquah-Busia Tradition in the Politics of Ghana: The Origins, Mission and Achievements of the New Patriotic Party* (Accra: Unimax Macmillan, 2010), 187–94.

5 E. G. K. Deletsa, "National Democratic Congress Launched," *People's Daily Graphic*, June 11, 1992.

6 Breda Atta-Quayson and Kobby Asmah, "Adu-Boahen Wins NPP Presidential Ticket," *People's Daily Graphic*, August 17, 1992; Joe Bradford Nyinah, "Rawlings Accepts NDC Offer," *People's Daily Graphic*, September 21, 1992.

7 National Democratic Congress, "Vote NDC for Sustainable Development," *People's Daily Graphic*, September 18, 1992.

8 K. N. Arkaah, cited in Mike Atiadevey, "Ghanaians Urged to Rally Behind NDC," *People's Daily Graphic*, October 5, 1992. The NCP/NDC alliance proved controversial with other Nkrumahist parties and activists with ties dating back to the Nkrumah era, with some prominent Nkrumah-era figures petitioning Nkrumahists to support Boahen and the NPP; see, for instance, "Nkrumahist Parties Cautioned on Alliances," *People's Daily Graphic*, October 7, 1992.

9 "NPP Holds Rally at Ho," *People's Daily Graphic*, September 14, 1992.

10 Friends of Adu Boahen, "Women of Ghana," *People's Daily Graphic*, October 17, 1992.

11 Breda Atta-Quayson, "Massive Turn-Out Expected," *People's Daily Graphic*, November 3, 1992.

12 Kojo Sam and James Mensah, "Massive Turn-Out of Voters Recorded at Polls," *People's Daily Graphic*, November 4, 1992; "Ghanaians Vote Early," *People's Daily Graphic*, November 4, 1992.

13 "Rawlings Continues to Maintain Lead," *People's Daily Graphic*, November 5, 1992.

14 "INEC Declares Rawlings Winner," *People's Daily Graphic*, November 6, 1992.

15 Kwabena Ofosuhene, "Candidates Complain of Rigging," *People's Daily Graphic*, November 6, 1992.

16 Joe Bradford Nyinah, "Rawlings Calls on Leaders of Losing Parties to Abandon Antagonistic Posture," *People's Daily Graphic*, November 7, 1992.

17 Kwaku Baka, "Post-election Reflections," *People's Daily Graphic*, November 9, 1992.

18 New Patriotic Party, *The Stolen Verdict: Ghana, November 1992 Presidential Election: A Report of the New Patriotic Party* (Accra: The Party, 1993), 9, 88–9, quotes on 9 and 89.

19 Adu Boahen, "A Note on the Ghanaian Elections," *African Affairs* 94, no. 375 (1995): 278, 279. Emphasis in original.

20 "Curfew in Kumasi," *People's Daily Graphic*, November 5, 1992.

21 "Police Storm NPP Office," *People's Daily Graphic*, November 5, 1992.

22 "NDC Official Abducted, Set Ablaze," *People's Daily Graphic*, November 10, 1992.

23 "Alhaji Imoro Adam Dies in London," *People's Daily Graphic*, November 23, 1992.

24 Joint Statement by the NDC, NCP, and Egle Party, quoted in "Three Parties Call for Arms to Protect Members," *People's Daily Graphic*, November 11, 1992.

25 Michael Crabbe, "NDC Leaders Deny Story," *People's Daily Graphic*, November 12, 1992.

26 "'No Plans for State of Emergency,'" *People's Daily Graphic*, November 16, 1992.

27 "Dec. 22 is New Date … for Parliamentary Election," *People's Daily Graphic*, November 21, 1992.

28 "Parliamentary Poll Now Shifted to December 29," *People's Daily Graphic*, December 2, 1992.

29 Obed Yao Asamoah, *The Political History of Ghana (1950–2013): The Experience of a Non-Conformist* (Bloomington, IN: AuthorHouse, 2014), 437.

30 Jerry John Rawlings, quoted in Joe Bradford Nyinah and Siisi Quainoo, "The Revolution Continues Unabated, Says Rawlings," *People's Daily Graphic*, January 1, 1993.

31 Debrah Fynn and Joe Okyere, "Akwaaba, Fourth Republic," *People's Daily Graphic*, January 8, 1993.

32 David Johnson, "Ghana: The 'Rising Star' of Inequality," *Review of African Political Economy*, April 28, 2016, https://roape.net/2016/04/28/ghana-rising-star-inequality/ (accessed January 25, 2023). The cedi went through a redenomination in 2007, converting what previously was the (second) GH¢10,000 note to the new (third) GH¢1 note, with equivalent changes to higher denomination banknotes.

33 John Agyeman Kufour, quoted in "Why We Went HIPC-Kufuor," *Public Agenda*, April 2, 2001.

34 [John Dramani Mahama], speech reproduced in "2014 State of the Nation Address by H. E. John Dramani Mahama," *Ghanaian Chronicle*, March 10, 2014.

35 Masahudu Ankiilu Kunateh, "Ghana Heads Back to HIPC," *Ghanaian Chronicle*, June 11, 2014.

36 "Ghana Going to the IMF is a Mistake—TUC," *Ghanaian Times*, July 5, 2022; "Ghana IMF Loan Outcry Pressures Government over Economy," *Radio France Internationale*, July 19, 2022, https://www.rfi.fr/en/business-and-tech/20220719-ghana-imf-loan-outcry-pressures-government-over-economy (accessed January 25, 2023).

37 Onyekachi Wambu, "Looking to Ghana," *New African*, February 2021.

38 Susan Mohammad, "A Beacon of Democracy in Africa," *Maclean's*, January 19, 2009.

39 Adama Gaye, "Democracy's March Through Africa," *Newsweek International*, January 22, 2001.

40 Ibid.

41 I. K. Acheampong, "Address by Col. I. K. Acheampong, Chairman of the National Redemption Council and Commissioner for Finance, Economic Planning and Defence, to the Staff of the Ministry of Finance and Economic Planning on Monday, February 7, 1972," in Col. I. K. Acheampong, *Speeches and Interviews* (n.p.: n.d.), 29.

42 See, for instance, Ndabaningi Sithole, "One-Party versus Two-Party System," *Voice of Africa*, September 1961; Convention People's Party, *Programme of the Convention People's Party for Work and Happiness* (Accra: Central Committee of the Party, 1962), 5.

43 Prince Yao Boateng, in Republic of Ghana, National Assembly, *Parliamentary Debates*, ser. 1, September 11, 1962, vol. 28, col. 174; Sulemana Ibun Iddrissu, in Republic of Ghana, National Assembly, *Parliamentary Debates*, ser. 1, September 11, 1962, vol. 28, col. 170. See also Jeffrey S. Ahlman, *Living with Nkrumahism: Nation, State, and Pan-Africanism in Ghana* (Athens, OH: Ohio University Press, 2017), 155–6.

44 Abena Ampofoa Asare, *Truth without Reconciliation: A Human Rights History of Ghana* (Philadelphia, PA: University of Pennsylvania Press, 2018).

45 W. E. B. Du Bois, "The African Roots of the War," in *W. E. B. Du Bois Reader*, ed. David Levering Lewis (New York: Owl Books, 1995), 642–51; originally published in *Atlantic Monthly* 115, no. 5 (May 1915): 707–14; Walter Rodney, *How Europe Underdeveloped Africa*, 2nd ed. (Washington, DC: Howard University Press, [1972] 1982); Howard French, *Born in Blackness: Africa, Africans, and the Making of the Modern World, 1471 to the Second World War* (New York: Liveright, 2021).

46 Carola Lentz, "Performing the Nation and Staging Ethnic Diversity in Ghanaian National-Day Celebrations," *Ghana Studies* 25 (2022): 3–32.

47 "Ghana's Cedi Now the World's Worst-Performing Currency as Kenya's Shilling Also Struggles," *Africanews.com*, October 18, 2023, https://www.africanews.com/2022/10/18/ghanas-cedi-now-the-worlds-worst-performing-currency-as-kenyas-shilling-also-struggles/ (accessed January 25, 2023).

48 Christian Akorlie and Cooper Inveen, "Ghana to Default on Most External Debt as Economic Crisis Worsens," *Reuters*, December 20, 2022, https://www.reuters.com/world/africa/ghana-announces-external-debt-payment-suspension-slipping-into-default-2022-12-19/ (accessed January 25, 2023).

49 Adwoa Preiman, Twitter Thread, November 28, 2022, https://twitter.com/blendnwhip/status/1597204776349229056 (accessed January 25, 2023).

50 See, for instance, Nana Akufo-Addo on his official Facebook page, "Fundraiser for the Construction of the National Cathedral of Ghana," February 9, 2019, https://www.facebook.com/watch/?v=242057660062965 (accessed January 25, 2023).

51 Mordecai Thiombiano, Duncan Amoah, Bobie Ansah, Mensah Thompson, Osei Kofi Acquah, Ishaq Awudu, Kojo Gold, Rex Omar, and Selorm Dramani, "Maiden Press Conference by 'Arise Ghana' to Address Critical Issues of Political and Socio-Economic Importance to Our Dear Nation," May 25, 2022, https://www.facebook.com/AriseGhanaofficial/photos/pcb.100896875979944/100896405979991/ (accessed January 24, 2023).

52 Jaysim Hanspal and Jonas Nyabor, "Police Now Hunt for Arise Ghana! Leaders after Protests Turn Violent," *The Africa Report*, https://www.theafricareport.com/218884/police-now-hunt-for-arise-ghana-leaders-after-protests-turn-violent/ (accessed January 25, 2023).

BIBLIOGRAPHY

Archives

Ghana

Public Records and Archives Administration Department—Accra
Public Records and Archives Administration Department—Cape Coast
Public Records and Archives Administration Department—Kumasi
Public Records and Archives Administration Department—Sekondi
Public Records and Archives Administration Department—Sunyani
Public Records and Archives Administration Department—Tamale

United Kingdom

British Library
The National Archives of the United Kingdom

United States

Howard University, Moorland-Spingarn Research Center
Library of Congress
Northwestern University Libraries, Melville J. Herskovits Library of African Studies
New York Public Library, Schomburg Center for Research in Black Culture
Princeton University Archives
University of Massachusetts—Amherst, Special Collections and Archives
Yale University, Beinecke Rare Book and Manuscript Library
Yale University Library, Manuscripts and Archives

Databases

British Library, Endangered Archive Project, Public Records and Archives
    Administration—Tamale (EAP 541), https://eap.bl.uk/project/EAP541/search.
Food and Agriculture Organization of the United Nations, FAOSTATE Statistics Database.
    [Rome?]: Food and Agriculture Organization, 2018, http://www.fao.org/faostat/
    en/?#data/QC.
Hansard. United Kingdom Parliament. https://hansard.parliament.uk.
Slave Voyages: The Trans-Atlantic Slave Trade Database, https://www.slavevoyages.org/
    voyage/database.

Government Reports and Documents

Colonial Office. *Report of the Commission of Enquiry into Disturbances in the Gold Coast, 1948*. London: His Majesty's Stationery Office, 1948.

Convention People's Party. *Programme of the Convention People's Party for Work and Happiness*. Accra: Central Committee of the Party, 1962.

Food and Agriculture Organization. *The State of Food and Agriculture 1983*. Rome: Food and Agriculture Organization of the United Nations, 1984.

[Ghana Public Relations Department.] *Second Milestone: A Record of Achievements of the Progress Party Government since It Came to Power Two Years Ago: October 1st, 1969–October 1st, 1971*. Accra: Ghana Public Relations Department, 1971.

[Government of Ghana.] *Ghana's External Debt Problem: Its Nature and Solution: Submitted by the Government of Ghana to the Creditor Countries* [April, 1970].

Government of Ghana. *Report of the Commission Appointed under the Commission of Enquiry Ordinance (CAP. 249): Enquiry into Matters Disclosed at the Trial of Captain Benjamin Awhaitey held on the 20th and 21st [sic] January, 1959, before a Court Martial Convened at Giffard Camp, Accra, and the Surrounding Circumstances*. Accra: Government Printer, 1959.

Government of Ghana. *Statement by the Government on the Report of the Commission Appointed to Enquire into the Matters Disclosed at the Trial of Captain Benjamin Awhaitey before a Court Martial, and the Surrounding Circumstances*. Accra: Government Printer, 1959.

Government of Ghana. *Second Development Plan, 1959–64*. Accra: Government Printer, 1959.

Government of Ghana, Ghana Statistical Service. *Ghana 2021 Population and Housing Census: General Report, Volume 3A: Population of Regions and Districts*. Accra: Ghana Statistical Service, 2021.

Government of Ghana, National Assembly. *Parliamentary Debates: Official Report: First Series*. Accra: State Publishing Company, 1957–1966.

Government of Ghana, National Assembly. *Parliamentary Debates: Official Report: Second Series*. Accra: State Publishing Company, 1969.

Government of Ghana, National Liberation Council. *Rebuilding the National Economy*. Accra: Ministry of Information, 1966.

Government of Gold Coast. *Accelerated Development Plan for Education, 1951*. Accra: Government Printer, 1951.

Government of Gold Coast. *Annual Report for 1896*, no. 220. London: Her Majesty's Stationery Office, 1897.

Government of Gold Coast. *Annual Report for 1901*, no. 375. London: Her Majesty's Stationery Office, 1902.

Government of Gold Coast. *Annual Report for 1902*, no. 397. London: Her Majesty's Stationery Office, 1903.

Government of Gold Coast. *Annual Report for 1914*, no. 859. London: Her Majesty's Stationery Office, 1915.

Government of Gold Coast. *Blue Book, 1850*. London: Her Majesty's Stationery Office, 1850.

Government of Gold Coast. *Census of Population, 1948: Reports and Tables*. Accra: Government Printing Department, 1950.

Government of Gold Coast. *Colonial Reports—Annual: Gold Coast: Report for 1901*. London: His Majesty's Stationery Office, 1902.

Government of Gold Coast. *Colonial Reports—Annual: Northern Territories of the Gold Coast: Report for 1913*, no. 807. London: His Majesty's Stationery Office, 1914.

Government of Gold Coast. *Colonial Reports—Annual: Northern Territories of the Gold Coast: Report for 1914*, no. 863. London: His Majesty's Stationery Office, 1915.

Government of Gold Coast. *Further Reports Relative to Economic Agriculture on the Gold Coast*, no. 1. London: Her Majesty's Stationery Office, 1891.

Government of Gold Coast. *Her Majesty's Colonial Possessions: Gold Coast: Economic Agriculture on the Gold Coast, 1889*, no. 110. London: Her Majesty's Stationery Office, 1890.

Government of Gold Coast. *The Development Plan, 1951: Being a Plan for the Economic and Social Development of the Gold Coast as Approved by the Legislative Assembly, September 1951*. Accra: Government Printing Department, 1951.

Government of the Gold Coast, Legislative Assembly. *Legislative Assembly Debates: Official Report*. Accra: Government Printing Department, 1951–56.

Government of the United Kingdom. *House of Lords Debates*.

International Bank for Reconstruction and Development, International Development Association, Africa Department, *Stabilization and Development in Ghana*, Report No. AF-57a, March 14, 1967.

National Redemption Council. *The Charter of the National Redemption Council*. [Accra]: The Council, [1972].

New Patriotic Party. *The Stolen Verdict: Ghana, November 1992 Presidential Election: A Report of the New Patriotic Party*. Accra: The Party, 1993.

Nigeria, Federal Ministry of Internal Affairs. *Illegal Immigrants*. [Lagos?]: External Publicity Division Department, 1983.

Provisional National Defence Council. *The P.N.D.C. Budget Statement and Economic Policy for 1986*. Accra: Ghana Publishing Corporation, 1986.

Republic of Ghana. *1962 Industrial Census Report, Volume I: Industry (Mining and Quarrying, Manufacturing, Construction, Electricity, Gas, and Steam)*. Accra: Central Bureau of Statistics, 1965.

Republic of Ghana. *Guidelines for Ghana's Return to Constitutional Rule: Nationwide Broadcast by the Head of State and Chairman of the PNDC, Flt.-Lt. Jerry John Rawlings, on the Eve of the 35th Independence Anniversary, 5th March, 1992*. Accra: Information Services Department, 1992.

Secretary of State for the Colonies. *Report of the Commission on the Marketing of West African Cocoa*. London: His Majesty's Stationery Office, 1938.

Thompson, H. N. *Gold Coast: Report on Forests*, no. 66. London: His Majesty's Stationery Office, 1910.

World Bank. *Ghana Policies and Program for Adjustment, Volume I: The Main Report*, Report no. 4702-GH, October 3, 1983.

Interviews

Abenkwan, Magnet. Koforidua, Eastern Region. May 26, 2008.

Asamoah, Lawrence. Koforidua, Eastern Region. May 26, 2008.

Nikoi-Oltai, Ben A. Accra, Greater Accra. November 28, 2007.

Sifah, N. Accra, Greater Accra. February 16, 2008.

Takyi-Micah, Eden Bentum. Accra, Greater Accra. March 17, 2008, May 10, 2008.

Tetteh, M. N. Accra, Greater Accra. March 8, 2008.

Microfilm Collections

Commonwealth Political Ephemera from the Institute of Commonwealth Studies, University of London, Phase I, Part 4: West Africa, Ghana (West Yorkshire, England: Altair, 1990).

Ivor Wilks-Phyllis Ferguson Collection of Material on Ghana (Chicago, IL: University of Chicago, Photopublication Department, 1974).

John F. Kennedy National Security Files, Africa: National Security Files, 1961–1963, First Supplement (Frederick, MD: University Publications of America, 1987).

Newspapers, Magazines, Other Periodicals

A Quarterly Token for Juvenile Subscribers: A Gift from the Church Missionary Society (London)
African Mail (London)
African Morning Post (Accra)
African Times (London)
Ashanti Pioneer (Kumasi)
Crisis (New York)
Daily Graphic (Accra)
Daily Times (Lagos)
Evening News (Accra)
Ghana Today (Accra)
Ghana Workers Bulletin (Accra)
Ghanaian Chronicle (Accra)
Ghanaian Times (Accra)
Glasgow Herald (Glasgow)
Gold Coast Aborigines (Cape Coast)
Gold Coast Chronicle (Accra)
Gold Coast Echo (Cape Coast)
Gold Coast Express (Accra)
Gold Coast Independent (Accra)
Gold Coast Leader (Cape Coast)
Gold Coast News (Cape Coast)
Maclean's (Toronto)
New African (London)
New York Times (New York)
Newsweek International (New York)
Party: CPP Journal (Accra)
People's Daily Graphic (Accra)
Public Agenda (Accra)
Radio France Internationale (Paris)
Royal Gazette and Sierra Leone Advertisers (Freetown)
Times of London (London)
Voice of Africa (Accra)
West Africa (London)
West African Mail (Liverpool)

West African Pilot (Lagos)
West African Review (London)

Websites

The Africa Report
Africanews.com
GhanaWeb
Graphic Online
Reuters

Published Books and Articles

A Native. *Marita: or the Folly of Love,* edited by Stephanie Newell. Leiden: Brill, 2002.

Abaka, Edmund. *"Kola is God's Gift": Agricultural Production, Export Initiatives, and the Kola Industry of Asante and the Gold Coast, c. 1820–1950.* Athens, OH: Ohio University Press, 2005.

Abaka, Edmund. *House of Slaves and "Door of No Return": Gold Coast/Ghana Slave Forts, Castles & Dungeons, and the Atlantic Slave Trade.* Trenton, NJ: Africa World, 2012.

Abu-Lughod, Janet. *Before European Hegemony: The World System A. D. 1250–1350.* Oxford: Oxford University Press, 1989.

Acheampong, I. K. *Speeches and Interviews.* N.p.: n.d.

Ackah, James Y. "Kaku Ackah and the Split of Nzema." MA thesis, University of Ghana, 1965.

Addo, Kwaku. *Illegal Aliens on the Run.* Cape Coast: Catholic Mission Press, 2000.

Adebanwi, Wale. *Nation as Grand Narrative: The Nigerian Press and the Politics of Meaning.* Rochester, NY: University of Rochester Press, 2016.

Adi, Hakim. *West Africans in Britain, 1900–1960: Nationalism, Pan-Africanism, and Communism.* London: Lawrence and Wishart, 1998.

Adi, Hakim. *African and Caribbean Peoples in Britain: A History.* London: Allen Lane, 2022.

Ahlman, Jeffrey S. "A New Type of Citizen: Youth, Gender, and Generation in the Ghanaian Builders Brigade." *Journal of African History* 53, no. 1 (2012): 87–105.

Ahlman, Jeffrey S. *Living with Nkrumahism: Nation, State, and Pan-Africanism in Ghana.* Athens, OH: Ohio University Press, 2017.

Ahlman, Jeffrey S. "'The Strange Case of Major Awhaitey': Conspiracy, Testimonial Evidence, and Narratives of Nation in Ghana's Postcolonial Democracy." *International Journal of African Historical Studies* 50, no. 2 (2017): 225–49.

Ahlman, Jeffrey S. *Kwame Nkrumah: Visions of Liberation.* Athens, OH: Ohio University Press, 2021.

Ajayi, J. F. Ade. "The Continuity of African Institutions under Colonialism." In *Emerging Themes of African History: Proceedings of the International Congress of African Historians held at University College, Dar es Salaam, October 1965,* edited by Terence Ranger. Dar es Salaam: East African Publishing House, 1968.

Akyeampong, Emmanuel Kwaku. *Between the Sea & Lagoon: An Eco-Social History of the Anlo of Southern Ghana, c. 1850 to Recent Times.* Athens, OH: Ohio University Press, 2001.

Akyeampong, Emmanuel Kwaku. "Race, Identity, and Citizenship in Black Africa: The Case of the Lebanese in Ghana." *Africa* 76, no. 3 (2006): 297–322.

Allman, Jean Marie. "'Hewers of Wood, Carriers of Water': Islam, Class, and the Politics on the Eve of Ghana's Independence." *African Studies Review* 34, no. 2 (1990): 1–26.

Allman, Jean Marie. *The Quills of the Porcupine: Asante Nationalism in an Emergent Ghana*. Madison, WI: University of Wisconsin Press, 1993.

Allman, Jean and John Parker. *Tongnaab: The History of a West African God*. Bloomington, IN: Indiana University Press, 2005.

Allman, Jean and Victoria Tashjian. "*I Will Not Eat Stone*": A Women's History of Colonial Asante. Portsmouth, NH: Heinemann, 2000.

Aluko, Olajide. "The Expulsion of Illegal Aliens from Nigeria: A Study of Nigeria's Decision-Making." *African Affairs* 84, no. 337 (1984): 539–60.

Amenumey, D. E. K. *The Ewe Unification Movement: A Political History*. Accra: Ghana Universities Press, 1989.

Amoah, Lloyd G. Adu. "Six Decades of Ghanaian Statecraft and Asia Relations: Strategies, Strains, and Successes." In *Politics, Governance, and Development in Ghana*, edited by Joseph R. A. Ayee. Lanham, MD: Lexington Books, 2019.

Anderson, Benedict. *Imagined Communities: Reflections on the Origin and Spread of Nationalism*, revised ed. New York: Verso, [1983] 1991.

Anquandah, James. "The People of Ghana: Their Origins and Culture." *Transactions of the Historical Society of Ghana*, new series 15 (2013): 1–25.

Anyemedu, Kwasi. "The Economic Policies of the PNDC." In *Ghana under the PNDC*, edited by E. Gyimah-Boadi. Dakar: CODESRIA, 1993.

Appiah, Kwame Anthony. *In My Father's House: Africa in the Philosophy of Culture*. Oxford: Oxford University Press, 1992.

Appiah, Peggy, Kwame Anthony Appiah, and Ivor Agyeman-Duah. *Bu Me Bɛ: Proverbs of the Akan*. Oxfordshire, UK: Ayebia Clarke, 2007.

Apter, David. *The Gold Coast in Transition*. Princeton, NJ: Princeton University Press, 1955.

Aremu, Johnson Olaosebikan and Adeyinka Theresa Ajayi. "Expulsion of Nigerian Immigrant Community from Ghana in 1969: Causes and Impact." *Developing Country Studies* 5, no. 10 (2014): 176–86.

Arhin, Kwame. "Aspects of the Ashanti Trade in the Nineteenth Century." *Africa* 40, no. 4 (1970): 363–70.

Arhin, Kwame, ed. *A Profile of Brong Kyempim: Essays on the Archeology, History, Language, and Politics of the Brong People of Ghana*. Legon: Institute of African Studies, University of Ghana, 1979.

Arhin, Kwame. "Chieftaincy, An Overview." In *Chieftaincy in Ghana: Culture, Governance, and Development*, edited by Irene K. Odotei and Albert K. Awedoba. Accra: Sub-Saharan Publishers, 2006. Published under the name Nana Arhin Brempong.

Armah, Ayi Kwei. *The Beautyful Ones are Not Yet Born*. Boston, MA: Houghton Mifflin, 1968.

Asamoah, Obed Yao. *The Political History of Ghana (1950–2013): The Experience of a Non-Conformist*. Bloomington, IN: AuthorHouse, 2014.

Asante, S. K. B. "The Neglected Aspects of the Activities of the Gold Coast Aborigines Rights Protection Society." *Phylon* 36, no. 1 (1975): 32–45.

Asare, Abena Ampofoa. *Truth without Reconciliation: A Human Rights History of Ghana*. Philadelphia, PA: University of Pennsylvania Press, 2018.

Attoh Ahuma, S. R. B. *The Gold Coast Nation and National Consciousness.* Liverpool: D. Marples, 1911.

Austen, Ralph A. *African Economic History: Internal Development and External Dependency.* Portsmouth, NH: Heinemann, 1987.

Austin, Dennis. *Politics in Ghana, 1946–1960.* London: Oxford University Press, 1964.

Austin, Dennis. *Ghana Observed: Essays on the Politics of a West African Republic.* Manchester: Manchester University Press, 1976.

Austin, Dennis and Robin Luckham, eds. *Politicians and Soldiers in Ghana, 1966–72.* London: Frank Cass, 1975.

Austin, Gareth. "Capitalists and Chiefs in the Cocoa Hold-Ups in South Asante, 1927–1938." *International Journal of African Historical Studies* 21, no. 1 (1988): 63–95.

Austin, Gareth. *Labour, Land, and Capital in Ghana: From Slavery to Free Labour in Asante, 1807–1956.* Rochester, NY: University of Rochester Press, 2005.

Awooner-Renner, Bankole. *West African Soviet Union.* London: WANS, 1946.

Ayee, Joseph R. A., ed. *Politics, Governance, and Development in Ghana.* Lanham, MD: Lexington Books, 2019.

Barbot, Jean. *Barbot on Guinea: The Writing of Jean Barbot on West Africa, 1678–1712,* edited by P. E. H. Hair, Adam Jones, and Robin Law, vols. 1–2. London: The Hakluyt Society, 1992.

Batsa, Kofi. *The Spark: Times Behind Me: From Kwame Nkrumah to Hilla Limann.* London: Rex Collings, 1985.

Beckman, Björn. *Organising the Farmers: Cocoa Politics and National Development in Ghana.* Uppsala: The Scandinavian Institute of African Studies, 1976.

Beltran, Alain, Léonard Laborie, Pierre Lanthier, and Stéphanie Le Gallic, eds. *Electric Worlds/Mondes électriques: Creations, Circulations, Tensions, Transitions (19th–21st C.).* Brussels: Peter Lang, 2016.

Bennion, F. A. R. *The Constitutional Law of Ghana.* London: Butterworth and Co., 1962.

Bing, Geoffrey. *Reap the Whirlwind: An Account of Kwame Nkrumah's Ghana from 1950 to 1966.* London: MacGibbon and Kee, 1968.

Birmingham, Walter, I. Neustadt, and E. N. Omaboe, eds. *A Study of Contemporary Ghana, Volume I: The Economy of Ghana.* London: George Allen & Unwin, 1966.

Blay, J. Benibengor. *Gold Coast Mines Employees' Union.* Ilfracombe, UK: Arthur H. Stockwell, 1950.

Bloom, Peter J., Takyiwaa Manuh, and Stephan F. Miescher, eds. *Modernization as Spectacle in Africa.* Bloomington, IN: Indiana University Press, 2014.

[Blyden, Edward Wilmot.] *Africa and the Africans: Proceedings on the Occasion of a Banquet Given at the Holborn Restaurant, August 15th 1903 to Edward W. Blyden LL.D by West Africans in London.* London: C. M. Phillips, 1903.

Boafo-Arthur, Kwame. "Ghana: Structural Adjustment, Democratization, and the Politics of Continuity." *African Studies Review* 42, no. 2 (1999): 41–72.

Boahen, A. Adu. *The Ghanaian Sphinx: Reflections on the Contemporary History of Ghana, 1972–1987.* Accra: Sankofa Educational, 1992.

Boahen, A. Adu. "A Note on the Ghanaian Elections." *African Affairs* 5, no. 375 (1995): 277–80.

Boahen, A. Adu, Emmanuel Akyeampong, Nancy Lawler, T. C. McCaskie, and Ivor Wilks,, eds. *"The History of Ashanti Kings and the Whole Country Itself" and Other Writings.* Oxford: Oxford University Press, 2008.

Bonne III, Nii Kwabena. *Milestones in the History of the Gold Coast: Autobiography of Nii Kwabena III, Osu Alata Mantse, also Nana Owusu Akenten III, Oyokohene of Techiman Ashanti.* N.p.: Diplomatist, n.d.

Bosman, William. *A New and Accurate Description of the Coast of Guinea Divided into the Gold, the Slave, and Ivory Coasts.* London: Ballantyne Books, [1705] 1907.

Botchwey, Kwesi. *Summary of P.N.D.C.'s Budget Statement and Economic Policy for 1983.* N.p.: 1983.

Bowdich, T. Edward. *Mission from Cape Castle to Ashantee, with a Descriptive Account of that Kingdom.* London: Griffith & Farran, 1873.

Brydon, Lynne. "Ghanaian Responses to the 1983 Nigerian Expulsions." *African Affairs* 84, no. 337 (1985): 561–85.

Brydon, Lynne. "Constructing Avatime: Questions of History and Identity in a West African Polity, c. 1690s to the Twentieth Century." *Journal of African History* 49, no. 1 (2008): 23–42.

Burbank, Jane and Frederick Cooper. *Empires in World History: Power and the Politics of Difference.* Princeton, NJ: Princeton University Press, 2010.

Busia, K. A. *Report on a Social Survey of Sekondi-Takoradi.* London: Crown Agents for the Colonies, 1950.

Byfield, Judith A., Carolyn A. Brown, Timothy Parsons, and Ahmad Alawad Sikainga, eds. *Africa and the World War II.* Cambridge: Cambridge University Press, 2015.

Byfield, Judith A. *Great Upheaval: Women and Nation in Postwar Nigeria.* Athens, OH: Ohio University Press, 2021.

Caldwell, John C. *African Rural–Urban Migration: The Movement to Ghana's Towns.* New York: Columbia University Press, 1969.

Callinicos, Luli. *Oliver Tambo: Beyond the Engeli Mountains.* Cape Town: David Philip Publishers, 2004.

Carstensen, Edward. *Closing the Books: Governor Edward Carstensen on Danish Guinea, 1842–1850,* translated by Tove Storsveen. Legon: Sub-Saharan Publishers, 2010.

Carter, Gwendolen, ed. *Politics in Africa: Seven Cases.* New York: Harcourt, Brace & World, 1966.

Casely Hayford, J. E. *Gold Coast Institutions: With Thoughts Upon a Healthy Imperial Policy for the Gold Coast and Ashanti.* London: Sweet and Maxwell, 1903.

Casely Hayford, J. E. "Introduction." In Edward Wilmot Blyden, *Africa and the Africans: Proceedings on the Occasion of a Banquet Given at the Holborn Restaurant, August 15th 1903 to Edward W. Blyden LL.D by West Africans in London.* London: C. M. Phillips, 1903.

Casely Hayford, J. E. *Ethiopia Unbound: Studies in Race Emancipation,* 2nd ed. London: Frank Cass, 1969.

Chatterjee, Partha. *Nationalist Thought and the Colonial World: A Derivative Discourse.* Minneapolis, MN: University of Minnesota Press, 1993.

Chatterjee, Partha. *The Nation and Its Fragments: Colonial and Postcolonial Histories.* Princeton, NJ: Princeton University Press, 1993.

Chazan, Noami. *An Anatomy of Ghanaian Politics: Managing Political Recession, 1969–1982.* Boulder, CO: Westview Press, 1983.

Chouin, Gérard. "The 'Big Bang' Theory Reconsidered: Framing Early Ghanaian History." *Transactions of the Historical Society of Ghana,* new series 14 (2012): 13–40.

Chouin, Gérard and Christopher R. Decorse. "Prelude to the Atlantic Trade: New Perspectives on Southern Ghana's Pre-Atlantic History (800–1500)." *Journal of African History* 51, no. 2 (2010): 123–45.

Claridge, W. Walton. *A History of the Gold Coast and Ashanti from the Earliest Times to the Commencement of the Twentieth Century,* vols 1–2. London: John Murray, 1915.

Clark, Gracia. *Onions are My Husband: Survival and Accumulation by West African Market Women*. Chicago, IL: University of Chicago Press, 1994.

Coe, Cati. "Educating an African Leadership: Achimota and the Teaching of African Culture in the Gold Coast." *Africa Today* 49, no. 3 (2002): 21–44.

Cole, Catherine M. *Ghana's Concert Party Theatre*. Bloomington, IN: Indiana University Press, 2001.

Cooper, Frederick. *Plantation Slavery on the East Coast of Africa*. Portsmouth, NH: Heinemann, 1997.

Cooper, Frederick. *Citizenship, Inequality, and Difference: Historical Perspectives*. Princeton, NJ: Princeton University Press, 2018.

Cowan, E. A. *Evolution of Trade Unionism in Ghana*. Accra: Ghana Trades Union Congress, [1960?].

Crisp, Jeff. "Union Atrophy and Worker Revolt: Labour Protest at Tarkwa Goldfields, Ghana, 1968–1969." *Canadian Journal of African Studies* 14, no. 1/2 (1979): 265, 267–93.

Crisp, Jeff. *The Story of an African Working Class: Ghanaian Miners' Struggles, 1870–1980*. London: Zed Books, 1984.

Crummey, Donald. *Farming and Famine: Landscape Vulnerability in Northeast Ethiopia, 1889–1991*, edited by James McCann. Madison, WI: University of Wisconsin Press, 2018.

Daaku, K. Y., comp. *Oral Traditions of Adanse*. Legon: Institute of African Studies, University of Ghana, 1969.

[Daaku, K. Y.], comp. *UNESCO Research Project on Oral Traditions: Denkyira*, no. 2. Legon: Institute of African Studies, University of Ghana, 1970.

[Daaku, K. Y.], comp. *UNESCO Research Project on Oral Traditions, No. 4, Part II: Sefwi-Wiawso* Legon: Institute of African Studies, University of Ghana, 1974.

Daly, Samuel Fury Childs. "Ghana Must Go: Nativism and the Politics of Expulsion in West Africa, 1969–1985." *Past & Present* (2022): https://doi.org/10.1093/pastj/gtac006.

Danquah, Francis. *Cocoa Disease and Politics in Ghana, 1909–1966*. New York: Peter Lang, 1995.

Danquah, J. B. *Gold Coast: Akan Laws and Customs and the Akim Abuakwa Constitution*. London: George Routledge & Sons, 1928.

Danquah, J. B. *The Akan Doctrine of God: A Fragment of Gold Coast Ethics and Religion*. London: Lutterworth Press, 1944.

Danso-Boafo, Kwaku. *The Political Biography of Dr. Kofi Abrefa Busia*. Accra: Ghana Universities Press, 1996.

Davidson, Basil. *The Black Man's Burden: Africa and the Curse of the Nation-State*. New York: Three Rivers, 1992.

Dei, George J. S. "Coping with the Effects of the 1982–1983 Drought in Ghana: The View from the Village." *Africa Development/Afrique et Développement* 13, no. 1 (1988): 107–22.

de Moraes Faias, P. F. "Silent Trade: Myth and Historical Evidence." *History in Africa* 1 (1974): 9–24.

Derrick, Jonathan. "West Africa's Worst Year of Famine." *African Affairs* 83, no. 332 (1984): 281–99.

Dickson, K. B. "Development of the Copra Industry in Ghana." *Journal of Tropical Geography* 19 (1964): 27–34.

Doortmont, Michel R. *The Pen-Pictures of Modern Africans and African Celebrities by Charles Francis Hutchinson: A Collective Biography of Elite Society in the Gold Coast Colony*. Leiden: Brill, 2005.

Drake, St. Clair and Leslie Alexander Lacy. "Government versus the Unions: The Sekondi-Takoradi Strike, 1961." In *Politics in Africa: Seven Cases*, edited by Gwendolen Carter. New York: Harcourt, Brace & World, 1966.

Du Bois, W. E. B. "The African Roots of the War." In *W. E. B. Du Bois: A Reader*, edited by David Levering Lewis. New York: Owl Books, 1995.

Dumett, Raymond. "The Rubber Trade of the Gold Coast and Asante in the Nineteenth Century: African Innovation and Market Responsiveness." *Journal of African History* 12, no. 1 (1971): 79–101.

Dumett, Raymond. "Africa's Strategic Minerals during the Second World War." *Journal of African History* 26, no. 4 (1985): 381–408.

Eades, J. S. *Strangers and Trades: Yoruba Migrants, Markets, and the State in Northern Ghana*. Trenton, NJ: Africa World, 1994.

Ellis, Stephen. "Writing History of Contemporary Africa." *Journal of African History* 43, no. 1 (2002): 1–26.

Equiano, Olaudah. *The Interesting Narrative of the Life of Olaudah Equiano; or Gustavus Vassa, the African*. 2nd ed. London: T. Wilkins, 1789.

Esseks, J. D. "Economic Policies." In *Politicians and Soldiers in Ghana, 1966–1972*, edited by Dennis Austin and Robin Luckham. London: Frank Cass, 1975.

Essien, Kwame. *Brazilian-African Diaspora in Ghana: The Tabom, Slavery, Dissonance of Memory, Identity, and Locating Home*. East Lansing, MI: Michigan State University Press, 2016.

Falola, Toyin. *Violence in Nigeria: The Crisis of Religious Politics and Secular Ideologies*. Rochester, NY: University of Rochester Press, 1998.

Falola, Toyin and Matthew M. Heaton. *A History of Nigeria*. Cambridge: Cambridge University Press, 2008.

Fanon, Frantz. *The Wretched of the Earth*, translated by Constance Farrington. New York: Grove, 1963.

Feinberg, Harvey M. "Africans and Europeans in West Africa: Elminans and Dutchman on the Gold Coast during the Eighteenth Century." *Transactions of the American Philosophical Society* 79, no. 7 (1989): i–xvi, 1–186.

Ferguson, James. *Expectations of Modernity: Myths and Meaning of Urban Life on the Zambian Copperbelt*. Berkeley, CA: University of California Press, 1999.

Ferrell, Lacy. "'We Were Mixed with All Types': Educational Migration in the Northern Territories of Colonial Ghana." In *Children on the Move: Past & Present Experiences of Migration*, edited by Elodie Razy and Marie Rodet. Rochester, NY: Boydell & Brewer, 2016.

Fordwor, Kantinka K. *The Danquah-Busia Tradition in the Politics of Ghana: The Origins, Mission and Achievements of the New Patriotic Party*. Accra: Unimax Macmillan, 2010.

Fortes, M., R. W. Steel, and P. Ady. "Ashanti Survey, 1945–46: An Experiment in Social Research." *Geographical Journal* 110, no. 4/6 (1947): 149–77.

French, Howard. *Born in Blackness: Africa, Africans, and the Making of the Modern World, 1471 to the Second World War*. New York: Liveright, 2021.

Fuller, Harcourt. *Building the Ghanaian Nation-State: Kwame Nkrumah's Symbolic Nationalism*. New York: Palgrave Macmillan, 2014.

Fynn, John Kofi, comp. *Oral Traditions of Fante States: Edina (Elmina)*. Legon: Institute of African Studies, University of Ghana, 1974.

Geiss, Immanuel. *The Pan-African Movement: A History of Pan-Africanism in America, Europe, and Africa*, translated by Ann Keep. New York: Africana, [1968] 1974.

George, Betty Stein. *Education in Ghana*. Washington, DC: Government Printing Office, 1976.

Gerits, Frank. "Anticolonial Capitalism: How Ghana Came to Embrace Market-Led Development Theory (the 1970s–1990s)." *Southern Journal of Contemporary History* 47, no. 1 (2002): 4–26.

Gerits, Frank. "The Ideological Scramble for Africa: The US, Ghanaian, French, and British Competition for Africa's Future, 1953–1963." PhD diss., Florence, Italy: European University Institute, 2014.

Getz, Trevor R. and Liz Clarke. *Abina and the Important Men: A Graphic History*, 2nd ed. Oxford: Oxford University Press, 2015.

Getz, Trevor R. and Lindsay Ehrisman. "The Marriages of Abina Mansah: Escaping the Boundaries of 'Slavery' as a Category of Historical Analysis." *Journal of West African History* 1, no. 1 (2015): 93–118.

Girdner, Janet, Victor Olounsola, Myrna Froning, and Emmanuel Hansen. "Ghana's Agricultural Food Policy: Operation Feed Yourself." *Food Policy* 5, no. 1 (1980): 14–25.

Gocking, Roger S. *Facing Two Ways: Ghana's Coastal Communities under Colonial Law*. Lanham, MD: University Press of America, 1999.

Goldsworthy, David. "Ghana's Second Republic: A Post-Mortem." *African Affairs* 72, no. 286 (1973): 8–25.

Gorman, Daniel. *Imperial Citizenship: Empire and the Question of Belonging*. Manchester: Manchester University Press, 2006.

Gravil, Roger. "The Nigerian Aliens Expulsion Order of 1983." *African Affairs* 84, no. 337 (1985): 523–37.

Gray, P. O. "The Pan-African Conference." *New Africa* 2, no. 5 (1900): 8–9.

Green, Toby. *A Fistful of Shells: West Africa from the Rise of the Slave Trade to the Age of Revolution*. London: Penguin, 2020.

Greene, Sandra E. *West African Narratives of Slavery: Texts from Late Nineteenth-Century and Early Twentieth-Century Ghana*. Bloomington, IN: Indiana University Press, 2011.

Grilli, Matteo. *Nkrumaism and African Nationalism: Ghana's Pan-African Foreign Policy in the Age of Decolonization*. New York: Palgrave Macmillan, 2018.

Grischow, Jeff and Holger Weiss. "Colonial Famine Relief and Development Policies: Towards an Environmental History of Northern Ghana." *Global Environment* 4, no. 7/8 (2011): 50–97.

Grove, A. T. "The State of Africa in the 1980s." *The Geographical Journal* 152, no. 2 (1986): 193–203.

Gyimah-Boadi, E., ed. *Ghana under the PNDC*. Dakar: CODESRIA, 1993.

Hansen, Emmanuel. "Public Policy and the Food Question in Ghana." *Africa Development/Afrique et Développement* 6, no. 3 (1981): 99–115.

Hansen, Emmanuel. *Ghana under Rawlings: Early Years*. London: Malthouse, 1991.

Hart, Jennifer. *Ghana on the Go: African Mobility in the Age of Motor Transportation*. Bloomington, IN: Indiana University Press, 2016.

Hartman, Saidiya. *Lose Your Mother: A Journey along the Atlantic Slave Route*. New York: Farrar, Straus, and Giroux, 2007.

Harvey, David. *A Brief History of Neoliberalism*. Oxford: Oxford University Press, 2005.

Haywood, Col. A. and Brig. F. A. S. Clarke. *The History of Royal West African Frontier Force*. Aldershot: Gale & Polden, 1964.

Herbst, Jeffrey I. *The Politics of Reform, 1982–1991*. Berkeley, CA: University of California Press, 1993.

Hess, Janet Berry. "Imagining Architecture: The Structure of Nationalism in Accra, Ghana." *Africa Today* 47, no. 2 (2000): 35–58.

Hill, Polly. *The Gold Coast Cocoa Farmer: A Preliminary Survey*. Oxford: Oxford University Press, 1956.

Hill, Polly. *Migrant Cocoa-Farmers of Southern Ghana: A Study in Rural Capitalism*. Cambridge: Cambridge University Press, [1963] 1970.

Hill, Polly. *Studies in Rural Capitalism*. Cambridge: Cambridge University Press, 1970.

Hippisley, John. *Essays: I. On the Populousness [sic] of Africa: II. On the Trade at the Forts on the Gold Coast; III. On the Necessity of Erecting a Fort at Cape Appolonia*. London: T. Lownds, 1764.

Hobsbawn, E. J. *Nation and Nationalism since 1780: Programme, Myth, Reality*. Cambridge: Cambridge University Press, 1990.

Hobsbawn, Eric and Terence Ranger, eds. *The Invention of Tradition*. Cambridge: Cambridge University Press, 1983.

Hodgson, Dorothy L. and Sheryl A. McCurdy, eds. *"Wicked Women" and the Reconfiguration of Gender in Africa*. Portsmouth, NH: Heinemann, 2001.

Holbrook, Wendell Patrick. "The Impact of the Second World War on the Gold Coast, 1939–1945." PhD diss., Princeton, NJ: Princeton University, 1978.

Hopkins, A. G. *An Economic History of West Africa*. New York: Columbia University Press, 1973.

Horton, Africanus B. *Letters on the Political Condition of the Gold Coast since the Exchange of Territory between the English and the Dutch Government, on January 1, 1868 together with a Short Account of the Ashantee War, 1863–4, and the Awoonah War, 1886*. London: Frank Cass, 1970.

Howe, Russell Warren. "Gold Coast into Ghana." *Phylon Quarterly* 18, no. 2 (1957): 155–61.

Hunwick, J. O., ed. *Proceedings of the Seminar on Ghanaian Historiography and Historical Review: 20th–22nd May, 1976*. Legon: Department of History, University of Ghana, 1977.

Hutchful, Eboe. *The IMF and Ghana: The Confidential Record*. London: Zed Books, 1987.

Iandolo, Alessandro. *Arrested Development: The Soviet Union in Ghana, Guinea, and Mali, 1955–1968*. Ithaca, NY: Cornell University Press, 2022.

Ipsen, Pernille. *Daughters of the Trade: Atlantic Slavers and Interracial Marriage on the Gold Coast*. Philadelphia, PA: University of Pennsylvania Press, 2015.

Israel, Andrienne M. "Ex-Servicemen at the Crossroads: Protest and Politics in Post-War Ghana." *Journal of Modern African Studies* 30, no. 2 (1992): 359–68.

Jackson, Jeanne-Marie. *The African Novel of Ideas: Philosophy and Individualism in the Age of Global Writing*. Princeton, NJ: Princeton University Press, 2021.

Jebuni, Charles D. and Abena D. Oduro. "Structural Adjustment Programme and the Transition to Democracy." In *Ghana: Transition to Democracy*, edited by Kwame A. Ninsin. Dakar: CODESRIA, 1998.

Jeffries, Richard. *Class, Power, and Ideology in Ghana: The Railwaymen of Sekondi*. Cambridge: Cambridge University Press, 1978.

Johnson, David. "Ghana: The 'Rising Star' of Inequality." *Review of African Political Economy*, April 28, 2016, https://roape.net/2016/04/28/ghana-rising-star-inequality/.

Justesen, Ole, ed. and Manley, James, trans. *Danish Sources for the History of Ghana, 1657–1753*, vols 1–2. Copenhagen: Det Kongelige Danske Videnskabernes Selskab, 2005.

Kay, G. B., ed. *The Political Economy of Colonialism in Ghana: Documents and Statistics, 1900–1960*. Aldershot: Gregg Revivals, 1992.

Kea, Ray A. *Settlements, Trade, and Polities in the Seventeenth-Century Gold Coast.* Baltimore, MD: Johns Hopkins University Press, 1982.

Kemp, David. *Nine Years at the Gold Coast.* London: Macmillan, 1898.

Killick, Tony. "External Trades." In *A Study of Contemporary Ghana, Volume I: The Economy of Ghana*, edited by Walter Birmingham, I. Neustadt, and E. N. Omaboe. London: George Allen & Unwin, 1966.

Killick, Tony. "Manufacturing and Construction." In *A Study of Contemporary Ghana, Volume I: The Economy of Ghana*, edited by Walter Birmingham, I. Neustadt, and E. N. Omaboe. London: George Allen & Unwin, 1966.

Killingray, David. "Repercussions of World War I in the Gold Coast," *Journal of African History* 19, no. 1 (1978): 39–59.

Killingray, David. "Soldiers, Ex-Servicemen, and Politics in the Gold Coast, 1939–50." *Journal of Modern African Studies* 21, no. 3 (1983): 523–34.

Killingray, David with Martin Plaut. *Fighting for Britain: African Soldiers in the Second World War.* Rochester, NY: Boydell & Brewer, 2010.

Kimble, David. *A Political History of Ghana: The Rise of Gold Coast Nationalism, 1850–1928.* Oxford: Clarendon, 1963.

Konadu, Kwasi. *The Akan Diaspora in the Americas.* Oxford: Oxford University Press, 2010.

Konadu, Kwasi. *Our Own Way in This Part of the World: Biography of an African Community, Culture, and Nation.* Durham, NC: Duke University Press, 2019.

Konings, Piet. *The State of Rural Class Formation in Ghana: A Comparative Analysis.* London: KPI, 1986.

Kraus, Jon. "Strikes and Labour Power in Ghana." *Development and Change* 10 (1979): 259–86.

Kyei, T. E. *Our Days Dwindle: Memories of My Childhood Days in Asante*, edited by Jean Allman. Portsmouth, NH: Heinemann, 2001.

Ladouceur, Paul André. *Chiefs and Politicians: The Politics of Regionalism in Northern Ghana.* London: Longman, 1979.

Lambert, Keri Grace. "Elastic Allegiances: Rubber, Development, and the Production of Sovereignties in Ghana, 1800–2017." PhD diss., New Haven, CT: Yale University, 2019.

Lambert, Keri Grace. "'It's All Work and Happiness on the Farms': Agricultural Development between the Blocs in Nkrumah's Ghana." *Journal of African History* 60, no. 1 (2019): 25–44.

Lapidus, Ira M. *A History of Islamic Societies*, 2nd ed. Cambridge: Cambridge University Press, 2002.

Laryea, A. D. Amare Quaye and Bernardin Senadza. "Trade and Exchange Rate Policies since Independence and Prospects for the Future." In *The Economy of Ghana Sixty Years after Independence*, edited by Ernest Aryeetey and Ravi Kanbur. Oxford: Oxford University Press, 2017.

Lawler, Nancy Ellen. *Soldiers, Airmen, Spies, and Whisperers: The Gold Coast in World War II.* Athens, OH: Ohio University Press, 2002.

Lawrance, Benjamin, ed. *The Ewe of Togo and Benin.* Accra: Woeli, 2005.

Lawrance, Benjamin, *Locality, Mobility, and "Nation": Periurban Colonialism in Togo's Eweland, 1900–1960.* Rochester, NY: University of Rochester Press, 2007.

Lentz, Carola. *Ethnicity and the Making of History in Northern Ghana.* Edinburgh: Edinburgh University Press, 2006.

Lentz, Carola. "Ghana@50: Celebrating the Nation, Debating the Nation." *Cahiers d'Etudes Africaines* 211 (2013): 519–46.

Lentz, Carola. "Performing the Nation and Staging Ethnic Diversity in Ghanaian National-Day Celebrations." *Ghana Studies* 25 (2022): 3–32.

Lentz, Carola and Jan Budniok. "Ghana@50: Celebrating the Nation: An Account from Accra." *Africa Spectrum* 42, no. 3 (2007): 531–41.

Levan, A. Carl and Patrick Ukata, eds. *The Oxford Handbook of Nigerian Politics*. Oxford: Oxford University Press, 2018.

Levtzion, Nehemia. *Muslims and Chiefs in West Africa: A Study of Islam in the Middle Volta Basin in the Pre-Colonial Period*. Oxford: Oxford University Press, 1968.

Levtzion, Nehemia. *Ancient Ghana and Mali*. New York: Africana Publishing, 1980.

Levtzion, Nehemia and J. F. P. Hopkins, eds. *Corpus of Early Arabic Sources for West African History*, translated by J. F. P. Hopkins. Cambridge: Cambridge University Press, 1981.

Levtzion, Nehemia and Randall L. Pouwels, eds. *The History of Islam in Africa*. Athens, OH: Ohio University Press, 2000.

Lewis, David Levering, ed. *W. E. B. Du Bois: A Reader*. New York: Owl Books, 1995.

Lewis, Pater. "Nigeria's Petreoleum Booms: A Changing Political Economy." In *The Oxford Handbook of Nigerian Politics*, edited by A. Carl Levan and Patrick Ukata. Oxford: Oxford University Press, 2018.

Lovejoy, Paul E. *Transformations in Slavery: A History of Slavery in Africa*, 3rd ed. Cambridge: Cambridge University Press, 2012.

Luckham, Robin. "The Constitutional Commission, 1966–69." In *Politicians and Soldiers in Ghana, 1966-1972*, edited by Dennis Austin and Robin Luckham. London: Frank Cass, 1975.

Lynn, Martin. *Commerce and Economic Change in West Africa: The Palm Oil Trade in the Nineteenth Century*. Cambridge: Cambridge University Press, 1997.

Mahama, John Dramani. *My First Coup d'Etat: And Other True Stories from the Lost Decades of Africa*. New York: Bloomsbury, 2012.

Malki, Isaac Xerxes. "Productive Aliens: Economic Planning and the Lebanese in Ghana, c. 1930–1972." *Mashriq & Mahjar* 1, no. 1 (2013): 85–114.

Mamdani, Mahmood. *Citizen and Subject: Contemporary Africa and the Legacy of Late Colonialism*. Princeton, NJ: Princeton University Press, 1996.

Manning, Patrick. "Slaves, Palm Oil, and Political Power on the West African Coast." *African Historical Studies* 2, no. 2 (1969): 279–88.

Manning, Patrick. *Slavery and African Life: Occidental, Oriental, and African Slave Trades*. Cambridge: Cambridge University Press, 1990.

McCaskie, T. C. *State and Society in Pre-Colonial Asante*. Cambridge: Cambridge University Press, 1995.

McCaskie, T. C. "Denkyira in the Making of Asante, c. 1660–1720." *Journal of African History* 48, no. 1 (2007): 1–25.

McCaskie, T. C. "Asante Origins, Egypt, and the Near East: An Idea and Its History." In *Recasting the Past: History Writing and Political Work in Modern Africa*, edited by Derek R. Peterson and Giacomo Macola. Athens, OH: Ohio University Press, 2009.

Metcalfe, G. E. *Maclean of the Gold Coast: The Life and Times of George Maclean, 1801-1847*. London: Oxford University Press, 1962.

Metcalfe, G. E., ed. *Great Britain and Ghana: Documents of Ghana History, 1807-1957*. Edinburgh: Thomas Nelson and Sons, 1964.

Miescher, Stephan F. "Building the City of the Future: Visions and Experiences of Modernity in Ghana's Akosombo Township." *Journal of African History* 53, no. 3 (2012): 367–90.

Miescher, Stephan F. "'No One Should be Worse Off': The Akosombo Dam, Modernization, and the Experience of Resettlement in Ghana." In *Modernization as Spectacle in Africa*, edited by Peter J. Bloom, Takyiwaa Manuh, and Stefan F. Miescher. Bloomington, IN: Indiana University Press, 2014.

Miescher, Stephan F. "The Akosombo Dam and the Quest for Rural Electrification in Ghana." In *Electric Worlds/Mondes électriques: Creations, Circulations, Tensions, Transitions (19th–21st C.)*, edited by Alain Beltran, Léonard Laborie, Pierre Lanthier, and Stéphanie Le Gallic. Brussels: Peter Lang, 2016.

Miescher, Stephan F. "Ghana's Akosombo Dam, Volta Lake Fisheries, & Climate Change." *Daedalus* 150, no. 4 (2021): 124–42.

Miescher, Stephan F. *A Dam for Africa: Akosombo Stories from Ghana*. Bloomington, IN: Indiana University Press, 2022.

Mikell, Gwendolyn. *Cocoa and Chaos in Ghana*. Washington, DC: Howard University Press, [1989] 1992.

Moghalu, Kingsley and Nonso Obikili. "Fiscal Policy during Boom and Bust." In *The Oxford Handbook of Nigerian Politics*, edited by A. Carl Levan and Patrick Ukata. Oxford: Oxford University Press, 2018.

Montgomery, Mary E. "The Eyes of the World Were Watching: Ghana, Great Britain, and the United States, 1957–1966." PhD diss., College Park, MD: Howard University of Maryland, 2004.

Morelle, Marie, Frédéric Le Marcis, and Julia Hornberger, eds. *Confinement, Punishment, and Prisons in Africa*. London: Hurst, 2021.

Mougoué, Jacqueline-Bethel Tchouta. *Gender, Separatist Politics, and Embodied Nationalism in Cameroon*. Ann Arbor, MI: University of Michigan Press, 2019.

Murillo, Bianca. *Market Encounters: Consumer Cultures in Twentieth-Century Ghana*. Athens, OH: Ohio University Press, 2017.

Mustakeem, Sowande'. *Slavery at Sea: Terror, Sex, and Sickness in the Middle Passage*. Urbana, IL: University of Illinois Press, 2016.

Mwakikagile, Godfrey. *Life under Nyerere*, 2nd ed. Dar es Salaam: New Africa, 2006.

Ninsin, Kwame, ed. *Ghana: Transition to Democracy*. Dakar: CODESRIA, 1998.

Nkrumah, Kwame. *Towards Colonial Freedom: Africa in the Struggle Against World Imperialism*. London: Farleigh, 1947.

Nkrumah, Kwame. *Ghana: An Autobiography of Kwame Nkrumah*. Edinburgh: Thomas Nelson and Sons, 1957.

Nkrumah, Kwame. *I Speak of Freedom: A Statement of African Ideology*. New York: Frederick A. Praeger, 1961.

Nkrumah, Kwame. *Africa Must Unite*. London: Panaf, 1963.

Nkrumah, Kwame. *Neo-Colonialism: The Last Stage of Imperialism*. London: Thomas Nelson and Sons, 1965.

Nkrumah-Boateng, Rodney. *Swords and Crosses: The Story of Opoku Ware School, 1952–2012*. N.p.: Opoku Ware Old Boys Association, n.d.

Nugent, Paul. *Big Men, Small Boys, and Politics in Ghana: Power, Ideology, and the Burden of History, 1982–1994*. Accra: Asempa Publishers, 1995.

Nugent, Paul. *Smugglers, Secessionists, and Loyal Citizens on the Ghana–Togo Frontier: The Lie of the Borderlands Since 1914*. Athens, OH: Ohio University Press, 2003.

Nugent, Paul. "A Regional Melting Pot: The Ewe and Their Neighbours in the Ghana-Togo Borderlands." In *The Ewe of Togo and Benin*, edited by Benjamin Lawrance. Accra: Woeli, 2005.

Nugent, Paul. *Boundaries, Communities, and State-Making in West Africa: The Centrality of the Margins.* Cambridge: Cambridge University Press, 2019.

Nworah, K. Dike. "The Politics of Lever's West African Concessions, 1907–1913." *International Journal of African Historical Studies* 5, no. 2 (1972): 248–64.

Odamtten, Harry N. K. *Edward W. Blyden's Intellectual Transformations: Afropublicanism, Pan-Africanism, Islam and the Indigenous West African Church.* East Lansing, MI: Michigan State University Press, 2019.

Odotei, Irene K. and Albert K. Awedoba, eds. *Chieftaincy in Ghana: Culture, Governance, and Development.* Accra: Sub-Saharan Publishers, 2006.

Ofori-Sarpong, E. "Impact of Drought in Ghana and Upper Volta (1970–1977)." Climatological Research Paper No. 1. Legon: Department of Geography, University of Ghana, 1980.

Ofori-Sarpong, E. "The 1981–1983 Drought in Ghana." *Singapore Journal of Tropical Geography* 7, no. 2 (1986): 108–27.

Okeke, Barbara E. *4 June: A Revolution Betrayed.* Enugu, Nigeria: Ikenga, 1982.

Olaniyi, Rashid. "The 1969 Ghana Exodus: Memory and Reminiscences of Yoruba Migrants." Unpublished ms., n.d.

Oquaye, Mike. *Politics in Ghana (1972–1979).* Accra: Tornado Publications, 1980.

Oquaye, Mike. *Politics in Ghana, 1982–1992: Rawlings, Revolution, and Populist Democracy.* Accra: Tornado Publications, 2004.

Organ, Edward J. *The Gold Coast Cocoa Industry & Its Recent Developments: A Paper Read at the Exhibition of Rubber, Other Tropical Products & Allied Industries, June 1921.* N.p.: Bourneville Works, 1921.

[Ormsby-Gore, W. G. A.] "Report by the Hon. W. G. A. Ormsby-Gore, M. P. (Parliamentary Under-Secretary of State for the Colonies), on his Visit to West Africa during the Year 1926." London: His Majesty's Stationery Office, 1926.

Osei-Opare, Nana. "Uneasy Comrades: Postcolonial Statecraft, Race, and Citizenship, Ghana-Soviet Relations, 1957–1966." *Journal of West African History* 5, no. 2 (2019): 85–112.

Osei-Opare, Nana. "'If You Trouble a Hungry Snake, You Will Force It to Bite You': Rethinking Postcolonial African Archival Pessimism, Worker Discontent, and Petition Writing in Ghana, 1957–66." *Journal of African History* 62, no. 1 (2021): 59–78.

Osei-Tutu, John K. "Contesting British Sovereignty in Cape Coast, Ghana: Insights from King John Aggery's Correspondences, 1865–72." *Transactions of the Historical Society of Ghana,* new series 7 (2003): 231–51.

Owusu, Maxwell. "Economic Nationalism, Pan-Africanism, and the Military: Ghana's National Redemption Council." *Africa Today* 22, no. 1 (1975): 31–50.

Pacheco Pereira, Duarte. *Esmeraldo de Situ Orbis,* edited and translated by George H. T. Kimble. London: The Hakluyt Society, 1936.

Panford, Kwamina. *IMF-World Bank and Labor's Burden in Africa: Ghana's Experience.* London: Praeger, 2001.

Parker, John. *Making the Town: Ga State and Society in Early Colonial Accra.* Portsmouth, NH: Heinemann, 2000.

Parsons, Timothy H. *The African Rank-and-File: Social Implications of Colonial Military Service in the King's African Rifles, 1902–1964.* Portsmouth, NH: Heinemann, 1999.

Pavanello, Mariano. "Foragers or Cultivators? A Discussion of Wilks's 'Big Bang' Theory of Akan History." *Journal of West African History* 1, no. 2 (2015): 1–26.

Peil, Margaret. "The Expulsion of West Africa Aliens." *Journal of Modern African Studies* 9, no. 2 (1971): 205–29.

Peil, Margaret. *The Ghanaian Factory Worker: Industrial Man in Africa*. Cambridge: Cambridge University Press, 1972.

Peil, Margaret. "Ghana's Aliens." *International Migration Review* 8, no. 3 (1974): 367–81.

Pellow, Deborah. "Coping Responses to Revolution in Ghana." *Cultures et développement: Revue Internationale des Sciences du Développement* 15, no. 1 (1983): 11–36.

Peterson, Derek R. and Giacomo Macola, eds. *Recasting the Past: History Writing and Political Work in Modern Africa*. Athens, OH: Ohio University Press, 2009.

Plageman, Nate. "'Accra is Changing, Isn't It?': Urban Infrastructure, Independence, and Nation in the Gold Coast's *Daily Graphic*, 1954–57." *International Journal of African Historical Studies* 43, no. 1 (2010): 137–59.

Plageman, Nate. *Highlife Saturday Night: Popular Music and Social Change in Urban Ghana*. Bloomington, IN: Indiana University Press, 2012.

Posnansky, Merrick. "Aspects of Early West African Trade." *World Archaeology* 6, no. 2 (1973): 149–62.

Posnansky, Merrick. "The Archaeological Foundations of the History of Ghana." In *Proceedings of the Seminar on Ghanaian Historiography and Historical Review: 20th–22nd May, 1976*, edited by J. O. Hunwick. Legon: Department of History, University of Ghana, 1977.

Preedy, V. R. and V. B. Patel, eds. *Handbook of Famine, Starvation, and Nutrient Deprivation*. Cham, Switzerland: Springer Nature Switzerland, 2019.

Prosperetti, Elisa Sophie. "Every Available Penny: Expectations, Education, and Development in Postcolonial West Africa." PhD diss., Princeton, NJ: Princeton University 2020.

Quarcoopome, S. S. "Urbanisation, Land Alienation and Politics in Accra." *Research Review NS* 8, nos. 1 and 2 (1992): 40–54.

Quarshie, Nana Osei. "Cocoa and Compliance: How Exemptions Made Mass Expulsion in Ghana, 1969–1972." Unpublished Ms., n.d.

Quarshie, Nana Osei. "Mass Expulsion as Internal Exclusion: Police Raids and the Imprisonment of West African Immigrants in Ghana, 1969–1974." In *Confinement, Punishment, and Prisons in Africa*, edited by Marie Morelle, Frédéric Le Marcis, and Julia Hornberger. London: Hurst, 2021.

Ranger, Terence, ed. *Emerging Themes of African History: Proceedings of the International Congress of African Historians held at University College, Dar es Salaam, October 1965*. Dar es Salaam: East African Publishing House, 1968.

Rathbone, Richard, ed. *Ghana*. Vol. 1, pts. 1 and 2, of *British Documents on the End of Empire*, ser. B. London: Her Majesty's Stationery Office, 1992.

Rathbone, Richard. *Nkrumah & the Chiefs: The Politics of Chieftaincy in Ghana, 1951–60*. Athens, OH: Ohio University Press, 2000.

Rawlings, Jerry John. *A Revolutionary Journey: Selected Speeches of Flt.-Lt. Jerry John Rawlings, Chairman of the Provisional National Defence Council, December 31, 1981–December 31, 1982*, vol. 1. Accra: Information Services Departments, n.d.

Rawlings, Jerry John. *Forging Ahead: Selected Speeches of Flt.-Lt. Jerry John Rawlings, Chairman of the Provisional National Defence Council —January 1st 1983–December 31st 1983*, vol. 2. Accra: Information Services Department, n.d.

Rawlings, Jerry John. *The New Momentum: Speeches of the Chairman of the PNDC, Flt-Lt. J. J. Rawlings, during the Fifth Anniversary Celebration of the 31st December Revolution*. [Accra]: Information Services Department, 1987.

Ray, Carina. "World War II and the Sex Trade in British West Africa." In *Africa and the World Wars II*, edited by Judith A. Byfield, Carolyn A. Brown, Timothy Parsons, and Ahmad Alawad Sikainga. Cambridge: Cambridge University Press, 2015.

Ray, Deborah Wing. "The Takoradi Route: Roosevelt's Prewar Venture beyond the Western Hemisphere." *Journal of American History* 62, no. 2 (1975): 340–58.

Razy, Elodie and Marie Rodet, eds. *Children on the Move: Past & Present Experiences of Migration*. Rochester, NY: Boydell & Brewer, 2016.

Reid, Richard J. *A History of Modern Uganda*. Cambridge: Cambridge University Press, 2017.

Reindorf, Carl Christian. *History of the Gold Coast and Asante: Based on Traditions and Historical Facts, Comprising a Period of More than Three Centuries from About 1500 to 1860*. Basel: privately printed, 1895.

Rimmer, Douglas. "New Industrial Relations in Ghana." *Industrial and Labor Relations Review* 14, no. 2 (1961): 206–26.

Rimmer, Douglas. *Staying Poor: Ghana's Political Economy, 1950–1990*. Oxford: Pergamon, 1992.

Robertson, Claire C. *Sharing the Same Bowl: A Socioeconomic History of Women and Class in Accra, Ghana*. Ann Arbor, MI: University of Michigan Press, 1984.

Robertson, Claire C. "Gender and Profiteering: Ghana's Market Women as Devoted Mothers and 'Human Vampire Bats.'" In *"Wicked Women" and the Reconfiguration of Gender in Africa*, edited by Dorothy L. Hodgson and Sheryl A. McCurdy. Portsmouth, NH: Heinemann, 2001.

Robertson, G. A. *Notes on Africa: Particularly Those Parts which are Situated between Cape Verd [sic] and the River Congo; Containing Sketches of the Geographical Situation— the Manners and Customs—the Trade, Commerce, and Manufacturers—and the Government and Policy of the Various Nations in This Extensive Tract; Also a View of Their Capabilities for the Reception of Civilization; With Hints for the Melioration of the Whole African Population*. [Boston, MA]: Adamant Media, [1819] 2007.

Robins, Jonathan E. *Oil Palm: A Global History*. Chapel Hill, NC: University of North Carolina Press, 2021.

Rodney, Walter. "Gold and Slaves on the Gold Coast." *Transactions of the Historical Society of Ghana* 10 (1969): 13–28.

Rodney, Walter. *How Europe Underdeveloped Africa*, 2nd ed. Washington, DC: Howard University Press, [1972] 1982.

Rømer, Ludewig Ferdinand. *A Reliable Account of the Coast of Guinea (1760)*, translated and edited by Selena Axelrod Winsnes. Oxford: Oxford University Press, 2000.

Salau, Mohammed Bashir. *Plantation Slavery in the Sokoto Caliphate*. Rochester, NY: University of Rochester Press, 2018.

Sampson, Magnus J. *Makers of Modern Ghana*, vol. 1. Accra: Anowuo Educational Publications, 1969.

Sarbah, John Mensah. *Fanti Customary Laws: A Brief Introduction to the Principles of the Native Laws and Customs of the Fanti and Akan Districts of the Gold Coast, with a Report of Some Cases thereon Decided in the Law Courts*. London: W. Clowes and Sons, 1904.

Sarbah, John Mensah. *Fanti National Constitution: A Short Treatise on the Constitution and Government of the Fanti, Asanti [sic], and Other Akan Tribes of West Africa together with a Brief Account of the Discovery of the Gold Coast by Portuguese Navigators; A Short Narrative of Early English Voyages; and a Study of the Rise of British Gold Coast Jurisdictions, etc., etcs.*, 2nd ed. London: Frank Cass, 1968.

Schauert, Paul. *Staging Ghana: Artistry and Nationalism in State Dance Ensembles.* Bloomington, IN: Indiana University Press, 2015.

Schneer, Jonathan. *London 1900: The Imperial Metropolis.* New Haven, CT: Yale University Press, 1999.

Sekyi, Kobina. *The Blinkards: A Comedy and the Anglo-Fanti: A Short Story.* Accra: Readwide Publications, 1997.

Shumway, Rebecca. *The Fante and the Transatlantic Slave Trade.* Rochester, NY: University of Rochester Press, 2011.

Shumway, Rebecca. "Castle Slaves of the Eighteenth-Century Gold Coast (Ghana)." *Slavery & Abolition* 35, no. 1 (2014): 84–98.

Skinner, Kate. *The Fruits of Freedom in British Togoland: Literacy, Politics, and Nationalism, 1914–2014.* Cambridge: Cambridge University Press, 2015.

Slobodian, Quinn. *Globalists: The End of Empire and the Birth of Neoliberalism.* Cambridge, MA: Harvard University Press, 2018.

Smith, Anthony D. *National Identity.* Las Vegas, NV: University of Nevada Press, 1991.

Sparks, Randy J. *Where the Negroes are Master: An African Port in the Era of the Slave Trade.* Cambridge, MA: Harvard University Press, 2014.

Staniland, Martin. *The Lions of Dagbon: Political Change in Northern Ghana.* Cambridge: Cambridge University Press, [1975] 2008.

St. Clair, William. *The Grand Slave Emporium: Cape Coast Castle and the British Slave Trade.* London: Profile Books, 2006.

Sundiata, I. K. "Prelude to Scandal: Liberia and Fernando Po, 1880–1930." *Journal of African History* 15, no. 1 (1974): 97–112.

Talton, Benjamin. *Politics of Social Change: The Konkomba Struggle for Political Equality.* New York: Palgrave Macmillan, 2010.

Tan, Chih Ming and Marc Rockmore. "Famine in Ghana and Its Impact." In *Handbook of Famine, Starvation, and Nutrient Deprivation,* edited by V. R. Preedy and V. B. Patel. Cham, Switzerland: Springer Nature Switzerland, 2019.

Thomas, Roger G. "Forced Labour in British West Africa: The Case of the Northern Territories of the Gold Coast, 1906–1927." *Journal of African History* 14, no. 1 (1973): 79–103.

Tignor, Robert L. *W. Arthur Lewis and the Birth of Development Economics.* Princeton, NJ: Princeton University Press, 2006.

Timothy, Bankole. *Kwame Nkrumah: His Rise to Power.* London: George Allen & Unwin, 1955.

Tsikata, Dzodzi. *Living in the Shadow of Large Dams: Long Term Responses of Downstream and Lakeside Communities of Ghana's Volta River Project.* Leiden: Brill, 2006.

Twumasi, Yaw. "J. B. Danquah: Towards an Understanding of the Social and Political Ideas of a Ghanaian Nationalist and Politician." *African Affairs* 77, no. 336 (1978): 73–88.

Valsecchi, Pierluigi. "The 'True Nzema': A Layered Identity." *Africa* 71, no. 3 (2001): 391–425.

Valsecchi, Pierluigi. "The Fall of Kaku Aka: Social and Political Change in the Mid-Nineteenth-Century Western Gold Coast." *Journal of West African History* 2, no. 1 (2016): 1–26.

Vaughan, Olufemi. *Nigerian Chiefs: Traditional Power in Modern Politics, 1890s–1990s.* Rochester, NY: University of Rochester Press, 2000.

Vaughan, Olufemi. *Religion and the Making of Nigeria.* Durham, NC: Duke University Press, 2016.

Vilgiate, Timothy. "Forestry and the 'World on Paper': Ideas of Science and Resistance to Forest Reservation on the Gold Coast in the Early Twentieth Century." *Ghana Studies* 23 (2020): 3–27.

Vogt, John. *Portuguese Rule on the Gold Coast, 1469–1682*. Athens, OH: University of Georgia Press, 1979.

Walters, Alexander. *My Life and Work*. New York: Fleming H. Revell, [1917].

Warren D. M. and K. O. Brempong. *Techiman Traditional State, Part 1: Traditional and Stool Histories*. Legon: Institute of African Studies, University of Ghana, 1971.

Weiss, Holger. "Crop Failures, Food Shortages, and Colonial Famine Relief Policies in the Northern Territories of the Gold Coast." *Ghana Studies* 6 (2003): 5–58.

Weiss, Holger. "Variations in the Colonial Representation of Islam and Muslims in Northern Ghana, ca. 1900–1930." *Journal of Muslim Minority Affairs* 25, no. 1 (2005): 73–95.

Wiemers, Alice. *Village Work: Development and Rural Statecraft in Twentieth-Century Ghana*. Athens, OH: Ohio University Press, 2021.

Wilks, Ivor. "The Northern Factor in Ashanti History: Begho and the Mande." *Journal of African History* 2, no. 1 (1961): 25–34.

Wilks, Ivor. *Asante in the Nineteenth Century: The Structure and Evolution of a Political Order*. Cambridge: Cambridge University Press, 1989.

Wilks, Ivor. *Forests of Gold: Essays on the Akan and the Kingdom of Asante*. Athens, OH: Ohio University Press, 1993.

Wilks, Ivor. "The Juula and the Expansion of Islam into the Forest." In *The History of Islam in Africa*, edited by Nehemia Levtzion and Randall L. Pouwels. Athens, OH: Ohio University Press, 2000.

Wilks, Ivor. *Akwamu 1640–1750: A Study of the Rise and Fall of a West African Empire*. Trondheim: Department of History, Norwegian University of Science and Technology, 2001.

Wilks, Ivor. "The Forest and the Twis." *Transactions of the Historical Society of Ghana*, new series 8 (2004): 1–81.

Williamson, Thora. *Gold Coast Diaries: Chronicles of Political Officers in West Africa, 1900–1919*, edited by Anthony Kirk-Greene. London: Radcliffe Press, 2000.

Wolf, Eric. *Europe and the People without History*. Berkeley, CA: University of California Press, 1982.

Wright, Richard. *Black Power: A Record of Reactions in a Land of Pathos*. New York: Harper and Brothers, 1954.

Yeebo, Zaya. "Ghana: Defence Committees and the Class Struggle." *Review of African Political Economy* 32 (1985): 64–72.

Yeebo, Zaya. *Ghana, The Struggle for Popular Power: Rawlings, Saviour or Demagogue*. London: New Beacon Books, 1991.

Young, Crawford. *The Politics of Cultural Pluralism*. Madison, WI: University of Wisconsin Press, 1976.

Young, Crawford. *The African Colonial State in Comparative Perspective*. New Haven, CT: Yale University Press, 1994.

Zeleke, Elleni Centime. *Ethiopia in Theory: Revolution and Knowledge Production, 1964–2016*. Chicago, IL: Haymarket, 2019.

INDEX